Cloud Computing Bible

Cloud Computing Bible

Barrie Sosinsky

WILEY

Wiley Publishing, Inc.

Cloud Computing Bible

Published by
Wiley Publishing, Inc.
10475 Crosspoint Boulevard
Indianapolis, IN 46256
www.wiley.com

Copyright © 2011 by Wiley Publishing, Inc., Indianapolis, Indiana

Published by Wiley Publishing, Inc., Indianapolis, Indiana

Published simultaneously in Canada

ISBN: 978-0-470-90356-8

10 9 8 7 6 5 4 3

For general information on our other products and services or to obtain technical support, please contact our Customer Care Department within the U.S. at (877) 762-2974, outside the U.S. at (317) 572-3993 or fax (317) 572-4002.

Library of Congress Control Number: 2010941512

This book is dedicated to my sister Gina Sosinsky, with love.

About the Author

Barrie Sosinsky has written about computers and technology for more than 25 years beginning with writing about personal computers for the Boston Computer Society in the early 1980s. He has published books on operating systems, applications, databases, desktop publishing, and networking for publishers such as Que, Sybex, Ventana, IDG, Wiley, and others and seen the industry change and reinvent itself several times. His last book was Wiley's *Networking Bible*.

At heart Barrie is a PC enthusiast. He loves building computers, finding and learning about new applications that allow him to do new things, and keeping up with the latest advances in the field of computer technology, which he believes is just in its infancy. Having lived long enough to see the Boston Red Sox win not one but two World Series, he remains committed to living long enough to see grandchildren and to see someone clone a wooly mammoth. To this list (replacing the Red Sox) he adds the new milestone of holding a universal translator in his hands; a device he believes will appear within this decade.

Barrie lives in Medfield Massachusetts about 25 miles southwest of Boston with his six cats Stormy, Shadow, Smokey, Scamper, Slate, and Spat as writing companions; Scout the wonder dog; his son Joseph; his daughter Allie; and his wife Carol; surrounded by pine trees, marauding deer, wild turkeys, and the occasional fox and coyote.

You can reach Barrie at bsosinsky@mindspring.com, where he welcomes your comments and suggestions.

Credits

Senior Acquisitions Editor
Stephanie McComb

Project Editor
Martin V. Minner

Technical Editor
Benjamin M. Schupak

Copy Editor
Gwenette Gaddis

Editorial Director
Robyn Siesky

Editorial Manager
Rosemarie Graham

Business Manager
Amy Knies

Senior Marketing Manager
Sandy Smith

Vice President and Executive Group Publisher
Richard Swadley

Vice President and Executive Publisher
Barry Pruett

Project Coordinator
Patrick Redmond

Graphics and Production Specialists
Nikki Gately
Andrea Hornberger

Quality Control Technician
Lindsay Littrell

Proofreading and Indexing
Evelyn Wellborn
Sherry Massey

Preface

Cloud Computing Bible is Wiley's general introduction to an important topic in large book format. A Bible is a book that is meant to be read by knowledgeable readers who are not subject matter experts in a topic but want to have an in-depth introduction to the various individual subjects contained within. It is assumed that the reader of this book may be a generalist, a developer, a system architect, a programmer, or perhaps something else, and therefore the content in a Bible must contain information for each member of this book's audience.

Cloud computing is a vast topic that encompasses many different subjects. To adequately describe what cloud computing offers, we must discuss infrastructure, service-oriented architectures, social networking, unique protocols, open and standard Application Programming Interfaces (APIs), and dozens of other topics. Even a large book can address many of these topics in only an introductory manner. However, this book tries to give you at least the basic information you need on all the related topics, as well as pointers to additional information sources.

In the last several years, many books have been published on cloud computing. Each book has attempted to present some element of the topic for a particular audience. In this book, I do not make the assumption that you are a particular type of reader, nor do I assume that you are approaching the topic with a fresh view. This Bible was written to serve as the introductory course in the topic at a university level, but it is not a textbook. You can pick up and read this book at any particular chapter because the material doesn't build upon itself.

Many topics in this book are unique to this book and are based on published information that is both current and timely. In researching this book, I attempted to bring into the discussion all the new trends, experiments, and products that have made cloud computing such a dynamic area.

Acknowledgments

I want to acknowledge the editorial team at Wiley for giving me the chance to do this book and to work with them again. I also want to thank my literary agent, Matt Wagner, for his assistance; without his vision, this book would not have been created. Finally, I want to thank my family for allowing me the time I spent away from them writing this book.

Contents at a Glance

Contents

Contents

Contents

Contents

Contents

Introduction

In the five months that I have been researching and writing *Cloud Computing Bible,* it has become clear to me that most people recognize that cloud computing is a big deal, even if they are not really clear why that is so. Every day newspaper and magazine articles and radio and TV stories report on cloud computing. The phrase "in the cloud" has entered into our colloquial language. You may have heard that the United States government has initiated a "cloud initiative," or that nearly 75 percent of the developers at Microsoft are currently working on "cloud-related" products, or that a phone or service stores its data in the cloud. The cloud is therefore this amorphous entity that is supposed to represent the future of modern computing.

In reality, the cloud is something that you have been using for a long time now; it is the Internet, along with all the associated standards and protocols that provide a set of Web services to you. When you draw the Internet as a cloud, you are representing one of the essential characteristics of cloud computing: abstraction. In the cloud, resources are pooled and partitioned as needed, and communications are standards-based.

The Internet was begun as a network of networks, with an architecture that was redundant and could survive massive disruption. What the original system architects of the Internet could not have anticipated is that the size of resources attached to it would become massively scalable, which is the second characteristic of cloud computing.

Google's infrastructure, for example, which is described in this book in Chapter 9, spans 30 datacenters around the world with over a million computers; infrastructure that Google now leases out to developers upon which applications may be staged. So the third and equally as important characteristic of cloud computing is that the cloud is a "utility" and that services are provided using a pay-as-you-go model.

A computing utility has been a dream of computer scientists and industry luminaries for several decades. With a utility model of computing, an application can start small and grow to be enormous overnight. This democratization of computing means that any application has the potential to scale, and that even the smallest seed planted in the cloud may be a giant.

Cloud computing will affect your life in the following ways in the next ten years:

- Applications in the cloud will replace applications that are local to your devices.
- Information will become cheaper, more ubiquitous, and easier to find because the cloud makes it cheaper to scale applications and connections to always-on networks such as wireless carriers that make the information always available.

- The cloud will enable new social services by connecting users via social networks that are constructed using multiple cloud services.

- New applications will be easier to create and will be based on standard modular parts.

- It will lessen the role that proprietary operating systems have in our daily computing.

- You will be connected through the cloud wherever you are and at all times.

Frankly, it is hard to predict what new capabilities the cloud may enable. The cloud has a trajectory that is hard to plot and a scope that reaches into so many aspects of our daily life that innovation can occur across a broad range.

Many technologically savvy people have told me they don't understand what the fuss about cloud computing is; in fact, they believe there is nothing new about cloud computing, at least from a technological standpoint. Indeed, they have a point. The technologies that enable cloud computing—system and resource virtualization, thin clients (browsers, for example), virtual private networks and tunneling, and others—are all technologies that existed before anyone ever began to talk about cloud computing. That is all true. Cloud computing is a revolutionary way of architecting and implementing services based on evolutionary changes. *Cloud Computing Bible* attempts to explain how this all came about.

How to Read This Book

Cloud Computing Bible is made up of 21 chapters in five parts. To read this book and get the most out of it, you should know about basic computer operations and theory. You should be able to turn a computer on and know what operating system is running, how processing and input/output is used, and be able to connect with a browser to different Web sites. You should understand the basic user interface elements used by many browsers, such as Microsoft Internet Explorer, Mozilla Firefox, Apple Safari, or Google Chrome.

These are basic skills without which it would be hard to effectively maximize the value contained in this book. If you don't have these skills, Wiley publishes a number of introductory computer books that will give them to you.

It doesn't matter which type of computer operating system you use because most of cloud computing is operating-system-neutral. Indeed, as time goes by, it may not matter whether you use a computer at all. Mobile devices such as smartphones and tablets are on their way to displacing computers in many venues. If you have some familiarity with smartphones, that would be helpful in understanding the last part of this book on mobile-based cloud applications, but it isn't a necessity.

Part I of the book, called "Examining the Value Proposition," defines what cloud computing is and why you should be interested in it. This vocabulary, along with description of cloud architectures and types, will allow you to discuss cloud computing in a standard way and serves to give you a framework over which you can place all the different service types that make cloud computing such a rich area.

Part II, called "Using Platforms," looks at the fundamental features that make a cloud computing application unique. You get a background in the concepts of abstraction and virtualization, along with methods for examining how applications are scaled. This part contains several chapters of vendor-specific services that are illustrative of different cloud computing models. In several chapters, I discuss vendors that are thought leaders in different fields of cloud computing. For infrastructure, I've chosen to highlight Amazon Web Services, and for platforms and services, you learn about the efforts of Google and Microsoft in cloud computing.

Part III, "Exploring Cloud Infrastructures," contains two chapters about managing the cloud and working with the cloud securely. The cloud builds on standard distributed networking technologies, applied over systems with large resources, often over federated systems and services.

In Part IV, "Understanding Services and Applications," the first two chapters describe Service Oriented Architecture and transactions—both of which are important principles in building cloud applications so they are efficient and interoperable—and moving applications to the cloud. The remaining chapters in Part IV describe different types of applications in common use in the cloud today. Those applications are the most highly developed ones in the cloud and have the largest number of users and services. The examples chosen are online backup and storage, Webmail, online productivity applications, messaging, and online media, particularly using streaming technologies.

The book rounds out with two chapters on "Using the Mobile Cloud," Part V. These chapters describe the rise of the smartphone and its predecessor, the feature phone. These phones are supported by a host of Web services. Since 2008, more traffic has been flowing over wireless networks than wired networks, so it would be hard to underestimate how much impact mobile devices have on the cloud. For vast portions of the world, the cell phone is the only computer most people will know. Mobile Web services use different protocols and technologies and can take into account location and other user profile information that can use the cloud to create a rich user experience.

Please dive into whatever chapter interests you. I hope you enjoy reading about cloud computing as much as I enjoyed writing about it.

Icons

The icons in this book offer you a chance to learn a little more about a topic, refer to a discussion elsewhere in the book, address a problem, or get a little more help. This book offers the following icons:

Caution

A Caution icon alerts you to a potential problem that you should be aware of. ■

Note

A Note icon points to a clarification or expansion of the topic being discussed. ■

Tip

Tips are shortcuts you can use to get something done more effectively. ■

Cross-Ref

A Cross-Ref icon provides a reference to related discussions that take place elsewhere in the book. ■

Because this isn't a how-to book, you will find fewer Cautions and Tips in this book than you might find in other Wiley Bibles. However, there are plenty of Notes and Cross-Refs to help guide you in these chapters.

Contacting Us

If, after reviewing this publication, you feel some important information was overlooked or you have any questions concerning cloud computing, you can contact us and let us know your views, opinions, complaints, or suggestions for the next revision.

You can reach the author, Barrie Sosinsky, at the following e-mail address: `bsosinsky@mind spring.com`.

Part I

Examining the Value Proposition

Defining Cloud Computing

Cloud computing refers to applications and services that run on a distributed network using virtualized resources and accessed by common Internet protocols and networking standards. It is distinguished by the notion that resources are virtual and limitless and that details of the physical systems on which software runs are abstracted from the user.

In an effort to better describe cloud computing, a number of cloud types have been defined. In this chapter, you learn about two different classes of clouds: those based on the deployment model and those based on the service model. The deployment model tells you where the cloud is located and for what purpose. Public, private, community, and hybrid clouds are deployment models.

Service models describe the type of service that the service provider is offering. The best-known service models are Software as a Service, Platform as a Service, and Infrastructure as a Service—the SPI model. The service models build on one another and define what a vendor must manage and what the client's responsibility is.

Cloud computing represents a real paradigm shift in the way in which systems are deployed. The massive scale of cloud computing systems was enabled by the popularization of the Internet and the growth of some large service companies. Cloud computing makes the long-held dream of utility computing possible with a pay-as-you-go, infinitely scalable, universally available system. With cloud computing, you can start very small and become big very fast. That's why cloud computing is revolutionary, even if the technology it is built on is evolutionary.

Not all applications benefit from deployment in the cloud. Issues with latency, transaction control, and in particular security and regulatory compliance are of particular concern.

Defining Cloud Computing

Cloud computing takes the technology, services, and applications that are similar to those on the Internet and turns them into a self-service utility. The use of the word "cloud" makes reference to the two essential concepts:

- **Abstraction:** Cloud computing abstracts the details of system implementation from users and developers. Applications run on physical systems that aren't specified, data is stored in locations that are unknown, administration of systems is outsourced to others, and access by users is ubiquitous.

- **Virtualization:** Cloud computing virtualizes systems by pooling and sharing resources. Systems and storage can be provisioned as needed from a centralized infrastructure, costs are assessed on a metered basis, multi-tenancy is enabled, and resources are scalable with agility.

Computing as a utility is a dream that dates from the beginning of the computing industry itself. A set of new technologies has come along that, along with the need for more efficient and affordable computing, has enabled an on-demand system to develop. It is these enabling technologies that are the focal point of this book.

Many people mistakenly believe that cloud computing is nothing more than the Internet given a different name. Many drawings of Internet-based systems and services depict the Internet as a cloud, and people refer to applications running on the Internet as "running in the cloud," so the confusion is understandable. The Internet has many of the characteristics of what is now being called cloud computing. The Internet offers abstraction, runs using the same set of protocols and standards, and uses the same applications and operating systems. These same characteristics are found in an intranet, an internal version of the Internet. When an intranet becomes large enough that a diagram no longer wishes to differentiate between individual physical systems, the intranet too becomes identified as a cloud.

Cloud computing is an abstraction based on the notion of pooling physical resources and presenting them as a virtual resource. It is a new model for provisioning resources, for staging applications, and for platform-independent user access to services. Clouds can come in many different types, and the services and applications that run on clouds may or may not be delivered by a cloud service provider. These different types and levels of cloud services mean that it is important to define what type of cloud computing system you are working with.

To help clarify how cloud computing has changed the nature of commercial system deployment, consider these three examples:

- **Google:** In the last decade, Google has built a worldwide network of datacenters to service its search engine. In doing so Google has captured a substantial portion of the world's advertising revenue. That revenue has enabled Google to offer free software to users based on that infrastructure and has changed the market for user-facing software. This is the classic Software as a Service case described in Chapter 8.

- **Azure Platform:** By contrast, Microsoft is creating the Azure Platform. It enables .NET Framework applications to run over the Internet as an alternate platform for Microsoft developer software running on desktops, which you will learn about in Chapter 10.

- **Amazon Web Services:** One of the most successful cloud-based businesses is Amazon Web Services, which is an Infrastructure as a Service offering that lets you rent virtual computers on Amazon's own infrastructure. AWS is the subject of Chapter 9.

These new capabilities enable applications to be written and deployed with minimal expense and to be rapidly scaled and made available worldwide as business conditions permit. This is truly a revolutionary change in the way enterprise computing is created and deployed.

Cloud Types

To discuss cloud computing intelligently, you need to define the lexicon of cloud computing; many acronyms in this area probably won't survive long. Most people separate cloud computing into two distinct sets of models:

- **Deployment models:** This refers to the location and management of the cloud's infrastructure.

- **Service models:** This consists of the particular types of services that you can access on a cloud computing platform.

This is a very useful demarcation that is now widely accepted.

The NIST model

The United States government is a major consumer of computer services and, therefore, one of the major users of cloud computing networks. The U.S. National Institute of Standards and Technology (NIST) has a set of working definitions (http://csrc.nist.gov/groups/SNS/cloud-computing/cloud-def-v15.doc) that separate cloud computing into service models and deployment models. Those models and their relationship to essential characteristics of cloud computing are shown in Figure 1.1.

The NIST model originally did not require a cloud to use virtualization to pool resources, nor did it absolutely require that a cloud support multi-tenancy in the earliest definitions of cloud computing. Multi-tenancy is the sharing of resources among two or more clients. The latest version of the NIST definition does require that cloud computing networks use virtualization and support multi-tenancy.

FIGURE 1.1

The NIST cloud computing definitions

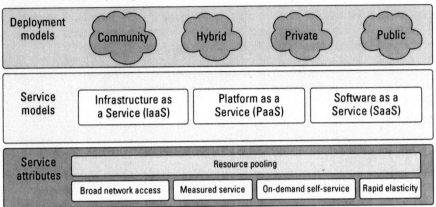

Because cloud computing is moving toward a set of modular interacting components based on standards such as the Service Oriented Architecture (described in Chapter 13), you might expect that future versions of the NIST model may add those features as well. The NIST cloud model doesn't address a number of intermediary services such as transaction or service brokers, provisioning, integration, and interoperability services that form the basis for many cloud computing discussions. Given the emerging roles of service buses, brokers, and cloud APIs at various levels, undoubtedly these elements need to be added to capture the whole story.

The Cloud Cube Model

The Open Group maintains an association called the Jericho Forum (https://www.open group.org/jericho/index.htm) whose main focus is how to protect cloud networks. The group has an interesting model that attempts to categorize a cloud network based on four dimensional factors. As described in its paper called "Cloud Cube Model: Selecting Cloud Formations for Secure Collaboration" (http://www.opengroup.org/jericho/cloud_cube_model_ v1.0.pdf), the type of cloud networks you use dramatically changes the notion of where the boundary between the client's network and the cloud begins and ends.

The four dimensions of the Cloud Cube Model are shown in Figure 1.2 and listed here:

- **Physical location of the data:** Internal (I) / External (E) determines your organization's boundaries.
- **Ownership:** Proprietary (P) / Open (O) is a measure of not only the technology ownership, but of interoperability, ease of data transfer, and degree of vendor application lock-in.

- **Security boundary:** Perimeterised (Per) / De-perimeterised (D-p) is a measure of whether the operation is inside or outside the security boundary or network firewall.
- **Sourcing:** Insourced or Outsourced means whether the service is provided by the customer or the service provider.

FIGURE 1.2

The Jericho Forum's Cloud Cube Model

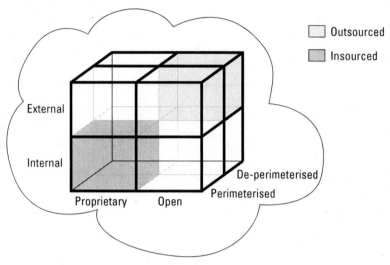

Taken together, the fourth dimension corresponds to two different states in the eight possible cloud forms: Per (IP, IO, EP, EO) and D-p (IP, IO, EP, EO). The sourcing dimension addresses the deliverer of the service. What the Cloud Cube Model is meant to show is that the traditional notion of a network boundary being the network's firewall no longer applies in cloud computing.

Deployment models

A deployment model defines the purpose of the cloud and the nature of how the cloud is located.

The NIST definition for the four deployment models is as follows:

- **Public cloud:** The public cloud infrastructure is available for public use alternatively for a large industry group and is owned by an organization selling cloud services.
- **Private cloud:** The private cloud infrastructure is operated for the exclusive use of an organization. The cloud may be managed by that organization or a third party. Private clouds may be either on- or off-premises.
- **Hybrid cloud:** A hybrid cloud combines multiple clouds (private, community of public) where those clouds retain their unique identities, but are bound together as a unit. A

hybrid cloud may offer standardized or proprietary access to data and applications, as well as application portability.

- **Community cloud:** A community cloud is one where the cloud has been organized to serve a common function or purpose.

    It may be for one organization or for several organizations, but they share common concerns such as their mission, policies, security, regulatory compliance needs, and so on. A community cloud may be managed by the constituent organization(s) or by a third party.

Figure 1.3 shows the different locations that clouds can come in. In the sections that follow, these different cloud deployment models are described in more detail.

FIGURE 1.3

Deployment locations for different cloud types

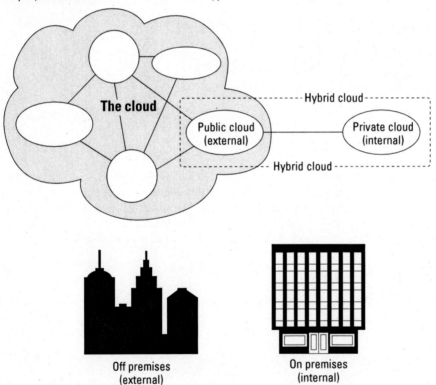

The United States Government, under the auspices of the General Services Administrator (GSA), launched a cloud computing portal called Apps.gov, as shown in Figure 1.4, with the purpose of providing cloud services to federal agencies. Described under the "U.S. Federal Cloud Computing

Initiative (http://www.scribd.com/doc/17914883/US-Federal-Cloud-Computing-Initiative-RFQ-GSA), the goal of the initiative is to make large portions of the federal government's apparatus available under a cloud computing model. This is a good example of a community cloud deployment, with the government being the community.

FIGURE 1.4

Apps.gov is the U.S. government's cloud computing system for its various agencies.

Apps.gov is also making available connections to free media services from its cloud, such as Twitter and YouTube. An example of this connection in practice is the YouTube channel created by the White House for citizens' outreach. You can find the White House channel at http://www.youtube.com/whitehouse and the general U.S. Government YouTube channel at http://www.youtube.com/usgovernment. You can see YouTube in action when you visit WhiteHouse.gov and click the video link that usually appears on that home page.

Service models

In the deployment model, different cloud types are an expression of the manner in which infrastructure is deployed. You can think of the cloud as the boundary between where a client's network, management, and responsibilities ends and the cloud service provider's begins. As cloud computing has developed, different vendors offer clouds that have different services associated with them. The portfolio of services offered adds another set of definitions called the service model.

There are many different service models described in the literature, all of which take the following form:

XaaS, or "*<Something>* as a Service"

Three service types have been universally accepted:

- **Infrastructure as a Service:** IaaS provides virtual machines, virtual storage, virtual infra-structure, and other hardware assets as resources that clients can provision.

  The IaaS service provider manages all the infrastructure, while the client is responsible for all other aspects of the deployment. This can include the operating system, applications, and user interactions with the system.

- **Platform as a Service:** PaaS provides virtual machines, operating systems, applications, services, development frameworks, transactions, and control structures.

  The client can deploy its applications on the cloud infrastructure or use applications that were programmed using languages and tools that are supported by the PaaS service pro-vider. The service provider manages the cloud infrastructure, the operating systems, and the enabling software. The client is responsible for installing and managing the application that it is deploying.

- **Software as a Service:** SaaS is a complete operating environment with applications, man-agement, and the user interface.

  In the SaaS model, the application is provided to the client through a thin client interface (a browser, usually), and the customer's responsibility begins and ends with entering and managing its data and user interaction. Everything from the application down to the infra-structure is the vendor's responsibility.

The three different service models taken together have come to be known as the SPI model of cloud computing. Many other service models have been mentioned: StaaS, Storage as a Service; IdaaS, Identity as a Service; CmaaS, Compliance as a Service; and so forth. However, the SPI ser-vices encompass all the other possibilities.

It is useful to think of cloud computing's service models in terms of a hardware/software stack. One such representation called the Cloud Reference Model is shown in Figure 1.5. At the bottom of the stack is the hardware or infrastructure that comprises the network. As you move upward in the stack, each service model inherits the capabilities of the service model beneath it. IaaS has the least levels of integrated functionality and the lowest levels of integration, and SaaS has the most.

Examples of IaaS service providers include:

- Amazon Elastic Compute Cloud (EC2)
- Eucalyptus
- GoGrid

- FlexiScale
- Linode
- RackSpace Cloud
- Terremark

All these vendors offer direct access to hardware resources. On Amazon EC2, considered the classic IaaS example, a client would provision a computer in the form of a virtual machine image, provision storage, and then go on to install the operating system and applications onto that virtual system. Amazon has a number of operating systems and some enterprise applications that they offer on a rental basis to customers in the form of a number of canned images, but customers are free to install whatever software they want to run. Amazon's responsibilities as expressed in its Service Level Agreement, which is published on Amazon's Web site, contractually obligates Amazon to provide a level of performance commensurate with the type of resource chosen, as well as a certain level of reliability as measured by the system's uptime.

FIGURE 1.5

The Cloud Reference Model

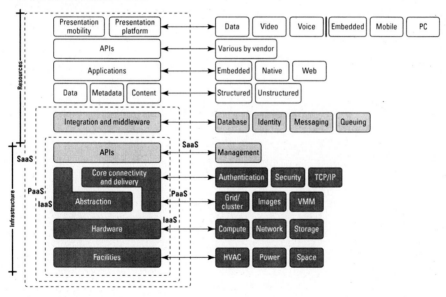

A PaaS service adds integration features, middleware, and other orchestration and choreography services to the IaaS model. Examples of PaaS services are:

- Force.com
- GoGrid CloudCenter

- Google AppEngine
- Windows Azure Platform

When a cloud computing vendor offers software running in the cloud with use of the application on a pay-as-you-go model, it is referred to as SaaS. With SaaS, the customer uses the application as needed and is not responsible for the installation of the application, its maintenance, or its upkeep. A good example of an SaaS offering is an online accounting package, with the online versions of Quicken and Quickbooks a prime example. Figure 1.6 shows a home page for QuickBooks Online plus on the Intuit.com Web site.

FIGURE 1.6

A home page for a Quickbooks customer on the Intuit.com Web site is an example of an SaaS service.

A client using an SaaS service might—as is the case for Quickbooks online—log into the service from his browser, create an account, and enter data into the system. Intuit.com has a service agreement that not only covers the performance of the hardware and software, but extends to protecting the data that they store for clients, and other fundamental characteristics.

Other good examples of SaaS cloud service providers are:

- GoogleApps
- Oracle On Demand
- SalesForce.com
- SQL Azure

These service model classifications start to get confusing rather quickly when you have a cloud service provider that starts out offering services in one area and then develops services that are classified as another type. For example, SalesForce.com started out as a Customer Relationship Management SaaS platform that allowed clients to add their own applications. Over time SalesForce.com opened an API called the Force API that allowed developers to create applications based on the SalesForce.com technologies. Force.com is thus their PaaS service.

As another example, take the PaaS offering that is the Windows Azure Platform. Windows Azure Platform allows .NET developers to stage their applications on top of Microsoft's infrastructure so that any application built with the .NET Framework can live locally, in Microsoft's cloud network, or some combination thereof. As Microsoft adds enterprise applications to its cloud service portfolio, as it has in the case of SQL Azure (and many other enterprise applications to come), these offerings fall under the rubric of being an SaaS service model.

Because a discussion of service models forms the basis for Chapter 4, I refer you to that chapter for a more in-depth discussion of this topic.

Examining the Characteristics of Cloud Computing

Cloud computing builds on so many older concepts in computer technology that it can be hard for people newly introduced to the concept to grasp that it represents a paradigm shift in computing. It's an evolutionary change that enables a revolutionary new approach to how computing services are produced and consumed.

Paradigm shift

When you choose a cloud service provider, you are renting or leasing part of an enormous infrastructure of datacenters, computers, storage, and networking capacity. Many of these datacenters are multi-million-dollar investments by the companies that run them. To give you some sense of scale, it has been estimated that a state-of-the-art microchip fabrication facility can cost anywhere from $2 to $5 billion. By comparison, a state of the art cloud computing datacenter can run in the range of $100 million. Most of the large cloud computing service providers have multiple datacenters located all over the world. An accurate count can be difficult to obtain, but in Chapter 9 the location of some 20 datacenters in Amazon Web Service's cloud are detailed. Google's cloud includes perhaps some 35 datacenters worldwide.

In the 1960s, military initiative aimed at miniaturizing electronics funded many of the semiconductor production lines that led to advanced microprocessors, dense memory arrays, and the sophisticated integrated circuit technology that makes computers, mobile devices, and so much more possible today. In the 1990s, the commercialization of the Internet gave rise to some very large companies that were forced to build very large computing infrastructures to support their businesses.

Amazon.com's infrastructure was built to support elastic demand so the system could accommodate peak traffic on a busy shopping day such as "Black Monday." Because much of the capacity was idle, Amazon.com first opened its network to partners and then as Amazon Web Services to customers.

Google's business has also grown exponentially and required the building of datacenters worldwide. One of its datacenters in Dalles, Oregon, built in 2006 on the banks of the Columbia River, is shown in Figure 1.7. It is the size of an American football field.

FIGURE 1.7

The Google Dalles, Oregon, datacenter shown in Google Earth is an industrial-sized information technology utility.

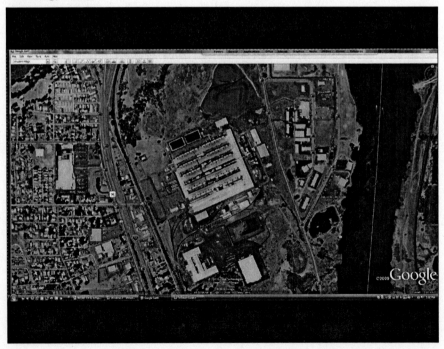

As these various datacenters grew in size, businesses have developed their datacenters as "green-field" projects. Datacenters have been sited to do the following:

- Have access to low cost power
- Leverage renewable power source
- Be near abundant water
- Be sited where high-speed network backbone connections can be made
- Keep land costs modest and occupation unobtrusive
- Obtain tax breaks
- Optimize the overall system latency

These characteristics make cloud computing networks highly efficient and capture enough margin to make utility computing profitable.

It has been estimated that the Internet consumes roughly 10 percent of the world's total power, so these companies are very big energy consumers. In some cases, such as Google, these companies may also become some of the major energy producers of the 21st century. Essentially what has happened is that the Internet has funded the creation of the first information technology utilities. That's why cloud computing is such a big deal.

According to the research firm IDC, the following areas were the top five cloud applications in use in 2010:

- Collaboration applications
- Web applications/Web serving
- Cloud backup
- Business applications
- Personal productivity applications

The last five years have seen a proliferation of services and productivity applications delivered on-line as cloud computing applications. Examples of the impact of cloud computing abound in your everyday life, although many people do not make the connection to what was once a straightforward client/server Internet deployment. Movement of these applications to the cloud has been transparent, and in many cases the older on-premises deployment is supported by the same applications hosted in the cloud.

For example, many people have used ChannelAdvisor.com for their auction listings and sales management. That site recently expanded its service to include a CRM connector to Salesforce.com. One of the largest call center operations companies is a cloud-based service, Liveops.com. Figure 1.8 shows the Liveops home page.

Cloud computing has shifted the economics of software delivery in a manner similar to the way that music downloads have shifted the delivery of commercial music. The cost advantages of cloud computing have enabled new software vendors to create productivity applications that they can make available to people at a much smaller cost than would be possible for shrink-wrapped software. Given the general demise of the big-box computer store along with many other traditional retail models, it has become increasingly difficult for vendors to get shelf space. You can visit your local Wal-Mart to get some sense of this issue.

In Chapter 16, "Working with Productivity Software," some of these applications are described. This new model of computer application delivery has allowed vendors like Google to offer complete office suites to individuals for free, supported by its advertiser subscription model. Even Google's business offerings have had some major successes against industry leader Microsoft Office. Last year, Los Angeles County switched to Google Docs.

FIGURE 1.8

Liveops.com is a cloud computing call center service.

Benefits of cloud computing

"The NIST Definition of Cloud Computing" by Peter Mell and Tim Grance (version 14, 10/7/2009) described previously in this chapter (refer to Figure 1.1) that classified cloud computing into the three SPI service models (SaaS, IaaS, and PaaS) and four cloud types (public, private, community, and hybrid), also assigns five essential characteristics that cloud computing systems must offer:

- **On-demand self-service:** A client can provision computer resources without the need for interaction with cloud service provider personnel.

- **Broad network access:** Access to resources in the cloud is available over the network using standard methods in a manner that provides platform-independent access to clients of all types.

  This includes a mixture of heterogeneous operating systems, and thick and thin platforms such as laptops, mobile phones, and PDA.

- **Resource pooling:** A cloud service provider creates resources that are pooled together in a system that supports multi-tenant usage.

  Physical and virtual systems are dynamically allocated or reallocated as needed. Intrinsic in this concept of pooling is the idea of abstraction that hides the location of resources such as virtual machines, processing, memory, storage, and network bandwidth and connectivity.

- **Rapid elasticity:** Resources can be rapidly and elastically provisioned.

  The system can add resources by either scaling up systems (more powerful computers) or scaling out systems (more computers of the same kind), and scaling may be automatic or manual. From the standpoint of the client, cloud computing resources should look limit-less and can be purchased at any time and in any quantity.

- **Measured service:** The use of cloud system resources is measured, audited, and reported to the customer based on a metered system.

  A client can be charged based on a known metric such as amount of storage used, number of transactions, network I/O (Input/Output) or bandwidth, amount of processing power used, and so forth. A client is charged based on the level of services provided.

While these five core features of cloud computing are on almost anybody's list, you also should consider these additional advantages:

- **Lower costs:** Because cloud networks operate at higher efficiencies and with greater utilization, significant cost reductions are often encountered.

- **Ease of utilization:** Depending upon the type of service being offered, you may find that you do not require hardware or software licenses to implement your service.

- **Quality of Service:** The Quality of Service (QoS) is something that you can obtain under contract from your vendor.

- **Reliability:** The scale of cloud computing networks and their ability to provide load balancing and failover makes them highly reliable, often much more reliable than what you can achieve in a single organization.

- **Outsourced IT management:** A cloud computing deployment lets someone else manage your computing infrastructure while you manage your business. In most instances, you achieve considerable reductions in IT staffing costs.

- **Simplified maintenance and upgrade:** Because the system is centralized, you can easily apply patches and upgrades. This means your users always have access to the latest software versions.
- **Low Barrier to Entry:** In particular, upfront capital expenditures are dramatically reduced. In cloud computing, anyone can be a giant at any time.

This very long list of benefits should make it obvious why so many people are excited about the idea of cloud computing. Cloud computing is not a panacea, however. In many instances, cloud computing doesn't work well for particular applications.

Disadvantages of cloud computing

While the benefits of cloud computing are myriad, the disadvantages are just as numerous. As a general rule, the advantages of cloud computing present a more compelling case for small organizations than for larger ones. Larger organizations can support IT staff and development efforts that put in place custom software solutions that are crafted with their particular needs in mind.

When you use an application or service in the cloud, you are using something that isn't necessarily as customizable as you might want. Additionally, although many cloud computing applications are very capable, applications deployed on-premises still have many more features than their cloud counterparts.

All cloud computing applications suffer from the inherent latency that is intrinsic in their WAN connectivity. While cloud computing applications excel at large-scale processing tasks, if your application needs large amounts of data transfer, cloud computing may not be the best model for you.

Additionally, cloud computing is a stateless system, as is the Internet in general. In order for communication to survive on a distributed system, it is necessarily unidirectional in nature. All the requests you use in HTTP: PUTs, GETs, and so on are requests to a service provider. The service provider then sends a response. Although it may seem that you are carrying on a conversation between client and provider, there is an architectural disconnect between the two. That lack of state allows messages to travel over different routes and for data to arrive out of sequence, and many other characteristics allow the communication to succeed even when the medium is faulty. Therefore, to impose transactional coherency upon the system, additional overhead in the form of service brokers, transaction managers, and other middleware must be added to the system. This can introduce a very large performance hit into some applications.

If you had to pick a single area of concern in cloud computing, that area would undoubtedly be privacy and security. When your data travels over and rests on systems that are no longer under your control, you have increased risk due to the interception and malfeasance of others. You can't count on a cloud provider maintaining your privacy in the face of government actions.

In the United States, an example is the National Security Agency's program that ran millions of phone calls from AT&T and Verizon through a data analyzer to extract the phone calls that matched its security criteria. VoIP is one of the services that is heavily deployed on cloud computing systems. Another example is the case of Google's service in China, which had been subject to a filter that removed content to which the Chinese government objected. After five years of operation, and after Google detected that Chinese hackers were accessing Gmail accounts of Chinese citizens, Google moved their servers for Google.ch to Hong Kong.

So while the cloud computing industry continues to address security concerns, if you have an application that works with sensitive data, you need to be particularly aware of the issues involved. Chapter 12, "Understanding Cloud Security," expands upon these points in more detail.

These days most organizations are faced with regulatory compliance issues of various kinds. In the United States, companies must comply with the accounting requirements of the Sarbanes-Oxley Act; health care providers comply with the data privacy rules of HIPAA, and so on. In Europe, the European Common Market has a raft of its own legislation for companies to deal with. Rules apply to data at rest, and different rules may apply to data in transit. If you stage your cloud computing deployment across states and countries, the bad news is that you may end up having to comply with multiple jurisdictions. Don't expect much support from the cloud system provider or from the governments involved. The laws of most regulatory agencies place the entire burden on the client. So when it comes to compliance, cloud computing is still the "Wild West" of computing.

Assessing the Role of Open Standards

When you consider the development of cloud computing to date, it is clear that the technology is the result of the convergence of many different standards. Cloud computing's promise of scalability completely changes the manner in which services and applications are deployed. Without standards, the industry creates proprietary systems with vendor lock-in, sometimes referred to as "stovepipe" clouds. Because clients do not want to be locked into any single system, there is a strong industry push to create standards-based clouds.

The cloud computing industry is working with these architectural standards:

- Platform virtualization of resources
- Service-oriented architecture
- Web-application frameworks
- Deployment of open-source software
- Standardized Web services
- Autonomic systems
- Grid computing

These standards help to enable different business models that cloud computing vendors can support, most notably Software as a Service (SaaS), Web 2.0 applications, and utility computing. These businesses require open standards so that data is both portable and universally accessible.

The race to create the first generation of open cloud platform technologies that will compete with proprietary technologies offered by companies such as Microsoft (Azure Platform) and VMware (vSphere) is already underway. Rackspace.com, one of the large IaaS cloud service providers, announced in July 2010 that it is initiating an open-source project called OpenStack that will begin with the code used to run its Cloud Files and Cloud Servers technologies. NASA has also donated some of the Nebula Cloud Platform technology that it developed. The software developed will be released under the Apache 2.0 license. Founding members of this project include AMD, Citrix, Dell, Intel, NTT Data, and several other cloud service providers. OpenStack.org's home page (http://www.openstack.org/) is shown in Figure 1.9.

The first two deliverables of the project are a distributed object store based on Rackspace Cloud Files and a scalable machine provisioning technology based on NASA Nebula and Rackspace Cloud Servers. OpenStack Compute software will automatically create large groups of virtual private servers on industry-standard systems. OpenStack Storage is the software that will create redundant object-based storage using clusters of commodity servers and storage systems.

FIGURE 1.9

OpenStack.org is an industry group seeking to create open cloud standards based on Rackspace.com and NASA technologies.

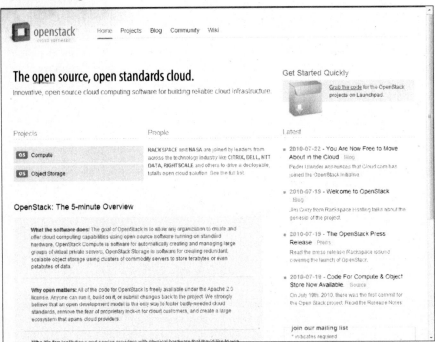

Eucalyptus (`http://open.eucalyptus.com/`) is a Linux-based software platform for creating cloud computing IaaS systems based on computer clusters. The project has an interface that can connect to Amazon's compute and storage cloud systems (EC2 and S3), and it maintains a private cloud as a sandbox for developers to work in. Eucalyptus works with a number of technologies for system virtualization, including VMware, Xen, and KVM. Eucalyptus is an acronym taken from the expression "Elastic Utility Computing Architecture for Linking Your Programs to Useful Systems." Most of the major Linux vendors support this project, which is based on the original work of Rich Wolski at the University of California at Santa Barbara. The company Eucalyptus Systems was formed in 2009 to support the commercialization of the Eucalyptus Cloud Computing Platform.

OpenStack and Eucalyptus are by no means unique; several other projects are underway to create open-source cloud platforms. There also are numerous research projects in the area. The IEEE Technical Committee on Services Computing (`http://tab.computer.org/tcsc/`) sponsors a conference in this area called CLOUD and has some working groups and publications in this area. Figure 1.10 shows the home page of TCSC.

FIGURE 1.10

The home page of the IEEE Technical Committee on Services Computing (`http://tab.computer.org/tcsc/`), which works with the cloud computing community to create standards

Summary

In this chapter, you learned what is meant by the term "cloud computing." Cloud computing defines systems that are virtualized and where resources are pooled so that customers can provision computing resources as needed.

To understand cloud computing and fully appreciate its subtleties, you need to categorize the different cloud types. The two types of cloud models are those based on where the cloud is deployed and those based on the types of services that clouds offer. In this chapter, you were introduced to these cloud types.

Cloud computing has a number of benefits and has attracted great industry and general interest. Cloud computing allows systems to be created cheaply with little upfront costs and to be scaled to massive sizes, when needed. Not all applications and services benefit from cloud computing, and I presented some of the factors that help you differentiate between successful deployments and those that are not.

In Chapter 2, "Assessing the Value Proposition," the economics of cloud computing are discussed.

Assessing the Value Proposition

In this chapter, the various attributes of cloud computing that make it a unique service are described. These attributes—scalability, elasticity, low barrier to entry, and a utility type of delivery—completely change how applications are created, priced, and delivered. I describe the factors that have led to this new model of computing. Early adopters of these services are those enterprises that can best make use of these characteristics.

To get a sense for the value of cloud computing, this chapter compares it to on-premises systems. From this perspective, a number of benefits for cloud computing emerge, along with many obstacles. I describe these factors in some detail. Aside from technological reasons, behavior considerations associated with cloud adoption are discussed.

Cloud computing is particularly valuable because it shifts capital expenditures into operating expenditures. This has the benefit of decoupling growth from cash on hand or from requiring access to capital. It also shifts risk away from an organization and onto the cloud provider.

This chapter describes how to begin to measure the costs of cloud computing and some of the tools that you can use to do so. The concept of optimization known as right-sizing is described, and cloud computing has some unique new capabilities in this area.

Service Level Agreements (SLAs) are an important aspect of cloud computing. They are essentially your working contract with any provider. Cloud computing is having impact on software licensing, which although not entirely settled is also described in this chapter.

IN THIS CHAPTER

Discovering the attributes that make cloud computing unique

Applying cloud computing when it is the best option

Measuring the costs associated with cloud computing systems

Learning about Service Level Agreements and Licensing

Measuring the Cloud's Value

Cloud computing presents new opportunities to users and developers because it is based on the paradigm of a shared multitenant utility. The ability to access pooled resources on a pay-as-you-go basis provides a number of system characteristics that completely alter the economics of information technology infrastructures and allows new types of access and business models for user applications.

Any application or process that benefits from economies of scale, commoditization of assets, and conformance to programming standards benefits from the application of cloud computing. Any application or process that requires a completely customized solution, imposes a high degree of specialization, and requires access to proprietary technology is going to expose the limits of cloud computing rather quickly. Applications that work with cloud computing are ones that I refer to as "low touch" applications; they tend to be applications that have low margins and usually low risk. The "high touch" applications that come with high margins require committed resources and pose more of a risk; those applications are best done on-premises.

A cloud is defined as the combination of the infrastructure of a datacenter with the ability to provision hardware and software: A service that concentrates on hardware follows the Infrastructure as a Service (IaaS) model, which is a good description for the Amazon Web Service described in Chapter 9. When you add a software stack, such as an operating system and applications to the service, the model shifts to the Software as a Service (SaaS) model. Microsoft's Windows Azure Platform, discussed in Chapter 10, is best described as currently using SaaS model. When the service requires the client to use a complete hardware/software/application stack, it is using the most refined and restrictive service model, called the Platform as a Service (PaaS) model. The best example of a PaaS offering is probably SalesForce.com. The Google App Engine discussed in Chapter 11 is another PaaS. As the Windows Azure Platform matures adding more access to Microsoft servers, it is developing into a PaaS model rather quickly.

Cross-Ref

Chapter 4, "Understanding Services and Applications by Type," describes a number of these XaaS service models. Cloud computing is in its wild and wooly frontier days, so it's best to take a few of the lesser known acronyms with a grain of salt. ∎

A cloud is an infrastructure that can be partitioned and provisioned, and resources are pooled and virtualized. If the cloud is available to the public on a pay-as-you-go basis, then the cloud is a public cloud, and the service is described as a utility. If the cloud is captive in an organization's infrastructure (network), it is referred to as a private cloud. When you mix public and private clouds together, you have a hybrid cloud. Any analysis of the potential of cloud computing must account for all these possibilities.

These are the unique characteristics of an ideal cloud computing model:

- **Scalability:** You have access to unlimited computer resources as needed.

   This feature obviates the need for planning and provisioning. It also enables batch processing, which greatly speeds up high-processing applications.

- **Elasticity:** You have the ability to right-size resources as required.

  This feature allows you to optimize your system and capture all possible transactions.

- **Low barrier to entry:** You can gain access to systems for a small investment.

  This feature offers access to global resources to small ventures and provides the ability to experiment with little risk.

- **Utility:** A pay-as-you-go model matches resources to need on an ongoing basis.

  This eliminates waste and has the added benefit of shifting risk from the client.

It is the construction of large datacenters running commodity hardware that has enabled cloud computing to gain traction. These datacenters gain access to low-cost electricity, high-network bandwidth pipes, and low-cost commodity hardware and software, which, taken together, represents an economy of scale that allows cloud providers to amortize their investment and retain a profit. It has been estimated that it costs around $100 million to create a datacenter with sufficient scale to be a cloud provider. At this scale, the resources for a large datacenter have been estimated to be between 35 percent and 20 percent lower than the pricing that is offered to medium-sized datacenters.

Note

Members of the UC Berkeley Reliable Adaptive Distribute System Laboratory have published a white paper summarizing the benefits of Cloud Computing called "Above the Clouds: A Berkeley View of Cloud Computing," which can be found at `http://www.eecs.berkeley.edu/Pubs/TechRpts/2009/EECS-2009-28.pdf`. This lab was funded by contributions from the major cloud providers and from the NSF, but it's a useful source of analytical data. ∎

The virtualization of pooled resources—processors or compute engines, storage, and network connectivity—optimizes these investments and allows the cloud provider to pass along these economies to customers. Pooling also blurs the differences between a small deployment and a large one because scale becomes tied only to demand.

Companies become cloud computing providers for several reasons:

- **Profit:** The economies of scale can make this a profitable business.

- **Optimization:** The infrastructure already exists and isn't fully utilized.

  This was certainly the case for Amazon Web Services.

- **Strategic:** A cloud computing platform extends the company's products and defends their franchise.

  This is the case for Microsoft's Windows Azure Platform.

- **Extension:** A branded cloud computing platform can extend customer relationships by offering additional service options.

  This is the case with IBM Global Services and the various IBM cloud services.

- **Presence:** Establish a presence in a market before a large competitor can emerge.

  Google App Engine allows a developer to scale an application immediately. For Google, its office applications can be rolled out quickly and to large audiences.

- **Platform:** A cloud computing provider can become a hub master at the center of many ISV's (Independent Software Vendor) offerings.

  The customer relationship management provider SalesForce.com has a development platform called Force.com that is a PaaS offering.

The development of cloud computing has been likened to the situation that has faced hardware companies that rely on proprietary silicon to produce their products: the AMDs, nVidias, eVGAs, and Apples of the world. Because a semiconductor fabrication facility costs several billion dollars to create, these companies were at a severe disadvantage to companies such as Intel or NEC, which could build their own fabs or fabrication facilities. (A *fab* is a facility that is a self-contained semiconductor assembly line.) Companies such as TSMC (Taiwan Semiconductor Manufacturing Company) have come along that provide fabrication based on customer designs, spreading their risk and optimizing their operation. Cloud computing is much the same.

Early adopters and new applications

Cloud computing is still in its infancy, but trends in adoption are already evident. In his white paper "Realizing the Value Proposition of Cloud Computing: CIO's Enterprise IT Strategy for the Cloud," Jitendra Pal Thethi, a Principle Architect for Infosys' Microsoft Technology Group, lists the following business types as the Top 10 adopters of cloud computing:

1. Messaging and team collaboration applications
2. Cross enterprise integration projects
3. Infrastructure consolidation, server, and desktop virtualization efforts
4. Web 2.0 and social strategy companies
5. Web content delivery services
6. Data analytics and computation
7. Mobility applications for the enterprise
8. CRM applications
9. Experimental deployments, test bed labs, and development efforts
10. Backup and archival storage

You can download Thethi's paper from: `http://www.infosys.com/cloud-computing/white-papers/Documents/realizing-value-proposition.pdf`.

As a group, early adopters are categorized by their need for ubiquity and access to large data sets.

Around 2000-2001, some companies began using the Internet to stage various types of user-facing applications such as office suites, accounting packages, games, and so forth. The first attempts by large ISPs to create utility computing date to that period. By 2005-2006, several Internet sites had become sufficiently large that they had developed extensive infrastructure for their own sites. The excess capacity in these sites began to be offered to partners and eventually to the general public.

The infrastructure cloud computing market was established as profitable so that by 2007-2008 many more vendors became cloud providers.

The nature of cloud computing should provide us with new classes of applications, some of which are currently emerging. Because Wide Area Network (WAN) bandwidth provides one of the current bottlenecks for distributed computing, one of the major areas of interest in cloud computing is in establishing content delivery networks (CDN). These solutions are also called edge networks because they cache content geographically.

Due to its scalability, cloud computing provides a means to do high-performance parallel batch processing that wasn't available to many organizations before. If a company must perform a complex data analysis that might take a server a month to do, then with cloud computing you might launch 100 virtual machine instances and complete the analysis in around 8 hours for the same cost. Processor-intensive applications that users currently perform on their desktops such as mathematical simulations in Mathematica and Matlab, graphic rendering in Renderman, and long encoding/decoding tasks are other examples of applications that could benefit from parallel batch processing and be done directly from the desktop. The economics must work out, but this approach is a completely new one for most people and is a game changer.

The relative ubiquity of cloud computing systems also enables emerging classes of interactive mobile applications. The large array of sensors, diagnostic, and mobile devices, all of which both generate data and consume data, require the use of large data sets and on-demand processing that are a good fit for the cloud computing model. Cloud computing also can provide access to multiple data sets that can support layered forms of information, the types of information you get when you view a mashup, such as the layers of information like Panoramio provided in the application Google Earth.

Note

A mashup is an application or Web page that combines data from two or more sources. Ajax (Asynchronous JavaScript and XML) is often used to create mashups. ■

The laws of cloudonomics

Joe Wienman of AT&T Global Services has concisely stated the advantages that cloud computing offers over a private or captured system. His article appeared on Gigaom.com at: `http://gigaom.com/2008/09/07/the-10-laws-of-cloudonomics/`. A summary of Wienman's "10 Laws of Cloudonomics" follows and his interpretation:

1. **Utility services cost less even though they cost more.**

   Utilities charge a premium for their services, but customers save money by not paying for services that they aren't using.

2. **On-demand trumps forecasting.**

   The ability to provision and tear down resources (de-provision) captures revenue and lowers costs.

3. **The peak of the sum is never greater than the sum of the peaks.**

   A cloud can deploy less capacity because the peaks of individual tenants in a shared system are averaged over time by the group of tenants.

4. **Aggregate demand is smoother than individual.**

   Multi-tenancy also tends to average the variability intrinsic in individual demand because the "coefficient of random variables" is always less than or equal to that of any of the individual variables. With a more predictable demand and less variation, clouds can run at higher utilization rates than captive systems. This allows cloud systems to operate at higher efficiencies and lower costs.

5. **Average unit costs are reduced by distributing fixed costs over more units of output.**

   Cloud vendors have a size that allows them to purchase resources at significantly reduced prices. (This feature was described in the previous section.)

6. **Superiority in numbers is the most important factor in the result of a combat (Clausewitz).**

   Weinman argues that a large cloud's size has the ability to repel botnets and DDoS attacks better than smaller systems do.

7. **Space-time is a continuum (Einstein/Minkowski).**

   The ability of a task to be accomplished in the cloud using parallel processing allows real-time business to respond quicker to business conditions and accelerates decision making providing a measurable advantage.

8. **Dispersion is the inverse square of latency.**

   Latency, or the delay in getting a response to a request, requires both large-scale and multi-site deployments that are a characteristic of cloud providers. Cutting latency in half requires four times the number of nodes in a system.

9. **Don't put all your eggs in one basket.**

   The reliability of a system with n redundant components and a reliability of r is $1-(1-r)n$. Therefore, when a datacenter achieves a reliability of 99 percent, two redundant datacenters have a reliability of 99.99 percent (four nines) and three redundant datacenters can achieve a reliability of 99.9999 percent (six nines). Large cloud providers with geographically dispersed sites worldwide therefore achieve reliability rates that are hard for private systems to achieve.

10. **An object at rest tends to stay at rest (Newton).**

    Private datacenters tend to be located in places where the company or unit was founded or acquired. Cloud providers can site their datacenters in what are called "greenfield sites." A *greenfield site* is one that is environmentally friendly: locations that are on a network backbone, have cheap access to power and cooling, where land is inexpensive, and the environmental impact is low. A network backbone is a very high-capacity network connection. On the Internet, an Internet backbone consists of the high-capacity routes and routers that are typically operated by an individual service provider such as a government or commercial entity. You can access a jump page of Internet backbone maps at: `http://www.nthelp.com/maps.htm`.

Cloud computing obstacles

Cloud computing isn't a panacea; nor is it either practical or economically sensible for many computer applications that you encounter. In practice, cloud computing can deviate from the ideals described in the previous list in many significant ways. The illusion of scalability is bounded by the limitations cloud providers place on their clients. Resource limits are exposed at peak conditions of the utility itself. As we all know, power utilities suffer brownouts and outages when the temperature soars, and cloud computing providers are no different. You see these outages on peak computing days such as Black Monday, which is the Monday after Thanksgiving in the United States when Internet Christmas sales traditionally start.

The illusion of low barrier to entry may be pierced by an inconsistent pricing scheme that makes scaling more expensive than it should be. You can see this limit in the nonlinearity of pricing associated with "extra large" machine instances versus their "standard" size counterparts. Additionally, the low barrier to entry also can be accompanied by a low barrier to provisioning. If you make a provisioning error, it can lead to vast costs.

Cloud computing vendors run very reliable networks. Often, cloud data is load-balanced between virtual systems and replicated between sites. However, even cloud providers experience outages. In the cloud, it is common to have various resources, such as machine instances, fail. Except for tightly managed PaaS cloud providers, the burden of resource management is still in the hands of the user, but the user is often provided with limited or immature management tools to address these issues.

Table 2.1 summarizes the various obstacles and challenges that cloud computing faces. These issues are described in various chapters in this book.

TABLE 2.1

Challenges and Obstacles to Cloud Computing

Subject Area	Captive	Cloud	Challenge
Accounting Management	Chargeback or Licensed	Usage	In private systems, costs associated with operations are fixed due to licenses and must be charged back to accounts based on some formula or usage model. For cloud computing, the pay-as-you-go usage model allows for costs to be applied to individual accounts directly.

(continued)

TABLE 2.1	*(continued)*		
Subject Area	**Captive**	**Cloud**	**Challenge**
Compliance	Policy-based	Proprietary	Compliance to laws and policies varies by geographical area. This requires that the cloud accommodate multiple compliance regimes.
Data Privacy	Bounded	Shared with cloud	To ensure data privacy in the cloud, additional security methods such as private encryption, VLANs, firewalls, and local storage of sensitive data is necessary.
Monitoring	Variable but under control	Limited	For private systems, any monitoring system the organization wishes to deploy can be brought to bear. Cloud computing models often have limited monitoring because it is vendor-defined.
Network Bottlenecks	Low	High	Network bottlenecks occur when large data sets must be transferred. This is the case for staging, replication, and other operations. On-premise operations use LANs that are better able to accommodate transfers than the WAN connections used in cloud computing.
Reputation	Individual	Shared	The reputation for cloud computing services for the quality of those services is shared by tenants. An outage of the cloud provider impacts individuals. Clouds often have higher reliability than private systems.
Security	Restricted	Federated	The different trust mechanisms require that applications be structured differently and that operations be modified to account for these differences.
Service Level Agreements (SLAs)	Customized	Cloud specific	Cloud SLAs are standardized in order to appeal to the majority of its audience. Custom SLAs that allow for multiple data sources are difficult to obtain or enforce. Cloud SLAs do not generally offer industry standard chargeback rates, and negotiations with large cloud providers can be difficult for small users. Business risks that aren't covered by a cloud SLA must be taken into account.
Software Stack	Customized	Commoditized	The cloud enforces standardization and lowers the ability of a system to be customized for need.

Subject Area	Captive	Cloud	Challenge
Storage	Scalable and high performance	Scalable but low performance	Enterprise class storage is under the control of an on-premise system and can support high speed queries. In cloud computing large data stores are possible but they have low bandwidth connection. High speed local storage in the cloud tends to be expensive.
Vendor Lock-in	Varies by company	Varies by platform	Vendor lock-in is a function of the particular enterprise and application in an on-premises deployment. For cloud providers, vendor lock-in increases going from the IaaS to SaaS to PaaS model. Vendor lock-in for a cloud computing solution in a PaaS model is very high.

Behavioral factors relating to cloud adoption

The issues described in Table 2.1 are real substantive issues that can be measured and quantified. However, a number of intrinsic properties of cloud computing create cognitive biases in people that are obstacles to cloud adoption and are worth mentioning. This goes for users as well as organizations. Duke University economist Dan Ariely, in his book *Predictably Irrational: The Hidden Forces that Shape Our Decisions* (Harper Collins, 2008), explores how people often make choices that are inconsistent based on expediency or human nature. Joe Weinman has expanded on these ideas and some others to formulate ten more "laws" for cloud computing adoption based on human behavior. You can read the original article at http://gigaom.com/2010/06/06/lazy-hazy-crazy-the-10-laws-of-behavioral-cloudonomics/.

The "10 Laws of Behavioral Cloudonomics" are summarized below:

1. **People are risk averse and loss averse.**

    Ariely argues that losses are more painful than gains are pleasurable. Cloud initiatives may cause the concerns of adoption to be weighed more heavily than the benefits accrued to improving total costs and achieving greater agility.

2. **People have a flat-rate bias.**

    Loss aversion expresses itself by preferences to flat-rate plans where risk is psychologically minimized to usage-based plans where costs are actually less.

    Weiman cites the work of Anja Lambrecht and Bernd Skiera, "Paying Too Much and Being Happy About It: Existence, Causes, and Consequences of Tariff-Choice Biases" (http://www.test2.marketing.wiwi.uni-frankfurt.de/fileadmin/Publikationen/Lambrecht_Skiera_Tariff-Choice-Biases-JMR.pdf) for this point.

3. **People have the need to control their environment and remain anonymous.**

   The need for environmental control is a primal directive. Loss of control leads to "learned helplessness" and shorter life spans.

   You can read about the research in this area in David Rock's Oxford Leadership Journal article "Managing with the Brain in Mind," found at http://www.oxfordleadership.com/journal/vol1_issue1/rock.pdf. The point about shorter life spans comes from the work of Judith Rodin and Ellen Langer, "Long-Term Effects of a Control-Relevant Intervention with the Institutionalized Aged" (http://capital2.capital.edu/faculty/jfournie/documents/Rodin_Judith.pdf), which appeared in the Journal of Personality and Social Psychology in 1977.

4. **People fear change.**

   Uncertainty leads to fear, and fear leads to inertia. This is as true for cloud computing as it is for investing in the stock market.

5. **People value what they own more than what they are given.**

   This is called the endowment effect. It is a predilection for existing assets that is out of line with their value to others. The cognitive science behind this principle is referred to as the choice-supportive bias (http://en.wikipedia.org/wiki/Choice-supportive_bias).

6. **People favor the status quo and invest accordingly.**

   There is a bias toward the way things have been and a willingness to invest in the status quo that is out of line with their current value. In cognitive science, the former attribute is referred to as the status quo bias (http://en.wikipedia.org/wiki/Status_quo_bias), while the latter attribute is referred to as an escalation of commitment (http://en.wikipedia.org/wiki/Escalation_of_commitment).

7. **People discount future risk and favor instant gratification.**

   Weinman argues that because cloud computing is an on-demand service, the instant gratification factor should favor cloud computing.

8. **People favor things that are free.**

   When offered an item that is free or another that costs money but offers a greater gain, people opt for the free item. Weinman argues that this factor also favors the cloud computing model because upfront costs are eliminated.

9. **People have the need for status.**

   A large IT organization with substantial assets is a visual display of your status; a cloud deployment is not. This is expressed as a pride of ownership.

10. **People are incapacitated by choice.**

    The Internet enables commerce to shift to a large inventory where profit can be maintained by many sales of a few items each, the so-called long tail. When this model is applied to cloud computing, people tend to be overwhelmed by the choice and delay adoption.

Measuring cloud computing costs

As you see, cloud computing has many advantages and disadvantages, and you can't always measure them. You can measure costs though, and that's a valuable exercise. Usually a commodity is cheaper than a specialized item, but not always. Depending upon your situation, you can pay more for public cloud computing than you would for owning and managing your private cloud, or for owning and using software as well. That's why it's important to analyze the costs and benefits of your own cloud computing scenario carefully and quantitatively. You will want to compare the costs of cloud computing to private systems.

The cost of a cloud computing deployment is roughly estimated to be

$$\text{Cost}_{\text{CLOUD}} = \Sigma(\text{UnitCost}_{\text{CLOUD}} \times (\text{Revenue} - \text{Cost}_{\text{CLOUD}}))$$

where the unit cost is usually defined as the cost of a machine instance per hour or another resource.

Depending upon the deployment type, other resources add additional unit costs: storage quantity consumed, number of transactions, incoming or outgoing amounts of data, and so forth. Different cloud providers charge different amounts for these resources, some resources are free for one provider and charged for another, and there are almost always variable charges based on resource sizing. Cloud resource pricing doesn't always scale linearly based on performance.

To compare your cost benefit with a private cloud, you will want to compare the value you determine in the equation above with the same calculation:

$$\text{Cost}_{\text{DATACENTER}} = \Sigma(\text{UnitCost}_{\text{DATACENTER}} \times (\text{Revenue} - (\text{Cost}_{\text{DATACENTER}}/\text{Utilization})))$$

Notice the additional term for Utilization added as a divisor to the term for $\text{Cost}_{\text{DATACENTER}}$. This term appears because it is assumed that a private cloud has capacity that can't be captured, and it is further assumed that a private cloud doesn't employ the same level of virtualization or pooling of resources that a cloud computing provider can achieve. Indeed, no system can work at 100 percent utilization because queuing theory states that as the system approaches 100 percent, the latency and response times go to infinity. Typical efficiencies in datacenters are between 60 and 85 percent. It is also further assumed that the datacenter is operating under averaged loads (not at peak capacity) and that the capacity of the datacenter is fixed by the assets it has.

There is another interesting aspect to the calculated costs associated with $Cost_{CLOUD}$ vs. $Cost_{DATACENTER}$: The costs associated with resources in the cloud computing model $Cost_{CLOUD}$ can be unbundled to a greater extent than the costs associated with $Cost_{DATACENTER}$. The $Cost_{DATACENTER}$ consists of the summation of the cost of each of the individual systems with all the associated resources, as follows:

$$Cost_{DATACENTER} = {}_1^n\Sigma(UnitCost_{DATACENTER} \times (Revenue - (Cost_{DATACENTER}/Utilization)))_{SYSTEMn},$$

where the sum includes terms for System 1, System 2, System 3, and so on.

The costs of a system in a datacenter must also include the overhead associated with power, cooling, and the physical plant. Estimates of these additional overheads indicate that over the lifetime of a system, overhead roughly doubles the cost of any system. For a server with a four-year lifetime, you would therefore need to include an overhead roughly equal to 25 percent of the system's acquisition cost.

The overhead associated with IT staff is also a major cost, but it's highly variable from organization to organization. It is not uncommon for the burden cost of a system in a datacenter to be 150 percent of the cost of the system itself.

The costs associated with the cloud model are calculated rather differently. Each resource has its own specific cost and many resources can be provisioned independently of one another. In theory, therefore, the $Cost_{CLOUD}$ is better represented by the equation:

$$Cost_{CLOUD} = {}_1^n\Sigma(UnitCost_{CLOUD} \times (Revenue - Cost_{CLOUD}))_{INSTANCEn} +$$
$${}_1^n\Sigma(UnitCost_{CLOUD} \times (Revenue - Cost_{CLOUD}))_{STORAGE\_UNITn} +$$
$${}_1^n\Sigma(UnitCost_{CLOUD} \times (Revenue - Cost_{CLOUD}))_{NETWORK\_UNITn} + \cdots$$

In practice, cloud providers offer packages of machine instances with a fixed relationship between a machine instances, memory allocation (RAM), and network bandwidth. Storage and transactions are unbundled and variable.

Many cloud computing providers have created their own cost calculators to support their customers. Amazon lets you create a simulated billing based on the machine instances, storage, transactions, and other resources that you provision. An example is the Amazon Simple Monthly Calculator (`http://calculator.s3.amazonaws.com/calc5.html`) shown in Figure 2.1. You can find similar calculators elsewhere or download a spreadsheet with the calculations built into it from the various sites.

FIGURE 2.1

The Amazon Web Service Simple Monthly Calculator

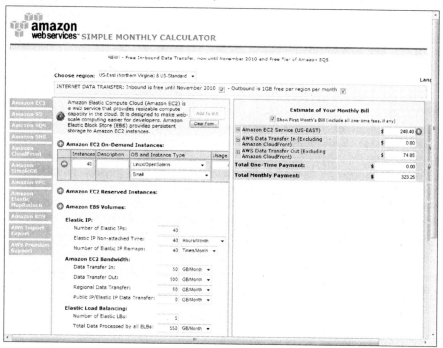

Avoiding Capital Expenditures

A major part of cloud computing's value proposition and its appeal is its ability to convert capital expenses (CapEx) to operating expenses (OpEx) through a usage pricing scheme that is elastic and can be right-sized. The conversion of real assets to virtual ones provides a measure of protection against too much or too little infrastructure. Essentially, moving expenses onto the OpEx side of a budget allows an organization to transfer risk to their cloud computing provider.

Capitalization may be the single largest reason that new businesses fail, and it is surely an impediment to established businesses starting new enterprises. Growth itself can be difficult when revenues don't cover the expansion and obtaining financing is difficult. A company wishing to grow would normally be faced with the following options:

- Buy the new equipment, and deploy it in-house

- Lease the equipment for a set period of time

- Outsource the operation to a managed-services organization

Capital expenditures must create the infrastructure necessary to capture the transactions that the business needs. However, if demand is variable, then it is an open question as to how much infrastructure is needed to support demand.

Cloud computing is also a good option when the cost of infrastructure and management is high. This is often the case with legacy applications and systems where maintaining the system capabilities is a significant cost.

Right-sizing

Consider an accounting firm with a variable demand load, as shown in Figure 2.2. For each of the four quarters of the tax year, clients file their quarterly taxes on the service's Web site. Demand for three of those quarters rises broadly as the quarterly filing deadline arrives. The fourth quarter that represents the year-end tax filing on April 15 shows a much larger and more pronounced spike for the two weeks approaching and just following that quarter's end. Clearly, this accounting business can't ignore the demand spike for its year-end accounting, because this is the single most important portion of the firm's business, but it needs to match demand to resources to maximize its profits.

FIGURE 2.2

Right-sizing demand to infrastructure

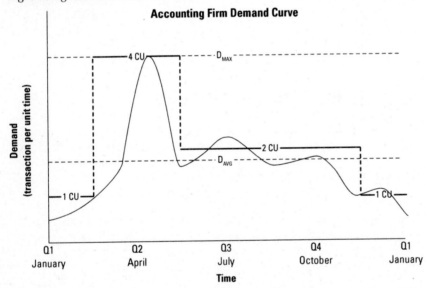

Buying and leasing infrastructure to accommodate the peak demand (or alternatively load) shown in the figure as D_{MAX} means that nearly half of that infrastructure remains idle for most of the time. Fitting the infrastructure to meet the average demand, D_{AVG}, means that half of the transactions in the

Q2 spike are not captured, which is the mission critical portion of this enterprise. More accurately using D_{AVG} means that during maximum demand the service is slowed to a crawl and the system may not be responsive enough to satisfy any of the users.

These limits can be a serious constraint on profit and revenue. Outsourcing the demand may provide a solution to the problem. But outsourcing essentially shifts the burden of capital expenditures onto the service provider. A service contract that doesn't match infrastructure to demand suffers from the same inefficiencies that captive infrastructure does.

The cloud computing model addresses this problem by allowing you to right-size your infrastructure. In Figure 2.2, the demand is satisfied by an infrastructure that is labeled in terms of a CU or "Compute Unit." The rule for this particular cloud provider is that infrastructure may be modified at the beginning of any month. For the low-demand Q1/Q4 time period, a 1 CU infrastructure is applied. On February 1st, the size is changed to a 4 CU infrastructure, which captures the entire spike of Q2 demand. Finally, on June 1st, a 2 CU size is applied to accommodate the typical demand DAVG that is experienced in the last half of Q2 through the middle of Q4. This curve-fitting exercise captures the demand nearly all the time with little idle capacity left unused.

Note

In reality, the major cloud providers provide machine instances in small slices that can be added within five minutes or less. A standard machine instance (virtual computer) might cost $0.10 or less an hour; a typical storage charge might be $0.10 per GB/month. It is this flexibility that has made cloud computing viable. Past efforts to push cloud computing such as the Intel Computing Services (circa 2000) approach required negotiated contracts and long commitments, which is why this service didn't gain traction. ■

If this deployment represented a single server, then 1 CU might represent a single dual-core processor, 2 CU might represent a quad-core processor, and 4 CU might represent a dual quad-core processor virtual system. Most cloud providers size their systems small, medium, and large in just this manner.

Right-sizing is possible when the system load is cyclical or in some cases when there are predictable bursts or spikes in the load. You encounter cyclical loads in many public facing commercial ventures with seasonal demands, when the load is affected by time zones, and at times that new products launch. Burst loads are less predictable. You can encounter bursts in systems that are gateways or hubs for traffic. In situations where demand is unpredictable and change can be rapid, right-sizing a cloud computing solution demands automated solutions. Amazon Web Services' Auto Scaling feature (`http://aws.amazon.com/autoscaling/`) for its EC2 service described in Chapter 9 is an example of such an automated solution. Shared systems with multiple tenants that need to scale are another example where right-sizing can be applied.

Computing the Total Cost of Ownership

The Total Cost of Ownership or TCO is a financial estimate for the costs of the use of a product or service over its lifetime, often broken out on a yearly or quarterly basis. In pitching cloud computing projects, it is common to create spreadsheets that predict the costs of using the cloud computing model versus performing the same functions in-house or on-premises.

To be really useful, a TCO must account for the real costs of items, but frequently they do not. For example, the cost of a system deployed in-house is not only the cost of acquisition and the cost of maintenance. A system consumes resources such as space in a datacenter or portion of your site, power, cooling, and management. All these resources represent an overhead that is often over-looked, either in error or for political reasons. When you account for monitoring and management of systems, you must account for the burdened cost of an IT employee, the cost of the hardware and software that is used for management, and other hidden costs.

The Wikipedia page on Total Cost of Ownership (`http://en.wikipedia.org/wiki/Total_cost_of_ownership`) contains a list of computer and software industries TCO elements that are a good place to start to build your own worksheet.

Note
A really thorough and meaningful TCO study should probably be done by an accountant or consultant with a financial background in this area to obtain meaningful results. ∎

You can find many examples of TCO wizards and worksheets for cloud systems. Microsoft maintains an economics page (`http://www.microsoft.com/windowsazure/economics/#tco_content`) for its Windows Azure Platform. One of the features on the page is a link to a TCO calculator that is based on an engine created by Alinean. In this calculator, you describe your business, its location and industry, and the level of activity (logins and connections) in the first step of the wizard. The Azure TCO Calculator shows you its recommendations for deployment, the Azure costs, and a report of its analysis as the last step of the wizard.

Figure 2.3 shows you a report for a hypothetical company with 10 servers on Azure. You can use this report to show graphs and print the report, and the factors it presents in this report may be useful to you.

Any discussion of Total Cost of Ownership provides an operational look at infrastructure deployment. A better metric for enterprises is captured by a Return on Investment or ROI calculation. To accurately measure an ROI, you need to capture the opportunities that a business has been able to avail itself of (or not), something that is accurate only in hindsight. The flexibility and agility of cloud computing allows a company to focus on its core business and create more opportunities.

FIGURE 2.3

The Microsoft Azure Platform ROI wizard provides a quick and dirty analysis of your TCO for a cloud deployment on Windows Azure in an attractive report format.

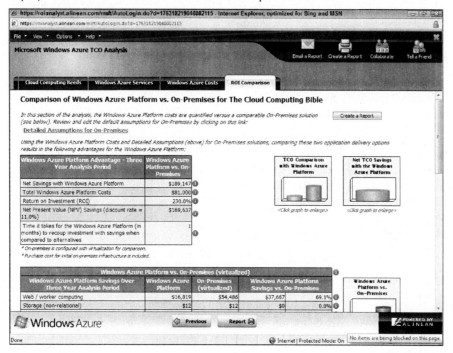

Specifying Service Level Agreements

A Service Level Agreement (SLA) is the contract for performance negotiated between you and a service provider. In the early days of cloud computing, all SLAs were negotiated between a client and the provider. Today with the advent of large utility-like cloud computing providers, most SLAs are standardized until a client becomes a large consumer of services.

Caution

Some SLAs are enforceable as contracts, but many are really agreements that are more along the lines of an Operating Level Agreement (OLA) and may not have the force of law. It's good to have an attorney review these documents before you make a major commitment to a cloud provider. ■

SLAs usually specify these parameters:

- Availability of the service (uptime)
- Response times or latency

- Reliability of the service components
- Responsibilities of each party
- Warranties

If a vendor fails to meet the stated targets or minimums, it is punished by having to offer the client a credit or pay a penalty. In this regard, an SLA should be like buying insurance, and like buying insurance, getting the insurer to pay up when disaster strikes can be the devil's work.

Microsoft publishes the SLAs associated with the Windows Azure Platform components at `http://www.microsoft.com/windowsazure/sla/`, which is illustrative of industry practice for cloud providers. Each individual component has its own SLA. The summary versions of these SLAs from Microsoft are reproduced here:

- **Windows Azure SLA:** "Windows Azure has separate SLA's for compute and storage. For compute, we guarantee that when you deploy two or more role instances in different fault and upgrade domains, your Internet facing roles will have external connectivity at least 99.95% of the time. Additionally, we will monitor all of your individual role instances and guarantee that 99.9% of the time we will detect when a role instance's process is not running and initiate corrective action."

Cross-Ref
The different components of the Windows Azure Platform are discussed in detail in Chapter 10. ■

- **SQL Azure SLA:** "SQL Azure customers will have connectivity between the database and our Internet gateway. SQL Azure will maintain a "Monthly Availability" of 99.9% during a calendar month. "Monthly Availability Percentage" for a specific customer database is the ratio of the time the database was available to customers to the total time in a month. Time is measured in 5-minute intervals in a 30-day monthly cycle. Availability is always calculated for a full month. An interval is marked as unavailable if the customer's attempts to connect to a database are rejected by the SQL Azure gateway."

- **AppFabric SLA:** "Uptime percentage commitments and SLA credits for Service Bus and Access Control are similar to those specified above in the Windows Azure SLA. Due to inherent differences between the technologies, underlying SLA definitions and terms differ for the Service Bus and Access Control services. Using the Service Bus, customers will have connectivity between a customer's service endpoint and our Internet gateway; when our service fails to establish a connection from the gateway to a customer's service endpoint, then the service is assumed to be unavailable. Using Access Control, customers will have connectivity between the Access Control endpoints and our Internet gateway. In addition, for both Service Bus and Access Control, the service will process correctly formatted requests for the handling of messages and tokens; when our service fails to process a request properly, then the service is assumed to be unavailable. SLA calculations will be based on an average over a 30-day monthly cycle, with 5-minute time intervals. Failures seen by a customer in the form of service unavailability will be counted for the purpose of availability calculations for that customer."

You can find Google's App Engine for Business SLA at `http://code.google.com/appengine/business/sla.html`. The SLA for Amazon Web Service Elastic Computer Cloud (EC2) is published at `http://aws.amazon.com/ec2-sla/`, and the SLA for Amazon Simple Storage Service (S3) may be found at `http://aws.amazon.com/s3-sla/`.

Some cloud providers allow for service credits based on their ability to meet their contractual levels of uptime. For example, Amazon applies a service credit of 10 percent off the charge for Amazon S3 if the monthly uptime is equal to or greater than 99 percent but less than 99.9 percent. When the uptime drops below 99 percent, the service credit percentage rises to 25 percent and this credit is applied to usage in the next billing period. Amazon Web Services uses an algorithm that calculates uptime based on the following formula:

Uptime = Error Rate/Requests

as measured for each 5-minute interval during a billing period. The error rate is based on internal server counters such as "InternalError" or "ServiceUnavailable." There are exclusions that limit Amazon's exposure.

Service Level Agreements are based on the usage model. Most cloud providers price their pay-as-you-go resources at a premium and issue standard SLAs only for that purpose. You can also purchase subscriptions at various levels that guarantee you access to a certain amount of purchased resources. The SLAs attached to a subscription often offer different terms. If your organization requires access to a certain level of resources, then you need a subscription to a service. A usage model may not provide that level of access under peak load conditions.

Defining Licensing Models

When you purchase shrink-wrapped software, you are using that software based on a licensing agreement called a EULA or End User License Agreement. The EULA may specify that the software meets the following criteria:

- It is yours to own.
- It can be installed on a single or multiple machines.
- It allows for one or more connections.
- It has whatever limit the ISV has placed on its software.

In most instances, the purchase price of the software is directly tied to the EULA.

For a long time now, the computer industry has known that the use of distributed applications over the Internet was going to impact the way in which companies license their software, and indeed it has. The problem is that there is no uniform description of how applications accessed over cloud networks will be priced. There are several different licensing models in play at the moment—and no clear winners.

It can certainly be argued that the use of free software is a successful model. The free use of software in the cloud is something that the open-source community can support, it can be supported as a line extension of a commercial product, or it can be paid for out of money obtained from other sources such as advertising. Google's advertising juggernaut has allowed it to create a portfolio of applications that users can access based on their Google accounts. Microsoft's free software in Windows Live is supported by its sales of the Windows operating system and by sales of the Microsoft Office suite.

In practice, cloud-based providers tend to license their applications or services based on user or machine accounts, but they do so in ways that are different than you might expect based on your experience with physical hardware and software. Many applications and services use a subscription or usage model (or both) and tie it to a user account. Lots of experimentation is going on in the publishing industry on how to price Internet offerings, and you can find the same to be true in all kinds of computer applications at the moment. Some services tie their licenses into a machine account when it makes sense. An example is the backup service Carbonite, where the service is for backing up a licensed computer. However, cloud computing applications rarely use machine licenses when the application is meant to be ubiquitous. If you need to access an application, service, or Web site from any location, then a machine license isn't going to be practical.

The impact of cloud computing on bulk software purchases and enterprise licensing schemes is even harder to gauge. Several analysts have remarked that the advent of cloud computing could lead to the end of enterprise licensing and could cause difficulties for software vendors going forward. It isn't clear what the impact on licensing will be in the future, but it is certainly an area to keep your eyes on.

Summary

In this chapter, you learned about the features that make cloud computing unique. It is both a new model and a new platform for computing. The idea of computing as a utility is as old as the computer industry itself, but it is the advent of low-cost datacenters that have really enabled this platform to thrive.

A cloud's unique features are scalability, elasticity, low barrier to entry, and a utility delivery of services. These features completely change the way in which applications and services are used. Cloud computing will enable the development of new types of applications, several of which were described in this chapter. Undoubtedly many new application types will arise that will be a complete surprise to us all. However, cloud computing has some limitations that were discussed as well.

To help you get a handle on cloud computing, this chapter stresses measurements of costs in comparison to private or on-premises systems. Cloud computing shifts capital expenditures into operating expenditures.

Cloud computing changes the nature of the service provider and its relationship to its client. You see this expressed in the Service Level Agreements (SLAs) and software licensing that are part of this new developing industry. There are many changes to come in these areas.

Chapter 3, "Understanding Cloud Architecture," is an in-depth look at the superstructure and plumbing that makes cloud computing possible. In that chapter, you learn about the standards and protocols used by the cloud computing industry.

Understanding Cloud Architecture

C loud computing is a natural extension of many of the design principles, protocols, plumbing, and systems that have been developed
over the past 20 years. However, cloud computing describes some
new capabilities that are architected into an application stack and are responsible for the programmability, scalability, and virtualization of resources.
One property that differentiates cloud computing is referred to as composability, which is the ability to build applications from component parts.

A platform is a cloud computing service that is both hardware and software.
Platforms are used to create more complex software. Virtual appliances are
an important example of a platform, and they are becoming a very important
standard cloud computing deployment object.

Cloud computing requires some standard protocols with which different layers of hardware, software, and clients can communicate with one another.
Many of these protocols are standard Internet protocols. Cloud computing
relies on a set of protocols needed to manage interprocess communications
that have been developed over the years. The most commonly used set of
protocols uses XML as the messaging format, the Simple Object Access
Protocol (SOAP) protocol as the object model, and a set of discovery and
description protocols based on the Web Services Description Language
(WSDL) to manage transactions.

Some completely new clients are under development that are specifically
meant to connect to the cloud. These clients have as their focus cloud applications and services, and are often hardened and more securely connected.
Two examples presented are Jolicloud and Google Chrome OS. They represent a new client model that is likely to have considerable impact.

Exploring the Cloud Computing Stack

Cloud computing builds on the architecture developed for staging large distributed network applications on the Internet over the last 20 years. To these standard networking protocols, cloud computing adds the advances in system virtualization that became available over the last decade. The cloud creates a system where resources can be pooled and partitioned as needed. Cloud architecture can couple software running on virtualized hardware in multiple locations to provide an on-demand service to user-facing hardware and software. It is this unique combination of abstraction and metered service that separates the architectural requirements of cloud computing systems from the general description given for an n-tiered Internet application.

Many descriptions of cloud computing describe it in terms of two architectural layers:

> A client as a front end
>
> The "cloud" as a backend

This is a very simplistic description because each of these two components is composed of several component layers, complementary functionalities, and a mixture of standard and proprietary protocols. Cloud computing may be differentiated from older models by describing an encapsulated information technology service that is often controlled through an Application Programming Interface (API), thus modifying the services that are delivered over the network.

A cloud can be created within an organization's own infrastructure or outsourced to another datacenter. While resources in a cloud can be real physical resources, more often they are virtualized resources because virtualized resources are easier to modify and optimize. A compute cloud requires virtualized storage to support the staging and storage of data. From a user's perspective, it is important that the resources appear to be infinitely scalable, that the service be measurable, and that the pricing be metered.

Composability

Applications built in the cloud often have the property of being built from a collection of components, a feature referred to as composability. A composable system uses components to assemble services that can be tailored for a specific purpose using standard parts. A composable component must be:

- **Modular:** It is a self-contained and independent unit that is cooperative, reusable, and replaceable.
- **Stateless:** A transaction is executed without regard to other transactions or requests.

It isn't an absolute requirement that transactions be stateless, some cloud computing applications provide managed states through brokers, transaction monitors, and service buses. In rarer cases, full transactional systems are deployed in the clouds, but these systems are harder to architect in a distributed architecture.

Although cloud computing doesn't require that hardware and software be composable, it is a highly desirable characteristic from a developer or user's standpoint, because it makes system design easier to implement and solutions more portable and interoperable.

There is a tendency for cloud computing systems to become less composable for users as the services incorporate more of the cloud computing stack. From the standpoint of an IaaS (Infrastructure as a Service) vendor such as Amazon Web Services, GoGrid, or Rackspace, it makes no sense to offer non-standard machine instances to customers, because those customers are almost certainly deploying applications built on standard operating systems such as Linux, Windows, Solaris, or some other well-known operating system.

In the next step up the cloud computing stack, PaaS (Platform as a Service) vendors such as Windows Azure or Google AppEngine may narrow the definition of standard parts to standard parts that work with their own platforms, but at least from the standpoint of the individual platform service provider, the intent is to be modular for their own developers.

When you move to the highest degree of integration in cloud computing, which is SaaS (Software as a Service), the notion of composability for users may completely disappear. An SaaS vendor such as Quicken.com or Salesforce.com is delivering an application as a service to a customer, and there's no particular benefit from the standpoint of the service provider that the customer be able to compose its own custom applications. A service provider reselling an SaaS may have the option to offer one module or another, to customize the information contained in the module for a client, to sell the service under their own brand, or to perform some other limited kind of customization, but modifications are generally severely limited.

This idea that composability diminishes going up the cloud computing stack is from the user's point of view. If you are a PaaS or SaaS service provider and your task is to create the platform or service presented to the developer, reseller, or user, the notion of working with a composable system is still a very powerful one. A PaaS or SaaS service provider gets the same benefits from a composable system that a user does—these things, among others:

- Easier to assemble systems
- Cheaper system development
- More reliable operation
- A larger pool of qualified developers
- A logical design methodology

You encounter the trend toward designing composable systems in cloud computing in the widespread adoption of what has come to be called the Service Oriented Architecture (SOA). The essence of a service oriented design is that services are constructed from a set of modules using standard communications and service interfaces. An example of a set of widely used standards describes the services themselves in terms of the Web Services Description Language (WSDL), data exchange between services using some form of XML, and the communications between the services using the SOAP protocol. There are, of course, alternative sets of standards.

Cross-Ref

SOA is described in detail in Chapter 13. ■

What isn't specified is the nature of the module itself; it can be written in any programming language the developer wants. From the standpoint of the system, the module is a black box, and only the interface is well specified. This independence of the internal workings of the module or component means it can be swapped out for a different model, relocated, or replaced at will, provided that the interface specification remains unchanged. That is a powerful benefit to any system or application provider as their products evolve.

Infrastructure

Most large Infrastructure as a Service (IaaS) providers rely on virtual machine technology to deliver servers that can run applications. Virtual servers described in terms of a machine image or instance have characteristics that often can be described in terms of real servers delivering a certain number of microprocessor (CPU) cycles, memory access, and network bandwidth to customers. Virtual machines are containers that are assigned specific resources. The software that runs in the virtual machines is what defines the utility of the cloud computing system.

Figure 3.1 shows the portion of the cloud computing stack that is defined as the "server." In the diagram, the API is shown shaded in gray because it is an optional component that isn't always delivered with the server. The VMM component is the Virtual Machine Monitor, also called a hypervisor. This is the low-level software that allows different operating systems to run in their own memory space and manages I/O for the virtual machines.

The notion of a virtual server presents to an application developer a new way of thinking about and programming applications. For example, when a programmer is creating software that requires several different tasks to be performed in parallel, he might write an application that creates additional threads of execution that must be managed by the application. When a developer creates an application that uses a cloud service, the developer can attach to the appropriate service(s) and allow the application itself to scale the program execution. Thus, an application such as a three-dimensional rendering that might take a long time for a single server to accomplish can be scaled in the cloud to many servers at once for a short period of time, accomplishing the task at a similar or lower price but at a much faster rate.

In future applications, developers will need to balance the architectural needs of their programs so their applications create new threads when it is appropriate or create new virtual machines. Applications will also need to be mindful of how they use cloud resources, when it is appropriate to scale execution to the cloud, how to monitor the instances they are running, and when not to expand their application's usage of the cloud. This will require a new way of thinking about application development, and the ability to scale correctly is something that will have to be architected into applications from the ground up.

FIGURE 3.1

This architectural diagram illustrates the portion of the cloud computing stack that is designated as the server.

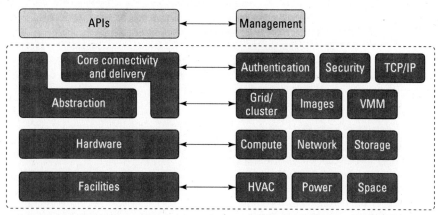

Platforms

A platform in the cloud is a software layer that is used to create higher levels of service. As you learned in Chapter 1, many different Platform as a Service (PaaS) providers offer services meant to provide developers with different capabilities. In Chapter 7, PaaS is explored more thoroughly, but for now it is useful to cite three of the major examples that are provided in this book:

● Salesforce.com's Force.com Platform

● Windows Azure Platform

● Google Apps and the Google AppEngine

These three services offer all the hosted hardware and software needed to build and deploy Web applications or services that are custom built by the developer within the context and range of capabilities that the platform allows. Platforms represent nearly the full cloud software stack, missing only the presentation layer that represents the user interface. This is the same portion of the cloud computing stack that is a virtual appliance and is shown in Figure 3.2. What separates a platform from a virtual appliance is that the software that is installed is constructed from components and services and controlled through the API that the platform provider publishes.

It makes sense for operating system vendors to move their development environments into the cloud with the same technologies that have been successfully used to create Web applications. Thus, you might find a platform based on a Sun xVM hypervisor virtual machine that includes a NetBeans Integrated Development Environment (IDE) and that supports the Sun GlassFish

Web stack programmable using Perl or Ruby. For Windows, Microsoft would be similarly interested in providing a platform that allowed Windows developers to run on a Hyper-V VM, use the ASP.NET application framework, support one of its enterprise applications such as SQL Server, and be programmable within Visual Studio—which is essentially what the Azure Platform does. This approach allows someone to develop a program in the cloud that can be used by others.

Platforms often come replete with tools and utilities to aid in application design and deployment. Depending upon the vendor, you may find developer tools for team collaboration, testing tools, instrumentation for measuring program performance and attributes, versioning, database and Web service integration, and storage tools. Most platforms begin by establishing a developer community to support the work done in the environment.

Note
To see the entire cloud computing stack, refer to Figure 1.5 in Chapter 1. ■

FIGURE 3.2

A virtual appliance is software that installs as middleware onto a virtual machine.

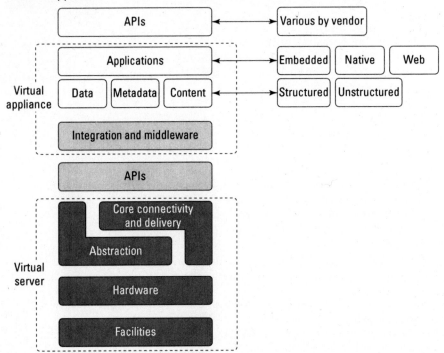

Just as a virtual appliance may expose itself to users through an API, so too an application built in the cloud using a platform service would encapsulate the service through its own API. Users would then interact with the platform, consuming services through that API, leaving the platform to manage and scale the service appropriately. Many platforms offer user interface development tools based on HTML, JavaScript, or some other technology. As the Web becomes more media-oriented, many developers have chosen to work with rich Internet environments such as Adobe Flash, Flex, or Air, or alternatives such as Windows Silverlight. A user interface abstracts away the platform API, making those services managed through the UI. Figure 3.3 shows the top portion of the cloud computing stack, which includes the API and the presentation functionality.

FIGURE 3.3

The top of the cloud computing interface includes the user interface and the API for the application layer.

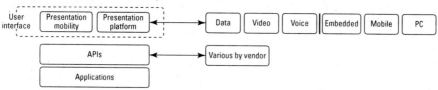

The Application Programming Interface is one of the key differentiators separating cloud computing from the older models of Internet applications, because it is the means for instantiating resources needed to support applications. An API can control data flow, communications, and other important aspects of the cloud application. Unfortunately, each cloud vendor has their own cloud API, none of them are standard, and the best you can hope for is that eventually the major cloud vendor's APIs will interoperate and exchange data. For now, the use of proprietary APIs results in vendor lock-in, which is why you are advised to choose systems that implement APIs based on open standards.

Virtual Appliances

Applications such as a Web server or database server that can run on a virtual machine image are referred to as virtual appliances. The name *virtual appliance* is a little misleading because it conjures up the image of a machine that serves a narrow purpose. Virtual appliances are software installed on virtual servers—application modules that are meant to run a particular machine instance or image type. A virtual appliance is a platform instance. Therefore, virtual appliances occupy the middle of the cloud computing stack (refer to Figure 3.2).

A virtual appliance is a common deployment object in the cloud, and it is one area where there is considerable activity and innovation. One of the major advantages of a virtual appliance is that you can use the appliances as the basis for assembling more complex services, the appliance being one of your standardized components. Virtual appliances remove the need for application configuration and maintenance from your list of system management chores.

You run across virtual appliances in IaaS systems such as Amazon's Elastic Compute Cloud (EC2), which is discussed in detail in Chapter 9. Amazon Machine Images are virtual appliances that have been packaged to run on the gird of Xen nodes that comprise the Amazon Web Service's EC2 system. Shown in Figure 3.4, the AMI library (`http://developer.amazonwebservices.com/connect/kbcategory.jspa?categoryID=171`) includes a variety of operating systems both proprietary and open source, a set of enterprise applications such as Oracle BPM, SQL Server, and even complete application stacks such as LAMP (Linux, Apache, MySQL, and PHP). Amazon has negotiated licenses from these vendors that are part of your per-use pricing when you run these applications on their servers.

Virtual appliances are far easier to install and run than an application that you must set up yourself. However, virtual appliances are also much larger than the application themselves would be because they are usually bundled with the operating system on which they are meant to run. An application that is 50 or 100MB might require a virtual appliance that is 500MB to 1GB in size. Usually, when a virtual appliance is created, the operating system is stripped of all excess functionality that isn't required by the appliance, because the appliance is meant to be used as is.

FIGURE 3.4

Amazon Machine Images are a collection of virtual appliances that you can install on their Xen hypervisor servers.

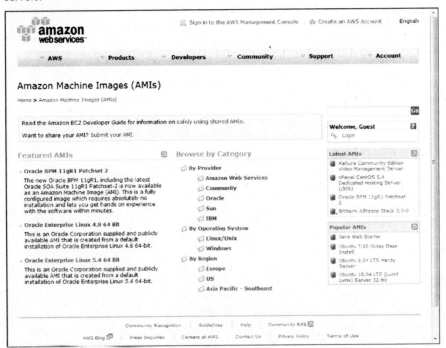

Virtual appliances have begun to affect the PC industry in much the same way that application stores have affected the cell phone industry. You can find various Web sites that either sell or distribute ready-to-use virtual appliances in various forms. Perhaps the best developed of these marketplaces is VMware's Virtual Appliances site (`http://www.vmware.com/appliances/`) shown in Figure 3.5. These appliances are certified by VMware to be ready to use in the enterprise.

Among the other places you can find virtual appliances are at the Web sites of the various operating system vendors, such as Ubuntu, Xen (`http://www.xen.org/`), and others, including these:

- **Bagvapp** (`http://bagside.com/bagvapp/`) offers virtual appliances, including ones based on Windows, all of which run on VMware Player.

- **HelpdeskLive** (`http://helpdesklive.info/download/VirtualBox%20 VDI%20free%20images.html`) offers various Linux distributions upon which you can build a virtual machine.

- **Jcinacio** (`http://www.jcinacio.com/`) has Ubuntu appliances.

FIGURE 3.5

VMware's Virtual Appliance marketplace (`http://www.vmware.com/appliances/`) sells virtual appliances that run on VMware's hypervisor in cloud computing applications.

- **Jumpbox** (`http://www.jumpbox.com`) offers open source virtual appliances installed by them as a managed service. Jumpbox offers virtual appliances for many applications including Bugzilla, DokuWiki, Drupal, Joomla!, Nagios, OpenVPN, PostgreSQL, Redmine, WordPress, and many others. Figure 3.6 shows the Jumpbox home page.

- **QEMU** (`http://www.qemu.org/`) is a CPU emulator and virtual machine monitor.

- **Parallels** (`http://ptn.parallels.com/ptn`) hosts a variety of appliances that includes Linux distros, server software, and other products.

- **ThoughtPolice** (`http://www.thoughtpolice.co.uk/vmware/`) offers appliances based on a variety of Linux distributions.

- **VirtualBox** (`http://www.virtualbox.org/`) is a virtual machine technology now owned by Oracle that can run various operating systems and serves as a host for a variety of virtual appliances.

- **Vmachines** (`http://www.vmachines.net/`) is a site with desktop, server, and security-related operating systems that run on VMware.

FIGURE 3.6

Jumpbox (`http://www.jumpbox.com/`) is an open-source virtual appliance installation and management service.

Converting a virtual appliance from one platform to another isn't an easy proposition. Efforts are underway to create file format standards for these types of objects that make this task easier. The best known of these file formats is the Open Virtualization Format (OVF), the work of the Distributed Management Task Force (DMTF) group. Nearly all major virtualization platform vendors support OVF, notably VMware, Microsoft, Oracle, and Citrix.

Cross-Ref

Chapter 5 describes virtual appliances in more detail and gives some examples of vendors offering these types of applications for cloud computing infrastructure development. ∎

Communication Protocols

Cloud computing arises from services available over the Internet communicating using the standard Internet protocol suite underpinned by the HTTP and HTTPS transfer protocols. The other protocols and standards that expose compute and data resources in the cloud either format data or communications in packets that are sent over these two transport protocols.

In order to engage in interprocess communication (IPC) processes, many client/server protocols have been applied to distributed networking over the years. Various forms of RPC (Remote Procedure Call) implementations (including DCOM, Java RMI, and CORBA) attempt to solve the problem of engaging services and managing transactions over what is essentially a stateless network. The first of the truly Web-centric RPC technologies was XML-RPC, which uses platform-independent XML data to encode program calls that are transported over HTTP, the networking transport to which nearly everyone is connected.

Note

You can find a full description of the common Internet protocol standards in *Networking Bible* by Barrie Sosinsky, Wiley, 2009. These protocols form the basis for much of the discussion in any good networking textbook. ∎

As Internet computing became more firmly entrenched over the last decade, several efforts began to better define methods for describing and discovering services and resources. The most widely used message-passing standard at the moment is the Simple Object Access Protocol (SOAP), which essentially replaces XML-RPC. SOAP uses XML for its messages and uses RPC and HTTP for message passing. SOAP forms the basis for most of the Web services stacks in use today. If you examine the XML file used in a SOAP transaction, you find that it contains a message and the instructions on how to use the message. The message has a set of rules that are translated into application instances and datatypes, and it defines the methods that must be used to initiate procedure calls and then return a response.

Several standards have emerged to allow the discovery and description of Web-based resources. The most commonly used model for discovery and description used with SOAP messaging is the Web Services Description Language (WSDL), a World Wide Web Consortium (http://www.w3.org/2002/ws/desc/) Internet standard. WSDL lets a Web service advertise itself in terms of a collection of endpoints or ports associated with a specific network address (URL) that can be addressed using XML messages to provide a service. In WSDL, a service is a container that performs a set of functions that are exposed to Web protocols. Taken together, the protocol and port are a binding to which messages are passed and operations are performed. A bound service is one that responds to any valid HTTP request sent to it. The important thing to remember about WSDL is that it defines a Web service's public interface.

Cross-Ref

Chapter 13, which describes Service Oriented Architecture, continues the discussion of these various components in building an application in the cloud from a component-based architecture. ■

Using WSDL and SOAP, a number of extensions were created that allow various Web services to describe additional sets of properties and methods that they could provide. These extensions fall under the name WS-*, or the "WS-star" specifications. A number of WS-* extensions are in common use, with the following being the most widely used:

- WS-Addressing
- WS-Discovery
- WS-Eventing
- WS-Federation
- WS-MakeConnection
- WS-Messaging
- WS-MetadataExchange
- WS-Notification
- WS-Policy
- WS-ResourceFramework
- WS-Security
- WS-Transfer
- WS-Trust

These different specifications provide a standard means of adding metadata to a SOAP message by modifying the message header while maintaining the message body structure. In this way, a standard method for metadata exchange is piggybacked onto the WSDL XML message. Each of these different WS-* specifications is in a different state of development.

You use these various WS-* services in your daily work. For example, the Web Services Dynamic Discovery specification (WS-Discovery) is a specification for multicast discovery on a LAN (Local Area Network) that is extended to Web services, most often as SOAP over UDP (User Datagram Protocol). When you open the Network Neighborhood in Windows and use the People Near Me feature, WS-Discovery goes into action and shows you discoverable resources.

These WS-* services carried over XML messages using the SOAP protocol access remote server applications in ways that are becoming increasingly complex. Whereas earlier methods for client/server provided a means through a gateway like CGI to access media content on servers, the current data communications burden servers with accepting and processing very complex requests or engaging their clients in sophisticated negotiations that seek to minimize the amount of processing that must be done and the information that must be exchanged as the response. None of this type of rich media servicing was ever envisaged in the construction of the Internet, and all of it is essentially a kludge.

Over the years, a variety of platform-specific RPC specifications, such as DCOM (Distributed Common Object Model) and CORBA (Common Object Response Broker Architecture), were developed to allow software components that ran on different computers to interoperate with one another. As SOAP and WS-* were developing, those protocols began to build into their specifications server application features from these other technologies in a more platform-independent protocol. What was really needed was a method for standardizing resources on the Web, which is where the idea of REST comes in.

REST stands for Representational State Transfer, and it owes its original description to the work of Roy Fielding, who was also a co-developer of the HTTP protocol. REST assigns a global identifier to a resource so there is a uniform method for accessing information sources. That identifier is a URI expressed in HTTP form. Given a resource then at a known address, various network clients in the form of what are called *user agents* can then communicate with that resource using HTTP commands (requests) to exchange information in the form of documents or files. Typical data transfers might use XML, text, an image file, a JSON document, or some other standard or agreed upon format to perform the data exchange. A transaction following the rules of REST is therefore considered to be RESTful, and this is the basis for cloud computing transactions to be initiated, processed, and completed in most modern implementations.

While REST is heavily used, it is not the only data interchange standard that is used by cloud services. Another example of a data exchange standard is the Atom or Atom Publishing Protocol (APP). Atom is a syndication format that allows for HTTP protocols to create and update information. Microsoft's ADO.NET Data Services Framework is another system for transferring data using a RESTful transaction and standard HTTP commands.

Cloud services span the gamut of computer applications: audio and video streaming, instant messaging, and so forth. Each of these areas uses protocols developed for network use and adapted for use by Web services. The impact of cloud computing on network communication is to encourage the use of open-network protocols in place of proprietary protocols.

For example, in the area of instant messaging, which is a major cloud service, the SIMPLE protocol (which stands for the Session Initiated Protocol for Instant Messaging and Presence Leveraging Extensions) is in widespread use today. SIMPLE is based on the IETF Session Initiation Protocol (SIP) standard and is an open standard. Although most early IM (Instant Messaging) services used proprietary standards, many IM services now support SIMPLE because without this support, it would be hard for the different services to interoperate. Similarly, in the area of VoIP, you find that the open XMPP or the Extensible Messaging and Presence Protocol is used.

Applications

Although the cloud computing stack encompasses many details that describe how clouds are constructed, it is not a perfect vehicle for expressing all the considerations that one must account for in any deployment. An important omission arises from the nature of distributed Web applications and the design of Internet protocols as a stateless service. The Internet was designed to treat each request made to a server as an independent transaction. Therefore, the standard HTTP commands are all atomic in nature: GET to read data, PUT to writedata, and so on.

While stateless servers are easier to architect and stateless transactions are more resilient and can survive outages, much of the useful work that computer systems need to accomplish are stateful. Here's the classic example. When you go to a reservation system to purchase something, you query inventory, reserve the item, and then pay for it. In a multiuser system, if you don't have a stateful system, you cannot know whether the item you reserved has already been taken by another user before you can enter your payment for the item. Should you decide you don't want the item at some later time, it is much easier to restore the item to inventory and return payments or make other adjustments if you can roll back all the steps as a transactional unit.

Much of the really hard development efforts that have gone into making the Web useful in commerce have centered around creating mechanisms to change a set of stateless transactions into stateful ones. The development of transaction servers, message queuing servers, and other middleware is meant to bridge this problem. Cloud computing is no exception to this problem, and to an extent it amplifies the problem by not only making transactions stateless but also virtualizing resources so transactions are always occurring in physically different locations. In cloud computing, a variety of constructs are brought to bear to solve these issues, but these are the two most important concepts:

- The notion of orchestration—that process flow can be choreographed as a service
- The use of what is referred to as a service bus that controls cloud components

In time, other methods for establishing transactional integrity may be developed that are better suited to cloud computing, but these are the standard methods that are now part of the Service Oriented Architecture. Chapter 13 takes up this topic in more detail, but it is something you should certainly keep in mind as you read through the intervening chapters.

Connecting to the Cloud

Clients can connect to a cloud service in a number of different ways. These are the two most common means:

- A Web browser
- A proprietary application

These applications can be running on a server, a PC, a mobile device, or a cell phone. What these devices have in common with either of these application types is that they are exchanging data over an inherently insecure and transient medium. There are three basic methods for securely connecting over a connection:

- Use a secure protocol to transfer data such as SSL (HTTPS), FTPS, or IPsec, or connect using a secure shell such as SSH to connect a client to the cloud.

- Create a virtual connection using a virtual private network (VPN), or with a remote data transfer protocol such as Microsoft RDP or Citrix ICA, where the data is protected by a tunneling mechanism.

- Encrypt the data so that even if the data is intercepted or sniffed, the data will not be meaningful.

The best client connections use two or more of these techniques to communicate with the cloud. In current browser technology, clients rely on the Web service to make available secure connections, but in the future, it is likely that cloud clients will be hardened so the client itself enforces a secure connection.

If you've ever logged into a hotel connection and browsed the network, you may find that often you can access systems on the network that haven't been protected with a firewall; an improperly configured firewall connection to the cloud is even worse. That has led people to drag portable routers with them, which provide a personal hardware firewall; many of these devices have VPN built directly into them.

Other solutions include using VPN software; here are three recommended solutions:

- Hotspot VPN (`http://www.hotspotvpn.com/`)

- AnchorFree Hotspot Shield (`http://hotspotshield.com/`)

- Gbridge (`http://www.gbridge.com/`), a third-party VPN based on Google's GoogleTalk infrastructure

Gbridge is an interesting solution that illustrates the use of VPN over a cloud connection. To use this product, you need to log into the GoogleTalk (or Gtalk) network and connect to another computer using your Google account. Gbridge allows additional people to join a connection when invited and supports collaborative features such as desktop sharing using the Virtual Network Computing (VNC) software, chat, live folder browsing, folder synchronization, and automated backup. Gbridge also works with applications deployed using Google Apps, allowing you to securely connect to these applications using a VPN. Figure 3.7 shows browsing a folder over a VPN connection using Gbridge's SecureShares feature.

FIGURE 3.7

Gbridge provides a means for securely connecting one computer to another using Gtalk. Shown here is the SecureShares folder-browsing feature.

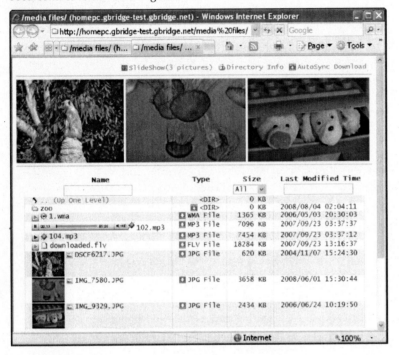

The Jolicloud Netbook OS

The popularity of ultralight netbooks and mobile phones has greatly expanded the potential audience of dedicated cloud computing devices, but until recently these devices ran standard operating systems such as Windows, Linux, and Macintosh on the PC and Android, IOS, and Windows Mobile (among others) on cell phones. The primary differentiation between these devices is whether or not they are capable of running video and animation (particularly Adobe Flash).

None of these portable devices has been optimized to connect securely to the cloud by narrowing the operating system functions to harden these devices. The French firm Jolicloud (http://www.jolicloud.com/) has recently released a lightweight version of Linux designed specifically to run connected to the cloud as a dedicated cloud client. Jolicloud 1.0 ("The Anywhere OS") can be loaded onto a netbook as the only operating system, or it can be set up as a dual boot system that shares files with a Windows partition.

Jolicloud concentrates on building a social platform with automatic software updates and installs. The application launcher is built in HTML 5 and comes preinstalled with Gmail, Skype, Twitter,

Firefox, and other applications. Any HTML 5 browser can be used to work with the Jolicloud interface. Jolicloud maintains a library or App Directory of over 700 applications as part of an app store. When you click to select an application, the company both installs and updates the application going forward, just as the iPhone manages applications on that device. Figure 3.8 shows the Jolicloud interface.

FIGURE 3.8

The Jolicloud cloud client operating system is a social networking platform for netbooks with a dedicated application store.

When you install Jolicloud on multiple devices, the system automatically synchronizes your applications so you are working with the same content on all your devices. You can manage your devices from any cloud-connected device. Your files are also unified in a single location, and the operating system provides access to shared storage cloud services such as box.net, Dropbox, and drop.io, among other services.

Chromium OS: The Browser as an Operating System

The Google Chrome OS is a Linux open-source operating system designed to be a robust cloud client. Unlike many other Linux distributions, Google's Chrome is not a software installation, but is shipped installed on validated hardware from Google-approved OEMs (Original Equipment Manufacturers), just as the Android operating system is shipped on a variety of phones. The intent is to have a tightly coupled hardware offering that supports features in the Chrome OS and that would be highly efficient. Early designs have shown Chrome running on tablet designs that would position it as an Apple iPad competitor running on netbook-type devices in the $300-400 range.

Note

An OEM or original equipment manufacturer builds systems from components and sells them under a brand name. ■

The expectation is that the first versions of Chrome systems will appear in late 2010, perhaps in both consumer and enterprise offerings. There is also an open-source version of this cloud client called Chromium (`http://www.chromium.org/chromium-os`), which shares the same code base. The Chromium architecture is built as a three-tier system with a hardware layer, the browser and window manager, and a set of system software and utilities.

The Chrome OS has been described as a hardened operating system because it incorporates a sandbox architecture for running applications and also performs automatic updates. Also included in the system is a version of remote desktop connection software that creates an encrypted connection like Microsoft's RDP, Citrix's ICA, or a VNC client. The Chrome OS hardware specification includes a Trusted Platform Module, which provides for a "trusted bootpath" along with a hardware switch that can be used to boot the system into a developer model. In that mode, some of the security features are turned off, allowing the user to reset the system.

Demonstrations of early prototypes of Chrome and Chromium OS systems have shown that they are capable of nearly instantaneous startup. Chromium Linux kernel has adopted the Upstart (`http://upstart.ubuntu.com/`) event-based replacement for the `init` daemon, which is used to launch services concurrently, restore stalled jobs, and perform delayed system startup. The fast boot time is possible because the device is devoid of most of the devices in modern PCs. Chromium has also adopted a set of security routines in firmware that run during startup and store the information necessary to perform verified system restoration.

Essentially, the Chrome OS looks like the Chrome browser. Chrome is interesting because Google has essentially stripped down the operating system to run one specific application that connects to the Internet. The user interface is similar to the Chrome Web browser and includes a media player that plays MP3, views JPEGs, and plays media content both online and offline. Adobe Flash is integrated directly into the Chrome OS, just as it is in the Chrome browser. When you launch Chrome, you see links to the major Google cloud applications such as Gmail, Google Apps, and YouTube, along with other major sites such as Facebook, Hulu, Pandora, Twitter, and others. Figure 3.9 shows an early demonstration of the Chrome OS, its multi-tab interface, and its application launcher utility. From this same demonstration is shown the Google Reader application with a page from *Alice in Wonderland*, displayed in Figure 3.10.

Google will include on Chromium the Google Cloud Print service that allows an application to print to any connected printer without accessing a printer driver. This system frees Chromium from having to develop hardware- and OS-specific print subsystems. Instead, a proxy is installed in Chrome that registers a printer with the service, and this proxy manages print jobs for the user.

The Chrome OS devices that appear, as well as the competitors such as the Apple iPad and a host of other similar devices from other system vendors, signal a sea change in the manner in which users access the cloud, and they represent the cloud's impact on the manner in which many users perform their daily work. It's anyone's guess how impactful these introductions will be, but it is clear that they are not simply another competitor to Windows and Macintosh desktop-oriented systems. They represent the move into a cloud-based future where applications run and data is stored remotely. Their success is likely to be contingent upon how fast consumers and businesses become comfortable with the idea of outsourcing these functions. In time, the transition is probably inevitable because the economies of scale and efficiency that cloud computing offers is too compelling to ignore.

FIGURE 3.9

The Chrome OS operating system's application launcher from an early demo of the product found at
`http://www.youtube.com/watch?v=ANMrzw7JFzA&feature=channel`

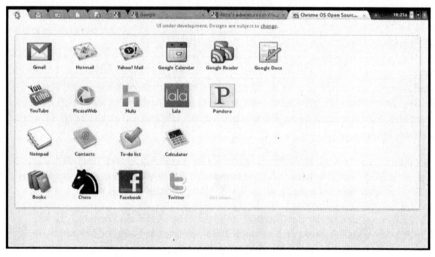

FIGURE 3.10

From the same source as Figure 3.9, this figure illustrates how the Google Reader appears within the Chrome OS as a tab.

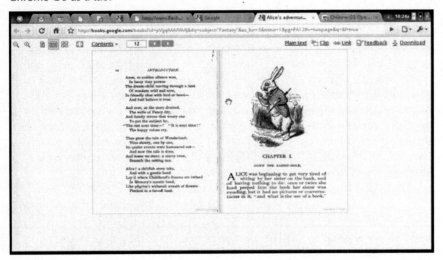

Summary

In this chapter, you learned about the various architectural layers that make up the cloud computing stack. Cloud computing may be seen to be an extension of older Internet standards, but it includes some new architecture. In particular, infrastructure components were described, as were platform components. Platform services are software-based and can include a class of applications referred to as virtual appliances.

The focus of the chapter was how all the different parts of cloud computing work together. Many of the important standards are aimed at managing transactions in the cloud and making components work together. This chapter took an initial look at SOAP, XML, and the various WSDL services.

The chapter ended by considering the development of a new class of cloud-connected clients. These clients, which are often hardware and software solutions like the Google Chrome OS, may have major impact in changing the model by which people connect to the Internet and get their work done. They have many advantages, but we will have to wait to see how readily consumers and businesses are willing to adopt this new computing paradigm.

In the next chapter, each of the different Internet service models is more closely described.

Understanding Services and Applications by Type

This chapter describes some of the different types of cloud computing models, categorized as a set of service models. You may think of cloud computing applications as being composed of a set of layers upon which distributed applications may be built or hosted. These layers include Infrastructure, Platform, and Software. Depending on the type and level of service being offered, a client can build on these layers to create cloud-based applications.

The service models described here—Infrastructure as a Service (IaaS), Software as a Service (SaaS), and Platform as a Service (PaaS)—are useful in categorizing not only cloud computing capabilities, but specific vendor offerings, products, and services. Infrastructure as a Service allows for the creation of virtual computing,systems or networks.

Software as a Service represents a hosted application that is universally available over the Internet, usually through a browser. With Software as a Service, the user interacts directly with the hosted software. SaaS may be seen to be an alternative model to that of shrink-wrapped software and may replace much of the boxed software that we buy today.

Platform as a Service is a cloud computing infrastructure that creates a development environment upon which applications may be build. PaaS provides a model that can be used to create or augment complex applications such as Customer Relation Management (CRM) or Enterprise Resource Planning (ERP) systems. PaaS offers the benefits of cloud computing and is often componentized and based on a service-oriented architecture model.

As cloud computing matures, several service types are being introduced and overlaid upon these architectures. The most fully developed of these service types is Identity as a Service (IDaaS). Identity as a Service provides authentication and authorization services on distributed networks. Infrastructure and supporting protocols for IDaaS are described in this chapter. Other service types such as Compliance as a Service (CaaS), provisioning, monitoring, communications, and many vertical services yet to be fully developed are touched upon in this chapter.

Defining Infrastructure as a Service (IaaS)

You can broadly partition cloud computing into four layers that form a cloud computing ecosystem, as shown in Figure 4.1. The Application layer forms the basis for Software as a Service (SaaS), while the Platform layer forms the basis for Platform as a Service (PaaS) models that are described in the next two sections. Infrastructure as a Service (IaaS) creates what may be determined to be a utility computing model, something that you can tap into and draw from as you need it without significant limits on the scalability of your deployment. You pay only for what you need when you need it. IaaS may be seen to be an incredibly disruptive technology, one that can help turn a small business into a large business nearly overnight. This is a most exciting prospect; one that is fueling a number of IaaS startups during one of the most difficult recessions of recent memory.

Infrastructure as a Service (IaaS) is a cloud computing service model in which hardware is virtualized in the cloud. In this particular model, the service vendor owns the equipment: servers, storage, network infrastructure, and so forth. The developer creates virtual hardware on which to develop applications and services. Essentially, an IaaS vendor has created a hardware utility service where the user provisions virtual resources as required.

FIGURE 4.1

The cloud computing ecosystem

Business Process (SOA)

Application Services

Platform Services

Infrastructure Services

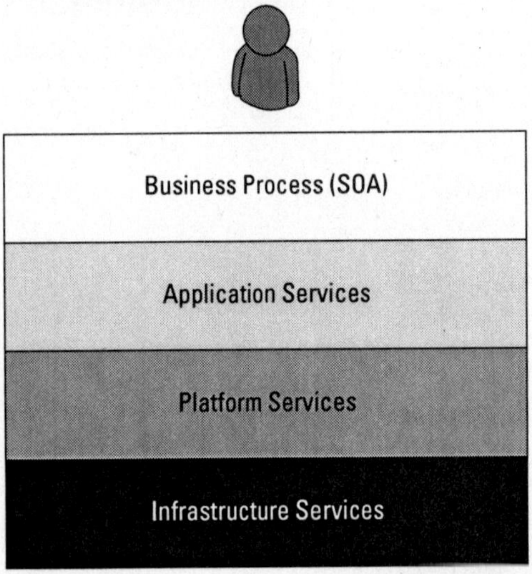

The developer interacts with the IaaS model to create virtual private servers, virtual private storage, virtual private networks, and so on, and then populates these virtual systems with the applications and services it needs to complete its solution. In IaaS, the virtualized resources are mapped to real systems. When the client interacts with an IaaS service and requests resources from the virtual systems, those requests are redirected to the real servers that do the actual work.

IaaS workloads

The fundamental unit of virtualized client in an IaaS deployment is called a *workload*. A workload simulates the ability of a certain type of real or physical server to do an amount of work. The work done can be measured by the number of Transactions Per Minute (TPM) or a similar metric against a certain type of system. In addition to throughput, a workload has certain other attributes such as Disk I/Os measured in Input/Output Per Second IOPS, the amount of RAM consumed under load in MB, network throughput and latency, and so forth. In a hosted application environment, a client's application runs on a dedicated server inside a server rack or perhaps as a standalone server in a room full of servers. In cloud computing, a provisioned server called an instance is reserved by a customer, and the necessary amount of computing resources needed to achieve that type of physical server is allocated to the client's needs.

Figure 4.2 shows how three virtual private server instances are partitioned in an IaaS stack. The three workloads require three different sizes of computers: small, medium, and large.

A client would reserve a machine equivalent required to run each of these workloads. The IaaS infrastructure runs these server instances in the data center that the service offers, drawing from a pool of virtualized machines, RAID storage, and network interface capacity. These three layers are expressions of physical systems that are partitioned as logical units. LUNs, the cloud interconnect layer, and the virtual application software layer are logical constructs. LUNs are logical storage containers, the cloud interconnect layer is a virtual network layer that is assigned IP addresses from the IaaS network pool, and the virtual application software layer contains software that runs on the physical VM instance(s) that have been partitioned from physical assets on the IaaS' private cloud.

From an architectural standpoint, the client in an IaaS infrastructure is assigned its own private network. The Amazon Elastic Computer Cloud (EC2), described in detail in Chapter 8, behaves as if each server is its own separate network—unless you create your own Virtual Private Cloud (an EC2 add-on feature), which provides a workaround to this problem. When you scale your EC2 deployment, you are adding additional networks to your infrastructure, which makes it easy to logically scale an EC2 deployment, but imposes additional network overhead because traffic must be routed between logical networks. Amazon Web Service's routing limits broadcast and multicast traffic because Layer-2 (Data Link) networking is not supported. Rackspace Cloud (http://www.rackspacecloud.com/) follows the AWS IP assignment model.

Other IaaS infrastructures such as the one Cloudscaling.com (http://www.cloudscaling.com) offers or a traditional VMWare cloud-assigned networks on a per-user basis, which allows for Level 2 networking options. The most prominent Level 2 protocols that you might use are tunneling options, because they enable VLANs.

FIGURE 4.2

A virtual private server partition in an IaaS cloud

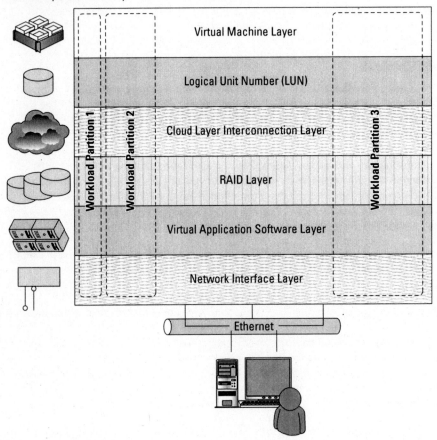

Consider a transactional eCommerce system, for which a typical stack contains the following components:

- Web server
- Application server
- File server
- Database
- Transaction engine

This eCommerce system has several different workloads that are operating: queries against the database, processing of business logic, and serving up clients' Web pages.

The classic example of an IaaS service model is Amazon.com's Amazon Web Services (AWS). AWS has several data centers in which servers run on top of a virtualization platform (Xen) and may be partitioned into logical compute units of various sizes. Developers can then apply system images containing different operating systems and applications or create their own system images. Storage may be partitions, databases may be created, and a range of services such a messaging and notification can be called upon to make distributed application work correctly.

Cross-Ref

Amazon Web Services offers a classic Service Oriented Architecture (SOA) approach to IaaS. You learn more about AWS in Chapter 9; a description of the Service Oriented Architecture approach to building distributed applications is described in Chapter 13. ■

Pods, aggregation, and silos

Workloads support a certain number of users, at which point you exceed the load that the instance sizing allows. When you reach the limit of the largest virtual machine instance possible, you must make a copy or clone of the instance to support additional users. A group of users within a particular instance is called a *pod*. Pods are managed by a Cloud Control System (CCS). In AWS, the CCS is the AWS Management Console.

Sizing limitations for pods need to be accounted for if you are building a large cloud-based application. Pods are aggregated into pools within an IaaS region or site called an *availability zone*. In very large cloud computing networks, when systems fail, they fail on a pod-by-pod basis, and often on a zone-by-zone basis. For AWS' IaaS infrastructure, the availability zones are organized around the company's data centers in Northern California, Northern Virginia, Ireland, and Singapore. A failover system between zones gives IaaS private clouds a very high degree of availability. Figure 4.3 shows how pods are aggregated and virtualized in IaaS across zones.

When a cloud computing infrastructure isolates user clouds from each other so the management system is incapable of interoperating with other private clouds, it creates an information silo, or simply a silo. Most often, the term *silo* is applied to PaaS offerings such as Force.com or QuickBase, but silos often are an expression of the manner in which a cloud computing infrastructure is architected. Silos are the cloud computing equivalent of compute islands: They are processing domains that are sealed off from the outside.

When you create a private virtual network within an IaaS framework, the chances are high that you are creating a silo. Silos impose restrictions on interoperability that runs counter to the open nature of build-componentized service-oriented applications. However, that is not always a bad thing. A silo can be its own ecosystem; it can be protected and secured in ways that an open system can't be. Silos just aren't as flexible as open systems and are subject to vendor lock-in.

FIGURE 4.3

Pods, aggregation, and failover in IaaS

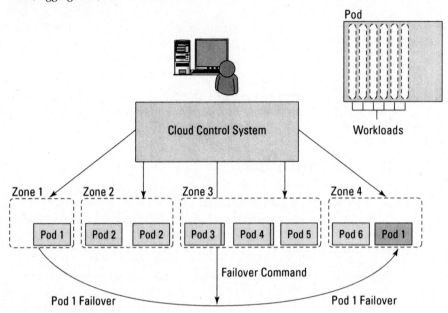

Defining Platform as a Service (PaaS)

The Platform as a Service model describes a software environment in which a developer can create customized solutions within the context of the development tools that the platform provides. Platforms can be based on specific types of development languages, application frameworks, or other constructs. A PaaS offering provides the tools and development environment to deploy applications on another vendor's application. Often a PaaS tool is a fully integrated development environment; that is, all the tools and services are part of the PaaS service. To be useful as a cloud computing offering, PaaS systems must offer a way to create user interfaces, and thus support standards such as HTLM, JavaScript, or other rich media technologies.

In a PaaS model, customers may interact with the software to enter and retrieve data, perform actions, get results, and to the degree that the vendor allows it, customize the platform involved. The customer takes no responsibility for maintaining the hardware, the software, or the development of the applications and is responsible only for his interaction with the platform. The vendor is responsible for all the operational aspects of the service, for maintenance, and for managing the product(s) lifecycle.

The one example that is most quoted as a PaaS offering is Google's App Engine platform, which is described in more detail in Chapter 8. Developers program against the App Engine using Google's published APIs. The tools for working within the development framework, as well as the structure of the file system and data stores, are defined by Google. Another example of a PaaS offering is

Force.com, Salesforce.com's developer platform for its SaaS offerings, described in the next section. Force.com is an example of an add-on development environment.

A developer might write an application in a programming language like Python using the Google API. The vendor of the PaaS solution is in most cases the developer, who is offering a complete solution to the customer. Google itself also serves as a PaaS vendor within this system, because it offers many of its Web service applications to customers as part of this service model. You can think of Google Maps, Google Earth, Gmail, and the myriad of other PaaS offerings as conforming to the PaaS service model, although these applications themselves are offered to customers under what is more aptly described as the Software as a Service (SaaS) model that is described below.

The difficulty with PaaS is that it locks the developer (and the customer) into a solution that is dependent upon the platform vendor. An application written in Python against Google's API using the Google App Engine is likely to work only in that environment. There is considerable vendor lock-in associated with a PaaS solution.

Defining Software as a Service (SaaS)

The most complete cloud computing service model is one in which the computing hardware and software, as well as the solution itself, are provided by a vendor as a complete service offering. It is referred to as the Software as a Service (SaaS) model. SaaS provides the complete infrastructure, software, and solution stack as the service offering. A good way to think about SaaS is that it is the cloud-based equivalent of shrink-wrapped software.

Software as a Service (SaaS) may be succinctly described as software that is deployed on a hosted service and can be accessed globally over the Internet, most often in a browser. With the exception of the user interaction with the software, all other aspects of the service are abstracted away.

Every computer user is familiar with SaaS systems, which are either replacements or substitutes for locally installed software. Examples of SaaS software for end-users are Google Gmail and Calendar, QuickBooks online, Zoho Office Suite, and others that are equally well known. SaaS applications come in all shapes and sizes, and include custom software such as billing and invoicing systems, Customer Relationship Management (CRM) applications, Help Desk applications, Human Resource (HR) solutions, as well as myriad online versions of familiar applications.

Many people believe that SaaS software is not customizable, and in many SaaS applications this is indeed the case. For user-centric applications such as an office suite, that is mostly true; those suites allow you to set only options or preferences. However, many other SaaS solutions expose Application Programming Interfaces (API) to developers to allow them to create custom composite applications. These APIs may alter the security model used, the data schema, workflow characteristics, and other fundamental features of the service's expression as experienced by the user. Examples of an SaaS platformwith an exposed API are Salesforce.com and Quicken.com. So SaaS does not necessarily mean that the software is static or monolithic.

SaaS characteristics

All Software as a Service (SaaS) applications share the following characteristics:

1. The software is available over the Internet globally through a browser on demand.

2. The typical license is subscription-based or usage-based and is billed on a recurring basis.

   In a small number of cases a flat fee may be changed, often coupled with a maintenance fee. Table 4.1 shows how different licensing models compare.

3. The software and the service are monitored and maintained by the vendor, regardless of where all the different software components are running.

   There may be executable client-side code, but the user isn't responsible for maintaining that code or its interaction with the service.

4. Reduced distribution and maintenance costs and minimal end-user system costs generally make SaaS applications cheaper to use than their shrink-wrapped versions.

5. Such applications feature automated upgrades, updates, and patch management and much faster rollout of changes.

6. SaaS applications often have a much lower barrier to entry than their locally installed competitors, a known recurring cost, and they scale on demand (a property of cloud computing in general).

7. All users have the same version of the software so each user's software is compatible with another's.

8. SaaS supports multiple users and provides a shared data model through a single-instance, multi-tenancy model.

   The alternative of software virtualization of individual instances also exists, but is less common.

TABLE 4.1

Shrink-Wrapped versus SaaS Licensing

	Shrink-Wrapped Software	Hybrid Model	SaaS
Licensing	Owned	Subscription (flat fee)	Metered subscription
Location	Locally installed	Available through an application	Cloud based
Management	Local IT staff	Application Service Provider (ASP)	Cloud vendor through a Service Level Agreement (SLA)

Open SaaS and SOA

A considerable amount of SaaS software is based on open source software. When open source software is used in a SaaS, you may hear it referred to as *Open SaaS*. The advantages of using open source software are that systems are much cheaper to deploy because you don't have to purchase the operating system or software, there is less vendor lock-in, and applications are more portable. The popularity of open source software, from Linux to APACHE, MySQL, and Perl (the LAMP platform) on the Internet, and the number of people who are trained in open source software make Open SaaS an attractive proposition. The impact of Open SaaS will likely translate into better profitability for the companies that deploy open source software in the cloud, resulting in lower development costs and more robust solutions.

A mature SaaS implementation based on SOA is shown in Figure 4.4.

FIGURE 4.4

A modern implement of SaaS using an Enterprise Service Bus and architected with SOA components

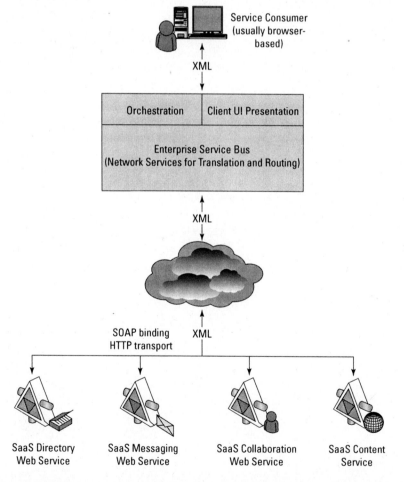

The componentized nature of SaaS solutions enables many of these solutions to support a feature called mashups. A mashup is an application that can display a Web page that shows data and supports features from two or more sources. Annotating a map such as Google maps is an example of a mashup. Mashups are considered one of the premier examples of Web 2.0, and that is technology's ability to support social network systems.

A mashup requires three separate components:

- An interactive user interface, which is usually created with HTML/XHTML, Ajax, JavaScript, or CSS.
- Web services that can be accessed using an API, and whose data can be bound and transported by Web service protocols such as SOAP, REST, XML/HTTP, XML/RPC, and JSON/RPC.
- Data transfer in the form of XML, KML (Keyhole Markup Language), JSON (JavaScript Object Notation), or the like.

Mashups are an incredibly useful hybrid Web application, one that SaaS is a great enabler for. The Open Mashup Alliance (OMA; see http://www.openmashup.org/) is a non-profit industry group dedicated to supporting technologies that implement enterprise mashups. This group supports the developing standard, the Enterprise Mashup Markup Language (EMML), which is a Domain Specific Language (DSL). This group predicts that the use of mashups will grow by a factor of 10 within just a few years.

Gartner Group predicts that approximately 25 percent of all software sold by 2011 will use the SAAS model, offered either by vendors or an intermediary party, sometimes referred to as an *aggregator*. An aggregator bundles SaaS applications from different vendors and presents them as part of a unified platform or solution.

Note

There's a notion that SaaS will eventually replace all locally installed software. However, owning software has several advantages that greatly inhibit this trend: You aren't exposed to the risk of an SaaS company going out of business; you aren't dependent upon the vagaries of an Internet connection; you aren't subject to the often much slower processing speed of a distributed computing model (compared to your local system).

I believe the introduction of SaaS applications will eventually drive down the price of major applications such as Microsoft Office and Adobe Photoshop because the most important functionality contained in commercial packages becomes available at equal quality online for a much lower cost. ■

SaaS examples abound, and while many SaaS offerings are based on proprietary software, a cloud computing service is required to be highly interoperable with other services and therefore easily replaced by a newer or better version of that software's function. When you think about this difference, visualize the situation involved for large enterprise applications such as CRM and ERP, which involve large application suites containing multiple interacting data stores. SaaS software based on the Service Oriented Architecture described in Chapter 13 has the potential of decoupling this integration, with all the attendant benefits.

Salesforce.com and CRM SaaS

Perhaps the best-known example of Software as a Service (SaaS) is the Customer Relationship Management software offered by Salesforce.com whose solution offers sales, service, support, marketing, content, analytical analysis, and even collaboration through a platform called Chatter. Salesforce.com was founded in 1999 by a group of Oracle executives and early adopters of many of the technologies that are becoming cloud computing staples.

Note

Sometimes people refer to this type of software as CaaS or CRaaS for Customer Relationship as a Service software. In cases where many different kinds of relationship data are maintained as a service, you might also see those types of services referred to as XaaS. ∎

Salesforce.com extended its SaaS offering to allow developers to create add-on applications, essentially turning the SaaS service into a Platform as a Service (PaaS) offering called the Force.com Platform. Applications built on Force.com are in the form of the Java variant called Apex using an XML syntax for creating user interfaces in HTML, Ajax, and Flex. Nearly a thousand applications now exist for this platform from hundreds of vendors. Figure 4.5 shows Salesforce.com's home page.

FIGURE 4.5

Salesforce.com is the largest SaaS provider of CRM software and a pioneer in this type of cloud computing software. This is the company's home page.

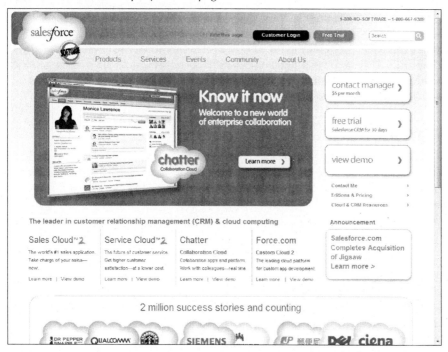

Defining Identity as a Service (IDaaS)

The establishment and proof of an identity is a central network function. An identity service is one that stores the information associated with a digital entity in a form that can be queried and managed for use in electronic transactions. Identity services have as their core functions: a data store, a query engine, and a policy engine that maintains data integrity.

Distributed transaction systems such as internetworks or cloud computing systems magnify the difficulties faced by identity management systems by exposing a much larger attack surface to an intruder than a private network does. Whether it is network traffic protection, privileged resource access, or some other defined right or privilege, the validated authorization of an object based on its identity is the central tenet of secure network design. In this regard, establishing identity may be seen as the key to obtaining trust and to anything that an object or entity wants to claim ownership of.

Services that provide digital identity management as a service have been part of internetworked systems from Day One. Like so many concepts in cloud computing, IDentity as a Service is a FLAVor (Four Letter Acronym) of the month, applied to services that already exist. The Domain Name Service can run on a private network, but is at the heart of the Internet as a service that provides identity authorization and lookup. The name servers that run the various Internet domains (.COM, .ORG, .EDU, .MIL, .TV, .RU, and so on) *are* IDaaS servers. DNS establishes the identity of a domain as belonging to a set of assigned addresses, associated with an owner and that owner's information, and so forth. If the identification is the assigned IP number, the other properties are its metadata.

You can categorize a myriad of services as IDaaS that run in the cloud. However, when most experts in the area of IDaaS define an identity service, they narrow the definition so the service must operate as a component according to the rules of a Service Oriented Architecture, as is defined in Chapter 13. This narrower definition restricts IDaaS to newer software services, services that interoperate, and therefore services that are standards based. It's best to keep this narrower definition in mind when you discuss IDaaS in a modern context.

What is an identity?

An identity is a set of characteristics or traits that make something recognizable or known. In computer network systems, it is one's digital identity that most concerns us. A digital identity is those attributes and metadata of an object along with a set of relationships with other objects that makes an object identifiable. Not all objects are unique, but by definition a digital identity must be unique, if only trivially so, through the assignment of a unique identification attribute. An identity must therefore have a context in which it exists.

This description of an identity as an object with attributes and relationships is one that programmer's would recognize. Databases store information and relationships in tables, rows, and columns, and the identity of information stored in this way conforms to the notion of an entity and a relationship—or alternatively under the notion of an object role model (ORM)—and database architects are always wrestling with the best way of reducing their data set to a basic set of identities. You can extend this notion to the idea of an identity having a profile and profiling services such as Facebook as being an extension of the notion of Identity as a Service in cloud computing.

An identity can belong to a person and may include the following:

- **Things you are:** Biological characteristics such as age, race, gender, appearance, and so forth
- **Things you know:** Biography, personal data such as social security numbers, PINs, where you went to school, and so on
- **Things you have:** A pattern of blood vessels in your eye, your fingerprints, a bank account you can access, a security key you were given, objects and possessions, and more
- **Things you relate to:** Your family and friends, a software license, beliefs and values, activities and endeavors, personal selections and choices, habits and practices, an iGoogle account, and more

To establish your identity on a network, you might be asked to provide a name and password, which is called a single-factor authentication method. More secure authentication requires the use of at least two-factor authentication; for example, not only name and password (things you know) but also a transient token number provided by a hardware key (something you have). To get to multifactor authentication, you might have a system that examines a biometric factor such as a fingerprint or retinal blood vessel pattern—both of which are essentially unique things you are. Multifactor authentication requires the outside use of a network security or trust service, and it is in the deployment of trust services that our first and most common IDaaS applications are employed in the cloud.

Of course, many things have digital identities. User and machine accounts, devices, and other objects establish their identities in a number of ways. For user and machine accounts, identities are created and stored in domain security databases that are the basis for any network domain, in directory services, and in data stores in federated systems. Network interfaces are identified uniquely by Media Access Control (MAC) addresses, which alternatively are referred to as Ethernet Hardware Addresses (EHAs). It is the assignment of a network identity to a specific MAC address that allows systems to be found on networks.

The manner in which Microsoft validates your installation of Windows and Office is called Windows Product Activation and creates an identification index or profile of your system, which is instructive. During activation, the following unique data items are retrieved:

- A 25-character software product key and product ID
- The uniquely assigned Global Unique Identifier or GUID
- PC manufacturer
- CPU type and serial number
- BIOS checksum
- Network adapter and its MAC address
- Display adapter
- SCSCI and IDE adapters
- RAM amount
- Hard drive and volume serial number

- Optical drive
- Region and language settings and user locale

From this information, a code is calculated, checked, and entered into the registration database. Each of these uniquely identified hardware attributes is assigned a weighting factor such that an overall sum may be calculated. If you change enough factors—NIC and CPU, display adapter, RAM amount, and hard drive—you trigger a request for a reactivation based on system changes. This activation profile is also required when you register for the Windows Genuine Advantage program. Windows Product Activation and Windows Genuine Advantage are cloud computing applications, albeit proprietary ones. Whether people consider these applications to be services is a point of contention.

Networked identity service classes

To validate Web sites, transactions, transaction participants, clients, and network services—various forms of identity services—have been deployed on networks. Ticket or token providing services, certificate servers, and other trust mechanisms all provide identity services that can be pushed out of private networks and into the cloud.

Identity protection is one of the more expensive and complex areas of network computing. If you think about it, requests for information on identity by personnel such as HR, managers, and others; by systems and resources for access requests; as identification for network traffic; and the myriad other requirements mean that a significant percentage of all network traffic is supporting an identification service. Literally hundreds of messages on a network every minute are checking identity, and every Ethernet packet contains header fields that are used to identify the information it contains.

As systems become even more specialized, it has become increasingly difficult to find the security experts needed to run an ID service. So Identity as a Service or the related hosted (managed) identity services may be the most valuable and cost effective distributed service types you can subscribe to.

Identity as a Service (IDaaS) may include any of the following:

- Authentication services (identity verification)
- Directory services
- Federated identity
- Identity governance
- Identity and profile management
- Policies, roles, and enforcement
- Provisioning (external policy administration)
- Registration
- Risk and event monitoring, including audits
- Single sign-on services (pass-through authentication)

The sharing of any or all of these attributes over a network may be the subject of different government regulations and in many cases must be protected so that only justifiable parties may have access to the minimal amount that may be disclosed. This level of access defines what may be called an identity relationship.

Note

The Burton Group (`http://www.burtongroup.com/`), **a well-known computer industry analyst firm located in Midvale, Utah, has a trademark on the term IaaS as defined as Identity as a Service for use in the publication of their research in this area. The Burton Group is a well-known authority in the field of network infrastructure, particularly directory services and more recently in cloud computing. In this book, I use the term IaaS as applied to Infrastructure as a Service and use IDaaS to identify Identity as a Service.** ∎

Identity system codes of conduct

Certain codes of conduct must be observed legally, and if not legally at the moment, then certainly on a moral basis. Cloud computing services that don't observe these codes do so at their peril. In working with IDaaS software, evaluate IDaaS applications on the following basis:

- **User control for consent:** Users control their identity and must consent to the use of their information.

- **Minimal Disclosure:** The minimal amount of information should be disclosed for an intended use.

- **Justifiable access:** Only parties who have a justified use of the information contained in a digital identity and have a trusted identity relationship with the owner of the information may be given access to that information.

- **Directional Exposure:** An ID system must support bidirectional identification for a public entity so that it is discoverable and a unidirectional identifier for private entities, thus protecting the private ID.

- **Interoperability:** A cloud computing ID system must interoperate with other identity services from other identity providers.

- **Unambiguous human identification:** An IDaaS application must provide an unambiguous mechanism for allowing a human to interact with a system while protecting that user against an identity attack.

- **Consistency of Service:** An IDaaS service must be simple to use, consistent across all its uses, and able to operate in different contexts using different technologies.

IDaaS interoperability

Identity as a Service provides an easy mechanism for integrating identity services into individual applications with minimal development effort, by allowing the identification logic and storage of an identity's attributes to be maintained externally. IDaaS applications may be separated from other distributed security systems by their compliance with SOA standards (as described in Chapter 13, "Understanding Service Oriented Architecture"), particularly if you want to have these services interoperate and be federated.

Therefore, cloud computing IDaaS applications must rely on a set of developing industry standards to provide interoperability. The following are among the more important of these services:

- **User centric authentication (usually in the form of information cards):** The OpenID and CardSpace specifications support this type of data object.

- **The XACML Policy Language:** This is a general-purpose authorization policy language that allows a distributed ID system to write and enforce custom policy expressions. XACML can work with SAML; when SAML presents a request for ID authorization, XACML checks the ID request against its policies and either allows or denies the request.

- **The SPML Provisioning Language:** This is an XML request/response language that is used to integrate and interoperate service provisioning requests. SPML is a standard of OASIS's Provision Services Technical Committee (PSTC) that conforms to the SOA architecture.

- **The XDAS Audit System:** The Distributed Audit Service provides accountability for users accessing a system, and the detection of security policy violations when attempts are made to access the system by unauthorized users or by users accessing the system in an unauthorized way.

Figure 4.6 shows how these different standards form an identity service framework.

Open standards that support an IDaaS infrastructure for cloud computing

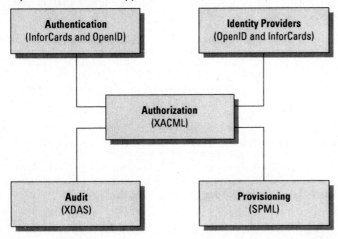

The Identity Governance Framework (IGF) is a standards initiative of the Liberty Alliance (http://www.projectliberty.org/) that is concerned with the exchange and control of identity information using standards such as WS-Trust, ID-WSF, SAML, and LDAP directory services. The Liberty Alliance was established by an industry group in 2001 with the purpose of promoting open identity interchanges through policy standards that applications can use to enforce privacy as well as to allow privacy auditing. In 2009, this group released its Client Attribute Requirements Markup Language (CARML) and a set of IGF Privacy Constraints that forms the basis of the open source project called Aristotle (`http://www.openliberty.org/wiki/index.php/ProjectAris`), which has as its goal the creation of an API for identity interchange.

User authentication

OpenID is a developing industry standard for authenticating "end users" by storing their digital identity in a common format. When an identity is created in an OpenID system, that information is stored in the system of any OpenID service provider and translated into a unique identifier. Identifiers take the form of a Uniform Resource Locator (URL) or as an Extensible Resource Identifier (XRI) that is authenticated by that OpenID service provider. Any software application that complies with the standard accepts an OpenID that is authenticated by a trusted provider. A very impressive group of cloud computing vendors serve as identity providers (or OpenID providers), including AOL, Facebook, Google, IBM, Microsoft, MySpace, Orange, PayPal, VeriSign, LiveJournal, Ustream, Yahoo!, and others.

The OpenID standard applies to the unique identity of the URL; it is up to the service provider to store the information and specify the forms of authentication required to successfully log onto the system. Thus an OpenID authorization can include not only passwords, but smart cards, hardware keys, tokens, and biometrics as well. OpenID is supported by the OpenID Foundation (`http://openid.net/foundation/`), a not-for-profit organization that promotes the technology.

These are samples of trusted providers and their URL formats:

- **Blogger:** *<username>*`.blogger.com` or *<blogid>*`.blogspot.com`
- **MySpace:** `myspace.com/`*<username>*
- **Google:** `https://www.google.com/accounts/o8/id`
- **Google Profile:** `google.com/profiles/`*<username>*
- **Microsoft:** `accountservices.passport.net/`
- **MyOpenID:** *<username>*`.myopenid.com`
- **Orange:** `openid.orange.fr/username` or simply `orange.fr/`
- **Verisign:** *<username>*`.pip.verisinglabs.com`
- **WordPress:** *<username>*`.wordpress.com`
- **Yahoo!:** `openid.yahoo.com`

After you have logged onto a trusted provider, that logon may provide you access to other Web sites that support OpenID. When you request access to a site through your browser (or another application that is referred to as a user-agent), that site serves as the "relying party" and requests of the server or server-agent that it verify the end-user's identifier. You won't need to log onto these other Web sites, if your OpenID is provided. Most trusted providers require that you indicate which Web sites you want to share your OpenID identifier with and the information is submitted automatically to the next site.

CardSpace is a Microsoft software client that is part of the company's Identity Metasystem and built into the Web Services Protocol Stack. This stack is built on the OASIS standards (WS-Trust, WS-Security, WS-SecurityPolicy, and WS-MetadataExchange), so any application that conforms with the OASIS WS- standards can interoperate with CardSpace. CardSpace was introduced with .NET Frameworks 3.0 and can be installed on Windows XP, Server 2003, and later. It is installed by default on Windows Vista and Windows 7.

CardSpace offers another way of authenticating users in the cloud. An Information Card may be requested with an HTML <OBJECT> tag, and the trusted Identity Provider then creates an encrypted and digitally signed token using the Security Token Service (STS) that is part of a WS-Trust request/reply mechanism. CardSpace may be seen as an alternative mechanism to the use of OpenID and SAML and is used to sign into those services as well as Windows Live ID accounts.

Cross-Ref

See Chapter 10 for more information on Windows Live. ■

Figure 4.7 shows a personal Identification Card that is stored locally on a Windows 7 system. Managed Information Cards are stored on a network service and can be made available to other cloud services upon demand.

FIGURE 4.7

This is a private CardSpace Identification Card. Managed Identification Cards that store similar information are stored on a network service and can be shared to the cloud.

Note

IBM and Novell both support Information Cards under the Web Service Protocol Stack, as well as SAML and OpenID through an industry initiative known at the Higgins Open Source Identity Framework (http://eclipse.org/higgins/), which uses the interface metaphor of an i-Card. The Higgins's home page is shown in Figure 4.8. Higgins develops a browser add-on that logs you into Web sites and manages digital identities. ∎

A CardSpace object called an Identity Selector stores a digital identity, making it available to Windows applications in the form of a visual Information Card that can be accepted by complying applications and Web sites. When a user selects an Information Card, the CardSpace software issues a request to validate the information from a Web service that returns a digitally signed XML token that contains the identity and its metadata. A personal or self-issued Information Card also can be created into which you can store biographical information. Personal Information Cards may or may not be managed by a trusted third party.

Before leaving the subject of digital identity services and formats, it is appropriate to mention some file format standards such as vCard, which stores identity data in the form of an electronic business card. Less frequently encountered is the vCard derivative hCard. vCard was an industry initiative in the mid-1990s as a means for identifying parties in e-mail exchanges.

FIGURE 4.8

The Higgins Open Source Identity Framework uses an i-Card metaphor and interoperable identity service APIs to create a vendor-neutral cloud-based authentication service.

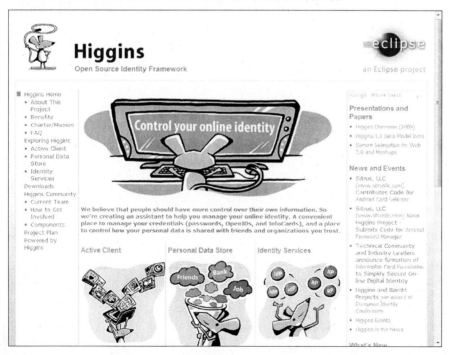

As e-mail platforms such as Lotus Notes and MS Exchange broadened the notion of e-mail to include calendars and appointments, the vCalendar format was created, which eventually was developed into iCalendar. The current version 3.0 of vCard is part of the vCardDAV working group within the IETF and through RFC 2425 and RFC 2426 is undergoing the process of standardization. vCard is more of an interchange file format for an identity than it is an identity trust-authorization service, which is why it is mentioned in passing here. To read more about vCard and vCalendar, go to http://www.imc.org/pdi/.

Authorization markup languages

Information requests and replies in cloud computing are nearly always in the form of XML replies or requests. XML files are text files and are self-describing. That is, XML files contain a schema that describes the data it contains or contains a point to another text file with its schema. A variety of specialized XML files are in the identity framework, the ones of note being XACML and SAML, shown in Figure 4.9.

The eXtensible Access Control Markup Language (XACML) is an OASIS standard (see http://xml.coverpages.org/xacml.html) for a set of policy statements written in XML that support an authentication process. A policy in XACML describes a subject element that requests an action from a resource. These three elements operate within an environment that also can be described in terms of an Action element. Subject and Action elements (which are terms of art in XACML) are elements that can have one or more attributes. Resources (which are services, system components, or data) have a single attribute, which is usually its URL.

The location at which policy is managed is referred to as the Policy Administration Point (PAP). Policy requests are passed through to the location where the policy logic can be executed, referred to as the Policy Decision Point (PDP). The result of the policy is transmitted through the PAP to the resource that acts on and enforces the PDP policy decision, which is referred to as the Policy Enforcement Point (PEP). An XACML engine also may access a resource that provides additional information that can be used to determine policy logic, called a Policy Information Point (PIP). Examples of PIP services are LDAP or Active Directory servers. A request for identification goes to the XACML engine, where it becomes a directive from the Policy Decision Point to the Policy Enforcement Point called an obligation.

The main method for exchanging information between an authentication and authorization service in a Service Oriented Architecture is the Security Assertion Markup Language (SAML). In SAML, a service provider passes a statement or set of statements (called assertions) to an identity provider that must be evaluated. The identity provider must determine if the principle or user requesting access is registered with the identity service and is who he claims to be.

SAML in most instances operates as a reply/request mechanism; it makes no demands on the identification service as to how the identity is authenticated. Should the identity provider validate the identity of the principle in the assertion, it passes a local authorization to the service provider, which then enforces an access-control judgment based on the authorization.

SAML integrates with XACML to implement a policy engine in a Service Oriented Architecture to support identity services authorization.

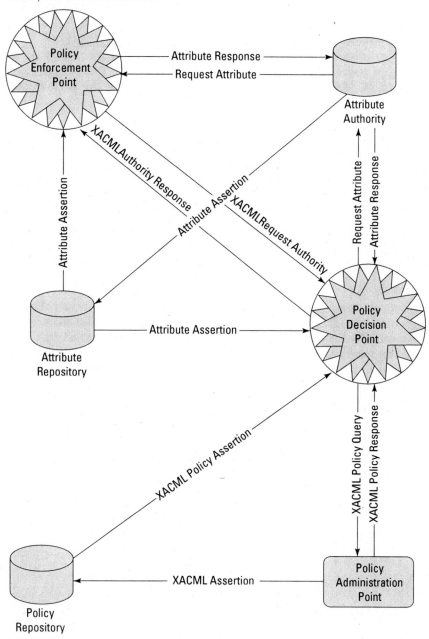

A SAML assertion is a security statement in the SAML file that makes a claim regarding authentication, attributes, or authorization. The statement is of this form:

Assertion X created at Time T by User U about Subject S is true when Conditions C are TRUE.

It is up to the identity provider to parse this statement and determine its validity. The SAML protocol request is often referred to as a query; the three different supported query types are an authentication query, an attribute query, and an authorization decision query. SAML requests use a SOAP binding; that is, the SAML request or response is embedded in a SOAP wrapper within an HTTP message.

SAML is used to provide a mechanism for a Web Browser Single Sign On (SSO). In this instance, a Web browser is the user agent, which requests access to a resource that is authorized by a SAML service provider. The service provider takes a request from a user for access to the resource and sends an authentication request to the SAML identity provider directly from the initiating user agent (Web browser). Figure 4.10 shows the SAML Single Sign On Request/Response mechanism.

The Service Provisioning Markup Language (SPML) is another of the OASIS open standards developed to provide for service provisioning. Provisioning is the process by which a resource is prepared for use, reserved, accessed, used, and then released when the transaction is completed. A classic example of provisioning a resource is the reservation and use of a phone line or a Virtual Private Network.

A provisioning system has three types of components: A Requesting Authority (RA) is the client, the Provisioning Service Point (PSP) is the cloud component that receives the request and returns a response to the RA, and a Provisioning Service Targets (PST) is the software application upon which the provisioning action is performed. The SPML provisioning system (which can be thought of as an architectural layer) means that identity information need only be entered into these three components once.

SPML is used to prepare Web services and applications for use, signal that the resource is available for use and waiting for instructions, and signal when the use or transaction has been completed. With SPML, a system can provide automated user and system access, enforce access rights, and make cloud computing services available across network systems. Without a provisioning system, a cloud computing system can be very inefficient and potentially unreliable.

SAML provides a mechanism by which a service requester can use a Single Sign On logon to access Web services securely.

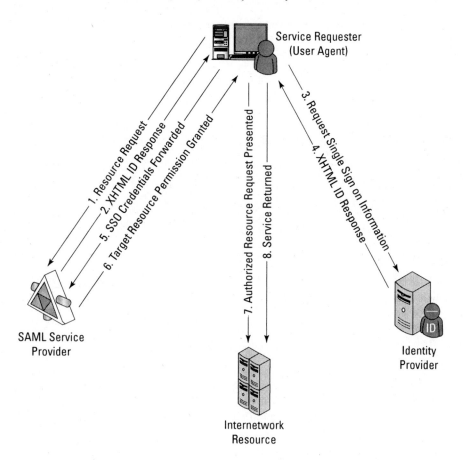

SAML Single Sign On Request/Response Mechanism

Defining Compliance as a Service (CaaS)

Cloud computing by its very nature spans different jurisdictions. The laws of the country of a request's origin may not match the laws of the country where the request is processed, and it's possible that neither location's laws match the laws of the country where the service is provided. Compliance is much more than simply providing an anonymous service token to an identity so they can obtain access to a resource. Compliance is a complex issue that requires considerable expertise.

While Compliance as a Service (CaaS) appears in discussions, few examples of this kind of service exist as a general product for a cloud computing architecture. A Compliance as a Service application would need to serve as a trusted third party, because this is a man-in-the-middle type of service. CaaS may need to be architected as its own layer of a SOA architecture in order to be trusted. A CaaS would need to be able to manage cloud relationships, understand security policies and procedures, know how to handle information and administer privacy, be aware of geography, provide an incidence response, archive, and allow for the system to be queried, all to a level that can be captured in a Service Level Agreement. That's a tall order, but CaaS has the potential to be a great value-added service.

In order to implement CaaS, some companies are organizing what might be referred to as "vertical clouds," clouds that specialize in a vertical market. Examples of vertical clouds that advertise CaaS capabilities include the following:

- **athenahealth** (`http://www.athenahealth.com/`) for the medical industry
- **bankserv** (`http://www.bankserv.com/`) for the banking industry
- **ClearPoint PCI** Compliance-as-a-Service for merchant transactions under the Payment Card Industry Data Security Standard
- **FedCloud** (`http://www.fedcloud.com/`) for government
- **Rackserve PCI** Compliant Cloud (`http://www.rackspace.com/`; another PCI CaaS service)

It's much easier to envisage a CaaS system built inside a private cloud where the data is under the control of a single entity, thus ensuring that the data is under that entity's secure control and that transactions can be audited. Indeed, most of the cloud computing compliance systems to date have been built using private clouds.

It is easy to see how CaaS could be an incredibly valuable service. A well-implemented CaaS service could measure the risks involved in servicing compliance and ensure or indemnify customers against that risk. CaaS could be brought to bear as a mechanism to guarantee that an e-mail conformed to certain standards, something that could be a new electronic service of a network of national postal systems—and something that could help bring an end to the scourge of spam.

Summary

In this chapter, you learned about cloud computing service types. Service types are models upon which distributed applications are created and hosted. The main service models in cloud computing are Infrastructure, Platform, and Software. Vendors offer services based on these different service models called Infrastructure as a Service (IaaS), Software as a Service (SaaS), and Platform as a Service (PaaS), which are helpful in understanding how products and services are organized.

Infrastructure as a Service is a hardware model in which you can create virtual computing systems or networks and deploy your applications on those servers. Software as a Service is a hosted application that is the cloud equivalent of a traditional desktop application. Platform as a Service is a development environment that builds upon an existing cloud computing application infrastructure. Other service types are possible. You learned about Identity as a Service (IDaaS), which enables secure transactions on a distributed network. In time many vertical services for cloud computing will appear.

Chapter 5, "Understanding Abstraction and Virtualization," considers some of the more important characteristics of cloud computing networks and applications.

Part II

Using Platforms

Understanding Abstraction and Virtualization

I n this chapter, I discuss different technologies that create shared pools of resources. The key to creating a pool is to provide an abstraction mechanism so that a logical address can be mapped to a physical resource. Computers use this technique for placing files on disk drives, and cloud computing networks use a set of techniques to create virtual servers, virtual storage, virtual networks, and perhaps one day virtual applications. Abstraction enables the key benefit of cloud computing: shared, ubiquitous access.

In this chapter, you learn about how load balancing can be used to create high performance cloud-based solutions. Google.com's network is an example of this approach. Google uses commodity servers to direct traffic appropriately.

Another technology involves creating virtual hardware systems. An example of this type of approach is hypervisors that create virtual machine technologies. Several important cloud computing approaches use a strictly hardware-based approach to abstraction. I describe VMware's vSphere infrastructure in some detail, along with some of the unique features and technologies that VMware has developed to support this type of cloud.

Finally, I describe some approaches to making applications portable. Application portability is a difficult proposition, and work to make applications portable is in its infancy. Two approaches are described, the Simple API and AppZero's Virtual Application Appliance (VAA). VAAs are containers that abstract an application from the operating system, and they offer the potential to make an application portable from one platform to another.

Using Virtualization Technologies

The dictionary includes many definitions for the word "cloud." A cloud can be a mass of water droplets, gloom, an obscure area, or a mass of similar particles such as dust or smoke. When it comes to cloud computing, the definition that best fits the context is "a collection of objects that are grouped together." It is that act of grouping or creating a resource pool that is what succinctly differentiates cloud computing from all other types of networked systems.

Not all cloud computing applications combine their resources into pools that can be assigned on demand to users, but the vast majority of cloud-based systems do. The benefits of pooling resources to allocate them on demand are so compelling as to make the adoption of these technologies a priority. Without resource pooling, it is impossible to attain efficient utilization, provide reasonable costs to users, and proactively react to demand. In this chapter, you learn about the technologies that abstract physical resources such as processors, memory, disk, and network capacity into virtual resources.

When you use cloud computing, you are accessing pooled resources using a technique called virtualization. Virtualization assigns a logical name for a physical resource and then provides a pointer to that physical resource when a request is made. Virtualization provides a means to manage resources efficiently because the mapping of virtual resources to physical resources can be both dynamic and facile. Virtualization is dynamic in that the mapping can be assigned based on rapidly changing conditions, and it is facile because changes to a mapping assignment can be nearly instantaneous.

These are among the different types of virtualization that are characteristic of cloud computing:

- **Access:** A client can request access to a cloud service from any location.
- **Application:** A cloud has multiple application instances and directs requests to an instance based on conditions.
- **CPU:** Computers can be partitioned into a set of virtual machines with each machine being assigned a workload. Alternatively, systems can be virtualized through load-balancing technologies.
- **Storage:** Data is stored across storage devices and often replicated for redundancy.

To enable these characteristics, resources must be highly configurable and flexible. You can define the features in software and hardware that enable this flexibility as conforming to one or more of the following mobility patterns:

- **P2V:** Physical to Virtual
- **V2V:** Virtual to Virtual
- **V2P:** Virtual to Physical
- **P2P:** Physical to Physical
- **D2C:** Datacenter to Cloud

- **C2C:** Cloud to Cloud
- **C2D:** Cloud to Datacenter
- **D2D:** Datacenter to Datacenter

The techniques used to achieve these different types of virtualization are the subject of this chapter. According to Gartner ("Server Virtualization: One Path that Leads to Cloud Computing," by Thomas J. Bittman, 10/29/2009, Research Note G00171730), virtualization is a key enabler of the first four of five key attributes of cloud computing:

- **Service-based:** A service-based architecture is where clients are abstracted from service providers through service interfaces.
- **Scalable and elastic:** Services can be altered to affect capacity and performance on demand.
- **Shared services:** Resources are pooled in order to create greater efficiencies.
- **Metered usage:** Services are billed on a usage basis.
- **Internet delivery:** The services provided by cloud computing are based on Internet protocols and formats.

Load Balancing and Virtualization

One characteristic of cloud computing is virtualized network access to a service. No matter where you access the service, you are directed to the available resources. The technology used to distribute service requests to resources is referred to as *load balancing*. Load balancing can be implemented in hardware, as is the case with F5's BigIP servers, or in software, such as the Apache `mod_proxy_balancer` extension, the Pound load balancer and reverse proxy software, and the Squid proxy and cache daemon. Load balancing is an optimization technique; it can be used to increase utilization and throughput, lower latency, reduce response time, and avoid system overload.

The following network resources can be load balanced:

- Network interfaces and services such as DNS, FTP, and HTTP
- Connections through intelligent switches
- Processing through computer system assignment
- Storage resources
- Access to application instances

Without load balancing, cloud computing would very difficult to manage. Load balancing provides the necessary redundancy to make an intrinsically unreliable system reliable through managed redirection. It also provides fault tolerance when coupled with a failover mechanism. Load balancing is nearly always a feature of server farms and computer clusters and for high availability applications.

A load-balancing system can use different mechanisms to assign service direction. In the simplest load-balancing mechanisms, the load balancer listens to a network port for service requests. When a request from a client or service requester arrives, the load balancer uses a scheduling algorithm to assign where the request is sent. Typical scheduling algorithms in use today are round robin and weighted round robin, fastest response time, least connections and weighted least connections, and custom assignments based on other factors.

A session ticket is created by the load balancer so that subsequent related traffic from the client that is part of that session can be properly routed to the same resource. Without this session record or persistence, a load balancer would not be able to correctly failover a request from one resource to another. Persistence can be enforced using session data stored in a database and replicated across multiple load balancers. Other methods can use the client's browser to store a client-side cookie or through the use of a rewrite engine that modifies the URL. Of all these methods, a session cookie stored on the client has the least amount of overhead for a load balancer because it allows the load balancer an independent selection of resources.

The algorithm can be based on a simple round robin system where the next system in a list of systems gets the request. Round robin DNS is a common application, where IP addresses are assigned out of a pool of available IP addresses. Google uses round robin DNS, as described in the next section.

Advanced load balancing

The more sophisticated load balancers are workload managers. They determine the current utilization of the resources in their pool, the response time, the work queue length, connection latency and capacity, and other factors in order to assign tasks to each resource. Among the features you find in load balancers are polling resources for their health, the ability to bring standby servers online (priority activation), workload weighting based on a resource's capacity (asymmetric loading), HTTP traffic compression, TCP offload and buffering, security and authentication, and packet shaping using content filtering and priority queuing.

An Application Delivery Controller (ADC) is a combination load balancer and application server that is a server placed between a firewall or router and a server farm providing Web services. An Application Delivery Controller is assigned a virtual IP address (VIP) that it maps to a pool of servers based on application specific criteria. An ADC is a combination network and application layer device. You also may come across ADCs referred to as a content switch, multilayer switch, or Web switch.

These vendors, among others, sell ADC systems:

- A10 Networks (http://www.a10networks.com/)
- Barracuda Networks (http://www.barracudanetworks.com/)
- Brocade Communication Systems (http://www.brocade.com/)
- Cisco Systems (http://www.cisco.com/)
- Citrix Systems (http://www.citrix.com/)

- F5 Networks (`http://www.f5.com/`)
- Nortel Networks (`http://www.nortel.com/`)
- Coyote Point Systems (`http://www.coyotepoint.com/`)
- Radware (`http://www.radware.com/`)

An ADC is considered to be an advanced version of a load balancer as it not only can provide the features described in the previous paragraph, but it conditions content in order to lower the workload of the Web servers. Services provided by an ADC include data compression, content caching, server health monitoring, security, SSL offload and advanced routing based on current conditions. An ADC is considered to be an application accelerator, and the current products in this area are usually focused on two areas of technology: network optimization, and an application or framework optimization. For example, you may find ADC's that are tuned to accelerate ASP.NET or AJAX applications.

An architectural layer containing ADCs is described as an Application Delivery Network (ADN), and is considered to provide WAN optimization services. Often an ADN is comprised of a pair of redundant ADCs. The purpose of an ADN is to distribute content to resources based on application specific criteria. ADN provide a caching mechanism to reduce traffic, traffic prioritization and optimization, and other techniques. ADN began to be deployed on Content Delivery Networks (CDN) in the late 1990s, where it added the ability to optimize applications (application fluency) to those networks. Most of the ADC vendors offer commercial ADN solutions.

In addition to the ADC vendors in the list above, these are additional ADN vendors, among others:

- Akamai Technologies (`http://www.akamai.com/`)
- Blue Coat Systems (`http://www.bluecoat.com/`)
- CDNetworks (`http://www.cdnetworks.com/`)
- Crescendo Networks (`http://www.crescendonetworks.com/`)
- Expand Networks (`http://www.expand.com/`)
- Juniper Networks (`http://www.juniper.net/`)

Google's cloud is a good example of the use of load balancing, so in the next section let's consider how Google handles the many requests that they get on a daily basis.

The Google cloud

According to the Web site tracking firm Alexa (`http://www.alexa.com/topsites`), Google is the single most heavily visited site on the Internet; that is, Google gets the most hits. The investment Google has made in infrastructure is enormous, and the Google cloud is one of the largest in use today. It is estimated that Google runs over a million servers worldwide, processes a billion search requests, and generates twenty petabytes of data per day.

Google is understandably reticent to disclose much about its network, because it believes that its infrastructure, system response, and low latency are key to the company's success. Google never gives datacenter tours to journalists, doesn't disclose where its datacenters are located, and obfuscates the locations of its datacenters by wrapping them in a corporate veil. Thus, the discretely named Tetra LLC (limited liability company) owns the land for the Council Bluffs, Iowa, site, and Lapis LLC owns the land for the Lenoir, North Carolina, site. This makes Google infrastructure watching something akin to a sport to many people.

So what follows is what we think we know about Google's infrastructure and the basic idea behind how Google distributes its traffic by pooling IP addresses and performing several layers of load balancing.

Google has many datacenters around the world. As of March 2008, Rich Miller of DataCenterKnowledge.com wrote that Google had at least 12 major installations in the United States and many more around the world. Google supports over 30 country specific versions of the Google index, and each localization is supported by one or more datacenters. For example, Paris, London, Moscow, Sao Paolo, Tokyo, Toronto, Hong Kong, Beijing and others support their countries' locale. Germany has three centers in Berlin, Frankfurt, and Munich; the Netherlands has two at Groningen and Eemshaven. The countries with multiple datacenters store index replicas and support network peering relationships. Network peering helps Google have low latency connections to large Internet hubs run by different network providers.

You can find a list of sites as of 2008 from Miller's FAQ at `http://www.datacenter knowledge.com/archives/2008/03/27/google-data-center-faq/`.

Based on current locations and the company's statements, Google's datacenters are sited based on the following factors (roughly in order of importance):

1. Availability of cheap and, if possible, renewable energy

2. The relative locations of other Google datacenters such that the site provides the lowest latency response between sites

3. Location of nearby Internet hubs and peering sites

4. A source of cooling water

5. The ability to purchase a large area of land surrounding the site

    Speculation on why Google purchases large parcels of land ranges from creating a buffer zone between the datacenter and surrounding roads and towns or possibly to allow for building wind farms when practical.

6. Tax concessions from municipalities that lower Google's overhead

Google maintains a pool of hundreds of IP addresses, all of which eventually resolve to its Mountain View, California, headquarters. When you initiate a Google search, your query is sent to a DNS server, which then queries Google's DNS servers. The Google DNS servers examine the pool of addresses to determine which addresses are geographically closest to the query origin and uses a round robin policy to assign an IP address to that request. The request usually goes to the nearest datacenter, and that IP address is for a cluster of Google servers. This DNS assignment acts as a first level of IP virtualization, a pool of network addresses have been load balanced based on geography.

A Google cluster can contain thousands of servers. Google servers are racks of commodity (low cost) 1U or 2U servers containing 40 to 80 servers per rack with one switch per rack. Each switch is connected to a core gigabit switch. Google servers run a customized version of Linux with applications of several types.

When the query request arrives at its destination, a Google cluster is sent to a load balancer, which forwards that request to a Squid proxy server and Web cache dameon. This is the second level of IP distribution, based on a measure of the current system loading on proxy servers in the cluster. The Squid server checks its cache, and if it finds a match to the query, that match is returned and the query has been satisfied. If there is no match in the Squid cache, the query is sent to an individual Google Web Server based on current Web server utilizations, which is the third level of network load balancing, again based on utilization rates.

It is the Google Web Servers that perform the query against the Google index and then format the results into an HTML page that is returned to the requester. This procedure then performs two more levels of load balancing based on utilization rates.

Google's secret sauce is its in-memory inverted index and page rank algorithm. Google's GoogleBot (a spider or robot) crawls the Web and collects document information. Some details of the search and store algorithm are known. Google looks at the title and first few hundred words and builds a word index from the result. Indexes are stored on an index server.

Some documents are stored as snapshots (PDF, DOC, XLS, and so on), but lots of information is not addressed in the index. Each document is given a unique ID ("docid"), and the content of the document is disassembled into segments called shards, subjected to a data compression scheme and stored on a document server. The entire index is maintained in system memory partitioned over each instance of the index's replicas. A page rank is created based on the significant links to that page.

Queries are divided into word lists, and the Google algorithm examines the words and the relationships of one word to another. Those word relationships are mapped against the main index to create a list of documents, a feature called an inverted index. In an inverted index, words are mapped to documents, which can be done very quickly when the index is fully kept in memory.

The Web server takes the result of a query and composes the Web page from that result. Ads included on the page are from ad servers, which provide Google's AdSense and AdWords services. The query also is presented to a spelling server to provide suggestions for alternative spellings to include in the search result. Certain keywords, data input patterns, and other strings are recognized as having special operational significance. For example entering "2 plus 2" initiates Google's calculator program, and a ten-digit number returns a reverse phone lookup using the phonebook program. These programs are supported by special application servers.

Google doesn't use hardware virtualization; it performs server load balancing to distribute the processing load and to get high utilization rates. The workload management software transfers the workload from a failed server over to a redundant server, and the failed server is taken offline. Multiple instances of various Google applications are running on different hosts, and data is stored on redundant storage systems.

Understanding Hypervisors

Load balancing virtualizes systems and resources by mapping a logical address to a physical address. Another fundamental technology for abstraction creates virtual systems out of physical systems. If load balancing is like playing a game of hot potato, then virtual machine technologies is akin to playing slice and dice with the potato.

Given a computer system with a certain set of resources, you can set aside portions of those resources to create a virtual machine. From the standpoint of applications or users, a virtual machine has all the attributes and characteristics of a physical system but is strictly software that emulates a physical machine. A system virtual machine (or a hardware virtual machine) has its own address space in memory, its own processor resource allocation, and its own device I/O using its own virtual device drivers. Some virtual machines are designed to run only a single application or process and are referred to as process virtual machines.

A virtual machine is a computer that is walled off from the physical computer that the virtual machine is running on. This makes virtual machine technology very useful for running old versions of operating systems, testing applications in what amounts to a sandbox, or in the case of cloud computing, creating virtual machine instances that can be assigned a workload. Virtual machines provide the capability of running multiple machine instances, each with their own operating system.

From the standpoint of cloud computing, these features enable VMMs to manage application provisioning, provide for machine instance cloning and replication, allow for graceful system failover, and provide several other desirable features. The downside of virtual machine technologies is that having resources indirectly addressed means there is some level of overhead.

Virtual machine types

A low-level program is required to provide system resource access to virtual machines, and this program is referred to as the hypervisor or Virtual Machine Monitor (VMM). A hypervisor running on bare metal is a Type 1 VM or native VM. Examples of Type 1 Virtual Machine Monitors are LynxSecure, RTS Hypervisor, Oracle VM, Sun xVM Server, VirtualLogix VLX, VMware ESX and ESXi, and Wind River VxWorks, among others. The operating system loaded into a virtual machine is referred to as the guest operating system, and there is no constraint on running the same guest on multiple VMs on a physical system. Type 1 VMs have no host operating system because they are installed on a bare system.

An operating system running on a Type 1 VM is a full virtualization because it is a complete simulation of the hardware that it is running on.

Note

Not all CPUs support virtual machines, and many that do require that you enable this support in the BIOS. For example, AMD-V processors (code named Pacifica) and Intel VT-x (code named Vanderpool) were the first of these vendor's 64-bit offerings that added this type of support. ■

Some hypervisors are installed over an operating system and are referred to as Type 2 or hosted VM. Examples of Type 2 Virtual Machine Monitors are Containers, KVM, Microsoft Hyper V, Parallels Desktop for Mac, Wind River Simics, VMWare Fusion, Virtual Server 2005 R2, Xen, Windows Virtual PC, and VMware Workstation 6.0 and Server, among others. This is a very rich product category. Type 2 virtual machines are installed over a host operating system; for Microsoft Hyper-V, that operating system would be Windows Server. In the section that follows, the Xen hypervisor (which runs on top of a Linux host OS) is more fully described. Xen is used by Amazon Web Services to provide Amazon Machine Instances (AMIs).

Figure 5.1 shows a diagram of Type 1 and Type 2 hypervisors.

On a Type 2 VM, a software interface is created that emulates the devices with which a system would normally interact. This abstraction is meant to place many I/O operations outside the virtual environment, which makes it both programmatically easier and more efficient to execute device I/O than it would be inside a virtual environment. This type of virtualization is sometimes referred to as *paravirtualization,* and it is found in hypervisors such as Microsoft's Hyper-V and Xen. It is the host operating system that is performing the I/O through a para-API.

FIGURE 5.1

VMware's vSphere cloud computing infrastructure model

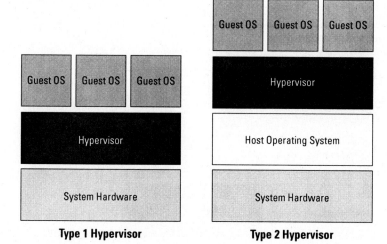

Type 1 Hypervisor   Type 2 Hypervisor

Figure 5.2 shows the difference between emulation, paravirtualization, and full virtualization. In emulation, the virtual machine simulates hardware, so it can be independent of the underlying system hardware. A guest operating system using emulation does not need to be modified in any way. Paravirtualization requires that the host operating system provide a virtual machine interface for the guest operating system and that the guest access hardware through that host VM. An operating system running as a guest on a paravirtualization system must be ported to work with the host interface. Finally, in a full virtualization scheme, the VM is installed as a Type 1 Hypervisor directly onto the hardware. All operating systems in full virtualization communicate directly with the VM hypervisor, so guest operating systems do not require any modification. Guest operating systems in full virtualization systems are generally faster than other virtualization schemes.

The Virtual Machine Interface (VMI) open standard (`http://vmi.ncsa.uiuc.edu/`) that VMware has proposed is an example of a paravirtualization API. The latest version of VMI is 2.1, and it ships as a default installation with many versions of the Linux operating system.

Note

Wikipedia maintains a page called "Comparison of platform virtual machines" at `http://en.wikipedia.org/wiki/Comparison_of_platform_virtual_machines`. **The page contains a table of features of the most common Virtual Machine Managers. ■**

You are probably familiar with process or application virtual machines. Most folks run the Java Virtual Machine or Microsoft's .NET Framework VM (called the Common Language Runtime or CLR) on their computers. A process virtual machine instantiates when a command begins a process, the VM is created by an interpreter, the VM then executes the process, and finally the VM exits the system and is destroyed. During the time the VM exists, it runs as a high-level abstraction.

FIGURE 5.2

Emulation, paravirtualization, and full virtualization types

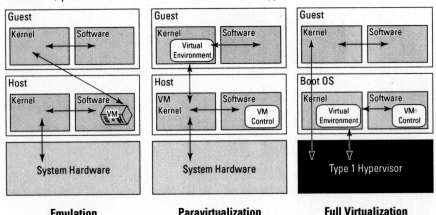

Applications running inside an application virtual machine are generally slow, but these programs are very popular because they provide portability, offer rich programming languages, come with many advanced features, and allow platform independence for their programs. Although many cloud computing applications provide process virtual machine applications, this type of abstraction isn't really suitable for building a large or high-performing cloud network, with one exception.

The exception is the process VMs that enable a class of parallel cluster computing applications. These applications are high-performance systems where the virtual machine is operating one process per cluster node, and the system maintains the necessary intra-application communications over the network interconnect. Examples of this type of system are the Parallel Virtual Machine (PVM; see `http://www.csm.ornl.gov/pvm/pvm_home.html`) and the Message Passing Interface (MPI; see `http://www.mpi-forum.org/`). Some people do not consider these application VMs to be true virtual machines, noting that these applications can still access the host operating system services on the specific system on which they are running. The emphasis on using these process VMs is in creating a high-performance networked supercomputer often out of heterogeneous systems, rather than on creating a ubiquitous utility resource that characterizes a cloud network.

Some operating systems such as Sun Solaris and IBM AIX 6.1 support a feature known as *operating system virtualization*. This type of virtualization creates virtual servers at the operating system or kernel level. Each virtual server is running in its own virtual environment (VE) as a virtual private server (VPS). Different operating systems use different names to describe these machine instances, each of which can support its own guest OS. However, unlike true virtual machines, VPS must all be running the same OS and the same version of that OS. Sun Solaris 10 uses VPS to create what is called Solaris Zones. With IBM AIX, the VPS is called a System Workload Partition (WPAR). This type of virtualization allows for a dense collection of virtual machines with relatively low overhead. Operating system virtualization provides many of the benefits of virtualization previously noted in this section.

VMware vSphere

VMware vSphere is a management infrastructure framework that virtualizes system, storage, and networking hardware to create cloud computing infrastructures. vSphere is the branding for a set of management tools and a set of products previously labeled VMware Infrastructure. vSphere provides a set of services that applications can use to access cloud resources, including these:

- **VMware vCompute:** A service that aggregates servers into an assignable pool
- **VMware vStorage:** A service that aggregates storage resources into an assignable pool
- **VMware vNetwork:** A service that creates and manages virtual network interfaces
- **Application services:** Such as HA (High Availability) and Fault Tolerance
- **vCenter Server:** A provisioning, management, and monitoring console for VMware cloud infrastructures

Figure 5.3 shows an architectural diagram of a vSphere cloud infrastructure.

FIGURE 5.3

VMware's vSphere cloud computing infrastructure model

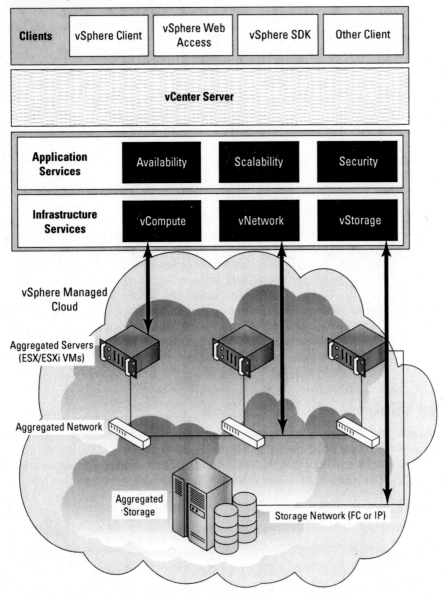

A vSphere cloud is a pure infrastructure play. The virtualization layer that abstracts processing, memory, and storage uses the VMware ESX or ESXi virtualization server. ESX is a Type 1 hypervisor; it installs over bare metal (a clean system) using a Linux kernel to boot and installs the vmkernel hypervisor (virtualization kernel and support files). When the system is rebooted, the vmkernel loads first, and then the Linux kernel becomes the first guest operating system to run as a virtual machine on the system and contains the service console.

VMware is a very highly developed infrastructure and the current leader in this industry. A number of important add-on products are available for cloud computing applications. These are among the more notable products:

- **Virtual Machine File System (VMFS):** A high-performance cluster file system for an ESX/ESXi cluster.

- **VMotion:** A service that allows for the migration of a virtual machine from one physical server to another physical server while the virtual server runs continuously and without any interruption of ongoing transactions.

  The ability to live migrate virtual machines is considered to be a technological tour de force and a differentiator from other virtual machine system vendors.

- **Storage VMotion:** A product that can migrate files from one datastore to another datastore while the virtual machine that uses the datastore continues to run.

- **Virtual SMP:** A feature that allows a virtual machine to run on two or more physical processors at the same time.

- **Distributed Resource Scheduler (DRS):** A system for provisioning virtual machines and load balancing processing resources dynamically across the different physical systems that are in use. A part of the DRS called the distributed power management (DPM) module can manage the power consumption of systems.

- **vNetwork Distributed Switch (DVS):** A capability to maintain a network runtime state for virtual machines as they are migrated from one physical system to another. DVS also monitors network connections, provides firewall services, and enables the use of third-party switches such as the Cisco Nexus 1000V to manage virtual networks.

You can get a better sense of how the different resources are allocated by vSphere into a virtual set of components by examining Figure 5.4. Physical computers can be standalone hosts or a set of clustered systems. In either case, a set of virtual machines can be created that is part of a single physical system or spans two or more physical systems.

You can define a group of VMs as a Resource Pool (RP) and, by doing so, manage those virtual machines as a single object with a single policy. Resource Pools can be placed into a hierarchy or nested and can inherit properties of their parent RP. As more hosts or cluster nodes are added or removed, vSphere can dynamically adjust the provisioning of VMs to accommodate the policy in place. This fine tuning of pooled resources is required to accommodate the needs of cloud computing networks.

FIGURE 5.4

Virtual infrastructure elements

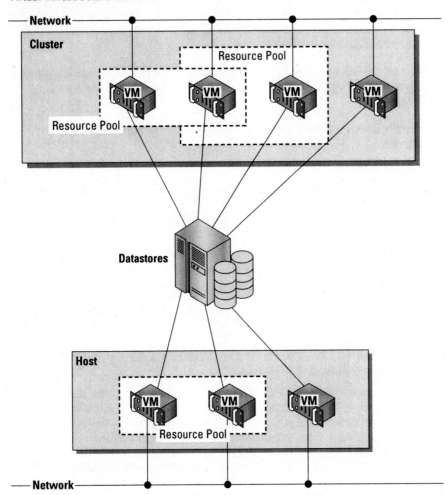

The datastore shown at the center of Figure 5.4 is a shared storage resource. These storage resources can be either Direct Attached Storage (DAS) of a server using SCSI, SAS, or SATA connections, Fibre Channel disk arrays/SANs, iSCSI disk arrays/SANs, or Network Attached Storage (NAS) disk arrays. Although the lines drawn between the datastore and different VMs indicate a direct connection, with the exception of DAS, the other storage types are shared storage solutions.

Storage virtualization is most commonly achieved through a mapping mechanism where a logical storage address is translated into a physical storage address. Block-based storage such as those used in SANs use a feature called a Logical Unit Identifier (LUN) with specific addresses stored in the form of an offset called the Logical Block Address (LBA). The address space mapping then maps the address of the logical or virtual disk (vdisk) to the logical unit on a storage controller. Storage virtualization may be done in software or in hardware, and it allows requests for virtualized storage to be redirected as needed.

Similarly, network virtualization abstracts networking hardware and software into a virtual network that can be managed. A virtual network can create virtual network interfaces (VNICs) or virtual LANs (VLANS) and can be managed by a hypervisor, operating system, or external management console. In a virtualized infrastructure such as the one presented in this section, internal network virtualization is occurring and the hypervisor interacts with networking hardware to create a pseudo-network interface. External network virtualization can be done using network switches and VLAN software.

The key feature that makes virtual infrastructure so appealing for organizations implementing a cloud computing solution is flexibility. Instantiating a virtual machine is a very fast process, typically only a few seconds in length. You can make machine images of systems in the configuration that you want to deploy or take snapshots of working virtual machines. These images can be brought on-line as needed.

Understanding Machine Imaging

In the preceding sections, you have seen how the abstractions that cloud computing needs can be achieved through redirection and virtualization. A third mechanism is commonly used to provide system portability, instantiate applications, and provision and deploy systems in the cloud. This third mechanism is through storing the state of a systems using a system image.

Cross-Ref

Backing up to the cloud often involves imaging or snapshot applications; this process is described in Chapter 15, "Working with Cloud-Based Storage." ■

A system image makes a copy or a clone of the entire computer system inside a single container such as a file. The system imaging program is used to make this image and can be used later to restore a system image. Some imaging programs can take snapshots of systems, and most allow you to view the files contained in the image and do partial restores.

Note

The one open standard for storing a system image is the Open Virtualization Format (OVF; see `http://www.dmtf.org/standards/published_documents/DSP0243_1.1.0.pdf`) that is published by the Distributed Task Format (DMTF; `http://www.dmtf.org/`). Some notable virtualization vendors, such as VMware, Microsoft, Citrix, and Oracle (Sun), are supporting this effort. ■

A prominent example of a system image and how it can be used in cloud computing architectures is the Amazon Machine Image (AMI) used by Amazon Web Services to store copies of a virtual machine. Because this is a key feature of Amazon's Elastic Compute Cloud and is discussed in detail in Chapter 9, I briefly mention it here. An AMI is a file system image that contains an operating system, all appropriate device drivers, and any applications and state information that the working virtual machine would have.

When you subscribe to AWS, you can choose to use one of its hundreds of canned AMIs or to create a custom system and capture that system's image to an AMI. An AMI can be for public use under a free distribution license, for pay-per-use with operating systems such as Windows, or shared by an EC2 user with other users who are given the privilege of access.

Cross-Ref

Refer to Chapter 9, "Using Amazon Web Services," for more information about AMIs and their uses in the EC2 service. ■

The AMI file system is not a standard bit-for-bit image of a system that is common to many disk imaging programs. AMI omits the kernel image and stores a pointer to a particular kernel that is part of the AWS kernel library. Among the choices are Red Hat Linux, Ubuntu, Microsoft Windows, Solaris, and others. Files in AMI are compressed and encrypted, and an XML file is written that describes the AMI archive. AMIs are typically stored in your Amazon S3 (Simple Storage System) buckets as a set of 10MB chunks.

Machine images are sometimes referred to as "virtual appliances"—systems that are meant to run on virtualization platforms. AWS EC2 runs on the Xen hypervisor, for example. The term *virtual appliance* is meant to differentiate the software image from an operating virtual machine. The system image contains the operating system and applications that create an environment. Most virtual appliances are used to run a single application and are configurable from a Web page. Virtual appliances are a relatively new paradigm for application deployment, and cloud computing is the major reason for the interest in them and for their adoption. This area of WAN application portability and deployment, and of WAN optimization of an application based on demand, is one with many new participants. Certeon (`http://www.certeon.com/`), Expand Networks (`http://www.expand.com/`), and Replify (`http://www.replify.com/`) are three vendors offering optimization appliances for VMware's infrastructure.

Porting Applications

Cloud computing applications have the ability to run on virtual systems and for these systems to be moved as needed to respond to demand. Systems (VMs running applications), storage, and network assets can all be virtualized and have sufficient flexibility to give acceptable distributed WAN application performance. Developers who write software to run in the cloud will undoubtedly want the ability to port their applications from one cloud vendor to another, but that is a much more difficult proposition. Cloud computing is a relatively new area of technology, and the major vendors have technologies that don't interoperate with one another.

The Simple Cloud API

If you build an application on a platform such as Microsoft Azure, porting that application to Amazon Web Services or GoogleApps may be difficult, if not impossible. In an effort to create an interoperability standard, Zend Technologies has started an open source initiative to create a common application program interface that will allow applications to be portable. The initiative is called the Simple API for Cloud Application Services (`http://www.simplecloud.org/`), and the effort has drawn interest from several major cloud computing companies. Among the founding supporters are IBM, Microsoft, Nivanix, Rackspace, and GoGrid.

Simple Cloud API has as its goal a set of common interfaces for:

- **File Storage Services:** Currently Amazon S3, Windows Azure Blob Storage, Nirvanix, and Local storage is supported by the Storage API. There are plans to extend this API to Rackspace Cloud Files and GoGrid Cloud Storage.

- **Document Storage Services:** Amazon SimpleDB and Windows Azure Table Storage are currently supported. Local document storage is planned.

- **Simple Queue Services:** Amazon SQS, Windows Azure Queue Storage, and Local queue services are supported.

Zend intends to add the interface to their open source PHP Framework (`http://www.frame work.zend.com`) as the Zend_Cloud framework component. Vendors such as Microsoft and IBM are supplying adapters that will use part of the Simple Cloud API for their cloud application services.

AppZero Virtual Application Appliance

Applications that run in datacenters are captive to the operating systems and hardware platforms that they run on. Many datacenters are a veritable Noah's Ark of computing. So moving an application from one platform to another isn't nearly as simple as moving a machine image from one system to another.

The situation is further complicated by the fact that applications are tightly coupled with the operating systems on which they run. An application running on Windows, for example, isn't isolated from other applications. When the application loads, it often loads or uses different Dynamic Link Libraries (DLL), and it is through the sharing or modification of DLLs that Windows applications get themselves in trouble. Further modifications include modifying the registry during installation. These factors make it difficult to port applications from one platform to another without lots of careful work. If you are a Platform as a Service (PaaS) application developer, you are packaging a complete software stack that includes not only your application, but the operating system and application logic and rules as well. Vendor lock-in for you application is assured.

The ability to run an application from whatever platform you want is not one of the characteristics of cloud computing, but you can imagine that it is a very attractive proposition. While the Simple Cloud API is useful for applications written in PHP, other methods may be needed to make applications easily portable. One company working on this problem is AppZero (`http://www. appzero.com/`), and its solution is called the Virtual Application Appliance (VAA).

The AppZero solution creates a virtual application appliance as an architectural layer between the Windows or the UNIX operating system and applications. The virtualization layer serves as the mediator for file I/O, memory I/O, and application calls and response to DLLs, which has the effect of sandboxing the application. The running application in AppZero changes none of the registry entries or any of the files on the Windows Server.

VAA creates a container that encapsulates the application and all the application's dependencies within a set of files; it is essentially an Application Image for a specific OS. Dependencies include DLL, service settings, necessary configuration files, registry entries, and machine and network settings. This container forms an installable server-side application stack that can be run after installation, but has no impact on the underlying operating system. VAAs are created using the AppZero Creator wizard, managed with the AppZero Admin tool, and may be installed using the AppZero Director, which creates a VAA runtime application. If desired, an application called AppZero Dissolve removes the VAA virtualization layer from the encapsulated application and installs that application directly into the operating system.

Note

Microsoft App-V (`http://www.microsoft.com/windows/enterprise/products/mdop/app-v.aspx`**) and VMware ThinApp (**`http://www.vmware.com/products/thinapp/`**) are two application delivery platforms, but their main focus is on desktop installations and not on server deployment in the cloud.** ■

Installations can be done over the network after the AppZero application appliance is installed. Therefore, with this system, you could run applications on the same Windows Server and eliminate one application from interfering with another; applications would be much more easily ported from one Windows system to another. AppZero's approach provides the necessary abstraction layer that frees an application from its platform dependence.

An interesting use of VAAs involves segmenting an application into several VAAs, some of which are read-only runtime components, while others can be modified. When backing up or replicating VAAs in a cloud, you would need to synchronize only those VAAs that are modified. In many instances, the portion of an application that changes is only a very small component of large applications, which means that this technique can greatly reduce the amount of data required to replicate a VM in the cloud.

AppZero envisages using VAAs to create what it calls a *stateless cloud*. In a stateless cloud, the application's state information is stored on a network share where it is available to run on different cloud systems as needed. This approach allows the cloud system to run with a VM containing a clean operating system (like AWS does now) and provisioned by the VAA. This approach should greatly reduce the number of complete system images that cloud vendors and cloud users should need to store to support their work; it also should make the running of applications on secure, well-performing VEs easier to achieve.

Summary

In this chapter, you learned about some of the more important characteristics of cloud computing networks and applications, including ubiquitousness and on-demand service. To enable a cloud service, you need to create a pool of resources you can call on. The key techniques for enabling this are abstraction and virtualization. Abstraction maps a logical identity or address to a physical identity or address. Changes to the underlying systems, therefore, do not affect the client requesting a service.

Several different methods for abstraction have been considered. A widely used technique is load balancing. With load balancing, system requests are directed to appropriate systems on demand. All large cloud networks use some form of load balancing. You learned about some of the details of Google's load balancing for queries.

Another technology virtualizes hardware. You learned about the different types of hypervisors—software that can serve as a virtualization layer for operating systems accessing the underlying hardware. As an example of hardware virtualization VMware's vSphere infrastructure was considered. vSphere can create virtual machines, virtual datastores, and virtual networks, and move these resources about while the system is active. vSphere is a potent cloud-building technology.

System imaging also can be useful in creating and instantiating machine instances. A brief explanation of Amazon Machine Instances was given.

Finally, the topic of application portability was considered. Applications are hard to move from platform to platform, because they are bound up with the operating system on which they run. Eventually, applications will be as portable as virtual machines. A cloud programming interface was described, as was an application delivery appliance.

In Chapter 6, "Capacity Planning," the idea of system workloads is described. Understanding this concept allows you to scale your systems correctly, choose the right type of infrastructure, and do availability planning. Some of the key performance metrics for cloud computing "right sizing" are described.

Capacity Planning

C apacity planning seeks to match demand to available resources. Capacity planning examines what systems are in place, measures their performance, and determines patterns in usage that enables the planner to predict demand. Resources are provisioned and allocated to meet demand.

Although capacity planning measures performance and in some cases adds to the expertise needed to improve or optimize performance, the goal of capacity planning is to accommodate the workload and not to improve efficiency. Performance tuning and optimization is not a primary goal of capacity planners.

To successfully adjust a system's capacity, you need to first understand the workload that is being satisfied and characterize that workload. A system uses resources to satisfy cloud computing demands that include processor, memory, storage, and network capacity. Each of these resources has a utilization rate, and one or more of these resources reaches a ceiling that limits performance when demand increases.

It is the goal of a capacity planner to identify the critical resource that has this resource ceiling and add more resources to move the bottleneck to higher levels of demand.

Scaling a system can be done by scaling up vertically to more powerful systems or by scaling out horizontally to more but less powerful systems. This is a fundamental architectural decision that is affected by the types of workloads that cloud computing systems are being asked to perform. This chapter presents some of these tradeoffs.

Network capacity is one of the hardest factors to determine. Network performance is affected by network I/O at the server, network traffic from the cloud to Internet service providers, and over the last mile from ISPs to homes and offices. These factors are also considered.

Capacity Planning

Capacity planning for cloud computing sounds like an oxymoron. Why bother doing capacity planning for a resource that is both ubiquitous and limitless? The reality of cloud computing is rather different than the ideal might suggest; cloud computing is neither ubiquitous, nor is it limitless. Often, performance can be highly variable, and you pay for what you use. That said, capacity planning for a cloud computing system offers you many enhanced capabilities and some new challenges over a purely physical system.

A capacity planner seeks to meet the future demands on a system by providing the additional capacity to fulfill those demands. Many people equate capacity planning with system optimization (or performance tuning, if you like), but they are not the same. System optimization aims to get more production from the system components you have. Capacity planning measures the maximum amount of work that can be done using the current technology and then adds resources to do more work as needed. If system optimization occurs during capacity planning, that is all to the good; but capacity planning efforts focus on meeting demand. If that means the capacity planner must accept the inherent inefficiencies in any system, so be it.

Note
Capacity and performance are two different system attributes. With capacity, you are concerned about how much work a system can do, whereas with performance, you are concerned with the rate at which work gets done. ■

Capacity planning is an iterative process with the following steps:

1. Determine the characteristics of the present system.

2. Measure the workload for the different resources in the system: CPU, RAM, disk, network, and so forth.

3. Load the system until it is overloaded, determine when it breaks, and specify what is required to maintain acceptable performance.

   Knowing when systems fail under load and what factor(s) is responsible for the failure is the critical step in capacity planning.

4. Predict the future based on historical trends and other factors.

5. Deploy or tear down resources to meet your predictions.

6. Iterate Steps 1 through 5 repeatedly.

Defining Baseline and Metrics

The first item of business is to determine the current system capacity or workload as a measurable quantity over time. Because many developers create cloud-based applications and Web sites based on a LAMP solution stack, let's use those applications for our example in this chapter.

LAMP stands for:

- Linux, the operating system

- Apache HTTP Server (http://httpd.apache.org/), the Web server based on the work of the Apache Software Foundation

- MySQL (http://www.mysql.com), the database server developed by the Swedish company MySQL AB, owned by Oracle Corporation through its acquisition of Sun Microsystems

- PHP (http://www.php.net/), the Hypertext Preprocessor scripting language developed by The PHP Group

Note
Either Perl or Python is often substituted for PHP as the scripting language used. ■

These four technologies are open source products, although the distributions used may vary from cloud to cloud and from machine instance to machine instance. On Amazon Web Services, machine instances are offered for both Red Hat Linux and for Ubuntu. LAMP stacks based on Red Hat Linux are more common than the other distributions, but SUSE Linux and Debian GNU/Linux are also common. Variants of LAMP are available that use other operating systems such as the Macintosh, OpenBSD (OpAMP), Solaris (SAMP), and Windows (WAMP).

Although many other common applications are in use, LAMP is good to use as an example because it offers a system with two applications (APACHE and MySQL) that can be combined or run separately on servers. LAMP is one of the major categories of Amazon Machine Instances that you can create on the Amazon Web Service (see Chapter 9).

Baseline measurements

Let's assume that a capacity planner is working with a system that has a Web site based on APACHE, and let's assume the site is processing database transactions using MySQL. There are two important overall workload metrics in this LAMP system:

- **Page views** or hits on the Web site, as measured in hits per second

- **Transactions** completed on the database server, as measured by transactions per second or perhaps by queries per second

In Figure 6.1, the historical record for the Web server page views over a hypothetical day, week, and year are graphed. These graphs are created by summing the data from the different servers contained in the performance Web logs of the site or measuring throughput from the system based on an intervening service (such as a proxy server). What Figure 6.1 shows is a measure of the *overall* workload of the Web site involved.

Tip

Your performance logs are a primary source of data that everyone should have available for planning purposes, but they are not the only source of performance measurements. A number of companies offer services that can monitor your Web service's performance. For example, sites such as Alertra (`http://www.alertra.com`), Keynote (`http://www.keynote.com`), Gomez (`http://www.gomez.com`), PingDom (`http://www.pingdom.com`), and SiteUpTime (`http://www.siteuptime.com`) can monitor your Web pages to determine their response, latency, uptime, and other characteristics. Gomez and Keynote expose your site data visually as a set of dashboard widgets. Because these are third-party services, many Web services use these sites as the compliance monitor for Service Level Agreements (SLAs). ■

Notice several things about the graphs in Figure 6.1. A typical daily log (shown on top) shows two spikes in demand, one that is centered around 10 AM EST when users on the east coast of the United States use the site heavily and another at around 1 PM EST (three hours later; 10 AM PST) when users on the west coast of the United States use the site heavily. The three-hour time difference is also the difference between Eastern Standard Time and Pacific Standard Time.

These daily performance spikes occur on workdays, but the spikes aren't always of equal demand, as you can see from the weekly graph, shown in the middle of Figure 6.1. On weekends (Saturday and Sunday), the demand rises through the middle of the day and then ebbs later. Some days show a performance spike, as shown on the Tuesday morning section of the weekly graph. A goal of capacity planning (and an important business goal) is to correlate these performance spikes and dips with particular events and causations. Also, at some point your traffic patterns may change, so you definitely want to evaluate these statistics on an ongoing basis.

The yearly graph, at the bottom of Figure 6.1, shows that the daily averages and the daily peaks rise steadily over the year and, in fact, double from January 1st at the start of the year to December 31st at year end. Knowing this, a capacity planner would need to plan to serve twice the traffic while balancing the demands of peak versus average loads. However, it may not mean that twice the resources need to be deployed. The amount of resources to be deployed depends upon the characterization of the Web servers involved, their potential utilization rates, and other factors.

Caution

In predicting trends, it is important that the time scale be selected appropriately. A steady sure rise in demand over a year is much more accurate in predicting future capacity requirements than a sharp spike over a day or a week. Forecasting based on small datasets is notoriously inaccurate. You can't accurately predict the future (no one can), but you can make good guesses based on your intuition. ■

The total workload might be served by a single server instance in the cloud, a number of virtual server instances, or some combination of physical and virtual servers.

FIGURE 6.1

A Web servers' workload measured on a day, a week, and over the course of a year

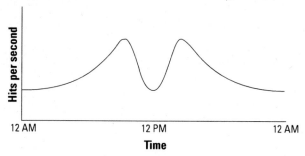

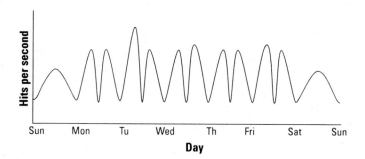

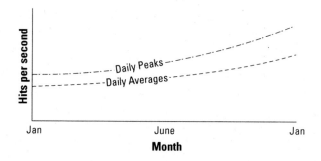

A number of important characteristics are determined by these baseline studies:

- W_T, the total workload for the system per unit time

  To obtain W_T, you need to integrate the area under the curve for the time period of interest.

- WAVG, the average workload over multiple units of time

  To obtain W_{AVG}, you need to sum various W_Ts and divide by the number of unit times involved. You may also want to draw a curve that represents the mean work done.

- W_{MAX}, the highest amount of work recorded by the system

  This is the highest recorded system utilization. In the middle graph of Figure 6.1, it would be the maximum number recorded on Tuesday morning.

- W_{TOT}, the total amount of work done by the system, which is determined by the sum of W_T (ΣW_T)

A similar set of graphs would be collected to characterize the database servers, with the workload for those servers measured in transactions per second. As part of the capacity planning exercise, the workload for the Web servers would be correlated with the workload of the database servers to determine patterns of usage.

The goal of a capacity planning exercise is to accommodate spikes in demand as well as the overall growth of demand over time. Of these two factors, the growth in demand over time is the most important consideration because it represents the ability of a business to grow. A spike in demand may or may not be important enough to an activity to attempt to capture the full demand that the spike represents.

System metrics

Notice that in the previous section, you determined what amounts to application-level statistics for your site. These measurements are an aggregate of one or more Web servers in your infrastructure. Capacity planning must measure system-level statistics, determining what each system is capable of, and how resources of a system affect system-level performance.

In some instances, the capacity planner may have some influence on system architecture, and the impact of system architecture on application- and system-level statistics may be examined and altered. Because this is a rare case, let's focus on the next step, which defines system performance.

A machine instance (physical or virtual) is primarily defined by four essential resources:

- CPU
- Memory (RAM)
- Disk
- Network connectivity

Each of these resources can be measured by tools that are operating-system-specific, but for which tools that are their counterparts exist for all operating systems. Indeed, many of these tools were written specifically to build the operating systems themselves, but that's another story. In Linux/ UNIX, you might use the `sar` command to display the level of CPU activity. `sar` is installed in Linux as part of the `sysstat` package. In Windows, a similar measurement may be made using the Task Manager, the data from which can be dumped to a performance log and/or graphed.

Some tools give you a historical record of performance, which is particularly useful in capacity planning. For example, the popular Linux performance measurement tool `RRDTool` (the Round Robin Database tool; `http://oss.oetiker.ch/rrdtool/`) is valuable in this regard.

RRDTool is a utility that can capture time-dependent performance data from resources such as a CPU load, network utilization (bandwidth), and so on and store the data in a circular buffer. It is commonly used in performance analysis work.

A time interval in RRDTool is called a step, with the value in a step referred to as a primary data point (PDP). When a function is applied to a data point (average, minimum, maximum, and so on), the function is referred to as a Consolidation Function (CF), and the value obtained is a Consolidated Data Point (CDP). An interval is stored in the Round Robin Archive (RRA), and when that interval is filled, it is replaced by new step data. RRDTool includes a graphical front end for displaying performance results visually. RRDTool is widely used for a number of different purposes. Figure 6.2 shows some of the examples from a gallery of RRDTool graphs found at http://oss.oetiker.ch/rrdtool/gallery/.

FIGURE 6.2

RRDTool lets you create historical graphs of a wide variety of performance data. Some samples are shown in the gallery at http://oss.oetiker.ch/rrdtool/gallery/.

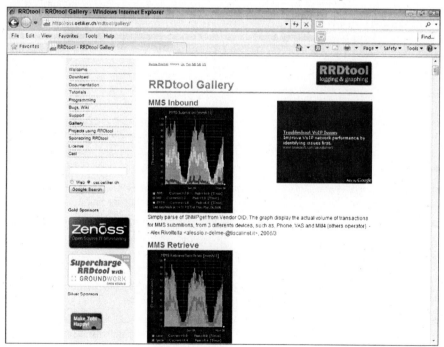

Table 6.1 lists some LAMP performance testing tools.

TABLE 6.1

LAMP Performance Monitoring Tools

Tool Name	Web Site	Developer	Description
Alertra	http://www.alertra.com	Alertra	Web site monitoring service
Cacti	http://www.cacti.net	Cacti	Open source RRDTool graphing module
Collectd	http://www.collectd.org/	collectd	System statistics collection daemon
Dstat	http://dag.wieers.com/home-made/dstat/	DAG	System statistics utility; replaces vmstat, iostat, netstat, and ifstat
Ganglia	http://www.ganglia.info	Ganglia	Open source distributed monitoring system
Gomez	http://www.gomez.com	Gomez	Commercial third-party Web site performance monitor
GraphClick	http://www.arizona-software.ch/graphclick/	Arizona	A digitizer that can create a graph from an image
GroundWork	http://www.groundworkopensource.com/	Groundwork's Open Source	Network monitoring solution
Hyperic HQ	http://www.hyperic.com	Spring Source	Monitoring and alert package for virtualized environments
Keynote	http://www.keynote.com	Keynote	Commercial third-party Web site performance monitor
Monit	http://www.tildeslash.com/monit	Monit	Open source process manager
Munin	http://munin.projects.linpro.no/	Munin	Open source network resource monitoring tool
Nagios	http://www.nagios.org	Nagios	Metrics collection and event notification tool
OpenNMS	http://www.opennms.org	OpenNMS	Open source network management platform
Pingdom	http://www.pingdom.com	Pingdom	Uptime and performance monitor
RRDTool	http://www.RRDTool.org/	Oetiker+Partner AG	Graphing and performance metrics storage utility
SiteUpTime	http://www.siteuptime.com	SiteUpTime	Web site monitoring service
Zabbix	http://www.zabbix.com	Zabbix	Performance monitor
ZenOSS	http://www.zenoss.com/	Zenoss	Operations monitor, both open source and commercial versions

Load testing

Examining your server under load for system metrics isn't going to give you enough information to do meaningful capacity planning. You need to know what happens to a system when the load increases. Load testing seeks to answer the following questions:

1. What is the maximum load that my current system can support?

2. Which resource(s) represents the bottleneck in the current system that limits the system's performance?

   This parameter is referred to as the resource ceiling. Depending upon a server's configuration, any resource can have a bottleneck removed, and the resource ceiling then passes onto another resource.

3. Can I alter the configuration of my server in order to increase capacity?

4. How does this server's performance relate to your other servers that might have different characteristics?

Note

Load testing is also referred to as performance testing, reliability testing, stress testing, and volume testing. ■

If you have one production system running in the cloud, then overloading that system until it breaks isn't going to make you popular with your colleagues. However, cloud computing offers virtual solutions. One possibility is to create a clone of your single system and then use a tool to feed that clone a recorded set of transactions that represent your application workload.

Two examples of applications that can replay requests to Web servers are HTTPerf (http:// hpl.hp.com/research/linux/httperf/) and Siege (http://www.joedog.org/ JoeDog/Siege), but both of these tools run the requests from a single client, which can be a resource limitation of its own. You can run Autobench (http://www.xenoclast.org/auto bench/) to run HTTPerf from multiple clients against your Web server, which is a better test.

You may want to consider these load generation tools as well:

- HP LodeRunner (https://h10078.www1.hp.com/cda/hpms/display/main/ hpms_content.jsp?zn=bto&cp=1-11-126-17^8_4000_100__)

- IBM Rational Performance Tester (http://www-01.ibm.com/software/ awdtools/tester/performance/)

- JMeter (http://jakarta.apache.org/jmeter)

- OpenSTA (http://opensta.org/)

- Micro Focus (Borland) SilkPerfomer (http://www.borland.com/us/products/ silk/silkperformer/index.html)

Load testing software is a large product category with software and hardware products. You will find load testing useful in testing the performance of not only Web servers, but also application servers, database servers, network throughput, load balancing servers, and applications that rely on client-side processing.

When you have multiple virtual servers that are part of a server farm and have a load balancer in front of them, you can use your load balancer to test your servers' resource ceilings. This technique has the dual advantages of allowing you to slowly increment traffic on a server and to use real requests while doing so. Most load balancers allow you to weight the requests going to a specific server with the goal of serving more requests to more powerful systems and fewer requests to less powerful systems. Sometimes the load balancer does this optimization automatically, and other times you can exert manual control over the weighting.

Whatever method you use to load a server for performance testing, you must pick a method that is truly representative of real events, requests, and operations. The best approach is to incrementally alter the load on a server with the current workload. When you make assumptions such as using a load balancer to serve traffic based on a condition that summarizes the traffic pattern instead of using the traffic itself, you can get yourself into trouble.

Problems with load balancers have led to some spectacular system failures because those devices occupy a central controlling site in any infrastructure. For example, if you assume that traffic can be routed based on the number of connections in use per server and your traffic places a highly variable load based on individual requests, then your loading measurements can lead to dramatic failures when you attempt to alter your infrastructure to accommodate additional loads.

Resource ceilings

Whatever performance measurement tool you use, the goal is to create a set of resource utilization curves similar to the ones shown in Figure 6.3 for individual server types in your infrastructure. To do this, you must examine the server at different load levels and measure utilization rates.

The graphs in Figure 6.3 indicate that over a certain load for a particular server, the CPU (A), RAM (B), and Disk I/O (C) utilization rates rise but do not reach their resource ceiling. In this instance, the Network I/O (D) reaches its maximum 100-percent utilization at about 50 percent of the tested load, and this factor is the current system resource ceiling.

Network I/O is often a bottleneck in Web servers, and this is why, architecturally, Web sites prefer to scale out using many low-powered servers instead of scaling up with fewer but more powerful servers. You saw this play out in the previous chapter where Google's cloud was described. Adding more (multi-homing) or faster network connections can be another solution to improving Web servers' performance.

Unless you alter the performance of the server profiled in Figure 6.3 to improve it, you are looking at a maximum value for that server's workload of W_{Smax}, as shown in the dashed line at the 50-percent load point in graph D. At this point, the server is overloaded and the system begins to fail. Some amount of failure may be tolerable in the short term, provided that the system can recover and not too many Web hits are lost, but this is a situation that you really want to minimize. You can consider W_{Sn} to be the server's red line, the point at which the system should be generating alerts or initiating scripts to increase capacity.

FIGURE 6.3

Resource utilization curves for a particular server

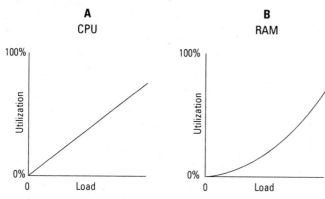

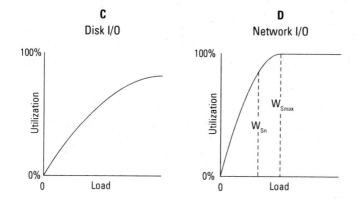

Notice that I have not discussed whether these are physical or virtual servers. The parameter you are most interested in is likely to be the overall system capacity, which is the value of W_T.

W_T is the sum over all the Web servers in your infrastructure:

$$W_T = \Sigma(W_{SnP} \ W_{SnV})$$

In this equation, W_{SnP} represents the workload of your physical server(s) and W_{SnV} is the workload of the virtual servers (cloud-based server instances) of your infrastructure. The amount of overhead you allow yourself should be dictated by the amount of time you require to react to the challenge and to your tolerance for risk. A capacity planner would define a value W_T such that there is suffi-cient overhead remaining in the system to react to demand that is defined by a number greater than W_{MAX} by bringing more resources on-line. For storage resources that tend to change slowly, a planner might set the red line level to be 85 percent of consumption of storage; for a Web server, that utilization percentage may be different. This setting would give you a 15-percent safety factor.

There are more factors that you might want to take into account when considering an analysis of where to draw the red line. When you load test a system, you are applying a certain amount of overhead to the system from the load testing tool—a feature that is often called the "observer effect." Many load testers work by installing lightweight agents on the systems to be tested. Those agents themselves impact the performance you see; generally though, their impact is limited to a few percent. Additionally, in order to measure performance, you may be forced to turn on various performance counters. A performance counter is also an agent of sorts; the counter is running a routine that measures some aspect of performance such as queue length, file I/O rate, numbers of READs and WRITEs, and so forth. While these complications are second order effects, it's always good to keep this in mind and not over-interpret performance results.

Before leaving the topic of resource ceilings, let's consider a slightly more complicated case that you might encounter in MySQL database systems. Database servers are known to exhibit resource ceilings for either their file caches or their Disk I/O performance. To build high-performance applications, many developers replicate their master MySQL database and create a number of slave MySQL databases. All READ operations are performed on the slave MySQL databases, and all WRITE operations are performed on the master MySQL database. Figure 6.4 shows this sort of database architecture.

A master/slave database system has two competing processes and the same server that are sharing a common resource: READs and WRITEs to the master/slave databases, and replication traffic between the master database and all the slave databases. The ratio of these transactions determines the WSn for the system, and the WSn you derive is highly dependent upon the system architecture. These types of servers reach failure when the amount of WRITE traffic in the form of INSERT, UPDATE, and DELETE operations to the master database overtakes the ability of the system to replicate data to the slave databases that are servicing SELECT (query/READ) operations.

The more slave databases there are, the more actively the master database is being modified and the lower the WS for the master database is. This system may support no more than 25-35 percent transactional workload as part of its overall capacity, depending upon the nature of the database application you are running.

You increase the working capacity of a database server that has a Disk I/O resource ceiling by using more powerful disk arrays and improving the interconnection or network connection used to connect the server to its disks. Disk I/O is particularly sensitive to the number of spindles in use, so having more disks equals greater performance. Keep in mind that your ability to alter the performance of disk assets in a virtual or cloud-based database server is generally limited.

Tip

A master/slave MySQL replication architectural scheme is used for smaller database applications. As sites grow and the number of transactions increases, developers tend to deploy databases in a federated architecture. The description of Google's cloud in Chapter 5 describes this approach to large databases, creating what are called sharded databases. ■

Resource contention in a database server

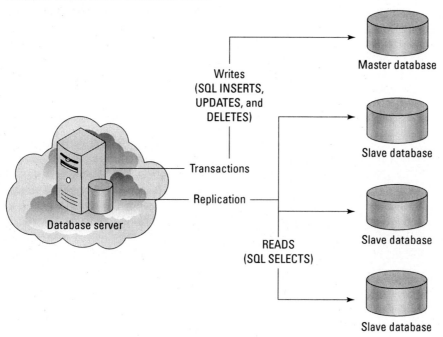

So far you've seen two cases. In the first case, a single server has a single application with a single resource ceiling. In the second case, you have a single server that has a single application with two competing processes that establish a resource ceiling. What do you do in a situation where your server runs the full LAMP stack and you have two or more applications running processes each of which has its own resource ceiling? In this instance, you must isolate each application and process and evaluate their characteristics separately while trying to hold the other applications' resource usage at a constant level. You can do this by examining identical servers running the application individually or by creating a performance console that evaluates multiple factors all at the same time. Remember, real-world data and performance is always preferred over simulations.

As your infrastructure grows, it becomes more valuable to create a performance console that lets you evaluate your KPIs (Key Performance Indicators) graphically at an instant. Many third-party tools offer performance consoles, and some tools allow you to capture their state so you can restore it at a later point. An example of a performance analysis tool that lets you save its state is the Microsoft Management Console (MMC). In the Amazon Web Service, the statistics monitoring tool is called Amazon CloudWatch, and you can create a performance monitoring console from the statistics it collects.

Server and instance types

One goal of capacity planning is to make growth and shrinkage of capacity predictable. You can greatly improve your chances by standardizing on a few hardware types and then well characterizing those platforms. In a cloud infrastructure such as Amazon Web Server, the use of different machine instance sizes is an attempt to create standard servers. Reducing the variability between servers makes it easier to troubleshoot problems and simpler to deploy and configure new systems.

As much as possible, you also should assign servers standardized roles and populate those servers with identical services. A server with the same set of software, system configuration, and hardware should perform similarly if given the same role in an infrastructure. At least that's the theory.

In practice, cloud computing isn't quite as mature as many organizations' physical servers, and in practice, there is more performance variability in cloud machine instances than you might expect. This variability may be due to your machine instances or storage buckets being moved from one system to another system. Therefore, you should be attentive to the increase in potential for virtual system variability and build additional safety factors into your infrastructure. System instances in a cloud can fail, and it is up to the client to recognize these failures and react accordingly. Virtual machines in a cloud are something of a black box, and you should treat them as such because you have no idea what the underlying physical reality of the resources you are using represents.

Capacity planning seeks to compare the capability of one system against another system and to choose the solution that is not only the right size but provides the service with the best operational parameters at the lowest cost. In Figure 6.5, a graph of different server types is shown, with some hypothetical physical servers plotted against Amazon Machine Instance types. This type of graph allows you to add the appropriate server type to your infrastructure while performing a cost analysis of the deployment.

An Amazon Machine Instance (AMI) is described as follows:

- **Micro Instance:** 633 MB memory, 1 to 2 EC2 Compute Units (1 virtual core, using 2 CUs for short periodic bursts) with either a 32-bit or 64-bit platform

- **Small Instance (Default):** 1.7GB memory, 1 EC2 Compute Unit (1 virtual core with 1 EC2 Compute Unit), 160GB instance storage (150GB plus 10GB root partition), 32-bit platform, I/O Performance: Moderate, and API name: m1.small

- **High-Memory Quadruple Extra Large Instance:** 68.4GB of memory, 26 EC2 Compute Units (8 virtual cores with 3.25 EC2 Compute Units each), 1,690GB of instance storage, 64-bit platform, I/O Performance: High, and API name: m2.4xlarge

- **High-CPU Extra Large Instance:** 7GB of memory, 20 EC2 Compute Units (8 virtual cores with 2.5 EC2 Compute Units each), 1,690GB of instance storage, 64-bit platform, I/O Performance: High, API name: c1.xlarge

View this at http://aws.amazon.com/ec2/instance-types/; I expand on this in Chapter 9.

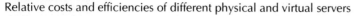

FIGURE 6.5

Relative costs and efficiencies of different physical and virtual servers

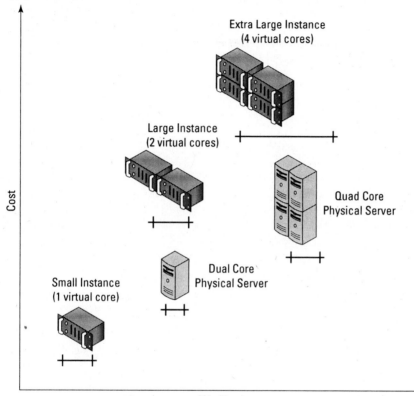

While you may not know what exactly EC2 Compute Unit or I/O Performance High means, at least we can measure these performance claims and attach real numbers to them. Amazon says that an EC2 Compute Unit is the equivalent of a 1.0-1.2 GHz 2007 Opteron or 2007 Xeon processor, but adds that "Over time, we may add or substitute measures that go into the definition of an EC2 Compute Unit, if we find metrics that will give you a clearer picture of compute capacity." What they are saying essentially is that this was the standard processor their fleet used as its baseline, and that over time more powerful systems may be swapped in. Whatever the reality of this situation, from the standpoint of capacity planning, all you should care about is measuring the current performance of systems and right-sizing your provisioning to suit your needs.

In cloud computing, you can often increase capacity on demand quickly and efficiently. Not all cloud computing infrastructures automatically manage your capacity for you as Amazon Web Service's Auto Scaling (`http://aws.amazon.com/autoscaling/`) feature does. At this point in the maturity of the industry, some systems provide automated capacity adjustments, but most do not.

Nor are you guaranteed to be provided with the needed resources from a cloud vendor at times you might need it most. For example, Amazon Web Services' infrastructure runs not only clients' machine instances, but also Amazon.com's machine instances as well as Amazon.com's partners' instances. If you need more virtual servers on Black Monday to service Web sales, you may be out of luck unless you have an SLA that guarantees you the additional capacity. Finding an SLA that you can rely on is still something of a crap shoot. If you are in the position of having to maintain the integrity of your data for legal reasons, this imposes additional problems and constraints.

Cloud computing is enticing. It is easy to get started and requires little up-front costs. However, cloud computing is not cheap. As your needs scale, so do your costs, and you have to pay particular attention to costs as you go forward. At the point where you have a large cloud-based infrastructure, you may find that it is more expensive to have a metered per-use cost than to own your own systems. The efficiencies of cloud computing, as I describe more fully in Chapter 2, aren't necessarily in the infrastructure itself. Most of the long-term efficiencies are realized in the reduced need for IT staff and management, the ability to react quickly to business opportunities, and the freeing of a business from managing networked computer systems to concentrate on their core businesses. So while the Total Cost of Ownership (TCO) of a cloud-based infrastructure might be beneficial, it might be difficult to convince the people paying the bills that this is really so.

Network Capacity

If any cloud-computing system resource is difficult to plan for, it is network capacity. There are three aspects to assessing network capacity:

- Network traffic to and from the network interface at the server, be it a physical or virtual interface or server
- Network traffic from the cloud to the network interface
- Network traffic from the cloud through your ISP to your local network interface (your computer)

This makes analysis complicated. You can measure factor 1, the network I/O at the server's interface with system utilities, as you would any other server resource. For a cloud-based virtual computer, the network interface may be a highly variable resource as the cloud vendor moves virtual systems around on physical systems or reconfigures its network pathways on the fly to accommodate demand. But at least it is measurable in real time.

To measure network traffic at a server's network interface, you need to employ what is commonly known as a network monitor, which is a form of packet analyzer. Microsoft includes a utility called the Microsoft Network Monitor as part of its server utilities, and there are many third-party products in this area. The site Sectools.org has a list of packet sniffers at http://sectools.org/sniffers.html. Here are some:

- Wireshark (http://www.wireshark.org/), formerly called Ethereal
- Kismet (http://www.kismetwireless.net/), a WiFi sniffer
- TCPdump (http://www.tcpdump.org/)

- Dsniff (http://www.monkey.org/~dugsong/dsniff/)
- Ntop (http://www.ntop.org/)
- EtherApe (http://etherape.sourceforge.net/)

Regardless of which of these tools you use, the statistics function of these tools provides a measurement of network capacity as expressed by throughput. You can analyze the data in a number of ways, including specific applications used, network protocols, traffic by system or users, and so forth all the way down to, in some cases, the content of the individual packets crossing the wire.

Note

Alternative names for packet analyzer include network analyzer, network traffic monitor, protocol analyzer, packet sniffer, and Ethernet sniffer, and for wireless networks, wireless or wifi sniffer, network detector, and so on. To see a comparison chart of packet analyzers on Wikipedia, go to http://en.wikipedia.org/wiki/Comparison_of_packet_analyzers. ■

Factor 2 is the cloud's network performance, which is a measurement of WAN traffic. A WAN's capacity is a function of many factors:

- Overall system traffic (competing services)
- Routing and switching protocols
- Traffic types (transfer protocols)
- Network interconnect technologies (wiring)
- The amount of bandwidth that the cloud vendor purchased from an Internet backbone provider

Again, factor 2 is highly variable and unlike factor 1, it isn't easy to measure in a reliable way.

Tools are available that can monitor a cloud network's performance at geographical different points and over different third-party ISP connections. This is done by establishing measurement systems at various well-chosen network hubs.

Apparent Networks, a company that makes WAN network monitoring software, has set up a series of these points of presence at various Internet hubs and uses its networking monitoring software called PathView Cloud to collect data in a display that it calls the Cloud Performance Scorecard (http://www.apparentnetworks.com/CPC/scorecard.aspx). Figure 6.6 shows this Web page populated with statistics for some of the cloud vendors that Apparent Networks monitors. You can use PathView Cloud as a hosted service to evaluate your own cloud application's network performance at these various points of presence and to create your own scorecard of a cloud network. Current pricing for the service is $5 per network path per month. The company also sells a small appliance that you can insert at locations of your choice and with which you can perform your own network monitoring.

The last factor, factor 3, is the connection from the backbone through your ISP to your local system, a.k.a. "The Internet." The "Internet" is not a big, fat, dumb pipe; nor is it (as former Senator Ted Stevens of Alaska proclaimed) "a series of tubes." For most people, their Internet connection is more like an intelligently managed thin straw that you are desperately trying to suck information out of. So factor 3 is measurable, even if the result of the measurement isn't very encouraging, especially to your wallet.

Internet connectivity over the last mile (to the home) is the Achilles heel of cloud computing. The scarcity of high-speed broadband connections (particularly in the United States) and high pricing are major impediments to the growth of cloud computing. Many organizations and communities will wait on the sidelines before embracing cloud computing until faster broadband becomes available. Indeed, this may be the final barrier to cloud computing's dominance.

That's one of the reasons that large cloud providers like Google are interested in building their own infrastructure, in promoting high-speed broadband connectivity, and in demonstrating the potential of high-speed WANs. Google is running a demonstration project called Google Fibre for Communities (`http://www.google.com/appserve/fiberrfi/public/overview`) that will deliver 1 gigabit-per-second fiber to the home. The few lucky municipalities chosen (with 50,000 to 500,000 residents) for the demonstration project will get advanced broadband applications, many of which will be cloud-based. The winners of this contest have yet to be announced, but they are certain to be highly sought after (see Figure 6.7).

FIGURE 6.6

Apparent Networks' Cloud Performance Center provides data on WAN throughput and uptime at Internet network hubs.

You are not in Kansas anymore. To petition Google for a Fiber for Communities network, Topeka, Kansas, became Google for a day, and Google returned the favor.

Topeka

Scaling

In capacity planning, after you have made the decision that you need more resources, you are faced with the fundamental choice of scaling your systems. You can either scale vertically (scale up) or scale horizontally (scale out), and each method is broadly suitable for different types of applications.

To scale vertically, you add resources to a system to make it more powerful. For example, during scaling up, you might replace a node in a cloud-based system that has a dual-processor machine instance equivalence with a quad-processor machine instance equivalence. You also can scale up when you add more memory, more network throughput, and other resources to a single node. Scaling out indefinitely eventually leads you to an architecture with a single powerful supercomputer.

Vertical scaling allows you to use a virtual system to run more virtual machines (operating system instance), run more daemons on the same machine instance, or take advantage of more RAM (memory) and faster compute times. Applications that benefit from being scaled up vertically include those applications that are processor-limited such as rendering or memory-limited such as certain database operations—queries against an in-memory index, for example.

Horizontal scaling or scale out adds capacity to a system by adding more individual nodes. In a system where you have a dual-processor machine instance, you would scale out by adding more dual-processor machines instances or some other type of commodity system. Scaling out indefinitely leads you to an architecture with a large number of servers (a server farm), which is the model that many cloud and grid computer networks use.

Horizontal scaling allows you to run distributed applications more efficiently and is effective in using hardware more efficiently because it is both easier to pool resources and to partition them. Although your intuition might lead you to believe otherwise, the world's most powerful computers are currently built using clusters of computers aggregated using high speed interconnect technologies such as InfiniBand or Myrinet. Scale out is most effective when you have an I/O resource ceiling and you can eliminate the communications bottleneck by adding more channels. Web server connections are a classic example of this situation.

These broad generalizations between scale up and scale out are useful from a conceptual stand-point, but the reality is that there are always tradeoffs between choosing one method for scaling your cloud computing system versus the other. Often, the choice isn't so clear-cut. The pricing model that cloud computing vendors now offer their clients isn't fully mature at the moment, and you may find yourself paying much more for a high-memory extra-large machine instance than you might pay for the equivalent amount of processing power purchased with smaller system equivalents. This has always been true when you purchase physical servers, and it is still true (but to a much smaller extent) when purchasing virtual servers. Cost is one factor to pay particular attention to, but there are other tradeoffs as well. Scale out increases the number of systems you must manage, increases the amount of communication between systems that is going on, and introduces additional latency to your system.

Summary

In this chapter, you learned about how to match capacity to demand. To do this, you must mea-sure performance of your systems, predict demand, and understand demand patterns. You must them allocate resources to meet demands. When demand is higher, you must provision additional resources, and when demand is lower, you must tear down resources currently in place.

Cloud computing's use of virtual resources offers exciting new ways to flexibly respond to demand challenges. Cloud computing also poses some new risks and makes additional demands on the capacity planner that this chapter discusses.

The key to capacity planning is through measurement of current system performance and the col-lection of a meaningful historical data set. This chapter described some of the tools you need to perform these analyses, a general approach you must take, and how to act based on the results you find.

In Chapter 7, I more fully explore the Platform as a Service (PaaS) model that provides a new application delivery paradigm. PaaS is the delivery of a complete computer platform as well as an application stack. You can use systems of these types to create solutions that you use or offer to others as a service. Because the infrastructure and architecture is already in place, PaaS allows you to concentrate on a very specific service that leverages the investment already made by the PaaS vendor. Chapter 7 describes some of these types of services, the application frameworks used in PaaS, and some of the programming tools in place.

Exploring Platform as a Service

The Platform as a Service model provides the tools within an environment needed to create applications that can run in a Software as a Service model. For this reason, some overlap between vendors has created Software as a Service products, and those vendors have broadened their services to make their Web applications more customizable. Salesforce. com, the largest CRM application service company in the world, is an example, with Force.com being its PaaS (Platform as a Service) offering.

Applications developed in PaaS systems can be composite business applications, data portals, or mashups with data derived from multiple sources. PaaS environments can offer integrated lifecycle management or *anchored lifecycle applications*. An integrated system provides a broad range of tools for customization, whereas an anchored system is based on already established software.

Application frameworks are a particularly powerful tool for creating cloud computing applications. For this reason, many vendor products are based on this model. In other chapters, you learn about Google AppEngine and Windows Azure Platform. This chapter presents several examples of PaaS systems that can create captive hosted applications, portable applications, extended blogs or content management systems, or rich Internet data applications. Some of the sites you learn about in this chapter with PaaS tools include Drupal, Eccentex AppBase, LongJump, SquareSpace, and WaveMaker.

Each of these systems or tools presents a very different aspect of cloud application development. What all these tools have in common is that they are standards-based.

Defining Services

In many ways, the Platform as a Service model is the most interesting of all the hosted services in cloud computing. IaaS offers a service that is akin to installing an application on a computer. That computer is virtual, of course, but it is still a computer. By the time you are using an SaaS model, the software is pretty well mapped out for you. You can do some modest customization, some branding perhaps, but the software's capabilities and design has largely been worked out.

With Platform as a Service systems, you are given a toolkit to work with, a virtual machine to run your software on, and it is up to you to design the software and its user-facing interface in a way that is appropriate to your needs. So PaaS systems range from full-blown developer platforms like Windows Azure Platform to systems like Drupal, Squarespace, Wolf, and others where the tools are modules that are very well developed and require almost no coding. Many Content Management Systems (CMS) are essentially PaaS services where you get standard parts and can build Web sites and other software like Tinker Toys.

Thus you find that PaaS models span a broad range of services, including these, among others:

- **Application development:** A PaaS platform either provides the means to use programs you create in a supported language or offers a visual development environment that writes the code for you.
- **Collaboration:** Many PaaS systems are set up to allow multiple individuals to work on the same projects.
- **Data management:** Tools are provided for accessing and using data in a data store.
- **Instrumentation, performance, and testing:** Tools are available for measuring your applications and optimizing their performance.
- **Storage:** Data can be stored in either the PaaS vendor's service or accessed from a third-party storage service.
- **Transaction management:** Many PaaS systems provide services such as transaction managers or brokerage service for maintaining transaction integrity.

PaaS systems exist to allow you to create software that can be hosted as SaaS systems or to allow for the modification of existing SaaS applications. You've seen many examples of PaaS systems already, and whole chapters are dedicated to vendor-specific PaaS platforms. The next chapter describes the Google AppEngine, which is a system for deploying Web applications on Google infrastructure. Chapter 10 describes the Windows Azure Platform with its emphasis on creating Windows applications using the .NET Framework on Microsoft infrastructure.

A good PaaS system has certain desirable characteristics that are important in developing robust, scalable, and hopefully portable applications. On this list would be the following attributes:

- Separate of data management from the user interface
- Reliance on cloud computing standards

- An integrated development environment (IDE)
- Lifecycle management tools
- Multi-tenant architecture support, security, and scalability
- Performance monitoring, testing, and optimization tools

The more vibrant the associated market of a PaaS's third-party add-ons, applications, tools, and services, the better they are. These extras allow you to extend your application by buying functionality, which is almost always cheaper than having to roll your own.

Salesforce.com versus Force.com: SaaS versus PaaS

There can be no better example illustrating the difference between a SaaS and PaaS system than that of Salesforce.com and Force.com. Salesforce.com is a Web application suite that is an SaaS. Force.com is Salesforce.com's PaaS platform for building your own services.

Salesforce.com was formed by several Oracle employees in 1999 to create a hosted Customer Relationship Management (CRM) system. CRM has long been one of Oracle's core database services. The Salesforce.com team created hosted software based on a cloud computing model: pay as you go, simple to use, and multifunctional. The Salesforce.com platform looks like a typical Web site such as Amazon.com, with a multi-tabbed interface—each tab being an individual application.

Shown in Figure 7.1 is a Salesforce.com portal with the multi-tabbed interface exposing the different applications.

FIGURE 7.1

In Salesforce.com, each tab is an application, and data is shared. Shown here is a dashboard view.

Some of the applications included in the site are:

- Accounts and Contact
- Analytics and Forecasting
- Approvals and Workflow
- Chatter (Instant Messaging/Collaboration)
- Content Library
- E-mail and Productivity
- Jigsaw Business Data
- Marketing and Leads
- Opportunities and Quotes
- Partner Relationship
- Sales
- Service and Support

Which tabs you see, and how capable each hosted application is, depends on the level of service you purchase from Salesforce.com, as well as the particular type of bundle you buy. Salesforce.com tailors its SaaS for individual industries.

As Salesforce.com developed its SaaS production, it became obvious that many customers wanted to extend their Salesforce.com applications beyond what an SaaS offering would allow. Salesforce.com developed a PaaS platform known as Force.com, which allows developers to create applications that could be added to Salesforce.com's offerings and hosted on Salesforce.com's infrastructure.

Figure 7.2 shows the Force.com platform page at Salesforce.com.

Force.com uses a Java-based programming language called Apex for its application building, and it has an interface builder called Visualforce that allows a developer to create interfaces using HTML, Flex, and AJAX. Visualforce uses an XML-type language in its visual interface builder. Using the Force.com platform, more than 1,000 applications have been created and are offered for sale on Salesforce.com's AppExchange, which has greatly enhanced its PaaS offerings. These applications can show up as customizable tabs for different functions in customer applications or as a set of S-controls that are JavaScript widgets.

Because Salesforce.com is browser-based, it is platform-independent. However, the company has extended its audience to mobile devices, such as the Android, Blackberry, iPhone, and Windows Mobile Devices. It also has a server product that supports Salesforce.com applications in-house called the Resin Application Server.

Force.com has been a major hit and has served as the model from many of the PaaS systems of today. The company Salesforce.com is a recognized thought leader in the field of cloud computing. It is a $1.3 billion company as of 2009, with over 2 million subscribers.

FIGURE 7.2

Force.com's Web site (`http://www.salesforce.com/platform/`) leads to a set of developer tools as well as a gallery of sites built on this PaaS.

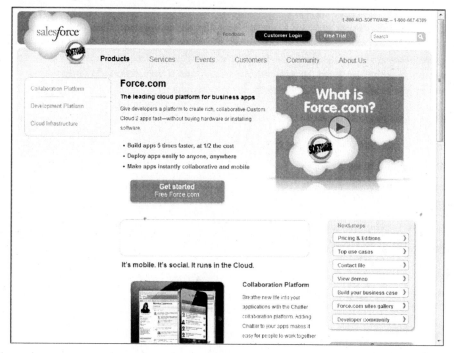

Application development

A PaaS provides the tools needed to construct different types of applications that can work together in the same environment. These are among the common application types:

- Composite business applications
- Data portals
- Mashups of multiple data sources

A *mashup* is a Web page that displays data from two or more data sources. The various landmarks and overlays you find in Google Earth, or annotated maps, are examples of mashups.

These applications must be able to share data and to run in a multi-tenant environment. To make applications work together more easily, a common development language such as Java or Python is usually offered. The more commonly used the language is, the more developers and developer services are going to be available to help users of platform applications. The use of application frameworks such as Ruby on Rails is useful in making application building easier and more powerful.

Most of the application building tools in this chapter create their own frameworks. Many are based on visual tools, and often these tools allow developers to extend applications using a common language for Web application development. These applications almost always adopt a Service Oriented Architecture model and use SOAP/REST with XML data exchange.

All PaaS application development must take into account lifecycle management. As an application ages, it must be upgraded, migrated, grown, and eventually phased out or ported. Many PaaS vendors offer systems that are integrated lifecycle development platforms. That is, the vendor provides a full software development stack for the programmer to use, and it isn't expected that the developer will need to go outside of the service to create his application.

An integrated lifecycle platform includes the following:

- The virtual machine and operating system (often offered by an IaaS)
- Data design and storage
- A development environment with defined Application Programming Interfaces
- Middleware
- Testing and optimization tools
- Additional tools and services

Google AppEngine, Microsoft Windows Azure Platform, Eccentex AppBase, LongJump, and Wolf are examples of integrated lifecycle platforms. The latter three services are described in this chapter. Refer to Chapter 8 to read about AppEngine, and see Chapter 10 to learn about Azure.

Some PaaS services allow developers to modify existing software. These services are referred to as *anchored lifecycle platforms*. Examples of an anchored lifecycle platform are QuickBooks.com and Salesforce.com. The applications in these two services are fixed, but developers can customize which applications the users see, how those applications are branded, and a number of features associated with the different applications. An anchored service offers less customization, but has a faster development cycle and may be less prone to software errors.

Using PaaS Application Frameworks

Application frameworks provide a means for creating SaaS hosted applications using a unified development environment or an *integrated development environment* (IDE). PaaS IDEs run the gamut from a tool that requires a dedicated programming staff to create and run to point-and-click graphical interfaces that any knowledgeable computer user can navigate and create something useful with.

In selecting the six different examples of Web sites and application building PaaS systems, a full range of user experience is considered. Many Web sites are based on the notion of information management and organization; they are referred to as *content management systems* (CMS). A database is a content management system, but the notion of a Web site as a CMS adds a number of special features to the concept that includes rich user interaction, multiple data sources, and extensive customization and extensibility. The Drupal CMS was chosen as an example of this type of PaaS because it is so extensively used and has broad industry impact, and it is a full-strength developer tool.

Whereas Drupal is used in major Web sites and organizes vast amounts of information, the site Squarespace.com was chosen to illustrate a point-and-click CMS system aimed at supporting individuals, small businesses, and other small organizations. Squarespace is often associated with blogging tools (as is Drupal), but it is more than that. Squarespace works with photos, imports information from other social tools, and allows very attractive Web sites to be created by average users.

Caution

The portability of the applications you create in a PaaS is an extremely valuable feature. If your service goes out of business, being able to port an application by simply redeploying that application to another IaaS can be a lifesaver. ∎

Eccentex AppBase, LongJump, and Wolf were chosen as examples of developer-oriented services aimed at users and developers who want to create Web-based applications based on Service Oriented Architecture protocols and services. These services vary in some details, but they have these common characteristics:

- They separate data-handling from presentation (user interface).
- They offer tools for establishing business objects or entities and the relationships between them.
- They support the incorporation of business rules, logic, and actions.
- They provide tools for creating data entry controls (forms), views, and reports.
- They provide instrumentation, tools for measuring application performance.
- They support packaging and deployment of applications.

These services differ in which language they use, support for different rendering technologies, and in other features. For the most part, they provide point-and-click tools where snippets of code provide exception programming. These services are extensible and customizable through application code. The goal of these services is to create portable applications, although each service includes a hosting platform for developed applications. Some cloud application platforms such as WorkXpress (http://www.workxpress.com) describe their environment as a 5GL PaaS (Fifth Generation) as opposed to something like Force.com, which they call a 3GL/4GL PaaS because 5GL environments have no programming requirement and you can host your application anywhere.

A 5GL programming language solves problems by acting on constraints and inputs and then uses intelligence to solve the problem. By comparison a 4GL programming language requires the programmer to build modules to solve specific problems. For a description of early programming language generations you may want to read the following reference: http://en.wikipedia.org/wiki/Programming_language_generations.

Drupal

Drupal (`http://drupal.org/`) is a content management system (CMS) that is used as the backend to a large number of Web sites worldwide. The software is an open-source project that was created in the PHP programming language. Drupal is really a programming environment for managing content, and it has elements of blogging and collaboration software as part of its distribution. Drupal is offered to the public under the GNU General Public License version 2 and is used by many prominent Web sites. The Drupal core is the standard distribution, with the current version being 6.19; version 7.0 is in preview.

Drupal is in this section because it is a highly extensible way to create Web sites with rich features. Druplas has a large developer community that has created nearly 6,000 third-party add-ons called *contrib modules*. Several thousand Drupal developers worldwide come together twice a year at the DrupalCon convention. It's a vibrant community of users and developers.

The number of Web sites that use Drupal is really quite remarkable, and many of them are very well known. Drupal is very popular with government agencies and with media companies, but its reach extends into nearly any industry, organization, and business type you can think of. Some of these sites are beautifully constructed. A short list of sites includes att.com, data.gov.uk, gouvernement.fr, intel.com, lucasfilms.com, mattel.com, thenation.com, whitehouse.gov, and ubuntu.com. Drupal has a gallery of screenshots of sites and features on its Web site, but for a better look at some of the more attractive sites, go to the Showcase of Popular Web sites Developed Using Drupal CMS (`http://artatm.com/2010/02/showcase-of-popular-website-developed-using-drupal/`), shown in Figure 7.3.

You find Drupal applications running on any Web server that can run PHP 4.4.0 and later. The most common deployments are on Apache, but you also can find Drupal on Microsoft IIS and other Unix Web servers. To store content, Drupal must be used with a database. Because LAMP installations are a standard Web deployment platform, the database most often used is MySQL. Other SQL databases work equally well.

The Drupal core by itself contains a number of modules that provide for the following:

- Auto-updates
- Blogs, forums, polls, and RSS feeds
- Multiple site management
- OpenID authentication
- Performance optimization through caching and throttling
- Search
- User interface creation tools
- User-level access controls and profiles
- Themes
- Traffic management
- Workflow control with events and triggers

FIGURE 7.3

Artatm.com has a gallery of some of the more attractive and well-known sites built with Drupal.

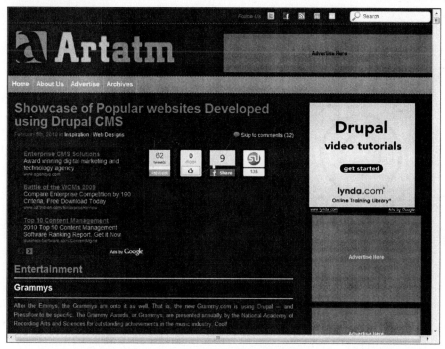

Drupal is modular and exposes its functionality through a set of published APIs. The contrib modules can be added to Drupal to replace other modules, enhance capabilities, or provide entirely new features. Third-party modules include messaging systems, visual editors, a content construction kit (CCK) for database schema extension, views, and panels. CCK Fields API is in the latest version of Drupal, version 7.0.

Drupal is reputed to be somewhat difficult to learn, and new versions often break old features. It is much more widely used than its competitor Joomla! (http://www.joomla.org/), and Drupal seems to have better performance than Joomla! as well. Another open source competitor in the content management space is eZ Publish (http://ez.no/).

Eccentex AppBase 3.0

Eccentex is a Culver City, California, company founded in 2005 that has a PaaS development platform for Web applications based on SOA component architecture to create what it calls Cloudware applications using its AppBase architecture. Figure 7.4 shows the AppBase platform page.

FIGURE 7.4

The Eccentex AppBase (`http://www.eccentex.com/platform/platform.html`) PaaS application delivery platform creates SOA applications that work on several different IaaS vendors.

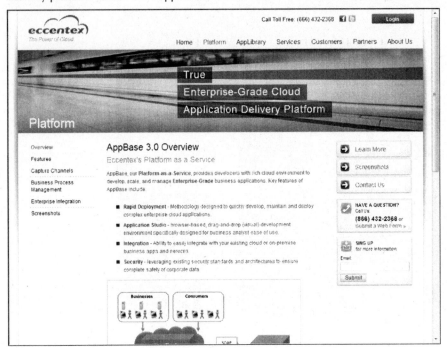

AppBase includes a set of different tools for building these applications, including the following:

- **Business Objects Build:** This object database has the ability to create rich data objects and create relationships between them.

- **Presentation Builder:** This user interface (UI) builder allows you to drag and drop visual controls for creating Web forms and data entry screens and to include the logic necessary to automate what the user sees.

- **Business Process Designer:** This tool is used to create business logic for your application. With it, you can manage workflow, integrate modules, create rules, and validate data.

- **Dashboard Designer:** This instrumentation tool displays the real-time parameters of your application in a visual form.

- **Report Builder:** This output design tool lets you sort, aggregate, display, and format report information based on the data in your application.

- **Security Roles Management:** This allows you to assign access rights to different objects in the system, to data sets, fields, desktop tabs, and reports. Security roles can be assigned in groups without users, and users can be added later as the application is deployed.

Figure 7.5 shows the AppBase architecture with the various tools identified. You can view a set of screenshots that illustrate the different tools and some features in the build process at http://www.eccentex.com/platform/screenshots.html.

FIGURE 7.5

AppBase's architecture with the different tools and modules shown

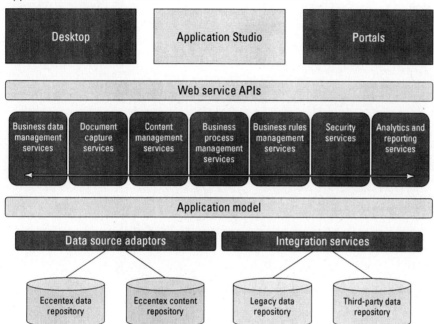

Applications that you create are deployed with the AppBase Application Revision Management console. The applications you create in AppBase, according to the company, may be integrated with Amazon S3 Web Services (storage), Google AppEngine (PaaS), Microsoft Windows Azure (PaaS), Facebook, and Twitter.

LongJump

LongJump (http://www.longjump.com/) is a Sunnyvale, California, company hosting service created in 2003 with a PaaS application development suite. Its development environment is based on Java and uses REST/SOAP APIs. Figure 7.6 shows the LongJump platform page.

FIGURE 7.6

LongJump's PaaS (http://www.longjump.com/index.php?option=com_content&view=artic
le&id=8&Itemid=57) is based on standard Java/JavaScript, SOAP, and REST.

LongJump creates browser-based Web applications that are database-enabled. Like other products mentioned in this section, LongJump comes with an Object Model Viewer, forms, reports, layout tools, dashboards, and site management tools. Access control is based on role- and rule-based access, and it allows for data-sharing between teams and between tenants. LongJump comes with a security policy engine that has user and group privileges, authentication, IP range blocking, SSO, and LDAP interoperability. Applications are packaged using a packaging framework that can support a catalog system, XML package file descriptions, and a distribution engine.

LongJump extends Java and uses a Model-View-Controller architecture (MVC) for its framework in the Developer Suite. The platform uses Java Server Pages (JSP), Java, and JavaScript for its various components and its actions with objects built with Java classes. Objects created in custom classes are referenced using POJO (Plain Old Java Object). Localization is supported using a module called the Translation Workbench that includes specified labels, errors, text, controls, and messaging text files (and header files) that allow them to be modified by a translation service to support additional languages. The development environment supports the Eclipse (http://www.eclipse.org/) plug-in for creating widgets using Java standard edition.

Squarespace

Squarespace (http://www.squarespace.com/), shown in Figure 7.7, is an example of a next-generation Web site builder and deployment tool that has elements of a PaaS development environment. The applications are built using visual tools and deployed on hosted infrastructure.

Squarespace presents itself, among other things, as:

- A blogging tool
- A social media integration tool
- A photo gallery
- A form builder and data collector
- An item list manager
- A traffic and site management and analysis tool

The platform has more than 20 core modules that you can add to your Web site. Squarespace sites can be managed on the company's iPhone app.

FIGURE 7.7

Squarespace lets you create beautiful hosted Web sites with a variety of capabilities with visual tools alone.

With Squarespace, users have created some very visually beautiful sites. Users tend to fall into these categories: personal Web sites, portfolios, and business brand identification. Although Squarespace positions itself as a competitor to blogging sites such as Wordpress (http:// wordpress.org/), Tumblr (http://www.tumblr.com/), Posterous (https:// posterous.com/), and other sites of their ilk, the site borders on a full content management system with a variety of useful and eclectic features.

WaveMaker

WaveMaker (http://www.wavemaker.com/) is a visual rapid application development environment for creating Java-based Web and cloud Ajax applications. The software is open-source and offered under the Apache license. WaveMaker is a WYSIWYG (What You See is What You Get) drag-and-drop environment that runs inside a browser. The metaphor used to build applications is described as the Model-View-Controller system of application architecture. In this regard, WaveMaker has some similarities to PowerBuilder (http://www.sybase.com/products/ internetappdevttools/powerbuilder).

Figure 7.8 shows the WaveMaker home page. A gallery of features is accessible from that page.

FIGURE 7.8

WaveMaker is a visual development environment for creating Java-based cloud applications.

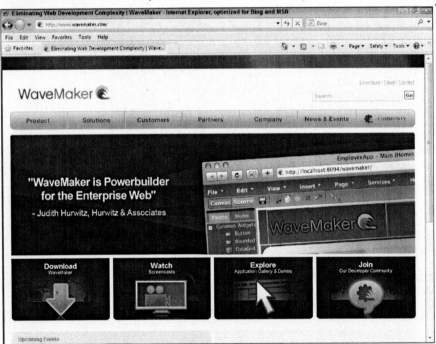

WaveMaker is a framework that creates applications that can interoperate with other Java frameworks and LDAP systems, including the following:

- Dojo Toolkit 1.0 (`http://dojotoolkit.org/`), a JavaScript library or toolbox
- LDAP directories
- Microsoft Active Directory
- POJO (Plain Old Java Object)
- Spring Framework (`http://www.springsource.org/`), an open-source application framework for Java that now also includes ACEGI

The visual builder tool is called Visual Ajax Studio, and the development server is called the WaveMaker Rapid Deployment Server for Java applications. When you develop within the Visual Ajax Studio, a feature called LiveLayout allows you to create applications while viewing live data. The data schema is prepared within a part of the tool called LiveForms. Mashups can be created using the Mashup Tool, which integrates applications using Java Services, SOAP, REST, and RSS to access databases.

Applications developed in WaveMaker run on standard Java servers such as Tomcat, DojoToolkit, Spring, and Hibernate. A 4GL version of WaveMaker also runs on Amazon EC2, and the development environment can be loaded on an EC2 instance as one of its machine images.

Wolf Frameworks

Many application frameworks like Google AppEngine and the Windows Azure Platform are tied to the platform on which they run. You can't build an AppEngine application and port it to Windows Azure without completely rewriting the application. There isn't any particular necessity to build an application framework in this way, but it suits the purpose of these particular vendors: for Google to have a universe of Google applications that build on the Google infrastructure, and for Microsoft to provide another platform on which to extend .NET Framework applications for their developers.

If you are building an application on top of an IaaS vendor such as AWS, GoGrid, or RackSpace, what you really want are application development frameworks that are open, standards-based, and portable. Wolf Frameworks is an example of a PaaS vendor offering a platform on which you can build an SaaS solution that is open and cross-platform. Wolf Frameworks (`http://www.wolfframeworks.com/`) was founded in Bangalore, India, in 2006, and it has offices in the United States.

Wolf Frameworks is based on the three core Windows SOA standard technologies of cloud computing:

- AJAX, asynchronous Java
- XML
- .NET Framework

Wolf Frameworks uses a C# engine and supports both Microsoft SQL Server and MySQL database. Applications that you build in Wolf are 100-percent browser-based and support mashable and multisource overlaid content. Figure 7.9 shows the Wolf Frameworks home page.

The Wolf platform is interesting in a number of ways. Wolf has architected its platform so applications can be built without the need to write technical code. It also allows application data to be written to the client's database server of choice, and data can be imported or exported from a variety of data formats. In Wolf, you can view your Business Design of the software application that you build in XML.

Wolf supports forms, search, business logic and rules, charts, reports, dashboards, and both custom and external Web pages. After you create entities and assign their properties, you create business rules with a rules designer. You can automate tasks via business rules. There are tools for building the various site features such as forms, reports, dashboards, and so on. Connections to the datacenter are over a 128-bit encrypted SSL connection, with authentication, access control, and a transaction history and audit trail. Security to multiple modules can be made available through a Single Sign-On (SSO) mechanism.

FIGURE 7.9

Wolf Frameworks offers an open platform based on SOA standards for building portable SaaS solutions.

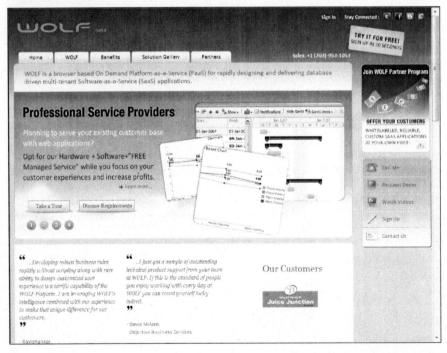

In Wolf, the data and transaction management conforms to the business rules you create. The data and UI rendering are separate systems. Thus, you can change the UI as you need to without affecting your stored data. Wolf lets you work with Adobe Flash or Flex or with Microsoft Silverlight. You can also use third-party on- or off-premises applications with your SaaS application. A backup system lets you back up data with a single click. Figure 7.10 shows the WOLF platform architecture.

These features enable Wolf developers to create a classic multitenant SOA application without the need for high-level developer skills. These applications are interoperable, portable from one Windows virtual machine to another, and support embedded business applications. You can store your Wolf applications on a private server or in the Wolf cloud.

FIGURE 7.10

The Wolf platform architecture; source: `http://www.wolfframeworks.com/platform.asp`.

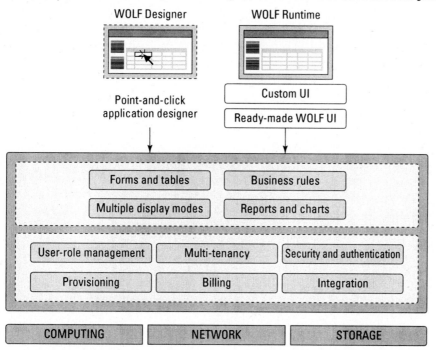

Summary

In this chapter, you learned about one of the core service models in cloud computing: Platform as a Service. With PaaS, the goal is to create hosted scalable applications that are used in a Software as a Service model. For this reason, some vendors start out offering SaaS systems and then broaden them to make them more customizable and programmable as PaaS systems.

Applications built using PaaS tools need to be standards-based. They often are constructed using similar sets of tools: data object and relationship builders; process and business logic systems; forms, views, and reporting tools; and more. This chapter looked at some of the better-known PaaS systems and considered what those tools have in common. You learned about a number of tools in this chapter, including Drupal, Eccentex AppBase, Force.com, LongJump, Squarespace, Wolf, and some others.

Chapter 8 continues the discussion of PaaS by describing one of the largest PaaS systems in use today: Google's AppEngine.

Using Google Web Services

G oogle is the prototypical cloud computing services company, and it supports some of the largest Web sites and services in the world. In this chapter, you learn about Google's applications and services for users and the various developer tools that Google makes available.

At the center of Google's core business is the company's search technology. Google uses automated technology to index the Web. It makes its search service available to users as a standard search engine and to developers as a collection of special search tools limited to various areas of content. The application of Google's searches to content aggregation has led to enormous societal changes and to a growing trend of disintermediation.

The most important commercial part of Google's activities is its targeting advertising business: AdWords and AdSense. Google has developed a range of services including Google Analytics that supports its targeted advertising business.

Google applications are cloud-based applications. The range of application types offered by Google spans a variety of types: productivity applications, mobile applications, media delivery, social interactions, and many more. The different applications are listed in this chapter. Google has begun to commercialize some of these applications as cloud-based enterprise application suites that are being widely adopted.

Google has a very large program for developers that spans its entire range of applications and services. Among the services highlighted are Google's AJAX APIs, the Google Web Toolkit, and in particular Google's relatively new Google Apps Engine hosting service. Using Google App Engine, you can create Web applications in Java and Python that can be deployed on Google's infrastructure and scaled to a large size.

Exploring Google Applications

Few companies have had as much impact on their industries as Google has had on the computer industry and on the Internet in particular. Some companies may have more Internet users (Microsoft comes to mind) or have a stock valuation higher than Google (Apple currently fits that description), but Google remains both a technology and thought leader for all things Internet. For a company whose motto is "Don't be evil," the impact of consumer tracking and targeted advertising, free sourcing applications, and the relentless assault on one knowledge domain after another has had a profound impact on the lives of many people. I call it the Google Effect.

The bulk of Google's income comes from the sales of target advertising based on information that Google gathers from your activities associated with your Google account or through cookies placed on your system using its AdWords system. In 2009, Google's revenue was $23.6 billion, and it controlled roughly 65 percent of the search market through its various sites and services. The company is highly profitable, and that has allowed Google to create a huge infrastructure as well as launch many free cloud-based applications and services that this chapter details. These applications are offered mostly on a free usage model that represents Google's Software as a Service portfolio. A business model that offers cloud-based services for free that are "good enough" is very compelling. While Google is slowly growing a subscription business selling these applications to enterprises, its revenue represents only a small but growing part of Google's current income.

Google's cloud computing services falls under two umbrellas. The first and best-known offerings are an extensive set of very popular applications that Google offers to the general public. These applications include Google Docs, Google Health, Picasa, Google Mail, Google Earth, and many more. You can access a jump table of Google's cloud-based user applications by following the "More" and "Even More" links on Google's home page to the More Google Products page at http://www.google.com/intl/en/options/ shown in Figure 8.1; these features are described in Table 8.1.

Because I cover many of these products in other chapters in this book, the focus in this chapter is to survey the applications that Google offers, to understand why Google offers them as services, and to gain some insight into their potential future role. Google's cloud-based applications have put many other vendors' products—such as office suites, mapping applications, image-management programs, and many other categories of traditional shrink-wrapped software—under considerable pressure.

The second of Google's cloud offerings is its Platform as a Service developer tools. In April 2008, Google introduced a development platform for hosted Web applications using Google's infrastructure called the Google App Engine (GAE). The goal of GAE is to allow developers to create and deploy Web applications without worrying about managing the infrastructure necessary to have their applications run. GAE applications may be written using many high-level programming languages (most prominently Java and Python) and the Google App Engine Framework, which lowers the amount of development effort required to get an application up and running. Goggle also allows a certain free level of service so that the application must exceed a certain level of processor load, storage usage, and network bandwidth (Input/Output) before charges are assessed.

FIGURE 8.1

More Google Products equals fewer commercial products.

Google App Engine applications must be written to comply with Google's infrastructure. This narrows the range of application types that can be run on GAE; it also makes it very hard to port applications to GAE. After an application is deployed on GAE, it is also difficult to port that application to another platform. Even with all these limitations, the Google App Engine provides developers a low-cost option on which to create an application that can run on a world-class cloud infrastructure—with all the attendant benefits that this type of deployment can bestow.

Surveying the Google Application Portfolio

It is fair to say that nearly all the products in Google's application and service portfolio are cloud computing services in that they all rely on systems staged worldwide on Google's one million plus servers in nearly 30 datacenters. Roughly 17 of the 48 services listed leverage Google's search engine in some specific way. Some of these search-related sites search through selected content such as Books, Images, Scholar, Trends, and more. Other sites such as Blog Search, Finance, News, and some others take the search results and format them into an Aggregation page. Figure 8.2 shows one of these aggregation pages: Google Finance.

Google's Finance page at `http://www.google.com/finance/` is an example of an aggregation page provided by results from Google's search engine.

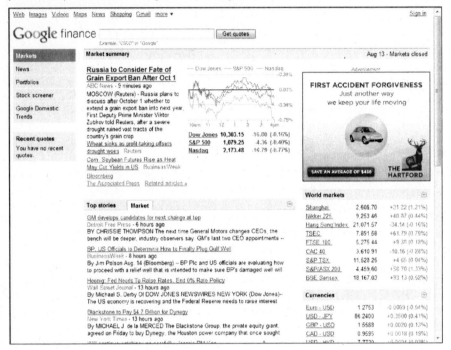

Indexed search

Google's search technology is based on automated page indexing and information retrieval by Web crawlers, also called spiders or robots. Content on pages is scanned up to a certain number of words and placed into an index. Google also caches copies of certain Web pages and stores copies of documents it finds such as DOC or PDF files in its cache.

Google uses a patented algorithm to determine the importance of a particular page based on the number of quality links to that page from other sites, along with other factors such as the use of keywords, how long the site has been available, and traffic to the site or page. That factor is called the PageRank, and the algorithm used to determine PageRank is a trade secret. Google is always tweaking the algorithm to prevent Search Engine Optimization (SEO) strategies from gaming the system. Based on this algorithm, Google returns what is called a Search Engine Results Page (SERP) for a query that is parsed for its keywords.

It is really important to understand what Google (and other search engines) offers and what it doesn't offer. Google does not search all sites. If a site doesn't register with the search engine or isn't the target of a prominent link at another site, that site may remain undiscovered. Any site can place directions in their ROBOTS.TXT file indicating whether the site can be searched or not, and if so what pages can be searched. Google developed something called the Sitemaps protocol, which lets a Web site list in an XML file information about how the Google robot can work with the site. Sitemaps can be useful in allowing content that isn't browsable to be crawled; they also can be useful as guides to finding media information that isn't normally considered, such as AJAX, Flash, or Silverlight media. The Sitemaps protocol has been widely adopted in the industry.

Note

While dynamic content presented in AJAX isn't normally indexed, Google now has a procedure that helps the Google engine crawl this information. You can read about it at: `http://code.google.com/web/ajaxcrawling/`. ∎

The dark Web

Online content that isn't indexed by search engines belongs to what has come to be called the "Deep Web"—that is, content on the World Wide Web that is hidden. Any site that suppresses Web crawlers from indexing it is part of the Deep Web. You need go no further than the world's number two Web site, Facebook, for a prominent example of a site that isn't indexed in search engines.

Entire networks exist that aren't searchable, particularly peer-to-peer networks. Ian Clarke's Freenet, which is a P2P network, supports both "darknet" and "opennet" connections. Freenet (`http://freenetproject.org/`) has been downloaded by millions of people.

The Deep Web includes:

- Database generated Web pages or dynamic content
- Pages without links
- Private or limited access Web pages and sites
- Information contained in sources available through executable code such as JavaScript
- Documents and files that aren't in a form that can be searched, which includes not only media files, but information in non-standard file formats

Although efforts are underway to enable information on the Deep Web to be searchable, the amount of information stored that is not accessible is many times larger than the amount of information that can currently be accessed. Some estimates at the size of the Dark Web suggest that it could be an order of magnitude larger than the content contained in the world's search engines.

It is always a good idea to keep these search engine limitations in mind when you work with this technology.

Aggregation and disintermediation

Aggregation pages are a great user service, but they are very controversial—as are a number of Google's search applications and services. It has long been argued that Google's display of information from various sites violates copyright laws and damages content providers. In several lawsuits, Google successfully defended its right to display capsule information under the Digital Millennium Copyright Act, while in other instances Google responds to requests from interested parties to remove information from its site.

The Authors Guild's filed a class action suit in 2005 regarding unauthorized scanning and copying of books for the creation of the Google Books feature. Google reached a negotiated agreement with the Authors Guild that specified Google's obligations under the fair use exemption. Google argues that the publicity associated with searchable content adds value to that content, and it is clear that this is an argument that will continue into the future.

What is clear is that Google has been a major factor in a trend referred to as disintermediation. Disintermediation is the removal of intermediaries such as a distributor, agent, broker, or some similar functionary from a supply chain. This connects producers directly with consumers, which in many cases is a very good thing. However, disintermediation also has the unfortunate side effect of impacting organizations such as news collection agencies (newspapers, for example), publishers, many different types of retail outlets, and many other businesses, some of which played a positive role in the transactions they were involved in.

Google began to introduce productivity applications starting in 2004 with Gmail. The expansion of these services has continued unabated ever since. Some of these applications are homegrown, but many of them were acquired by acquisition. An example of an acquired product is Writely, the online word processor that is now at the heart of Google Docs and is described in Chapter 14.

Productivity applications and services

These products store your information online in a form that Google can use to build a profile of your activities, and it is unclear how the company uses the information it stores. Google states that your information is never viewed individually by humans, and the company lists its policies in the Privacy Center, which you can find at http://www.google.com/privacypolicy.html. Google has been vigilant in protecting its privacy reputation, but the collection of such a large amount of personal data must give any thoughtful person reason for pause.

Note

Space considerations preclude a more complete description of Google applications and services. Several books treat this topic in detail, including *Google Apps For Dummies* by Ryan Teeter and Karl Barksdale, Wiley, 2008. ■

Table 8.1 lists the current Google "products" listed on its Even More page.

TABLE 8.1

Google Products

Product Name	URL	Google Description
Alerts	`http://www.google.com/alerts?hl=en`	Sends a periodic e-mail alert to you based on your search term. Search news, blogs, discussions, video, or everything.
Blog Search	`http://www.google.com/blogsearch?hl=en`	Displays an aggregation page from blogs.
Blogger	`http://www.blogger.com/start?hl=en`	A blogging site for personal blogs. See Chapter 18 for a description of blogging services.
Books	`http://books.google.com/books?hl=en`	A vast library of book content in the public domain and previews of copyrighted material.
Calendar	`http://www.google.com/calendar/render?hl=en`	Calendar service for managing schedules and events and sharing them with others.
Chrome	`http://www.google.com/chrome?hl=en&brand=CHMI`	Google's browser and operating system wannabe.
Checkout	`http://checkout.google.com/`	A payment processing system.
Code	`http://code.google.com/intl/en/`	Developer tools and resources. Described more fully later in this chapter.
Custom Search	`http://www.google.com/coop/cse/?hl=en`	Creates a custom search utility for a particular Web site.
Desktop	`http://desktop.google.com/en/?ignua=1`	Indexes content on your local drive for fast searches. Adds a sidebar with gadgets.
Directory	`http://www.google.com/dirhp?hl=en`	Search the Web by topics, a la Yahoo!
Docs	`http://docs.google.com/`	Online productivity applications. Described in Chapter 16.
Earth	`http://earth.google.com/intl/en/`	An online atlas and mapping service with mashups.
Finance	`http://www.google.com/finance`	A financial news aggregation service and site.
GOOG-411	`http://www.google.com/goog-411/`	Mobile phone search.
Google Health	`http://www.google.com/health/`	Health information management system.

(continued)

TABLE 8.1 (continued)

Product Name	URL	Google Description
Groups	`http://www.google.com/grphp?hl=en`	Discussion groups on specific topics.
iGoogle	`http://www.google.com/ig?hl=en&source=mpes`	AJAX customized home page.
Images	`http://images.google.com/imghp?hl=en`	Web image search.
Knol	`http://knol.google.com/k?hl=en`	Short articles submitted by users.
Labs	`http://labs.google.com/`	A collection of applications and utilities under development and testing.
Orkut	`https://www.orkut.com/`	Social media service with instant messaging. Described in Chapter 18.
Maps	`http://maps.google.com/?hl=en`	Mapping and direction service.
Maps for Mobile	`http://www.google.com/mobile/default/maps.html`	Mapping and direction service. Works with GPS on mobile devices.
Mobile	`http://www.google.com/mobile/`	Mobile search using voice and location.
News	`http://news.google.com/news?ned=en`	News aggregation service and Web site.
Pack	`http://pack.google.com/?hl=en`	Free Windows-based software selected by Google, including Chrome, apps, Desktop, Earth, Picasa, Adobe Reader, Talk, RealPlayer, Skype, and others.
Patent Search	`http://www.google.com/patents?hl=en`	Patent and trademark search of the United States Patents and Trademark Office.
Picasa	`http://picasa.google.com/intl/en/`	Photo-editing and management software.
Product Search	`http://www.google.com/products`	Shopping search function.
Reader	`http://www.google.com/reader/view/?hl=en&source=mmm-en`	An RSS reader.
Scholar	`http://www.google.com/schhp?hl=en`	Search site for research and scholarly work from many disciplines.
Search for Mobile	`http://www.google.com/mobile/default/search.html`	Google's search application optimized for mobile devices.
Sites	`http://sites.google.com/`	Web site and wiki creation and staging tool.
SketchUp	`http://sketchup.google.com/intl/en/`	Allows users to create 3D models and share them with others.

Product Name	URL	Google Description
Talk	`http://www.google.com/talk/`	Instant messaging and chat utility. Can be integrated in Gmail.
Toolbar	`http://toolbar.google.com/intl/en/`	Provides search features inside different browsers.
Translate	`http://translate.google.com/?hl=en`	Language translation utility.
Trends	`http://www.google.com/trends`	Statistical information on different search terms.
Videos	`http://video.google.com/?hl=en`	Searches for videos on the Web.
Voice	`http://voice.google.com/`	Free phone service, formerly called Grand Central. Described in Chapter 19.
Web Search	`http://www.google.com/webhp?hl=en`	Google's core Web search engine of indexed pages sorted with page rank.
Web Search Features	`http://www.google.com/intl/en/help/features.html`	A help page for special Web searches in Google.
YouTube	`http://www.youtube.com/`	Flash video sharing site. Described in Chapter 19.

Source: `http://www.google.com/intl/en/options/`.

Enterprise offerings

As Google has built out its portfolio, it has released special versions of its products for the enterprise. The following are among Google's products aimed at the enterprise market:

- **Google Commerce Search** (`http://www.google.com/commercesearch/`): This is a search service for online retailers that markets their products in their site searches with a number of navigation, filtering, promotion, and analytical functions.

- **Google Site Search** (`http://www.google.com/sitesearch/`): Google sells its search engine customized for enterprises under the Google Site Search service banner. The user enters a search string in the site's search, and Google returns the results from that site.

- **Google Search Appliance** (`http://www.google.com/enterprise/gsa`): This server can be deployed within an organization to speed up both local (Intranet) and Internet searching. The three versions of the Google Search Appliance can store an index of up to 300,000 (GB-1001), 10 million (GB-5005), or 30 million (GB-8008) documents. Beyond indexing, these appliances have document management features, perform custom searches, cache content, and give local support to Google Analytics and Google Sitemaps.

- **Google Mini** (`http://www.google.com/enterprise/mini/`): The Mini is the smaller version of the GSA that stores 300,000 indexed documents.

Google also has some success in marketing its productivity applications as office suites to organizations. Google uses different names for the different bundles under a branded program called Google Apps for Business (`http://www.google.com/apps/intl/en/business/index.html`). Figure 8.3 shows the home page for Google's various office suite bundles. The company has packages for governments, schools, non-profits, and ISPs (a reseller program). Google claims that some 8 million students now use Google Apps, and Google Apps has had some large government purchases, such as the City of Los Angeles.

For business and other organizations such as governmental agencies, the company has a branded Google Apps Premier Edition, which is a paid service. The different versions offer Gmail, Docs, and Calendar as core applications. The Premier Edition adds 25GB of Gmail storage, e-mail server synchronization, Groups, Sites, Talk, Video, enhanced security, directory services, authentication and authorization services, and the customer's own supported domain—all hosted in the cloud. Premium Edition also adds access to Google APIs and a 24/7 support service with a 99.9-percent uptime guarantee Service Level Agreement. The cost per use is $50 per user account/per year.

FIGURE 8.3

Google Apps for Business is the commercial versions of the company's productivity suites.

To support Google's Premier and Education Editions' Gmail, Google purchased the Postini archiving and discovery service. Google Postini Services (`http://www.google.com/postini/`) provides security services such as threat assessment, proactive link blocking and Web policy enforcement, e-mail message encryption, message archiving, and message discovery services. These are paid services that add from $12 to $45 per user/per year, based on the options chosen. Postini allows e-mail to be retained for up to 10 years and can be used to demonstrate regulatory compliance.

Many of Google's productivity applications are quite capable, but none is a state-of-the-art client you might expect to find in a locally installed office suite. When compared one-on-one to Microsoft Office applications, Google's online offerings give users the essential features for a fraction of the Microsoft Office price.

Most sophisticated users prefer Microsoft Office, but for the average user (that is most people) Google App bundles are good enough. When that low price is coupled with the collaborative tools and features Google offers, the value of Google Apps will be increasingly more appealing. We can reasonably expect that cloud-based productivity apps will put their shrink-wrapped competitors under great pressure. Microsoft's current strategy of putting crippled Office applications on the Web in Windows Live isn't going to be competitive.

AdWords

AdWords (`http://www.google.com/AdWords`) is a targeted ad service based on matching advertisers and their keywords to users and their search profiles. This service transformed Google from a competent search engine into an industry giant and is responsible for the majority of Google's revenue stream. AdWords' two largest competitors are Microsoft adcenter (`http://adcenter.microsoft.com/`) and Yahoo! Search Marketing (`http://searchmarketing.yahoo.com/`).

Ads are displayed as text, banners, or media and can be tailored based on geographical location, frequency, IP addresses, and other factors. AdWords ads can appear not only on Google.com, but on AOL search, Ask.com, and Netscape, along with other partners. Other partners belonging to the Google Display Network can also display AdSense ads. In all these cases, the AdWords system determines which ads to match to the user searches.

Here's how the system works: Advertisers bid on keywords that are used to match a user to their product or service. If a user searches for a term such as "develop abdominal muscles," Google returns products based on those terms. You might see an ad with Chuck Norris selling a modern-day version of a torture rack that, if it doesn't give you a six-pack, at least makes your wallet lighter. Up to 12 ads per search can be returned.

Google gets paid for the ad whenever a user clicks it. The system is referred to as pay-per-click advertising, and the success of the ad is measured by what is called the click-through rate (CTR). Google calculates a *quality score* for ads based on the CTR, the strength of the connection between the ad and the keywords, and the advertiser's history with Google. This quality score is a Google trade secret and is used to price the minimum bid of a keyword.

In 2007, Google purchased DoubleClick, an Internet advertising services company. DoubleClick helps clients create ads, provides hosting services, and tracks results for analysis. DoubleClick ads leave browser cookies on systems that collect information from users that determine the number of times a user has been exposed to a particular ad, as well as various system characteristics. Some spyware trackers flag DoubleClick cookies as spyware. Both AdWords and DoubleClick are sold as packages to large clients.

Google Analytics

Google Analytics (GA; `http://google.com/analytics`) is a statistical tool that measures the number and types of visitors to a Web site and how the Web site is used. It is offered as a free service and has been adopted by many Web sites. GA is built on the Urchin 5 analytical package that Google acquired in 2006. Figure 8.4 shows the Google Analytics home page.

According to Builtwith.com (`http://trends.builtwith.com/analytics/Google-Analytics`), Google Analytics was in use on 54 percent of the top 10,000 and 100,000, and 35 percent of the top one million of the world's Web sites. Builtwith.com speculates that Google Analytics JavaScript tag is the most widely used URL in the world today. The service BackendBattles.com (`http://www.backendbattles.com/backend/Google_Analytics`) sets GA's market share at 57 percent for the top 10,000 sites.

Google Analytics is the most widely used Web traffic analysis tool on the Internet.

Analytics works by using a JavaScript snippet called the Google Analytics Tracking Code (GATC) on individual pages to implement a *page tag*. When the page loads, the JavaScript runs and creates a first-party browser cookie that can be used to manage return visitors, perform tracking, test browser characteristics, and request tracking code that identifies the location of the visitor. GATC requests and stores information from the user's account. The code stored on the user's system acts like a beacon and collects visitor data that it sends back to GA servers for processing.

Among the visitors that can be tracked are those that land from search engines; referral links in e-mail, documents, and Web pages; display ads; PPC networks; and some other sources. GA aggregates the data and presents the information in a visual form. GA also is connected to the AdWords system so it can track the performance of particular ads in different contexts. You can view referral location statistics and time spent on a page, and you can filter by visitor site. GA lets you save and store up to 50 individual site profiles, provided the site has less than 5 million pageviews per month. This restriction is lifted for an AdWords subscription.

GA cookies are blocked by a number of technologies, such as Firefox Adblock and NoScript or by turning off JavaScript execution in other browsers. You also can delete GA cookies manually or block them, which also defeats the system.

Google Translate

Of all the Google applications, the one that might have significant immediate impact is Google Translate. Computer technology is very close to having the necessary hardware and software to realize the dream of a "universal translator" that the TV show *Star Trek* proposed some 45 years ago. The current version of Google Translate performs machine translation as a cloud service between two of your choice of 35 different languages. That's not truly universal, but until aliens appear, it will do for most people.

Google Translate was introduced in 2007 and replaced the SYSTRAN system that many other computer services utilize. The translation method uses a statistical approach that was first developed by Franz-Joseph Och in 2003. Och now heads the Translate effort at Google.

Translate uses what is referred to as a corpus linguistics approach to translation. You start off building a translation system for a language pair by collecting a database of words and then matching that database to two bilingual text corpuses. A text corpus or parallel collection is a database of word- and phrase-usage taken from the language in everyday use obtained by examining documents translated by professionals to software analysis. Among the documents that are analyzed are the translations of the United Nations and European Parliament, among others.

Google Translate can be accessed directly at `http://translate.google.com/translate_t?hl=en#`, where you can select the language pair to be translated. You can do the following:

- Enter text directly into the text box, and click the Translate button to have the text translated.

  If you select the Detect Language option, Translate tries to determine the language automatically and translate it into English.

- Enter a URL for a Web page to have Google display a copy of the translated Web page.

- Enter a phonetic equivalent for script languages.
- Upload a document to the page to have it translated.

Translate parses the document into words and phrases and applies its statistical algorithm to make the translation. As the service ages, the translations are getting more accurate, and the engine is being added to browsers such as Google Chrome and through extension into Mozilla Firefox. The Google Toolbar offers page translation as one of its options, selectable in the Tools settings.

The Google Translator Toolkit (`http://translate.google.com/toolkit`) shown in Figure 8.5 provides a means for using the Translate to perform translations that you can edit. Shown in the figure is the translation of an article from the English version of Wikipedia into Spanish. The toolkit provides access to tools to aid you in editing the translation.

Translation services have been in development for many years. IBM has had a large effort in this area, and the Microsoft Bing search engine also has a translation engine. There are many other translation engines, and some of them are even cloud-based like Google Translate. What makes Google's efforts potentially unique is the company's work in language transcription—that is, the conversion of voice to text. As part of Google Voice and its work with Android-based cell phones, Google is sampling and converting millions and millions of conversations. Combining these two Web services together could create a translation device based on a cloud service that would have great utility.

FIGURE 8.5

The Google Translator Toolkit lets you translate documents, Web pages, and other material from one language to another and provides tools to improve on the translation.

Exploring the Google Toolkit

Google has an extensive program that supports developers who want to leverage Google's cloud-based applications and services. These APIs reach into every corner of Google's business. Google's Code Home page for developers may be found at http://code.google.com and is shown in Figure 8.6. From this site, you can access developer tools, information on how to use its various APIs to include Google services in your own work, and technical resources.

FIGURE 8.6

Google's Code page at http://code.google.com/intl/en/

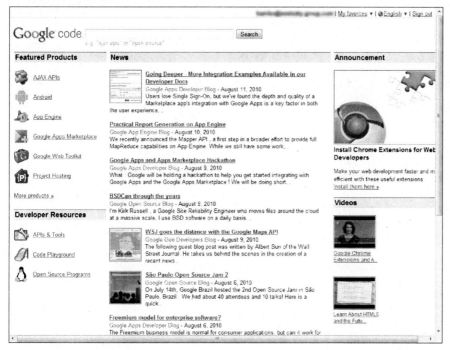

Google has a number of areas in which it offers development services, including the following:

- **AJAX APIs** (http://code.google.com/intl/en/apis/ajax/) are used to build widgets and other applets commonly found in places like iGoogle. AJAX provides access to dynamic information using JavaScript and HTML.

- **Android** (http://developer.android.com/index.html) is a phone operating system development.

- **Google App Engine** (`http://appengine.google.com/`) is Google's Platform as a Service (PaaS) development and deployment system for cloud computing applications.

- **Google Apps Marketplace** (`http://code.google.com/intl/en/googleapps/marketplace/`) offers application development tools and a distribution channel for cloud-based applications.

- **Google Gears** (`http://gears.google.com/`) is a service that provides offline access to online data.

  Google Gears includes a database engine installed on the client that caches data and synchronizes it. Gears allows cloud-based applications to be available to a client even when a network connection to the Internet isn't available. Using Gears, you could work on your mail in Gmail offline, for example.

- **Google Web Toolkit** (GWT; `http://code.google.com/webtoolkit`) is a set of development tools for browser-based applications.

  GWT is an open-source platform that has been used to create Google Wave and Google AdWords. GWT allows developers to create AJAX applications using Java or with the GWT compiler using JavaScript.

- **Project Hosting** (`http://code.google.com/intl/en/projecthosting/`) is a project management tool for managing source code.

The Google APIs

Most Google services are exposed by an API, which is why you find a version of Google's search engine, Google Maps, YouTube videos, Google Earth, AdWords, AdSense, and even elements of Google Apps exposed in many other Web sites. You can get to the listing of the Google APIs by clicking the More Products link on the Code page (refer to Figure 8.6). The page you see is `http://code.google.com/intl/en/more/`, which is shown in Figure 8.7.

Google's APIs can be categorized as belonging to the following categories:

- **Ads and AdSense:** These APIs allow Google's advertising services to be integrated into Web applications. The most commonly used services in this category are AdWords, AdSense, and Google Analytics.

- **AJAX:** The Google AJAX APIs provide a means to add content such as RSS feeds, maps, search boxes, and other information sources by including a snippet of JavaScript into your code.

- **Browser:** Google has several APIs related to building browser-based applications, including four for the Chrome browser. This category includes the Google Cloud Print API, the Installable Web Apps API for creating installation packages, the Google Web Toolkit for building AJAX applications using Java, and V8, which is a high-performance JavaScript engine.

- **Data:** The Data APIs are those that exchange data with a variety of Google services. The list of Google Data APIs includes Google Apps, Google Analytics, Blogger, Base, Book,

Calendar, Code Search, Google Earth, Google Spreadsheets, Google Notebook, and Picasa Web Albums.

● **Geo:** A number of APIs exist to give location-specific information hooking into maps and geo-specific databases. Some of the more popular APIs in this category include Google Earth, Directions, JavaScripts Maps, Maps API for Flash, and Static Maps.

● **Search:** The search APIs leverage Google's core competency and its central service. APIs such as Google AJAX Search, Book Search, Code Search, Custom Search, and Webmaster Tools Data APIs allow developers to include Google searches in their applications and web sites.

● **Social:** Many Google APIs are used for information exchange and communication tools. They support applications such as Gmail, Calendar, and others, and they provide a set of foundation services. The popular social APIs are Blogger Data, Calendar, Contacts, OpenSocial, Picasa, and YouTube.

FIGURE 8.7

Google's More Code page exposes the extensive set of APIs offered by Google for its various products.

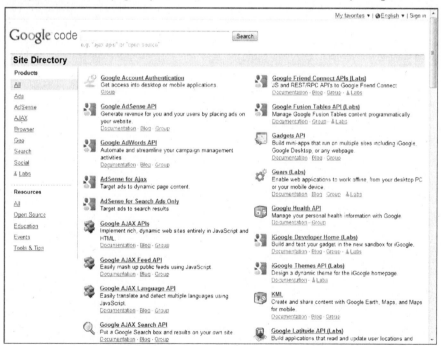

Table 8.2 summarizes the many different Google APIs.

TABLE 8.2

Google APIs

API Name	URL	Category	Google Description
Google Accounts Authentication	`http://code.google.com/apis/accounts/`	Infrastructure	Get access into desktop or mobile applications.
Google AdWords API	`http://code.google.com/apis/adwords/`	Ads	Automate and streamline your campaign management activities.
AdSense for AJAX	`http://code.google.com/apis/afa/`	Ads, AJAX	Target ads to dynamic page content.
AdSense for Search Ads Only	`http://code.google.com/apis/afs-ads-only/`	Ads	Target ads to search results.
Google AJAX APIs	`http://code.google.com/apis/ajax/`	AJAX	Implement rich, dynamic Web sites entirely in JavaScript and HTML.
Google AJAX Feed API	`http://code.google.com/apis/ajaxfeeds/`	AJAX	Easily mash up public feeds using JavaScript.
Google AJAX Language API	`http://code.google.com/apis/ajaxlanguage/`	AJAX	Easily translate and detect multiple languages using JavaScript.
Google AJAX Search API	`http://code.google.com/apis/ajaxsearch/`	AJAX, Search	Put a Google Search box and results on your own site.
Google Analytics	`http://code.google.com/apis/analytics/`	Ads	Track your site traffic, and write your own client applications that use Analytics data in the form of Google Data API feeds.
Android	`http://code.google.com/android/`	Infrastructure	Build mobile apps for Android, a software stack for mobile devices.
Google App Engine	`http://code.google.com/appengine/`	Infrastructure	Run your Web applications on Google's infrastructure.
Google Apps Script	`http://code.google.com/googleapps/appsscript/`	Productivity	Automate tasks across Google products.
BigQuery (Labs)	`http://code.google.com/apis/bigquery/`	Labs	Interactively analyze large datasets.
Google Apps	`http://code.google.com/googleapps/`	Productivity	Extend Google Apps, integrate with other systems, or build new apps.

API Name	URL	Category	Google Description
Google Apps Marketplace	`http://code.google.com/ googleapps/marketplace/`	Productivity	Sell integrated applications to millions of Google Apps users.
Gmail APIs and Tools	`http://code.google.com/ apis/gmail/`	Labs	Create gadgets for Gmail, and interact with the inbox.
Google Base Data API (Labs)	`http://code.google.com/ apis/base/`	Labs	Manage Google Base content programmatically.
Blogger Data API (Labs)	`http://code.google.com/ apis/blogger/`	Labs, Social	Enable your apps to view and update Blogger content.
Google Books Search APIs (Labs)	`http://code.google.com/ apis/books/`	Labs, Search	Search the complete index of Book Search, and integrate with its social features.
Google Buzz (Labs)	`http://code.google.com/ apis/buzz/`	Labs, Social	Share updates, photos, videos, and more, and start conversations about the things you find interesting.
Google Calendar APIs and Tools	`http://code.google.com/ apis/calendar/`	Social	Create and manage events, calendars, and gadgets for Google Calendar.
Chart Tools	`http://code.google.com/ apis/charttools/`	Productivity	Add charts and graphs to your Web page.
Google Checkout	`http://code.google.com/ apis/checkout/`	Infrastructure	Start selling on your Web site.
Chromium	`http://code.google.com/ chromium/`	Browser	Contribute to the open-source project behind Google Chrome.
Google Chrome Frame	`http://code.google.com/ chrome/chromeframe/`	Browser	Enable open Web technologies and Google Chrome's fast JavaScript implementation within Internet Explorer.
Google Chrome Extensions (Labs)	`http://code.google.com/ chrome/extensions/`	Browser, Labs	Modify and enhance the functionality of Google Chrome.
Installable Web Apps (Labs)	`http://code.google.com/ chrome/apps/`	Browser, Labs	Package your Web apps for installation in Google Chrome.
Closure Tools	`http://code.google.com/ closure/`	Labs	Create powerful and efficient JavaScript.
Google Cloud Print (Labs)	`http://code.google.com/ apis/cloudprint/`	Browser, Labs	Enable any app (Web, desktop, mobile) on any device to print to any printer.

(continued)

169

TABLE 8.2 *(continued)*

	URL	Category	Google Description
Google Code Search Data API (Labs)	http://code.google.com/apis/codesearch/	Labs, Search	Enable your apps to view data from Code Search.
Google Contacts API	http://code.google.com/apis/contacts/	Social	Allow your apps to view and update user contacts.
Google Coupon Feeds (Labs)	http://code.google.com/apis/coupons/	Labs	Provide coupon listings that are included in Google search results.
Google Custom Search API	http://code.google.com/apis/customsearch/	Ads, Search	Create a custom search engine for your Web site or a collection of Web sites.
Google DoubleClick for Publishers (Labs)	http://code.google.com/apis/dfp/	Ads, Labs	Build applications that interact directly with Google's next-generation display advertising platform.
Google Data Protocol	http://code.google.com/apis/gdata/	Infrastructure	A simple, standard protocol for reading and writing data on the Web.
Google Desktop APIs (Labs)	http://code.google.com/apis/desktop/	Labs, Search	Create gadgets and indexing plugins for Google Desktop.
Google Documents List Data API	http://code.google.com/apis/documents/	Infrastructure	Enable your apps to view and update your list of Google Documents.
Google Interactive Media Ads (Labs	http://code.google.com/apis/ima/	Ads, Labs	Google Interactive Media Ads enable publishers to request and display ads into video, audio, and game content.
Google Earth API	http://code.google.com/apis/earth/	AJAX, Geo	Embed Google Earth into your Web page.
Google Plugin for Eclipse	http://code.google.com/eclipse/	Infrastructure	Enjoy simplified development of GWT and App Engine projects in the Eclipse IDE.
Feedburner API (Labs)	http://code.google.com/apis/feedburner/	Labs	Interact with FeedBurner's feed management and awareness-generating capabilities.
Google Finance Data API (Labs)	http://code.google.com/apis/finance/	Labs	View and update Finance content in the form of Google Data API feeds.

	URL	Category	Google Description
Google Friend Connect APIs (Labs)	http://code.google.com/apis/friendconnect/	Labs, Social	JS and REST/RPC API's to Google Friend Connect.
Google Fusion Tables API (Labs)	http://code.google.com/apis/fusiontables/	Labs	Manage Google Fusion Tables content programmatically.
Gadgets API	http://code.google.com/apis/fusiontables/	Social	Build mini-apps that run on multiple sites, including iGoogle, Google Desktop, or any Web page.
Gears (Labs)	http://code.google.com/apis/gears/	AJAX, Labs	Enable Web applications to work offline, from your desktop PC, or your mobile device.
Google Health API	http://code.google.com/apis/health/	Productivity	Manage your personal health information with Google.
iGoogle Developer Home (Labs)	http://code.google.com/apis/igoogle/	Labs, Social	Build and test gadgets for iGoogle.
iGoogle Themes API (Labs)	http://code.google.com/apis/themes/	Labs	Design a dynamic theme for the iGoogle home page.
KML	http://code.google.com/apis/kml/	Geo	Create and share content with Google Earth, Maps, and Maps for mobile.
Google Latitude API (Labs)	http://code.google.com/apis/latitude/	Geo, Labs	Build applications that read and update user locations and location histories.
Google Libraries API	http://code.google.com/apis/libraries/	AJAX	Load open-source JavaScript libraries.
Google Moderator API (Labs)	http://code.google.com/apis/moderator/	Labs	Collect ideas, questions, and recommendations from audiences of any size.
Google Geocoding API	http://code.google.com/apis/maps/documentation/geocoding/	AJAX, Geo	Convert addresses from geographic coordinates.
Google Directions API	http://code.google.com/apis/maps/documentation/directions/	AJAX, Geo	Plot directions using a variety of transportation options.
Google JavaScript Maps API	http://code.google.com/apis/maps/documentation/javascript/	AJAX, Geo	Integrate Google's interactive maps with data on your site.

(continued)

TABLE 8.2 (continued)

	URL	Category	Google Description
Google Maps API for Flash	http://code.google.com/apis/maps/documentation/flash/	Geo	Integrate Google Maps in Flash applications.
OpenSocial	http://code.google.com/apis/opensocial/	AJAX, Social	Build social applications that work across many Web sites.
Orkut Developer Home	http://code.google.com/apis/orkut/	Social	Create social applications for the millions of global Orkut users.
Google Project Hosting	http://code.google.com/projecthosting/	Infrastructure	Host your open-source project on Google Code.
Picasa APIs (Labs)	http://code.google.com/apis/picasa/	Labs, Social	Create custom buttons and upload files to third-party services.
Picasa Web Albums Data API	http://code.google.com/apis/picasaweb/	Social	Include Picasa Web Albums in your application or Web site.
Google PowerMeter API (Labs)	http://code.google.com/apis/powermeter/	Labs	Integrate with Google PowerMeter.
Google Prediction API (Labs)	http://code.google.com/apis/predict/	Labs	Add predictions to your applications.
PubSubHubbub	http://code.google.com/apis/pubsubhubbub/	Labs, Social	Turn your Atom and RSS feeds into real-time streams.
reCAPTCHA (Labs)	http://code.google.com/apis/recaptcha/	AJAX, Labs	Digitize books with this anti-bot service.
Google Safe Browsing APIs (Labs)	http://code.google.com/apis/safebrowsing/	Labs	Download lists of suspected phishing and malware URLs.
Google Secure Data Connector	http://code.google.com/securedataconnector/	Infrastructure	Connect data from behind the firewall to Google Apps.
Google Sidewiki API	http://code.google.com/apis/sidewiki/	Labs, Social	Enable your apps to view data from Google Sidewiki.
Google Sites Data API	http://code.google.com/apis/sites/	Labs	Enable your apps to modify content within a Google Site.
Google SketchUp Ruby API	http://code.google.com/apis/sketchup/	Geo	Extend Google SketchUp with Ruby.
Social Graph API (Labs)	http://code.google.com/apis/socialgraph/	Labs, Social	Enable users to quickly add their public social connections to your site.

	URL	Category	Google Description
Google Static Maps API	`http://code.google.com/apis/maps/documentation/staticmaps/`	Geo	Embed a Google Maps image on your Web site without requiring JavaScript or any dynamic page loading.
Google Storage for Developers (Labs)	`http://code.google.com/apis/storage/`	Labs	Store and share your data in the Google cloud.
Google Talk for Developers (Labs)	`http://code.google.com/apis/talk/`	Labs, Social	Connect your client or network to the Google Talk network, add chatback, or customize the Google Talk gadget.
Google Transit Feed Specification	`http://code.google.com/transit/spec/transit_feed_specification.html`	Geo	Provide public transit route and schedule information for Google Maps and more.
Google Translator Toolkit Data API	`http://code.google.com/apis/gtt/`	Labs	Build applications that can access and update translation-related data.
V8	`http://code.google.com/apis/v8/`	Browser	Google's high-performance, open-source, JavaScript engine.
Google Wave API	`http://code.google.com/apis/wave`	Labs, Social	Build extensions for Google Wave or embed Google Waves in your site.
Google Web Elements	`http://www.google.com/webelements/`	Infrastructure	Add your favorite Google products to your own Web site.
Google Web Toolkit	`http://code.google.com/webtoolkit/`	AJAX, Browser	Build AJAX apps in the Java language.
Google Webmaster Tools Data API (Labs)	`http://code.google.com/apis/webmastertools/`	Labs, Search	View and update site information and Sitemaps in the form of feeds.
YouTube API	`http://code.google.com/apis/youtube/`	Social	Integrate YouTube videos into your Web site or application.

Source: `http://code.google.com/intl/en/more/`.

Working with the Google App Engine

Google App Engine (GAE) is a Platform as a Service (PaaS) cloud-based Web hosting service on Google's infrastructure. Figure 8.8 shows the GAE home page at `http://code.google.com/intl/en/appengine/`. This service allows developers to build and deploy Web applications and have Google manage all the infrastructure needs, such as monitoring, failover, clustering, machine instance management, and so forth. For an application to run on GAE, it must comply with Google's platform standards, which narrows the range of applications that can be run and severely limits those applications' portability.

GAE supports the following major features:

- Dynamic Web services based on common standards
- Automatic scaling and load balancing
- Authentication using Google's Accounts API
- Persistent storage, with query access sorting and transaction management features
- Task queues and task scheduling
- A client-side development environment for simulating GAE on your local system
- One of either two runtime environments: Java or Python

When you deploy an application on GAE, the application can be accessed using your own domain name or using the Google Apps for Business URL.

FIGURE 8.8

The Google App Engine page at `http://code.google.com/intl/en/appengine/`

Google App Engine currently supports applications written in Java and in Python, although there are plans to extend support to more languages in the future. The service is meant to be language-agnostic. A number of Java Virtual Machine languages are compliant with GAE, as are several Python Web frameworks that support the Web Server Gateway Interface (WSGI) and CGI. Google has its own Webapp framework designed for use with GAE. The AppScale (http://appscale.cs.ucsb.edu/) open-source framework also may be used for running applications on GAE.

To encourage developers to write applications using GAE, Google allows for free application development and deployment up to a certain level of resource consumption. Resource limits are described on Google's quota page at http://code.google.com/appengine/docs/quotas.html, and the quota changes from time to time.

Google uses the following pricing scheme:

- CPU time measured in CPU hours is $0.10 per hour.
- Stored data measured in GB per month is $0.15 per GB/month.
- Incoming bandwidth measured in GB is $0.10 per GB.
- Outgoing bandwidth measured in GB is $0.12 per GB.
- Recipients e-mailed is $0.0001 per recipient.

The pricing page for Google AppEngine may be found at: http://code.google.com/appengine/docs/billing.html. The current resource limits are shown in Table 8.3. Consumption of resources beyond the free limit is generally on a pay-as-you-go basis, although in certain circumstances, Google may allow for additional free usage. When you enable billing for an application deployed to GAE, you pay for consumption of CPU, network I/O, and other usage above the level of the free quotas that GAE allows.

TABLE 8.3

Apps Quota Limits

Resource Quotas	Free Default Quota	Billing Enabled Default Quota
Applications per developer	10	No fixed limit
Application size	150MB	No fixed limit
Bandwidth limit (in and out)	1GB (each), up to 56MB/minute	1GB free and 1,046GB max, up to 10GB/min rate
CPU usage	6.5 CPU-hours/day, up to 15 CPU-minutes/minute	6.5 CPU-hours/day free to 1,729 CPU-hours/day maximum, up to 72 CPU-minutes/minute maximum rate
Datastore API calls	10 million/day, up to 57,000 queries/min	200 million queries/day, up to 129 queries/min
Data received from API	115GB, up to 659MB/min	695GB, up to 1,484MB/min

(continued)

TABLE 8.3 *(continued)*		
Resource Quotas	**Free Default Quota**	**Billing Enabled Default Quota**
Data sent to API	12GB, up to 68MB/min	72GB, up to 153MB/min
Data storage	1GB	1GB free, no maximum
Datastore CPU Time	60 CPU-hours, up to 20 CPU-min/min	1,200 CPU-hours, up to 50 CPU-min/min
E-mails	2,000/day, up to 8 recipients/min	2,000 free to 7.4 million recipients max, up to 5,100 recipients/min
HTTP requests	1,300,000/day, up to 7,400 requests/minute	43,000,000 requests, up to 30,000 requests/min rate
Indexes	100	200
Storage per application (Blobstore)	1GB	1GB free, no limit
Storage API calls (Blobstore)	No free quota	140 million calls/day, up to 72,000 calls/min
Storage item limit	1GB	1 GB free, no maximum
Time per request allowed	30 sec	30 sec
URLFetch API calls	657,000/day up to 3,000 calls/min	46 million calls/day up to 32,000 calls/min

Source: http://code.google.com/appengine/docs/quotas.html.

Applications running in GAE are isolated from the underlying operating system, which Google describes as running in a sandbox. This allows GAE to optimize the system so Web requests can be matched to the current traffic load. It also allows applications to be more secure because applications can connect only to computers using the specified URLs for the e-mail and fetch services using HTTP or HTTPS over the standard well-known ports. URL fetch uses the same infrastructure that retrieves Web pages on Google. The mail service also supports Gmail's messaging system.

Applications also are limited in that they can only read files; they cannot write to the file system directly. To access data, an application must use data stored in the memcache (memory cache), the datastore, or some other persistent service. Memcache is a fast in-memory key-value cache that can be used between application instances. For persistent data storage of transactional data, the datastore is used. Additionally, an application responds only to a specific HTTP request—in real-time, part of a queue, or scheduled—and any request is terminated if the response requires more than 30 seconds to complete.

GAE has a distributed datastore system that supports queries and transactions. This datastore is non-relational or "schema-less," but it does store data objects or entities that are assigned properties. In your queries, you can use entities filtered by kind or type and also sorted by properties. You can find a list of the various property types at http://code.google.com/appengine/docs/python/datastore/typesandpropertyclasses.html; the list includes strings, booleans, float, datetime, blob, text, and other property types. Each application can structure its own sets of data entities. The datastore uses an optimistic concurrency control and maintains strong consistency. An application can execute transactions with multiple operations, and they either all succeed or fail as a unit. To support the distributed nature of the datastore, the concept of an entity group is employed. Transactions manage entities as a single group, and entity groups are stored together in the system so operations can be performed faster.

The App Engine relies on the Google Accounts API for user authentication, the same system used when you log into a Google account. This provides access to e-mail and display names within your app, and it eliminates the need for an application to develop its own authentication system. Applications can use the User API to determine whether a user belongs to a specific group and even whether that person is an administrator for your application.

Many applications have been built and are running on Google App Engine. To get some idea of the range of applications that have been developed, you may want to visit the Google App Engine Gallery. This gallery is found at `http://appgallery.appspot.com/` and is shown in Figure 8.9. It is searchable by keyword and category.

FIGURE 8.9

Google App Engine gallery page may be found at `http://appgallery.appspot.com/`.

Summary

In this chapter, you learned about all things Google. The range of applications and services that Google offers is truly impressive; the company is essentially a self-contained ecosystem. Google's empire is built on its highly regarded search engine. The company monetized search technology by attaching target advertising to searches that its users perform. This revenue has allowed Google to create a range of applications and services on the Web that are having real impact in society.

In this chapter, the applications and services were listed, as were the APIs that are built on these applications and services. Google makes nearly all the products accessible through its APIs. That is why you find Google's services on so many of the world's Web sites.

This chapter ended by describing Google App Engine, a Platform as a Service Web-hosting offering that allows you to create Web applications and deploy them on Google's own infrastructure. Development and deployment of these applications are free, as is some basic usage of the application. You can scale your applications on a pay-per-use basis to whatever size you need.

In Chapter 9, I examine the approach of Amazon Web Services in cloud computing. AWS offers a very different service model, operating as an Infrastructure as a Service (IaaS) provider.

Using Amazon Web Services

Amazon.com is one of the most important and heavily trafficked Web sites in the world. It provides a vast selection of products using an infrastructure based on Web services. As Amazon.com has grown, it has dramatically grown its infrastructure to accommodate peak traffic times. Over time the company has made its network resources available to partners and affiliates, which also has improved its range of products.

Starting in 2006, Amazon.com made its Web service platform available to developers on a usage-basis model. The technologies described in this chapter represent perhaps the best example of Web services achieved through the Service Oriented Architecture of components that you learn about in Chapter 13. Through hardware virtualization on Xen hypervisors, Amazon. com has made it possible to create private virtual servers that you can run worldwide. These servers can be provisioned with almost any kind of application software you might envisage, and they tap into a range of support services that not only make distributed cloud computing applications possible, but make them robust. Some very large Web sites are running on Amazon. com's infrastructure without their client audience being any the wiser.

Amazon Web Services is based on SOA standards, including HTTP, REST, and SOAP transfer protocols, open source and commercial operating systems, application servers, and browser-based access. Virtual private servers can provision virtual private clouds connected through virtual private networks providing for reasonable security and control by the system administrator.

AWS has a great value proposition: You pay for what you use. While you may not save a great deal of money over time using AWS for enterprise class Web applications, you encounter very little barrier to entry in terms of getting your site or application up and running quickly and robustly. AWS has much to teach us about the future of cloud computing and how virtual infrastructure can be best leveraged as a business asset.

IN THIS CHAPTER

Learning about Amazon Web Services

Instantiating Amazon Machine Images

Provisioning storage, databases, and other services

Learning about other AWS offerings

Realizing the potential of Infrastructure as a Service

Understanding Amazon Web Services

The Amazon is the world's largest river. Amazon.com is the world's largest online retailer with net sales in $24.51 billion, according to their 2009 annual report. The company is a long way past selling books and records. While Amazon.com is not the earth's biggest retailer (that spot is reserved for Wal-Mart), Amazon.com offers the largest number of retail product SKUs through a large ecosystem of partnerships. By any measure, Amazon.com is a huge business. To support this business, Amazon.com has built an enormous network of IT systems to support not only average, but peak customer demands. Amazon Web Services (AWS) takes what is essentially unused infrastructure capacity on Amazon.com's network and turns it into a very profitable business. Figure 9.1 shows the Amazon Web Services home page (http://aws.amazon.com/).

AWS is having enormous impact in cloud computing. Indeed, Amazon.com's services represent the largest pure Infrastructure as a Service (IAAS) play in the marketplace today. It is also one of the best examples of what is possible using a Service Oriented Architecture (SOA), which is described in Chapter 13. The structure of Amazon.com's Amazon Web Services (AWS) is therefore highly educational in understanding just how disruptive cloud computing can be to traditional fixed asset IT deployments, how virtualization enables a flexible approach to system rightsizing, and how dispersed systems can impart reliability to mission critical systems.

FIGURE 9.1

Amazon Web Services home page

For these reasons, even though Amazon.com's IaaS services are described in other chapters individually, this chapter provides background to the entire portfolio and shows why Amazon Web Services is a $500 million business that hosts eight of the top ten Facebook games (`http://gigaom.com/2010/08/02/amazon-web-services-revenues/`; and `http://venturebeat.com/2010/08/03/amazon-web-services-generating-an-estimated-500m-in-revenue-thanks-in-part-to-growth-of-social-games/`). In 2008 AWS claimed 330,000 unique accounts, although the press release for that claim has now disappeared.

Cross-Ref

In Chapter 4, "Understanding Services and Applications by Type," this form of cloud computing is defined as one that provides computer infrastructure usually in the form of a virtualized operating system environment. IaaS is characterized by virtual private servers running operating system and networked application instances, virtual storage, virtual data centers, and networks sold on a per-use or utility basis. ■

Amazon Web Services represents only a small fraction of Amazon's overall business sales at the moment, but it is a rapidly growing component. Amazon doesn't break down its sales by individual areas in its annual report, but according to Randy Bias who blogs on the site Cloudscaling.com (`http://cloudscaling.com/blog/cloud-computing/amazons-ec2-generating-220m-annually`) the largest component of Amazon's offerings is Amazon's Elastic Compute Cloud (EC2), which generates in excess of $220 million annually as of October 2009. EC2 is estimated to run on over 40,000+ servers worldwide divided into six availability zones. (You learn about EC2 later in this chapter.) EC2 is an Infrastructure as a Service (IaaS) play, a market that was pegged to be around $400-$600 M/year and growing 10%-20%/year even in the face of a dramatic market slowdown. Rackspace Cloud (`http://www.rackspacecloud.com/`), EC2's nearest competitor, is pegged to be around 10% the size of EC2 by Bias.

Amazon Web Service Components and Services

Amazon Web Services is comprised of the following components, listed roughly in their order of importance:

- **Amazon Elastic Compute Cloud** (EC2; `http://aws.amazon.com/ec2/`), is the central application in the AWS portfolio. It enables the creation, use, and management of virtual private servers running the Linux or Windows operating system over a Xen hypervisor. Amazon Machine Instances are sized at various levels and rented on a computing/hour basis. Spread over data centers worldwide, EC2 applications may be created that are highly scalable, redundant, and fault tolerant. EC2 is described more fully the next section. A number of tools are used to support EC2 services:

    Amazon Simple Queue Service (SQS; `http://aws.amazon.com/sqs/`) is a message queue or transaction system for distributed Internet-based applications. See "Examining the Simple Queue Service (SQS)" later in this chapter for a description of this AWS feature. In a loosely coupled SOA system, a transaction manager is required to ensure that messages are not lost when a component isn't available.

Amazon Simple Notification Service (SNS; `http://aws.amazon.com/sns/`) is a Web service that can publish messages from an application and deliver them to other applications or to subscribers. SNS provides a method for triggering actions, allowing clients or applications to subscribe to information (like RSS), or polling for new or changed information or perform updates.

EC2 can be monitored by **Amazon CloudWatch** (`http://aws.amazon.com/cloudwatch/`), which provides a console or command line view of resource utilization, site Key Performance Indexes (performance metrics), and operational indicators for factors such as processor demand, disk utilization, and network I/O. The metrics obtained by CloudWatch may be used to enable a feature called **Auto Scaling** (`http://aws.amazon.com/autoscaling/`) that can automatically scale an EC2 site based on a set of rules that you create. Autoscaling is part of Amazon Cloudwatch and available at no additional charge.

Amazon Machine Instances (AMIs) in EC2 can be load balanced using the **Elastic Load Balancing** (`http://aws.amazon.com/elasticloadbalancing/`) feature. The Load Balancing feature can detect when an instance is failing and reroute traffic to a healthy instance, even an instance in other AWS zones. The Amazon CloudWatch metrics request count and request latency that show up in the AWS console are used to support Elastic Load Balancing.

- **Amazon Simple Storage System** (S3; `http://aws.amazon.com/s3/`) is an online backup and storage system, which is described in "Working with Amazon Simple Storage System (S3)" later in this chapter.

  A high speed data transfer feature called AWS Import/Export (`http://aws.amazon.com/importexport/`) can transfer data to and from AWS using Amazon's own internal network to portable storage devices.

- **Amazon Elastic Block Store** (EBS; `http://aws.amazon.com/ebs/`) is a system for creating virtual disks (volume) or block level storage devices that can be used for Amazon Machine Instances in EC2.

- **Amazon SimpleDB** (`http://aws.amazon.com/simpledb/`) is a structured data store that supports indexing and data queries to both EC2 and S3. SimpleDB isn't a full database implementation, as you learn in "Exploring SimpleDB (S3)" later in this chapter; it stores data in "buckets" and without requiring the creation of a database schema. This design allows SimpleDB to scale easily. SimpleDB interoperates with both Amazon EC2 and Amazon S3.

- **Amazon Relational Database Service** (RDS; `http://aws.amazon.com/rds/`) allows you to create instances of the MySQL database to support your Web sites and the many applications that rely on data-driven services. MySQL is the "M" in the ubiquitous LAMP Web services platform (for Linux, APACHE, MySQL, and PERL), and the inclusion of this service allows developers to port applications, their source code, and databases directly over to AWS, preserving their previous investment in these technologies. RDS provides features such as automated software patching, database backups, and automated database scaling via an API call.

- **Amazon Cloudfront** (http://aws.amazon.com/cloudfront/) is an edge-storage or content-delivery system that caches data in different physical locations so that user access to data is enhanced through faster data transfer speeds and lower latency. Cloudfront is similar to systems such as Akamai.com, but is proprietary to Amazon.com and is set up to work with Amazon Simple Storage System (Amazon S3). Cloudfront is currently in beta, but has been well received in the trade press. See "Defining Cloudfront" later in this chapter for more details.

Cross-Ref

The importance of a message queue system for distributed applications is described in Chapter 13, "Understanding Service Oriented Architecture." ■

While the list above represents the most important of the AWS offerings, it is only a partial list—a list that is continually growing and very dynamic. A number of services and utilities support Amazon partners or the AWS infrastructure itself. These are the ones you may encounter:

- **Alexa Web Information Service** (http://aws.amazon.com/awis/) and **Alexa Top Sites** (http://aws.amazon.com/alexatopsites/) are two services that collect and expose information about the structure and traffic patterns of Web sites. This information can be used to build or structure Web sites, access related sites, analyze historical patterns for growth and relationships, and perform data analysis on site information. Alexa Top Sites can rank sites based on their usage and be used to structure awareness of site popularity into the structure of Web service you build.

- **Amazon Associates Web Services** (A2S) is the machinery for interacting with Amazon's vast product data and eCommerce catalog function. This service, which was called Amazon E-Commerce Service (ECS), is the means for vendors to add their products to the Amazon.com site and take orders and payments.

- **Amazon DevPay** (http://aws.amazon.com/devpay/) is a billing and account management service that can be used by businesses that run applications on top of AWS. DevPay provides a developer API that eliminates the need for application developers to build order pipelines, because Amazon does the billing based on your prices and then uses Amazon Payments to collect the payments.

- **Amazon Elastic MapReduce** (http://aws.amazon.com/elasticmapreduce/) is an interactive data analysis tool for performing indexing, data mining, file analysis, log file analysis, machine learning, financial analysis, and scientific and bioinformatics research. Elastic MapReduce is built on top of a Hadoop framework using the Elastic Compute Cloud (EC2) and Simple Storage Service (S3).

- **Amazon Mechanical Turk** (http://aws.amazon.com/mturk/) is a means for accessing human researchers or consultants to help solve problems on a contractual or temporary basis. Problems solved by this human workforce have included object identification, video or audio recording, data duplication, and data research. Amazon.com calls this type of work Human Intelligence Tasks (HITs). The Mechanical Turk is currently in beta.

- **AWS Multi-Factor Authentication** (AWS MFA; http://aws.amazon.com/mfa/) is a special feature that uses an authentication device you have in your possession to provide access to your AWS account settings. This hardware key generates a pseudo-random six-digit number when you press a button that you enter into your logon. This gives you two layers of protection: your user id and password (things you know) and the code from your hardware key (something you have). This multifactor security feature can be extended to Cloudfront and Amazon S3. The Enzio Time Token from Gemalto (http://online noram.gemalto.com/) is available for use with Amazon Web Service; the key costs $12.99.

  Secure access to your EC2 AMIs is controlled by passwords, Kerberos, and 509 Certificates.

- **Amazon Flexible Payments Service** (FPS; http://aws.amazon.com/fps/) is a payments-transfer infrastructure that provides access for developers to charge Amazon's customers for their purchases. Using FPS, goods, services, donations, money transfers, and recurring payments can be fulfilled. FPS is exposed as an API that sorts transactions into packages called Quick Starts that make this service easy to implement.

- **Amazon Fulfillment Web Services** (FWS; http://aws.amazon.com/fws/) allows merchants to fill orders through Amazon.com fulfillment service, with Amazon handling the physical delivery of items on the merchant's behalf. Merchant inventory is prepositioned in Amazon's fulfillment centers, and Amazon packs and ships the items. There is no charge for using Amazon FWS; fees for the Fulfillment by Amazon (FBA; http://www.amazon.com/gp/seller/fba/fulfillment-by-amazon.html) service apply. Between FBA and FWS, you can create a nearly virtual store on Amazon.com.

- **Amazon Virtual Private Cloud** (VPC; http://aws.amazon.com/vpc/) provides a bridge between a company's existing network and the AWS cloud. VPC connects your network resources to a set of AWS systems over a Virtual Private Network (VPN) connection and extends security systems, firewalls, and management systems to include their provisioned AWS servers. Amazon VPC is integrated with Amazon EC2, but Amazon plans to extend the capabilities of VPC to integrate with other systems in the Amazon cloud computing portfolio.

- **AWS Premium Support** (http://aws.amazon.com/premiumsupport/) is Amazon's technical support and consulting business. Through AWS Premium Support, subscribers to AWS can get help building or supporting applications that use EC2, S3, Cloudfront, VPC, SQS, SNS, SimpleDB, RDS, and the other services listed above. Service plans are available on a per-incidence, monthly, or unlimited basis at different levels of service.

With this overview of AWS components complete, let's look at the central part of Amazon Web Service's value proposition, the creation and deployment of virtual private servers using the Elastic Compute Cloud (EC2) service.

Working with the Elastic Compute Cloud (EC2)

Amazon Elastic Compute Cloud (EC2) is a virtual server platform that allows users to create and run virtual machines on Amazon's server farm. With EC2, you can launch and run server instances called Amazon Machine Images (AMIs) running different operating systems such as Red Hat Linux and Windows on servers that have different performance profiles. You can add or subtract virtual servers elastically as needed; cluster, replicate, and load balance servers; and locate your different servers in different data centers or "zones" throughout the world to provide fault tolerance. The term *elastic* refers to the ability to size your capacity quickly as needed.

The difference between an instance and a machine image is that an instance is the emulation of a hardware platform such as X86, IA64, and so on running on the Xen hypervisor. A machine image is the software and operating system running on top of the instance. A machine image may be thought of as the contents of a boot drive, something that you could package up with a program such as Ghost, Acronis, or TrueImage to create a single file containing the exact contents of a volume. A machine image should be composed of a hardened operating system with as few features and capabilities as possible and locked down as much as possible.

Consider a situation where you want to create an Internet platform that provides the following:

- A high transaction level for a Web application
- A system that optimizes performance between servers in your system
- Data driver information services
- Network security
- The ability to grow your service on demand

Implementing that type of service might require a rack of components that included the following:

- An application server with access to a large RAM allocation
- A load balancer, usually in the form of a hardware appliance such as F5's BIG-IP
- A database server
- Firewalls and network switches
- Additional rack capacity at the ISP

A physical implementation of these components might cost you something in the neighborhood of $25,000 depending upon the scale of your application. With AWS, you might be able to have an equivalent service for as little as $1,000 and have a high level of availability and reliability to boot. This difference may surprise you, but it is understandable when you consider that AWS can run its services with a much greater efficiency than your company would alone and therefore amortize its investment in hardware over several customers. That is the promise and the potential of cloud computing realized and why large Web sites such as Recovery.gov have moved to AWS.

Amazon Machine Images

AMIs are operating systems running on the Xen virtualization hypervisor. Each virtual private server is accorded a size rating called its *EC2 Compute Unit,* which is pegged to the equivalent of a 1.0–1.2 GHz 2007 Opteron or 2007 Xeon processor. Table 9.1 shows the current set of Instance types, which broadly fall into the following three classes:

1. **Standard Instances:** The standard instances are deemed to be suitable for standard server applications.

2. **High Memory Instances:** High memory instances are useful for large data throughput applications such as SQL Server databases and data caching and retrieval.

3. **High CPU Instances:** The high CPU instance category is best used for applications that are processor- or compute-intensive. Applications of this type include rendering, encoding, data analysis, and others.

TABLE 9.1

Amazon Machine Image Instance Types

Type	Compute Engine	RAM (GB)	Storage (GB)1	Platform	I/O Performance	API Name
Micro instance	Up to 2 EC2 Compute Units (1 virtual core) in short bursts	0.613	EBS (Elastic Block Storage) storage only	32-bit or 64-bit	Low	T1.micro
Standard instance – small (default)	1 EC2 Compute Unit (1 virtual core)	1.7	160	32-bit	Moderate	m1.small
Standard instance – large	4 EC2 Compute Units (2 virtual cores X 2 EC2 Units)	7.5	850	64-bit	High	m1.large
Standard instance – extra large	8 EC2 Compute Units (4 virtual cores X 2 EC2 Units)	15	1,690	64-bit	High	m1.xlarge
High Memory Double Extra Large Instance	13 EC2 Compute Units (4 virtual cores X 3.25 EC2 Units)	34.2	850	64-bit	High	m2.2xlarge

Type	Compute Engine	RAM (GB)	Storage (GB)1	Platform	I/O Performance	API Name
High Memory Quadruple Extra Large Instance	26 EC2 Compute Units (8 virtual cores X 3.25 EC2 Units)	68.4	1,690	64-bit	High	m2.4xlarge
High CPU Medium Instance	5 EC2 Compute Units (2 virtual cores X 2.5 EC2 Units)	1.7	350	32-bit	Moderate	c1.medium
High CPU Extra Large Instance	20 EC2 Compute Units (8 virtual cores X 2.5 EC2 Units)	7	1,690	64-bit	High	c1.xlarge

1. Storage is not persistent. All assigned storage is lost upon rebooting. To store data on AWS, you need to create a Simple Storage Service (S3) bucket or an Elastic Block Storage (EBS) volume.

Pricing models

The pricing of these different AMI types depends on the operating system used, which data center the AMI is located in (you can select its location), and the amount of time that the AMI runs. Rates are quoted based on an hourly rate. Additional charges are applied for:

- the amount of data transferred
- whether Elastic IP Addresses are assigned
- your virtual private server's use of Amazon Elastic Block Storage (EBS)
- whether you use Elastic Load Balancing for two or more servers
- other features

AMIs that have been saved and shut down incur a small one-time fee, but do not incur additional hourly fees.

The three different pricing models for EC2 AMIs are as follows:

- **On-Demand Instance:** This is the hourly rate with no long-term commitment.
- **Reserved Instances:** This is a purchase of a contract for each instance you use with a significantly lower hourly usage charge after you have paid for the reservation.
- **Spot Instance:** This is a method for bidding on unused EC2 capacity based on the current spot price. This feature offers a significantly lower price, but it varies over time or may not be available when there is no excess capacity.

Pricing varies by zone, instance, and pricing model. A chart of the different current prices may be found at `http://aws.amazon.com/ec2/`. This page also includes current Amazon Elastic Block Store volume and snapshot charges to Amazon S3, as well as data transfer rates. Figure 9.2 shows the AWS Simple Monthly Calculator that you can find at `http://calculator.s3.amazonaws.com/calc5.html` to help you estimate your monthly charges.

FIGURE 9.2

The Amazon Web Services Simple Monthly Calculator for determining system costs on AWS

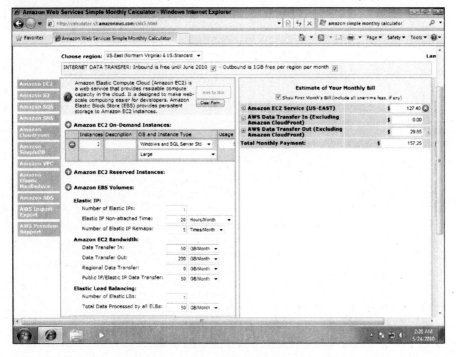

System images and software

You can choose to use a template AMI system image with the operating system of your choice or create your own system image that contains your custom applications, code libraries, settings, and data. Security can be set through passwords, Kerberos tickets, or certificates.

These operating systems are offered:

- Red Hat Enterprise Linux
- OpenSuse Linux
- Ubuntu Linux

- Sun OpenSolaris
- Fedora
- Gentoo Linux
- Oracle Enterprise Linux
- Windows Server 2003/2008 32-bit and 64-bit up to Data Center Edition
- Debian

Most of the system image templates that Amazon AWS offers are based on Red Hat Linux, Windows Server, Oracle Enterprise Linux, and OpenSolaris from the list above. Table 9.2 lists some of the more common enterprise applications that are available from AWS either as part of its canned templates or for use in building your own AMI system image. Hundreds of free and paid AMIs can be found on AWS.

TABLE 9.2

EC2 Enterprise Software Types

Application Type	Software
Application Development Environments	IBM sMash, JBoss Enterprise Application Platform, and Ruby on Rails
Application Servers	IBM WebSphere Application Server, Java Application Server, and Oracle WebLogic Server
Batch Processing	Condor, Hadoop, and Open MPI
Databases	IBM DB2, IBM Informix Dynamic Server, Microsoft SQL Server Standard 2005, MySQL Enterprise, and Oracle Database 11g
Video Encoding and Streaming	Windows Media Server and Wowza Media Server Pro
Web Hosting	Apache HTTP, IIS/ASP.Net, IBM Lotus Web Content Management, and IBM WebSphere Portal Server

When you create a virtual private server, you can use the Elastic IP Address feature to create what amounts to a static IP v4 address to your server. This address can be mapped to any of your AMIs and is associated with your AWS account. You retain this IP address until you specifically release it from your AWS account. Should a machine instance fail, you can map your Elastic IP Address to fail over to a different AMI. You don't need to wait until a DNS server updates the IP record assignment, and you can use a form to configure the reverse DNS record of the Elastic IP address change.

There are currently four different EC2 service zones or regions:

- US East (Northern Virginia)
- US West (Northern California)
- EU (Ireland)
- Asia Pacific (Singapore)

Creating an account and instance on EC2

The process for signing up for Amazon Web Services, creating an Amazon Machine Instance, and provisioning the image with software is relatively straightforward. You begin the process by clicking the Sign Up Now button on the Amazon Web Services home page (http://aws.amazon.com) shown in Figure 9.4. You see a page on which you name your account, provide a password, and select a payment option. If you have an Amazon.com user account, you can opt to use that account for your AWS account. After you create your account, you want to sign into the Amazon EC2 Management Console, where you see a dashboard similar to the one shown in Figure 9.3.

The AWS EC2 Management Console with no instances

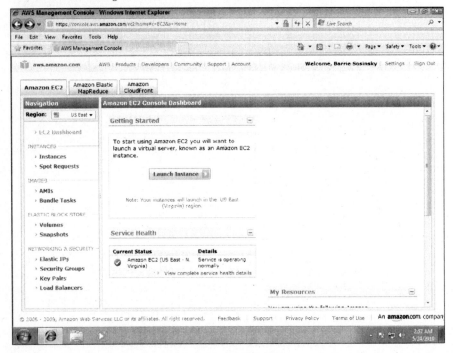

To create an AMI instance, do the following:

1. Click the Launch Instance button in the Getting Started Section to launch the Request Instances wizard shown in Figure 9.4.

2. Scroll the list to find the type of system image you want, and click Select.

3. Specify the Number of Instance(s) desired, the Availability Zone where the instance(s) should be located, the Instance type in the Instance Details step shown in Figure 9.5, and click Continue.

FIGURE 9.4

Select an Instance type from one of the templates shown, or create your own AMI in this step.

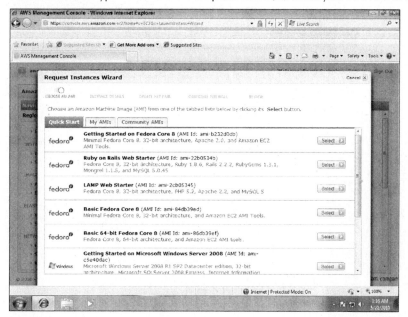

FIGURE 9.5

Fill in the instance details in this step.

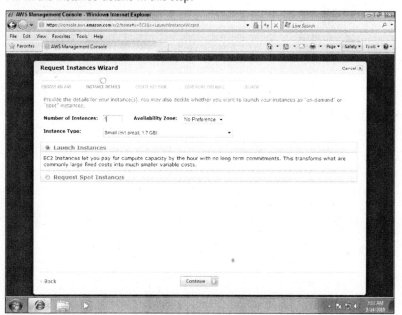

4. In the Advanced Instance Options step shown in Figure 9.6, enter an ID for the Kernel or RAM and enable CloudWatch, if desired; then click Continue.

In the Advanced Instance Options step, you can provide an identifier for your instance's kernel and RAM disk and enable the CloudWatch monitoring feature.

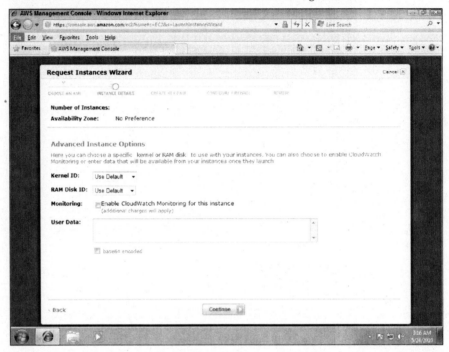

5. In the Create a Key Pair step, you are asked to either create a new key pair or apply a key pair that you have already created. Make a selection as shown in Figure 9.7, and click Continue.

    Creating a key pair generates a public/private key that you download from AWS. When you want to provide someone access to your secured server, you supply them with the private key they need to connect to the server.

6. The Configure Firewall page shown in Figure 9.8 allows you to set the applications that have access to your server, their transport protocols, ports, and the security group that can access your server. You can create a new security group or apply one that already exists.

FIGURE 9.7

For secure access to your AMI, you can assign a public/private key pair.

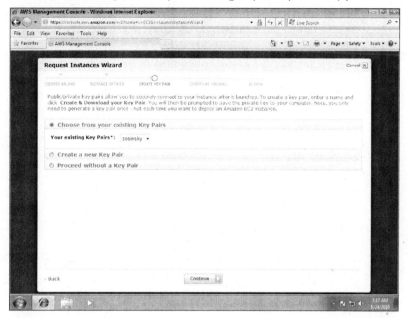

FIGURE 9.8

Firewall settings allow you to filter by service and protocol, as well as set a security group membership for access.

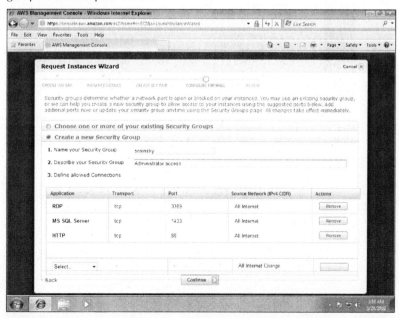

7. Click Continue to go the Review summary page shown in Figure 9.9; review the settings on that page and then click Continue again.

You are returned to the AWS Management Console, and your AMI is shown in the My Instances pane. The instance is created, and after a moment starts running, as shown in Figure 9.10.

8. After the instance is running, you need to connect to the instance. Use the Connect command on the Instance context menu, as shown in Figure 9.11. That menu also allows you to suspend, reboot, terminate (deleting or killing), clone, snapshot, set passwords, and perform other actions that are specific to the type of system image you created.

FIGURE 9.9

This Review page allows you to see the type of Amazon Machine Instance and the system image it will run before you create it.

FIGURE 9.10

The AWS Management Console with an active AMI showing

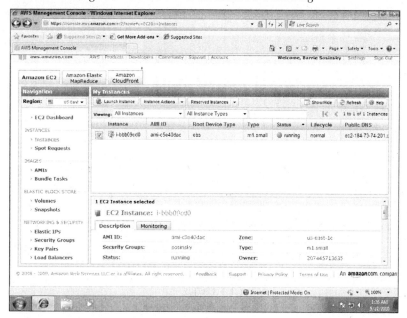

FIGURE 9.11

Context menu for a Windows system image running in an AMI

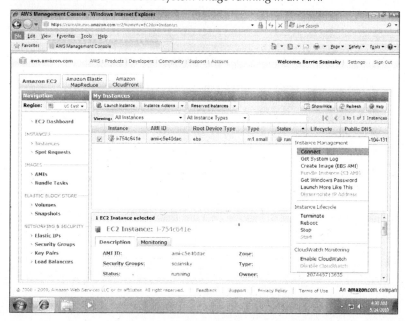

When you are finished creating an AMI instance, you can create a shortcut to directly connect with that instance. With Windows Server, that shortcut is a Microsoft Remote Desktop Connection (or Terminal Server Client), which connects to your server using the Remote Desktop Protocol. Other operating systems create different types of Virtual Private Network connections.

Working with Amazon Storage Systems

When you create an Amazon Machine Instance you provision it with a certain amount of storage. That storage is temporal, it only exists for as long as your instance is running. All of the data contained in that storage is lost when the instance is suspended or terminated, as the storage is reassigned to the pool for other AWS users to use. For this and other reasons you need to have access to persistent storage. The Amazon Simple Storage System provides block storage, but is set up in a way that is somewhat unique from other storage systems you may have worked with in the past.

Amazon Simple Storage System (S3)

Amazon S3's cloud-based storage system allows you to store data objects ranging in size from 1 byte up to 5GB in a flat namespace. In S3, storage containers are referred to as buckets, and buckets serve the function of a directory, although there is no object hierarchy to a bucket, and you save objects and not files to it. It is important that you do not associate the concept of a filesystem with S3, because files are not supported; only objects are stored. Additionally, you do not "mount" a bucket as you do a filesystem.

The S3 system allows you to assign a name to a bucket, but that name must be unique in the S3 namespace across all AWS customers. Access to an S3 bucket is through the S3 Web API (either with SOAP or REST) and is slow relative to a real-world disk storage system. S3's performance limits its use to non-operational functions such as data archiving and retrieval or disk backup. The REST API is preferred to the SOAP API, because it is easier to work with large binary objects with REST.

You can do the following with S3 buckets through the APIs:

- Create, edit, or delete existing buckets
- Upload new objects to a bucket and download them
- Search for and find objects and buckets
- Find metadata associate with objects and buckets
- Specify where a bucket should be stored
- Make buckets and objects available for public access

One tool commonly used to manage data for Amazon S3 is the s3cmd command line client (http://s3tools.org/s3cmd).

The S3 service is used by many people as the third level backup component in a 3-2-1 backup strategy. That is, you have your original data (1), a copy of your data (2), and an off-site copy of your data (3); the latter of these may be S3. In this regard, S3 acts as a direct competitor to Carbonite's backup system. One of the options available to you is versioning for Amazon S3. With versioning, every version of an object stored in an S3 bucket is retained, provided you enable the versioning feature. Any HTTP or REST operation such as PUT, POST, COPY, or DELETE creates a new object that is stored along with the older version. A GET operation retrieves the newest version of the object, but the ability to recover and undo actions is available. Versioning also can be used for preserving data and for archiving purposes.

Amazon S3 provides large quantities of reliable storage that is highly protected but to which you have low bandwidth access. S3 excels in applications where storage is archival in nature. For example, you find S3 in use by large photo sharing sites. In the next section you'll see Amazon's Elastic Block Storage or EBS. In EBS you create virtual drives that you can use with your machine instances in the same way that you would use a hard drive with a physical system. EBS tends to be used in transactional systems where high-speed data access is required.

Caution

Keep in mind that while Amazon S3 is highly reliable, it is not highly available. You can definitely get your data back from S3 at some point with guaranteed 100% fidelity, but the service is not always connected and experiences service outages. By comparison, an EBS volume is offered with an annual failure rate of 0.1% to 0.5%, about a factor of 10 better than typical disk drives you use in your own physical servers. ∎

Amazon Elastic Block Store (EBS)

The third of Amazon's data storage systems are devoted to Amazon Elastic Block Storage (EBS), which is a persistent storage service with a high operational performance. Advantages of EBS are that it can store file system information and its performance is higher and much more reliable than Amazon S3. That makes EBS valuable as an operational data storage medium for AWS. The cost of creating an EBS volume is also greater than creating a similarly sized S3 bucket.

An EBS volume can be used as an instance boot partition. The advantages of an EBS boot partition are that you can have a volume up to 1TB, retain your boot partition separately from your EC2 instance, and use a boot partition volume as a means for bundling an AMI into a single package. EBS boot partitions can be stopped and started, and they offer fast AMI boot times.

EBS is similar in concept to a Storage Area Network or SAN; you create block storage volumes varying in size from 1GB to 1TB and make those volumes available to your machine instances. The performance of a volume is dependent upon the network I/O and therefore varies as a function of the size of your instance (see Table 9.3), as well as the type of disk I/O operations (random, sequential, request size, and READS or WRITE) that are in progress.

When you create volumes, they appear first as raw block storage devices that must be formatted for use. A volume is mounted on a particular instance and is available to that instance alone; that is, volumes may not be shared between instances. Volumes may be located in the same zone as the AMI to which they are attached. Volumes appear as if they are devices (physical drives) when attached to an instance. You can mount multiple volumes on a single instance, if desired, and create striped RAID volumes for faster performance. The filesystem for mounted volumes appears when you open the volume, and you can install applications or copy data to mounted volumes as you would any physical disk.

EBS supports volume replication within the same availability zone, which can add an extra level of fault tolerance to the data set. The use of replication means that mirroring a volume won't add much additional fault tolerance. Snapshots are the recommended approach to improving your volume's reliability.

You can make an instance image or snapshot of your AMI, and these point-in-time snapshots are then copied out to Amazon S3. You can use these snapshots as system images to create new AMIs or to restore a volume (and instance) to that point-in-time snapshot when needed. You can share snapshots with other authorized users by using a volume's context menu in the AWS Management Console and selecting the Snapshot Permissions command.

When you create a new volume from an S3 snapshot, the data is slowly copied to the new volume. As you start working on the new volume, any missing data is downloaded preferentially as needed.

Each snapshot you take adds incremental changes to the previous snapshot, which means that while the first snapshot takes a fair amount of time, subsequent snapshots are usually executed quickly and with only a modest amount of extra storage space required.

Tip

EBS supports a special feature of AWS called a Public Data Set, which is a data repository that is made available at no extra charge to AWS customers; only the data transfer and compute fees are paid for working with the data set. Examples of Public Data Sets in use are the Annotated Human Genome map, U.S. Census Databases (1980, 1990, and 2000), UniGene transcript sequences, and Freebase.com data dump, among others. To learn more about Public Data Sets, see http://aws.amazon.com/publicdatasets/. ■

EBS is a service priced on the amount of storage space used, how long you use it, and the number of I/O requests made to the volume. You can use a utility like IOSTAT to measure I/O of your systems to estimate these transaction costs, which vary greatly by operating system and application. Amazon quotes an example of a medium-sized database of 100GB with 100 I/O per sec costing about $10 per month for the allocated storage and $26 per month for the I/O (there are 2.6 million seconds in a month). Snapshots are priced on the storage blocks used, not on the size of the volume being stored. Amazon also charges for the amount of data transferred to Amazon S3 during a snapshot.

Table 9.3 summarizes the various properties of the three different forms of EC2 data storage devices.

TABLE 9.3

EC2 Storage Type Properties

Property	AMI Instance	Amazon Simple Storage Service (S3)	Amazon Elastic Block Storage (EBS)	Amazon CloudFront
Adaptability	Medium	Low	High	Medium
Best usage	Transient data storage	Persistent or archival storage	Operational data storage	Data sharing and large data object streaming

Property	AMI Instance	Amazon Simple Storage Service (S3)	Amazon Elastic Block Storage (EBS)	Amazon CloudFront
Cost	Low	Medium	High	Low
Ease of use	Low	High	High	High
Data protection	Very Low	Very High	High	Low
Latency	Medium	Low	High	High
Least best used as	Persistent storage	Operational storage	For small I/O transfers	Operational data
Reliability	High	Medium	High	Medium
Throughput	Variable	Slow	High	High

CloudFront

Amazon CloudFront is referred to as a content delivery network (CDN), and sometimes called *edge computing*. In edge computing, content is pushed out geographically so the data is more readily available to network clients and has a lower latency when requested. You enable CloudFront through a selection in the AWS Management Console.

You can think of a CDN as a distributed caching system. CloudFront servers are located through-out the world—in Europe, Asia, and the United States. As such, CloudFront represents yet another level of Amazon cloud storage. A user requesting data from a CloudFront site is referred to the nearest geographical location. CloudFront supports "geo-caching" data by performing static data transfers and streaming content from one CloudFront location to another.

At the time this chapter was written CloudFront was in beta, but it has been well received. Direct competitors for CloudFront include Akamai Technologies (`http://www.akamai.com/`), Edgecast Networks (`http://www.edgecast.com/`), and Limelight Networks (`http://www.limelightnetworks.com/`). CloudFront's aggressive pricing model is expected to put pressure on these other services over time. Pricing for CloudFront is based on how much data is transferred to clients, and it doesn't require a service contract. You can estimate CloudFront's costs using the AWS Simple Monthly Calculator (refer to Figure 9.3); costs vary by region.

When you create a CloudFront implementation, a CloudFront domain name is registered for your domain name in the form `<domainname>.cloudfront.net`, and objects in the CloudFront domain can be mapped to your own domain. You store your source files on CloudNet servers in Amazon S3 buckets and then use the CloudFront API to register the S3 bucket with the CloudNet distribution. Then in your applications, Web pages, and links, you reference the distribution location.

CloudFront represents the last of the Amazon Web Services that store and serve objects and files. To store data in a way that makes it searchable and organizes it, Amazon offers two different database services that are covered in the next section.

Understanding Amazon Database Services

Amazon offers two different types of database services: Amazon SimpleDB, which is non-relational, and Amazon Relational Database Service (Amazon RDS), both of which were in beta at the time of this writing. Dynamic data access is a central element of Web services, particularly "Web 2.0" services, so although AMIs support several of the major databases, it isn't surprising that they would create their own databases as part of the AWS Service Oriented Architecture.

Amazon SimpleDB

Amazon SimpleDB is an attempt to create a high performance data store with many database features but without the overhead. This is analogous to the goals used to create the Amazon Simple Storage System (S3). The service is meant to be low touch, in that it abstracts many of the common concerns of database administrators for hardware requirements, software maintenance, indexing, and performance optimization.

To create a high performance "simple" database, the data store created is flat; that is, it is non-relational and joins are not supported. Data stored in SimpleDB domains doesn't require maintenances of a schema and is therefore easily scalable and highly available because replication is built into the system. Data is stored as collections of items with attribute-value pairs, and the system is akin to using the database function within a spreadsheet. To support replication, a set of two consistency functions are part of SimpleDB that check data across the different copies. Transactions are performed as a set of conditional PUTS and DELETES, and you can INSERT, REPLACE, or DELETE values for item attributes. These transaction capabilities do not enable features like ROLLBACK, but they allow you to create solutions that maintain optimistic concurrency control and will perform an INSERT based on the value of a counter or timestamp.

You grow a SimpleDB database by scaling out and creating additional data domains, and SimpleDB integrates with EC2 instances and S3 storage. Data objects stored in S3 can be queried in SimpleDB, returning information about the objects' metadata and pointers to the objects' location.

Data in SimpleDB is automatically indexed and may be queried as needed. The API is relatively simple, consisting of domain creation, put and get attributes, and SELECT statements. According to Amazon, query performance is near the level you would see for a database on a LAN, as access through a browser. Although a SimpleDB database is replicated and therefore made highly available and fault tolerant, the service lacks many of the speed enhancements available to relational systems. A data domain may be located geographically in any of AWS's regions.

The design goal was to remove as much of the database system maintenance as possible. In a Web services architecture, many applications don't require the performance level of a relational database. Among the featured uses of SimpleDB are data logging, online gaming, and metadata indexing. SimpleDB would not be the best choice for a high-volume transaction system. Data transfers within regions between SimpleDB and other AWS services are free. Service charges accrue based on SimpleDB Machine Hours and inter-regional data transfers.

The three areas of use for SimpleDB that Amazon Web Services highlights are: logging (http://aws.amazon.com/simpledb/usecases_logging/), online gaming (http://aws.amazon.com/simpledb/usecases_online_gaming/), and metadata indexing (http://aws.amazon.com/simpledb/usecases_metadata_indexing/).

Amazon Relational Database Service (RDS)

Amazon Relational Database Service is a variant of the MySQL5.1 database system, but one that is somewhat simplified. The purpose of RDS is to allow database applications that already exist to be ported to RDS and placed in an environment that is relatively automated and easy to use. RDS automatically performs functions such as backups and is deployable throughout AWS zones using the AWS infrastructure.

In RDS, you start by launching a database instance in the AWS Management Console and assigning the DB Instance class and size of the data store. The DB Instance is then connected to your MySQL database. Any database tool that works with MySQL 5.1 will work with RDS. Additionally, you can monitor your database usage as part of Amazon CloudWatch. Table 9.4 shows the different Instance Classes for an Amazon RDS database. Pricing is based on machine hour rates by class, by amount of storage per month, and per million requests.

TABLE 9.4

Amazon Relational Database Service Instance Class

Type1	Compute Engine	RAM (GB)	Platform	Price2
Small DB Instance (default)	1 EC2 Compute Unit (1 virtual core)	1.7	64-bit	$0.11
Large DB Instance	2 EC2 Compute Units (2 virtual cores X 2 EC2 Units)	7.5	64-bit	$0.44
Extra Large DB Instance	8 EC2 Compute Units (4 virtual cores X 2 EC2 Units)	15	64-bit	$0.88
Double Extra Large DB Instance	13 EC2 Compute Units (4 virtual cores X 3.25 EC2 Units)	34	64-bit	$1.55
Quadruple Extra Large DB Instance	26 EC2 Compute Units (8 virtual cores X 3.25 EC2 Units)	68	64-bit	$3.10

1. Storage available is from 5GB to 1TB.

2. Price for U.S. N. Virginia deployment for database machine; storage price is $0.10 per GB-month; and I/O rate price is $0.10 per 1 million requests for the same location. Data transfer rates also apply.

Among the important features of RDS is the automated point-in-time backup system for data in the database as well as for the MySQL transaction logs. Backups can be saved for up to eight days. In addition to backup, RDS supports database snapshots. A DB Snapshot is stored as a full database backup and is retained until you specifically delete it from your storage container. Snapshots may be scheduled or may be manually initiated by an administrator.

The deployment of RDS databases can be spread among multiple availability zones for increased fault tolerance and data availability. These so-called "Multi-AZ Deployments" can be automatically replicated and maintain a standby replica in another availability zone, with automatic failover when a database disruption is detected. The conversion of a single location RDS database to a Multi-DB deployment may be accomplished with a single API call. Other API calls support instance creation and maintenance, snapshots, and restores.

Choosing a database for AWS

In choosing a database solution for your AWS solutions, consider the following factors in making your selection:

- Choose SimpleDB when index and query functions do not require relational database support.
- Use SimpleDB for the lowest administrative overhead.
- Select SimpleDB if you want a solution that autoscales on demand.
- Choose SimpleDB for a solution that has a very high availability.
- Use RDS when you have an existing MySQL database that could be ported and you want to minimize the amount of infrastructure and administrative management required.
- Use RDS when your database queries require relation between data objects.
- Chose RDS when you want a database that scales based on an API call and has a pay-as-you-use-it pricing model.
- Select Amazon EC2/Relational Database AMI when you want access to an enterprise relational database or have an existing investment in that particular application.
- Use Amazon EC2/Relational Database AMI to retain complete administrative control over your database server.

Summary

In this chapter, Amazon Web Services (AWS) were described. AWS is the most successful example of a Service Oriented Architecture (SOA) that provides an Infrastructure as a Service (IaaS) cloud computing solution. With AWS, you can create virtual private servers using the Elastic Cloud Compute (EC2) service, dynamically size your servers and distribute them throughout the world, and create an application infrastructure that allows for very sophisticated and scalable applications.

The process for creating an Amazon Machine Instance (AMI) was described, as was the provisioning of various resources such as storage and databases for those instances. The range of services that AWS supports is wide and includes Content Delivery Networks (CDNs), messaging and notification systems, load balancing and replication, and many other services as well. AWS is among the most important developer platforms for building cloud computing applications, and the range of services and their point of development was described here.

Chapter 10, "Using Microsoft Web Services," describes the range of developer and user tools based in large part on Microsoft proprietary technologies such as .NET Framework, ASP.NET, and the Azure platform. Microsoft's cloud computing effort is considerable and falls midway between the approach taken by Google, which delivers applications that impact users, and Amazon.com, which delivers services that provide cloud computing infrastructure. In short, Amazon Web Services provide something for everyone.

10

Using Microsoft Cloud Services

Microsoft has a very extensive cloud computing portfolio under active development. Efforts to extend Microsoft products and third-party applications into the cloud are centered around adding more capabilities to existing Microsoft tools. Microsoft's approach is to view cloud applications as software plus service. In this model, the cloud is another platform and applications can run locally and access cloud services or run entirely in the cloud and be accessed by browsers using standard Service Oriented Architecture (SOA) protocols.

Microsoft calls their cloud operating system the Windows Azure Platform. You can think of Azure as a combination of virtualized infrastructure to which the .NET Framework has been added as a set of .NET Services. The Windows Azure service itself is a hosted environment of virtual machines enabled by a fabric called Windows Azure AppFabric. You can host your application on Azure and provision it with storage, growing it as you need it. Windows Azure service is an Infrastructure as a Service offering.

A number of services interoperate with Windows Azure, including SQL Azure (a version of SQL Server), SharePoint Services, Azure Dynamic CRM, and many of Windows Live Services comprising what is the Windows Azure Platform, which is a Platform as a Service cloud computing model. Eventually, many more services will be added, encompassing the whole range of Microsoft's offerings. This architecture positions Microsoft to either extend its product into the Web or to license its products, whichever way the cloud computing marketplace develops. From Microsoft's position and that of its developers, Windows Azure has lots of advantages.

Windows Live Services is a collection of applications and services that run on the Web. Some of these applications called Windows Live Essentials are add-ons to Windows and downloadable as applications. Other Windows

Live Services are standalone Web applications viewable in a browser. An important subset of these Windows Live Services is available to Windows Azure applications through the Windows Live Messenger Connect API. A set of Windows Live for Mobile applications also exists. These applications and services are more fully described in this chapter.

Exploring Microsoft Cloud Services

Microsoft CEO Steve Balmer recently said at a University of Washington speech that Microsoft was "betting our company" on the cloud. Balmer also claimed that about 70 percent of Microsoft employees were currently working on cloud-related projects and that the number was expected to rise to about 90 percent within a year. Plans to integrate cloud-based applications and services into the Microsoft product portfolio dominates the thinking at Microsoft and is playing a central role in the company's ongoing product development. The starting place for Microsoft's cloud computing efforts may be found at `Microsoft.com/cloud`, shown in Figure 10.1.

Microsoft has a vast array of cloud computing products and initiatives, and a number of industry-leading Web applications. Although services like America Online Instant Messenger (AIM) may garner mindshare in the United States, surprisingly Microsoft Messenger is the market leader in many other countries. Product by product in any category you can name—calendars, event managers, photo galleries, image editors, movie making, and so on—Microsoft has a Web application for it. Some of these products are also-rans, some are good, some are category leaders, and a few of them are really unique. What is also true is that Web apps are under very active development. Microsoft sees its on-line application portfolio as a way of extending its desktop applications to make the company pervasive and to extend its products' lives well into the future.

Going forward, Microsoft sees its future as providing the best Web experience for any type of device, which means that it structures its development environment so the application alters its behavior depending upon the device. For a mobile device, that would mean adjusting the user interface to accommodate the small screen, while for a PC the Web application would take advantage of the PC hardware to accelerate the application and add richer graphics and other features. That means Microsoft is pushing cloud development in terms of applications serving as both a service and an application. This duality—like light, both a particle and a wave—manifests itself in the way Microsoft is currently structuring its Windows Live Web products. Eventually, the company intends to create a Microsoft app store to sell cloud applications to users.

Microsoft Live is only one part of the Microsoft cloud strategy. The second part of the strategy is the extension of the .NET Framework and related development tools to the cloud. To enable .NET developers to extend their applications into the cloud, or to build .NET style applications that run completely in the cloud, Microsoft has created a set of .NET services, which it now refers to as the Windows Azure Platform. .NET Services itself had as its origin the work Microsoft did to create its BizTalk products.

FIGURE 10.1

Microsoft maintains a home page for cloud computing at `http://www.microsoft.com/cloud`.

Azure and its related services were built to allow developers to extend their applications into the cloud. Azure is a virtualized infrastructure to which a set of additional enterprise services has been layered on top, including:

- A virtualization service called Azure **AppFabric** that creates an application hosting environment. AppFabric (formerly .NET Services) is a cloud-enabled version of the .NET Framework.

- A high capacity non-relational storage facility called Storage.

- A set of virtual machine instances called Compute.

- A cloud-enabled version of SQL Server called SQL Azure Database.

- A database marketplace based on SQL Azure Database code-named "Dallas."

- An xRM (Anything Relations Management) service called Dynamics CRM based on Microsoft Dynamics.

- A document and collaboration service based on SharePoint called SharePoint Services.

- Windows Live Services, a collection of services that runs on Windows Live, which can be used in applications that run in the Azure cloud.

Eventually the entire Microsoft server portfolio will be available as a cloud-based application or service, including Exchange. So the Windows Azure Platform can be viewed in a sense as the next Microsoft operating system, the first one that is a cloud OS. The Microsoft vision for the Windows Azure Platform is shown in Figure 10.2, where the company sees applications developed in Visual Studio or through PHP and other languages deployed to the cloud, existing local (on-premises) applications interacting with Azure with standard SOA protocols (SOAP, REST, and XML), all running on the Windows Azure virtualized infrastructure.

The end result is pervasive computing available to users on the device of their choice. Just how Microsoft intends to integrate all these technologies into a unified offering is the story of this chapter.

FIGURE 10.2

The integrated vision for application development and deployment with Azure is illustrated in this overview page of the Azure platform (`http://www.microsoft.com/windowsazure/products/`).

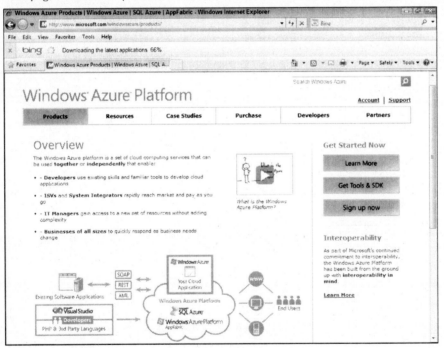

Defining the Windows Azure Platform

Azure is Microsoft's Infrastructure as a Service (IaaS) Web hosting service. Azure is a deep blue color, the color of the clear sky onto which you can paint clouds. Taken together as a unit, Windows Azure Platform becomes a Platform as a Service (PaaS) offering. Hence, you may run into some people calling Azure an infrastructure service and others calling it a platform; in context, both are correct. Compared to Amazon's and Google's cloud services, Azure (the service) is a competitor to AWS. Windows Azure Platform is a competitor to Google's App Engine.

Figure 10.3 shows the home page of the Windows Azure Platform found at `http://www.microsoft.com/windowsazure`.

A developer creates an Azure application by first logging onto the Azure portal from the Sign up now button shown in Figure 10.3, supplying a Windows Live ID, creating a hosted account, and provisioning a storage account. The completed application can then be made available to users as a hosted application or service.

FIGURE 10.3

Window Azure Platform's home page may be found at `http://www.microsoft.com/windowsazure`, and is shown in this figure.

The software plus services approach

Microsoft has a very different vision for cloud services than either Amazon or Google does. In Amazon's case, AWS is a pure infrastructure play. AWS essentially rents you a (virtual) computer on which to run your application. An Amazon Machine Image can be provisioned with an operating system, an enterprise application, or application stack, but that provisioning is not a prerequisite. An AMI is your machine, and you can configure it as you choose. AWS is a deployment enabler.

Google's approach with its Google App Engine (GAE) is to offer a cloud-based development platform on which you can add your program, provided that the program speaks the Google App Engine API and uses objects and properties from the App Engine framework. Google makes it possible to program in a number of languages, but you must write your applications to conform to Google's infrastructure. Google Apps lets you create a saleable cloud-based application, but that application can only work within the Google infrastructure, and the application is not easily ported to other environments.

Microsoft sees the cloud as being a complimentary platform to its other platforms. The company envisages a scenario where a Microsoft developer with an investment in an application wants to extend that application's availability to the cloud. Perhaps the application runs on a server, desktop, or mobile device running some form of Windows. Microsoft calls this approach *software plus services*.

The Windows Azure Platform allows a developer to modify his application so it can run in the cloud on virtual machines hosted in Microsoft datacenters. Windows Azure serves as a cloud operating system, and the suitably modified application can be hosted on Azure as a runtime application where it can make use of the various Azure Services. Additionally, local applications running on a server, desktop, or mobile device can access Windows Azure Services through the Windows Services Platform API.

Given that Microsoft owns the Office application market as well as the desktop OS market, this approach makes lots of sense. It is also quite possible that a hybrid application that can reside either locally or in the cloud will have lots of appeal not only to developers but to users who would prefer more control over their data and more security than the cloud might offer.

The Azure Platform

With Azure's architecture (shown in Figure 10.4), an application can run locally, run in the cloud, or some combination of both. Applications on Azure can be run as applications, as background processes or services, or as both. The Windows Azure service itself is shown as the oval in Figure 10.4 and is a cloud-based operating system with a fabric infrastructure of virtual machines hosted in Microsoft datacenters.

The Azure Windows Services Platform API uses the industry standard REST, HTTP, and XML protocols that are part of any Service Oriented Architecture cloud infrastructure to allow applications to talk to Azure. Developers can install a client-side managed class library that contains functions that can make calls to the Azure Windows Services Platform API as part of their applications. These

API functions have been added to Microsoft Visual Studio as part of Microsoft's Integrated Development Environment (IDE). There are plans to add IPsec connectivity to Azure in the near future. *IPsec* refers to the Internet Protocol Security protocol suite for creating a secure Internet connection between two endpoints. IPsec provides for authenticated communication using session-based negotiation and the exchange of cryptographic keys to enable encrypted communication to be sent and decrypted. IPsec is an IETF standard that is in wide use.

The Azure Service Platform hosts runtime versions of .NET Framework applications written in any of the languages in common use, such as Visual Basic, C++, C#, Java, and any application that has been compiled for .NET's Common Language Runtime (CLR). Azure also can deploy Web-based applications built with ASP.NET, the Windows Communication Foundation (WCF), and PHP, and it supports Microsoft's automated deployment technologies. Microsoft also has released SDKs for both Java and Ruby to allow applications written in those languages to place calls to the Azure Service Platform API to the AppFabric Service.

The Windows Azure service

Windows Azure is a virtualized Windows infrastructure run by Microsoft on a set of datacenters around the world. In Figure 10.4, the dashed oval encloses the portion of the Windows Azure Platform that is Azure itself—that is, the portion of the platform that is the IaaS part, which is shown in more detail in Figure 10.5.

Six main elements are part of Windows Azure:

- **Application:** This is the runtime of the application that is running in the cloud.
- **Compute:** This is the load-balanced Windows server computation and policy engine that allows you to create and manage virtual machines that serve either in a Web role and a Worker role.

  A Web role is a virtual machine instance running Microsoft IIS Web server that can accept and respond to HTTP or HTTPS requests. A Worker role can accept and respond to requests, but doesn't run IIS in that virtual machine. Worker roles can communicate with Azure Storage or through direct connections to clients.

- **Storage:** This is a non-relational storage system for large-scale storage.

  Azure Storage Service lets you create drives, manage queues, and store BLOBs (Binary Large Objects). You manipulate content in Azure Storage using the REST API, which is based on standard HTTP requests and is therefore platform-independent. Stored data can be read using GETs, written with PUTs, modified with POSTs, and removed with DELETE requests.

  Azure Storage plays the same role in Azure that Amazon Simple Storage Service (S3) plays in Amazon Web Services. For relational database services, SQL Azure may be used.

- **Fabric:** This is the Windows Azure Hypervisor, which is a version of Hyper-V that runs on Windows Server 2008.
- **Config:** This is a management service.
- **Virtual machines:** These are instances of Windows that run the applications and services that are part of a particular deployment.

FIGURE 10.4

The Windows Azure Platform extends applications running on other platforms to the cloud using Microsoft infrastructure and a set of enterprise services.

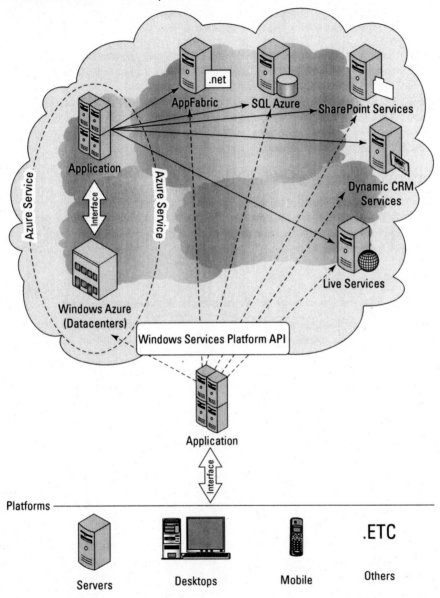

Windows Azure is a virtualized infrastructure that provides configurable virtual machines, independent storage, and a configuration interface.

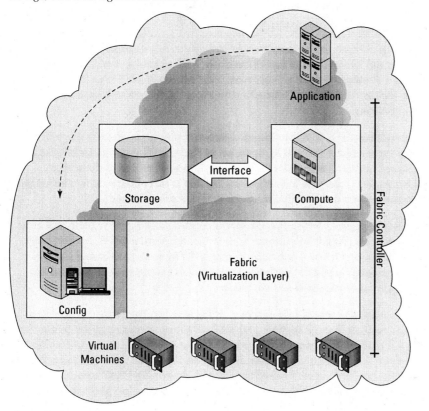

Table 10.1 shows the different Virtual Machine sizes available on Windows Azure.

Windows Azure Virtual Machine Sizes

VM Size1	CPU Cores	Memory (GB)	Disk Space for Local Storage Resources (GB)
Small	1	1.7	250
Medium	2	3.5	500
Large	4	7	1000
ExtraLarge	8	14	2000

1. Microsoft has not released information that would allow you to match VM sizes to physical systems based on real CPUs.

The portion of the Azure environment that creates and manages a virtual resource pool is called the Fabric Controller. Applications that run on Azure are memory-managed, load-balanced, replicated, and backed up through snapshots automatically by the Fabric Controller.

Windows Azure AppFabric

Azure AppFabric (http://msdn.microsoft.com/en-us/windowsazure/netservices.aspx) is a Service Bus and Access Control facility based on .NET technology for client requests to Web services on Azure. Previously, these services were called Microsoft .NET Services. Azure AppFabric supports the standard Service Oriented Architecture (SOA) protocols such as REST and SOAP and the WS- protocols.

The function of a service bus in an SOA is to expose distributed services as an endpoint with a specific URI that clients can request services from, as shown in Figure 10.6. A particular set of endpoints and its associated Access Control rules for an application is referred to as the service namespace. Each namespace is assigned a management key that is part of the security mechanism. The Service Bus service registry makes endpoints discoverable, if so configured.

Azure AppFabric manages requests by locating the service, communicating the request, and making the necessary connection possible by performing network address translation, opening appropriate ports in any intervening firewalls. AppFabric manages the transaction to ensure that it is completed and that a response is sent to the client. A service bus also can serve to negotiate the exchange of information between a client and the service.

Azure AppFabric acts as an SOA service bus, as shown in Figure 10.6. AppFabric can provide a negotiated traversal of services through firewalls and NATs as a relay service using the Service Bus' rendezvous address. A rendezvous address not only includes the service URI, but also includes the namespace of the service bus. Alternatively, if both applications comply to .NET Services a direct connection between the applications can be used instead with the required NAT traversal information for the direct connection provided by the relay service of the Service Bus. NAT (Network Address Traversal) is a system for creating and maintaining Internet connections for TCP or UDP traffic where the connection point is hidden behind a router or a firewall and routing is performed by one of several possible mechanisms.

Cross-Ref

In Chapter 13, "Understanding Service Oriented Architecture," the role of a service bus in a Service Oriented Architecture is more fully explored. ■

The Access Control portion of Azure AppFabric is a claims access control system that provides a token-based trust mechanism for identity management. An application or user, as shown on the right of Figure 10.7, presents a claim for a service from an application on the left. The Access Control examines the request, and if it finds it to be valid, it grants a security token to the client.

FIGURE 10.6

Azure AppFabric service pathways

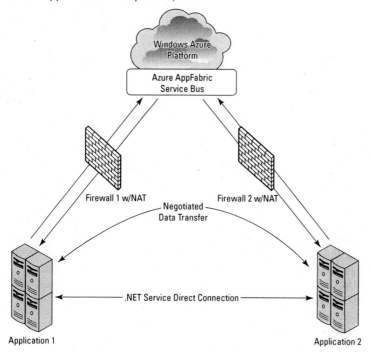

These steps are associated with Access Control:

1. The client requests authentication from Access Control.
2. Access Control creates a token based on the stored rules for server application.
3. A token is signed and returned to the client application.
4. The client presents the token to the service application.
5. The server application verifies the signature and uses the token to decide what the client application is allowed to do.

Access Control allows one application to trust the identity of another application. This mechanism can federate with identity providers such as Active Directory Federation Services (ADFS v2) to create distributed systems based on SOA.

Note

"AppFabric" is also used by Microsoft for the name of its local server deployment technology called Windows Server AppFabric (http://msdn.microsoft.com/en-us/windowsserver/ee695849.aspx). Windows Server AppFabric enables Web data caching for application data and provides managed services using WindowsWorkflow Foundation and the Windows Communication Foundation. There are plans to integrate Windows Server AppFabric into the Azure platform AppFabic. ■

FIGURE 10.7

Azure AppFabric Access Control enables secure application requests through a token mechanism.

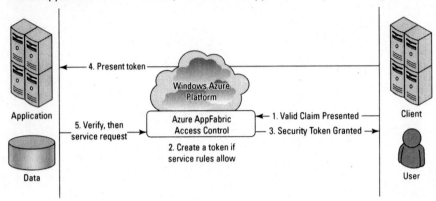

Microsoft likes to refer to the Azure AppFabric as an "Internet Service Bus" to differentiate it from the standard Enterprise Service Bus (ESB) that you find in SOA architectures. AppFabric has all the same components of an ESB, namely service orchestration, federated identity, access control, a namespace, service registry, and a messaging fabric, but it locates these components in the cloud. Often ESBs are located on LANs. According to Microsoft, this approach abstracts away from application developers the challenges related to NAT traversal, DDNS (Dynamic DNS), and UPnP. ESBs are described in Chapter 13; please refer to that chapter for further discussion on this topic.

Azure Content Delivery Network

The Windows Azure Content Delivery Network (CDN) is a worldwide content caching and delivery system for Windows Azure blob content. Currently, more than 18 Microsoft datacenters are hosting this service in Australia, Asia, Europe, South America, and the United States, referred to as endpoints. CDN is an edge network service that lowers latency and maximizes bandwidth by delivering content to users who are nearby.

Any storage account can be enabled for CDN. In order to share information stored in an Azure blob, you need to place the blob in a public blob container that is accessible to anyone using an anonymous sign-in. The Azure portal lists the domain name of the blob container in the form `http://<guid>.vo.msecnd.net/`. You also can register a custom domain name for a Windows Azure CDN endpoint.

For content in a public container named "Box" in the storage account named "MyAccount," a user would access the content with one of the following URLs:

- Windows Azure Blob services URL: `http://<MyAccount>.blob.core.windows.net/<Box>/`
- Windows Azure CDN URL: `http://<guid>.vo.msecnd.net/<Box>/`

When the Blob service URL is used, the request is redirected to the closest CDN endpoint to the client. The CDN service searches that location and serves the content; if the content isn't found, the CDN retrieves the Blob from the Blob service, caches the content, and then serves it to the user. Parameters can be set that determine how long content is cached (Time-To-Live, TTL), with the default being 72 hours.

SQL Azure

SQL Azure is a cloud-based relational database service that is based on Microsoft SQL Server. Initially, this service was called SQL Server Data Service. An application that uses SQL Azure Database can run locally on a server, PC, or mobile device, in a datacenter, or on Windows Azure. Data stored in an SQL Azure database is accessed using the Tabular Data Stream (TDS) protocol, the same protocol used for a local SQL Server database. SQL Azure Database supports Transact-SQL statements.

Azure data is replicated three times for data protection and writes are checked for consistency. SQL Azure eventually will support the Microsoft Sync Framework providing a facility for SQL Azure Databases to synchronize their data with local databases.

There is a current limit of 10GB for each SQL Azure Database. Queries against a single database are unified. However, if the storage size exceeds the limit, then data must be partitioned into logical sets and queries need to be structured to account for this partitioning. For example, names in a database might have to be partitioned A-K, L-R, and S-Z. SQL Azure Database is a shared database environment, and limitations are placed on how long a query can run or how many resources a query can use.

Note

Microsoft hopes to create a cloud-based global data marketplace using SQL Azure for stored information, a project that it has codenamed "Dallas." Applications will then be able to access both private and public domain data such as imagery, census data, statistical data, and other premium content using REST protocols. You can read about Microsoft's plans for Dallas at `http://www.microsoft.com/windowsazure/dallas/.` ■

From the standpoint of any application, an SQL Azure Database looks like and behaves like a local database with a few exceptions. The current exceptions are that the SQL Common Language Runtime (CLR) and support for spatial data were not included, although support will be added later for them. The biggest difference is that because SQL Azure is managed in the cloud, there are no administrative controls over the SQL engine. You can't shut the system down, nor can you directly interact with the SQL Servers.

Windows Azure pricing

Prices for working with the Windows Azure Platform are based either on a "consumption" (pay-as-you-go) model or through various contracts for levels of monthly service that Microsoft calls "commitments." When you exceed the subscription level of your commitment, the additional usage is charged on the consumption model.

Current pricing for Windows Azure is as follows:

- Compute: $0.12 / hour

- Storage: $0.15 / GB stored / month

- Storage transactions: $0.01 / 10K

- Data transfers (excluding CDN): $0.10 in / $0.15 out / GB ($0.30 in / $0.45 out / GB in Asia)

- CDN data transfers: $0.15 GB for North America and Europe ($0.20 GB elsewhere)

- CDN transactions: $0.01 / 10K

  A transaction is an application request.

In the Windows Azure Service Level Agreement, Microsoft states that it guarantees an external connectivity between two or more role instances that are located in different Azure domains of at least 99.95 percent uptime. The connection between storage and Microsoft's Content Delivery Network (CDN, described below) is stated to be at least 99.9 percent uptime.

SQL Azure charges are based on two different programs:

- Web Editions: Up to 1GB database = $9.99 / month; up to 5GB database = $49.95 / month

- Business Edition: Up to 10GB database = $99.99 / month; up to 20GB database = $199.98 / month; up to 30GB database = $299.97 / month; up to 40GB database = $399.96 / month; up to 50GB database = $499.95 / month

- Data transfers: $0.10 in / $0.15 out / GB ($0.30 in / $0.45 out / GB in Asia)

Note

The various consumption and subscription offers for the Windows Azure platform are summarized on the Pricing page at http://www.microsoft.com/windowsazure/pricing/. ■

These are the charges for Windows Azure Platform AppFabric:

- Access Control transactions of $1.99 / 100K transactions

- Service Bus connections: $3.99 per connection on a "pay-as-you-go" basis, $9.95 for a pack of 5 connections, $49.75 for a pack of 25 connections, $199 for a pack of 100 connections, and $995 for a pack of 500 connections

- Data transfers: $0.10 in / $0.15 out / GB ($0.30 in / $0.45 out / GB in Asia)

Given that Windows Azure is a relatively new service and that IaaS likely will become a very competitive market, pricing is sure to change over time. You should definitely check the pricing page for current pricing if you are thinking of deploying on Azure.

Microsoft offers a TCO calculator for the Windows Azure Platform that you may find useful in determining your costs and savings. To access the calculator use the following link: http://www.microsoft.com/windowsazure/economics/#tcoCompare-LB. The calculator was described in brief in Chapter 2, "Computing the Total Cost of Ownership."

Windows Live services

Windows Live is a collection of cloud-based applications and services, some of which can be used inside applications that run on Windows Azure Platform. Some Windows Live applications run as standalone applications and are available to users directly through a browser. Others are services that add capabilities to the Windows Azure Platform as part of Microsoft's software plus services strategy.

Microsoft has rolled out Windows Live in sets of releases they describe as four waves. The first wave was a rebranding of several Microsoft MSN applications and services in late 2005. More applications including Windows Mail, Windows Photo Gallery, and Windows Movie Maker were unbundled from Vista and rolled into a downloadable software suite called Windows Live Essentials. There has been continuous development, branding, marketing, and rebranding of the Windows Live portfolio that has had many people scratching their heads. Many Windows Live applications have been rolled into other services or discontinued entirely.

Here's what I believe the current situation is with Windows Live. If an application is bundled as part of an additional download for desktop users, it is part of the Windows Live Essentials package. Some applications that are part of Windows Live are standalone products, while others are extensions of existing Microsoft commercial software. An example of a standalone product would be Windows Live Calendar. An example of a cloud-based line extension is Windows Live Office, described more fully in Chapter 16.

Some parts of the Windows Live portfolio are shared applications and services that are accessible to developers, and those services are the Windows Live Services that are one component of the Windows Azure Platform. Developers access the services for Windows Live Services through a collection of APIs and controls called Windows Live Messenger Connect (previously called Live Services and Windows Live Dev). Using these APIs and controls, developers can add Windows Live Services capabilities and data to their application.

Note

To learn more about Windows Live Messenger Connect, visit the MSDN site's documentation found at
http://msdn.microsoft.com/en-us/library/ff749458.aspx. ■

Messenger Connect was released as part of the Windows Live Wave 4 at the end of June 2010, and it unites APIs such as Windows Live ID, Windows Live Contacts, and Windows Live Messenger Web Toolkit into a single API. Messenger Connect works with ASP.NET, Windows Presentation Foundation (WPF), Java, Adobe Flash, PHP, and Microsoft's Silverlight graphics rendering technology through four different methods:

- Messenger Connect REST API Service
- Messenger Connect .NET and Silverlight Libraries
- Messenger Connection JavaScript Libraries and Controls
- Web activity feeds, either RSS 2.0 or ATOM

Table 10.2 lists the current services that can be used by Windows Live Messenger Connect in applications and Web sites.

TABLE 10.2

Windows Live Services

Service Name	URL	Microsoft Description
Admin Center	Windows Live Admin Center SDK	A management utility for a domain using SOAP and RPC.
Alerts	Windows Live Alerts for RSS Feeds	Enables Windows Live Alerts from an RSS feed.
Alerts	Windows Live Alerts SDK	Allows developers to add Windows Live Alerts notification service to an application using SOAP.
Contacts	Windows Live Contacts API	Allows developers to use REST to query the Windows Live People Address Book, as well as to adjust permission to contact data based on the Windows Live ID Delegated Authentication protocol.
FeedSync	FeedSync	Synchronizes information obtained from RSS and ATOM sources.
Live Framework	Live Framework SDK	An API for building Live Mesh application based on Windows Live Services.
Live Framework	Live Framework Tools for Visual Studio	Includes the Live Mesh tools from Visual Studio 2008 and Visual Web Developer Express Edition 2008.
Messenger	Web Toolkit	UI controls for building Web applications using Windows Live Messenger.
Messenger	IM Control	A set of controls that can enable instant messaging in an application.
Messenger	Presence API	An API that can be used to indicate a Windows Live Messenger's presence and control instant messages to that person's browser using a set of HTTP commands.
Photo Gallery	Windows Live Photo Gallery SDK	Allows for the creation and editing of photos and videos using the Publishing Plug-in Platform of Windows Live Photo Gallery inside applications.
Spaces	Windows Live Spaces MetaWeblog API	An API that can use XML-RPC calls to get and send Weblog data.
Spaces	Windows Live Spaces API and Feeds	An API that integrates Windows Live Spaces, Windows Live Events, Windows Live Photos, and Windows Live Profile into applications.
Web Gadgets	Gadgets SDK	Lightweight, single-purpose applets that can run on Windows Live Personalized Experience and Windows Live Spaces.

Service Name	URL	Microsoft Description
Windows Live ID	Web Authentication	Used to integrate Windows Live ID authentication into a Web site.
Windows Live ID	Delegated Authentication	Allows an application to access data for an authenticated Windows Live ID user from Web services and sites that accept that authentication.
Windows Live ID	Client Authentication	An API for Windows Live ID sign-in from a desktop application.
Writer	Windows Live Writer SDK	Allows applications to incorporate the features of the Windows Live Writer in their application. Additional capabilities include features for creating and managing blogs, adding more content, and customizing the Windows Live Writer user interface.

Reference: Based on `http://en.wikipedia.org/wiki/Windows_Live_Messenger_Connect`. An API for Bing and the toolbar is also available as a service.

Using Windows Live

Windows Live includes several popular cloud-based services. The two best known and most widely used are Windows Live Hotmail and Windows Live Messenger, with more than 300 million users worldwide. Windows Live is based around five core services:

- E-mail
- Instant Messaging
- Photos
- Social Networking
- Online Storage

A user or application can consume Windows Live in a number of ways. Some Windows Live applications are entirely cloud-based Web services, so users can use these applications from within any browser. The Office Live applications described more fully in Chapter 16, "Microsoft Office Web Apps," is an example of this sort of service. Some of these services are aimed at mobile devices and are referred to as Windows Live for Mobile (described below), and they are consumed on conforming mobile devices. Some of these applications are client-side applications that you download from Windows Live for use on your desktop, of which Windows Live Essentials is the primary example.

You can access Windows Live services in one of the following ways:

- By navigating to the service from the command on the navigation bar at the top of Windows Live
- By directly entering the URL of the service
- By selecting the application from the Windows Live Essentials folder on the Start menu

If you haven't signed into Windows Live during your session, Windows Live requests that you do so before allowing you to proceed.

Table 10.3 lists the current offerings of Windows Live Services.

TABLE 10.3

Windows Live Services Offerings

Service Name	URL	Description
Windows Live Account	`http://account.live.com/`	Management service for Windows Live ID and relationships.
Windows Live Admin Center	`http://admin.live.com/`	E-mail hosting for Web site owners.
Windows Live Alerts	`http://alerts.live.com/`	Generates alerts sent to e-mail, mobile device, or Windows Messenger.
Windows Live Calendar	`http://calendar.live.com/`	Calendar service with appointments, meetings, and events; can be shared with others.
Windows Live Contacts	`http://contacts.live.com/`	Address book service with synchronization feature.
Windows Live Devices	`http://devices.live.com/`	Synchronization and remote access service for files stored on PCs and mobile devices.
Windows Live Essentials	`http://essentials.live.com/`	Downloadable applications that supplement Microsoft Windows.
Windows Live Family Safety	`http://fss.live.com/`	Allows you to manage and monitor your children's Internet activity so they can surf the Web more safely.
Windows Live Frameit	`http://frameit.live.com/`	Adds an RSS feed to digital photo frame devices.
Windows Live Gallery	`http://gallery.live.com/`	A collection of developer add-ons for Windows Live products.
Windows Live Groups	`http://groups.live.com/`	A group discussion, collaboration, sharing, and coordination tool.
Windows Live Home	`http://home.live.com/`	A personalization Web page and tool for Windows Live with status information and navigation features.
Windows Live Hotmail	`http://hotmail.com/`	A Web-based free e-mail service with contacts and calendar.
Windows Live ID	`http://login.live.com/`	A sign-on service shared by Windows Live applications.

Service Name	URL	Description
Windows Live Mail	http://mail.live.com	Desktop e-mail client with RSS; replaces Outlook Express and Windows Mail. You can use Live Mail to manage Gmail or Yahoo! Plus Mail accounts, as well as your POP e-mail services.
Windows Live Messenger	http://messenger.live.com/	Allows you to chat instantly with friends and family on your desktop, on the Web, and on your mobile phone.
Windows Live Messenger Companion	http://essentials.live.com/	Windows Live Essentials add-on for Internet Explorer; shares link to a page on the site you're visiting. You can see the page and add a comment.
Windows Live Movie Maker	http://essentials.live.com/	Allows you to create beautiful, memorable movies and then publish to the Web in a few clicks.
Windows Live Office	http://office.live.com/	Contains document creation and editing tools based on Office, Excel, PowerPoint, and OneNote with Windows Live SkyDrive storage.
Windows Live OneCare Safety Scanner	http://safety.live.com/	Consists of a PC scanner for viruses, spyware, and other malware. Features include disk cleaner, defragmenter, port scanner, and registry cleaner.
Windows Live Photo Gallery	http://photogallery.live.com/	Allows you to edit, organize, tag, and share your photos.
Windows Live Photos	http://photos.live.com/	Photo storage and sharing service. You can use the service to publish photos to third-party photo services.
Windows Live Profile	http://profile.live.com/	Profile information management service for user information.
Windows Live SkyDrive	http://skydrive.live.com/	Online file storage system service.
Windows Live Spaces	http://spaces.live.com/	Social networking, blogging, and photo-sharing site.
Windows Live Sync	http://sync.live.com/	File synchronization and sharing site based on Live Mesh; originally called folder share.
Windows Live Writer	http://writer.live.com/	Allows you to compose a blog post, add your photos and links to your videos, and then publish to the Web. You can post the blogs from Writer to Blogger, WordPress, and other services.

The following Windows Live services have been discontinued or rebranded:

- Windows Live Agent
- Windows Live Barcode
- Windows Live Call (now part of Windows Live Messenger)
- Windows Live Events
- Windows Live Expo
- Windows Live Favorites (now Part of Windows Live SkyDrive)
- Windows Live Help Community
- Windows Live Hotspot Locator (now MSN WiFi Hotspots)
- Windows Live OneCare (now Microsoft Security Essentials)
- Windows Live Personalized Experience
- Windows Live QnA (now MSN QnA)
- Windows Live Search Center (now Windows Search 4)
- Windows Live Shopping (now Bing Shopping)
- Windows Live Toolbar
- Windows Live TV
- Windows Live Video Messages
- Windows Live Web Messenger (now part of Windows Live Web services)
- Windows Live WiFi Center

Windows Live Essentials

Windows Live Essentials applications are a collection of client-side applications that must be downloaded and installed on a desktop. Some of these applications were once part of Windows and have been unbundled from the operating system; others are entirely new. Live Essentials rely on cloud-based services for their data storage and retrieval, and in some cases for their processing.

Windows Live Essentials currently includes the following:

- Family Safety
- Windows Live Messenger
- Photo Gallery
- Mail
- Movie Maker

The download page for Windows Live Essentials (`http://essentials.live.com/`) is shown in Figure 10.8. All the Windows Essentials are downloaded as a single file. This page also has links to download related software such as the Bing bar (which replaces the Windows Live Toolbar), Microsoft Office Outlook Connection, Office Live Add-in, and Microsoft Silverlight. When you install Windows Live Essentials, shortcuts for these programs are placed on the Windows Start menu.

Windows Live Essentials help alleviate a long-standing problem of Microsoft with Windows by allowing Microsoft to unbundle some of its add-on applications for the operating system so they don't compete with other vendors' products unfairly. Live Essentials moves these applications partially onto the cloud, while making them available easily as a download and a service. Shown in Figure 10.9 is Windows Live Family Safety, which is a Web filter and activity reporting tool for Windows accounts on a per-machine basis.

FIGURE 10.8

The Windows Live Essentials home page (`http://essentials.live.com/`) provides links to the downloads of Microsoft's cloud-based client-side applications, the application's own page, as well as links to download related software.

FIGURE 10.9

Windows Live Essentials is available from the Start menu as a set of commands.

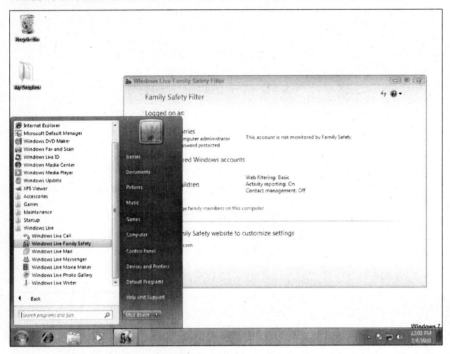

Windows Live Home

Windows Live Home is the central access page or portal for the Windows Live suite. An example is shown in Figure 10.10. The page provides navigation, lists activities, provides access to e-mail, shows your RSS feeds, and lists your account name and some related information. What you see on this page is customizable and depends on the services to which you are subscribed. The page can be themed, which changes the color, fonts, and look of the page.

These are the most commonly used features on Windows Live Home:

- Launching other Windows Live services
- Viewing e-mail headers from Hotmail and private messages from other users
- Viewing activity of people you follow
- Displaying weather information and RSS feed updates
- Managing calendars and events
- Viewing photos
- Modifying profile and relationships

Your personalized home page for Windows Live (`http://live.microsoft.com/home`) contains content and ads.

Windows Live for Mobile

Microsoft has a number of Windows Live services that are specifically meant to be run on mobile devices or cell phones that it calls Windows Live for Mobile (`http://mobile.live.com`). Some of these services run on the Windows Mobile platform, some are Web-based applications that conform to the lightweight Wireless Application Protocol (WAP) or on GPRS (General Packet Radio Service) browser, and some support SMS (Simple Message Service) systems. The current list of these services includes the following:

- Live Mesh Mobile
- Windows Live Calendar Mobile
- Windows Live Contacts Mobile
- Windows Live Groups Mobile
- Windows Live Home Mobile
- Windows Live Messenger Mobile

- Windows Live Office Mobile
- Windows Live Profile Mobile
- Windows Live SkyDrive Mobile
- Windows Live Spaces Mobile

To download these client applications on supported devices, go to `http://gowindowslive.com/mobile` and select the download.

Summary

In this chapter, I described Microsoft cloud computing strategy. Microsoft seeks to extend its products into the cloud using a software plus service approach. In this model, the cloud is yet another platform, and applications can run locally and access cloud services, run in the cloud and be made available through SOA standard protocols, or some combination of both.

Microsoft's cloud operating system is called Windows Azure. Windows Azure is a hosted environment of virtualized systems tied together in a fabric using a service called AppFabric. This is offered to developers in the form of an Infrastructure as a Service model similar to Amazon Web Services. To Windows Azure is added a cloud-enabled version of the .NET Framework originally called .NET Services, which are now part of Azure AppFabric. This approach lets developers extend their applications into the cloud using development tools that they already possess with the minimum amount of reconfiguration. Microsoft has added a number of additional services and the entire offering is now a Platform as a Service cloud model that Microsoft calls the Windows Azure Platform.

The other major component of Microsoft's cloud computing strategy is a collection of user applications and related services called Windows Live. Some Windows Live applications are client-side applications, many others are Web-based applications, some are mobile apps, and an important subset of these services is available to developers through the Windows Live Messenger Connect APIs. The various offering in Windows Live were discussed in this chapter.

In Chapter 11, "Managing the Cloud," you learn about some of the management tools used to work with cloud applications and methods used for application deployment.

Part III

Exploring Cloud Infrastructures

Managing the Cloud

Cloud computing deployments must be monitored and managed in order to be optimized for best performance. To the problems associated with analyzing distributed network applications, the cloud adds the complexity of virtual infrastructure. This is one of the most active areas of product development in the entire cloud computing industry, and this chapter introduces you to the different products in this nascent area.

Cloud management software provides capabilities for managing faults, configuration, accounting, performance, and security; this is referred to as FCAPS. Many products address one or more of these areas, and through network frameworks, you can access all five areas. Framework products are being repositioned to work with cloud systems.

Your management responsibilities depend on the particular service model for your cloud deployment. Cloud management includes not only managing resources in the cloud, but managing resources on-premises. The management of resources in the cloud requires new technology, but management of resources on-premises allows vendors to use well-established network management technologies.

The lifecycle of a cloud application includes six defined parts, and each must be managed. In this chapter, the tasks associated with each stage are described.

Efforts are underway to develop cloud management interoperability standards. One effort you learn about in this chapter is the DMTF's (Distributed Management Task Force) Open Cloud Standards Incubator. The goal of these efforts is to develop management tools that work with any cloud type. Another group called the Cloud Commons is developing a technology called the Service Measurement Index (SMI). SMI aims to deploy methods for measuring various aspects of cloud performance in a standard way.

IN THIS CHAPTER

Learning about network management software

Viewing the essential monitoring features

Using lifecycle management techniques

Discovering emerging network management interoperability standards

Administrating the Clouds

The explosive growth in cloud computing services has led many vendors to rename their products and reposition them to get in on the gold rush in the clouds. What was once a network management product is now a cloud management product. Nevertheless, this is one area of technology that is very actively funded, comes replete with interesting startups, has been the focus of several recent strategic acquisitions, and has resulted in some interesting product alliances. Let's join the party and see what all the fuss is about.

These fundamental features are offered by traditional network management systems:

- Administration of resources
- Configuring resources
- Enforcing security
- Monitoring operations
- Optimizing performance
- Policy management
- Performing maintenance
- Provisioning of resources

Network management systems are often described in terms of the acronym FCAPS, which stands for these features:

- Fault
- Configuration
- Accounting
- Performance
- Security

Most network management packages have one or more of these characteristics; no single package provides all five elements of FCAPS.

To get the complete set of all five of these management areas from a single vendor, you would need to adopt a network management framework. These large network management frameworks were industry leaders several years back: BMC PATROL, CA Unicenter, IBM Tivoli, HP OpenView, and Microsoft System Center. Network framework products have been sliced and diced in many different ways over the years, and they are rebranded from time to time. Today, for example, BMC PATROL is now part of BMC ProactiveNet Performance Management (`http://www.bmc.com/products/product-listing/ProactiveNet-Performance-Management.html`), HP OpenView has been split (`https://h10078.www1.hp.com/cda/hpms/display/main/hpms_content.jsp?zn=bto&cp=1-10^36657_4000_100`) into a set of HP Manager products.

The impact that cloud computing is having on network frameworks is profound. These five vendors have (or soon will have) products for cloud management. Computer Associates, for example, has completely repositioned its network management portfolio as an IT Management Software as a Service. Find the cloud products for these five large cloud vendors at the following URLs:

- BMC Cloud Computing (`http://www.bmc.com/solutions/esm-initiative/cloud-computing.html`)

- Computer Associates Cloud Solutions (`http://www.ca.com/us/cloud-computing.aspx`)

- HP Cloud Computing (`http://h20338.www2.hp.com/enterprise/w1/en/technologies/cloud-computing-overview.html`)

- IBM Cloud Computing (`http://www.ibm.com/ibm/cloud/`)

- Microsoft Cloud Services (`http://www.microsoft.com/cloud/`)

Figure 11.1 shows IBM Tivoli Service Automation Manager, a framework tool for managing cloud infrastructure.

FIGURE 11.1

Tivoli Service Automation Manager lets you create and stage cloud-based servers.

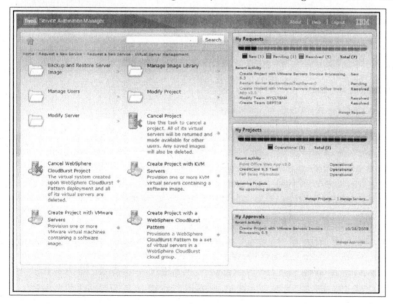

Management responsibilities

What separates a network management package from a cloud computing management package is the "cloudly" characteristics that cloud management service must have:

- Billing is on a pay-as-you-go basis.
- The management service is extremely scalable.
- The management service is ubiquitous.
- Communication between the cloud and other systems uses cloud networking standards.

To monitor an entire cloud computing deployment stack, you monitor six different categories:

1. End-user services such as HTTP, TCP, POP3/SMTP, and others
2. Browser performance on the client
3. Application monitoring in the cloud, such as Apache, MySQL, and so on
4. Cloud infrastructure monitoring of services such as Amazon Web Services, GoGrid, Rackspace, and others
5. Machine instance monitoring where the service measures processor utilization, memory usage, disk consumption, queue lengths, and other important parameters
6. Network monitoring and discovery using standard protocols like the Simple Network Management Protocol (SNMP), Configuration Management Database (CMDB), Windows Management Instrumentation (WMI), and the like

It's important to note that there are really two aspects to cloud management:

Managing resources *in the cloud*

Using the cloud to manage resources *on-premises*

When you move to a cloud computing architecture from a traditional networked model like client/ server or a three-tier architecture, many of the old management tasks for processes going on in the cloud become irrelevant or nearly impossible to manage because the tools to effectively manage resources of various kinds fall outside of your own purview. In the cloud, the particular service model you are using directly affects the type of monitoring you are responsible for.

Consider the case of an Infrastructure as a Service vendor such as Amazon Web Services or Rackspace. You can monitor your usage of resources either through their native monitoring tools like Amazon CloudWatch or Rackspace Control Panel or through the numerous third-party tools that work with these sites' APIs. In IaaS, you can alter aspects of your deployment, such as the number of machine instances you are running or the amount of storage you have, but you have very limited control over many important aspects of the operation. For example, your network bandwidth is locked into the type of instance you deploy. Even if you can provision more bandwidth, you likely have no control over how network traffic flows into and out of the system, whether there is packet prioritization, how routing is done, and other important characteristics.

The situation—as you move first to Platform as a Service (PaaS) like Windows Azure or Google App Engine and then onto Software as a Service (SaaS) for which Salesforce.com is a prime example—becomes even more restrictive. When you deploy an application on Google's PaaS App Engine cloud service, the Administration Console provides you with the following monitoring capabilities:

- Create a new application, and set it up in your domain.
- Invite other people to be part of developing your application.
- View data and error logs.
- Analyze your network traffic.
- Browse the application datastore, and manage its indexes.
- View the application's scheduled tasks.
- Test the application, and swap out versions.

However, you have almost no operational control. Essentially, Google App Engine lets you deploy the application and monitor it, and that's about it. All the management of devices, networks, and other aspects of the platform are managed by Google. You have even less control when you are selling software in the cloud, as you would with Salesforce.com.

Figure 11.2 graphically summarizes the management responsibilities by service model type.

The second aspect of cloud management is the role that cloud-based services can play in managing on-premises resources. From the standpoint of the client, a cloud service provider is no different than any other networked service. The full range of network management capabilities may be brought to bear to solve mobile, desktop, and local server issues, and the same sets of tools can be used for measurement.

Microsoft System Center is an example of how management products are being adapted for the cloud. System Center provides tools for managing Windows servers and desktops. The management services include an Operations Manager, the Windows Service Update Service (WSUS), a Configuration Manager for asset management, a Data Protection Manager, and a Virtual Machine Manager, among other components.

One of these service sets was called the System Center Online Desktop Manager (SCODM). Microsoft has taken SCODM and repositioned it as a cloud-based service for managing updates, monitoring PCs for license compliance and health, enforcing security policies, and using Forefront protect systems from malware, and the company has branded it as Windows Intune (`http://www.microsoft.com/windows/windowsintune/default.aspx`). From the client's standpoint, it makes little difference whether the service is in the cloud or on a set of servers in a datacenter. The benefit of a cloud management service accrues to the organization responsible for managing the desktops or mobile devices. Figure 11.3 shows an Overview screen from the beta version of Windows Intune. The product is due to be released in the first or second quarter of 2011.

FIGURE 11.2

Management responsibilities by service model type

	Hosted	Managed services	Cloud (IaaS)	Cloud (PaaS)	SaaS
Example(s)	Hosted infrastructure	Network VoIP	Amazon AWS, Rackspace Cloud server	Google App Engine Microsoft Azure	Salesforce.com
IT primary responsibilities					
Provider primary responsibilities		Varies by business agreement			
Shared responsibilities					

Business service/user satisfaction — Application — Database — Server — Operating system — Network

FIGURE 11.3

Intune is Microsoft's cloud-based management service for Windows systems.

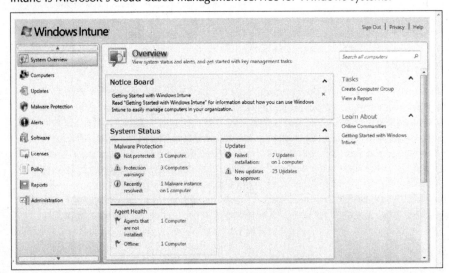

Lifecycle management

Cloud services have a defined lifecycle, just like any other system deployment. A management program has to touch on each of the six different stages in that lifecycle:

1. The definition of the service as a template for creating instances

   Tasks performed in Phase 1 include the creation, updating, and deletion of service templates.

2. Client interactions with the service, usually through an SLA (Service Level Agreement) contract

   This phase manages client relationships and creates and manages service contracts.

3. The deployment of an instance to the cloud and the runtime management of instances

   Tasks performed in Phase 3 include the creation, updating, and deletion of service offerings.

4. The definition of the attributes of the service while in operation and performance of modifications of its properties

   The chief task during this management phase is to perform service optimization and customization.

5. Management of the operation of instances and routine maintenance

   During Phase 5, you must monitor resources, track and respond to events, and perform reporting and billing functions.

6. Retirement of the service

   End of life tasks include data protection and system migration, archiving, and service contract termination.

Cloud Management Products

Cloud management software and services is a very young industry, and as such, it has a very large number of companies, some with new products and others with older products competing in this area. Table 11.1 shows some of the current players in this market, along with the products they either are offering or are promising in the very near future. When considering products in cloud management, you should be aware that—as in all new areas of technology—there is considerable churn as companies grow, get acquired, or fail along the way. It is entirely possible that if you return to this list a year or two after this book is published, half of these products or services will no longer exist as listed; you should keep this in mind.

TABLE 11.1

Cloud and Web Monitoring Solutions

Product	URL	Description
AbiCloud	`http://www.abiquo.com/`	Virtual machine conversion and management
Amazon CloudWatch	`http://aws.amazon.com/cloudwatch/`	AWS dashboard
BMC Cloud Computing Initiative	`http://www.bmc.com/solutions/esm-initiative/cloud-computing.html`	Cloud planning, lifecycle management, optimization, and guidance
CA Cloud Connected Management Suite	`http://www.ca.com/us/cloud-solutions.aspx`	CA Cloud Insight, CA Cloud Compose, CA Cloud Optimize, and CA Cloud Orchestrate are described below
Cacti	`http://www.cacti.net/`	Network performance graphing solution
CloudKick	`https://www.cloudkick.com/`	Cloud server monitoring
Dell Scalent	`http://www.scalent.com/index.php`	Virtualization provisioning system that will be rolled into Dell's Advanced Infrastructure Manager (AIM)
Elastra	`http://www.elastra.com/`	Federated hybrid cloud management software
Ganglia	`http://ganglia.info/`	Distributed network monitoring software
Gomez	`http://www.gomez.com/`	Web site monitoring and analytics
HP Cloud Computing	`http://h20338.www2.hp.com/enterprise/w1/en/technologies/cloud-computing-overview.html`	A variety of management products and services, both released and under development
Hyperic	`http://www.hyperic.com/`	Performance management for virtualized Java Apps with VMware integration
IBM Service Management and Cloud Computing	`http://www-01.ibm.com/software/tivoli/solutions/cloudcomputing/`	Various IBM Tivoli managers and monitors
Internetseer	`http://www.internetseer.com/home/index.xtp`	Web site monitoring service
Intune	`http://www.microsoft.com/windows/windowsintune/default.aspx`	Cloud-based Windows system management
Keynote	`http://www.keynote.com/`	Web, mobile, streaming, and customer test and measurement products

Product	URL	Description
ManageEngine OpManager	http://www.manageengine.com/network-performance-management.html	Network and server monitoring, server desk, event and security management
ManageIQ	http://www.manageiq.com/	Enterprise Virtualization Management Suite (EVM) that provides monitoring, provisioning, and cloud integration services
Managed Methods JaxView	http://managedmethods.com/	SOA management tool
Monit	http://mmonit.com/monit/	Unix system monitoring and management
Montis	http://portal.monitis.com/index.php/home	Cloud-based monitoring service
Morph	http://mor.ph/	Infrastructure management, provisioning, deployment, and monitoring tools
Nagios	http://www.nagios.org/	Network monitoring system
NetIQ	http://www.netiq.com/	Network management, monitoring, deployment, and security software
New Relic RPM	http://www.newrelic.com/	Java and Ruby application monitor and troubleshooting
Nimsoft	http://www.ca.com/us/products/detail/CA-Nimsoft-Monitoring-Solution.aspx	Cloud monitoring software
OpenQRM	http://www.openqrm.com/	Data center management platform
Pareto Networks	http://www.paretonetworks.com/	Cloud provisioning and deployment
Pingdom	http://www.pingdom.com/	Web site and server uptime and performing monitoring
RightScale	http://www.rightscale.com/	Automated virtual server scaling
ScienceLogic	http://www.sciencelogic.com/	Datacenter and cloud management solutions and appliances
Scout	http://scoutapp.com/	Hosted server management service
ServiceUptime	http://www.serviceuptime.com/	Web site monitoring service
Site24X7	http://site24x7.com/	Web site monitoring service
Solarwinds	http://www.solarwinds.com/	Network monitoring and management software

continued

TABLE 11.1 *(continued)*

Product	URL	Description
Tapinsystems	`http://www.tapinsystems.com/home`	Provisioning and management service
Univa UD	`http://univaud.com/index.php`	Application and infrastructure management software for hybrid multi-clouds
VMware Hyperic	`http://www.springsource.com/`	Performance management for VMware deployed Java applications
Webmetrics	`http://www.webmetrics.com/`	Web performance management, load testing, and application monitor for cloud services
WebSitePulse	`http://www.websitepulse.com/`	Server, Web site, and application monitoring service
Whatsup Gold	`http://www.whatsupgold.com/`	Network monitoring and management software
Zenoss	`http://www.zenoss.com/`	IT operations monitoring
Zeus	`http://www.zeus.com/`	Web-based application traffic manager

The core management features offered by most cloud management service products include the following:

- Support of different cloud types
- Creation and provisioning of different types of cloud resources, such as machine instances, storage, or staged applications
- Performance reporting including availability and uptime, response time, resource quota usage, and other characteristics
- The creation of dashboards that can be customized for a particular client's needs

Automated deployment on IaaS systems represents one class of cloud management services. One of the more interesting and successful vendors in this area is Rightscale (`http://www.right scale.com/`) whose software allows clients to stage and manage applications on AWS (Amazon Web Service), Eucalyptus, Rackspace, and the Chef Multicloud framework or a combination of these cloud types. Rightscale creates cloud-ready server templates and provides the automation and orchestration necessary to deploy them. Eucalyptus and Rackspace both use Amazon EC2 and S3 services, although Eucalyptus is open source and portable. RightScale server templates and the Rightscript technology are highly configurable and can be run under batch control. The RightScale user interface also provides real-time measurements of individual server instances.

Cloudkick (`https://www.cloudkick.com/`) is another infrastructure monitoring solution that is well regarded. Its service is noted for being agnostic and working with multiple vendor cloud platforms. The Cloudkick user interface is designed for rapid deployment assessment, and its at-a-glance-monitoring Insight module is particularly easy to use. Figure 11.4 shows the Insight module, and Figure 11.5 shows Cloudkick's real-time server visualization tool, which is one of the more interesting presentation tools we've seen. In Figure 11.5, the circles are servers with their location on the different axes based on observed metrics. Powerful servers are larger circles, and the colors indicate the current state of the server.

Users have commented on Cloudkick's instant launching being difficult, and both Cloudkick and RightScale are known to be easy to use with Linux virtual servers and less so with Windows instances.

FIGURE 11.4

Cloudkick's Insight module (`https://www.cloudkick.com/site_media/images/graphs2.png`) is powerful and particularly easy to use.

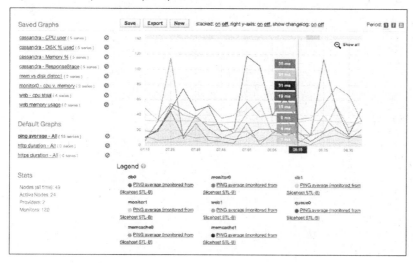

All of the service models support monitoring solutions, most often through interaction with the service API. Tapping into a service API allows management software to perform command actions that a user would normally perform. Some of these APIs are themselves scriptable, while in some cases, scripting is supported in the management software.

One key differentiator in monitoring and management software is whether the service needs to install an agent or it performs its service without an agent. The monitoring function normally can be performed through direct interaction with a cloud service or client using processes such as an HTTP GET or a network command like PING. For management functions, an agent is helpful in that it can provide needed hooks to manipulate a cloud resource. Agents also, as a general rule, are useful in helping to solve problems associated with firewall NAT traversal.

ManageIQ (`http://www.manageiq.com/`) and Service-now.com offer an integrated cloud stack that combines the ManageIQ Enterprise Virtualization Management Suite with Service-Now.com's ITSM SaaS service. The system has offers management, discovery, CMDB synchronization, and automated provisioning services. You can integrate these services into your Web applications using an open API that these companies offer.

The Cloudkick visualization demo (`https://www.cloudkick.com/viz/demo/`) provides a real-time graphical illustration of the state of monitored servers.

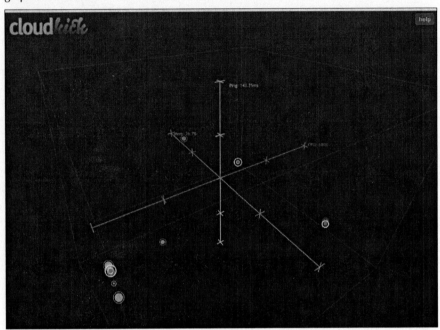

Distributed network applications often benefit from the deployment of a management appliance. Because cloud services tend to distribute applications across multiple sites, physical appliances need to be deployed in different locations—something that only cloud service providers can do. However, there has been a tendency to create virtual appliances, and those can be deployed as server instances wherever an application is deployed. Pareto Networks (`http://www.pareto networks.com/`) has a cloud computing service that can monitor and manage distributed network services using a physical or virtual appliance. The system can be used to control and provision network services. Pareto Networks plans to add an API to this service.

Emerging Cloud Management Standards

As it stands now, different cloud service providers use different technologies for creating and managing cloud resources. As the area matures, cloud providers are going to be under considerable pressure from large cloud users like the federal government to conform to standards and make their systems interoperable with one another. No entity is likely to want to make a major investment in a service that is a silo or from which data is difficult to stage or to extract. To this end, a number of large industry players such as VMware, IBM, Microsoft, Citrix, and HP have gotten together to create standards that can be used to promote cloud interoperability. In the section that follows, you learn about the work of the DMTF in this area.

Another effort just getting underway has been started by CA (the company formerly known as Computer Associates) in association with Carnegie Mellon called the Cloud Commons. This effort is aimed at creating an industry community and working group, and promoting a set of monitoring standards that were part of CA's cloud technology portfolio but are now open sourced.

DMTF cloud management standards

The Distributed Management Task Force (DMTF; see http://www.dmtf.org/) is an industry organization that develops industry system management standards for platform interoperability. Its membership is a "who's who" in computing, and since its founding in 1992, the group has been responsible for several industry standards, most notably the Common Information Model (CIM). The DMTF organizes itself into a set of working groups that are tasked with specifying standards for different areas of technology.

A recent standard called the Virtualization Management Initiative (VMAN) was developed to extend CIM to virtual computer system management. VMAN has resulted in the creation of the Open Virtualization Format (OVF), which describes a standard method for creating, packaging, and provisioning virtual appliances. OVF is essentially a container and a file format that is open and both hypervisor- and processor-architecture-agnostic. Since OVF was announced in 2009, vendors such as VirtualBox, AbiCloud, IBM, Red Hat, and VMWare have announced or introduced products that use OVF.

It was, therefore, a natural extension of the work that DMTF does in virtualization to solve management issues in cloud computing. DMTF has created a working group called the Open Cloud Standards Incubator (OCSI) to help develop interoperability standards for managing interactions between and in public, private, and hybrid cloud systems. The group is focused on describing resource management and security protocols, packaging methods, and network management technologies. The Web site of the Cloud Management group (http://dmtf.org/standards/cloud) is shown in Figure 11.6.

DMTF's cloud management efforts are really in their initial stages, but the group has broad industry support. Part of the group's task is to provide industry education, so you can find a number of white papers and technology briefs published on this site. It's an effort that's worth checking back with over time. Although the OCSI's work has not yet been joined by Amazon or Salesforce.com, a set of open standards that extend the use of industry standard protocols—such as the Common Information Model (CIM), the Open Virtualization Format (OVF), and WBEM—to the cloud are going to be hard for vendors to resist.

FIGURE 11.6

DMTF (http://dmtf.org/standards/cloud) has a large and important effort underway for developing cloud interoperability management standards.

Cloud Commons and SMI

CA Technologies (http://www.ca.com), the company once known as Computer Associates, has taken some of its technologies in measuring distributed network performance metrics and repositioned its products as the following:

- CA Cloud Insight, a cloud metrics measurement service
- CA Cloud Compose, a deployment service
- CA Cloud Optimize, a cloud optimization service
- CA Cloud Orchestrate, a workflow control and policy based automation service

Taken together, these products form the basis for CA's Cloud Connected Management Suite (http://www.ca.com/us/cloud-solutions.aspx).

CA has lots of experience in this area through its Unicenter management suite and the products that were spawned from it. The company also has invested in cloud vendors such as 3Tera,

Oblicore, and Cassatt to create their cloud services. CA acquired Nimsoft in March 2010. Nimsoft has a monitoring and management package called Nimsoft United Monitoring that creates a monitoring portal with customizable dashboards. The system can gather information from up to 100 types of data points and can work with both Google and Rackspace cloud deployments. Among the data points that can be monitored are resource usage and UPS status.

At the heart of CA Cloud Insight is a method for measuring different cloud metrics that creates what CA calls a Service Measurement Index or SMI. The SMI measures things like SLA compliance, cost, and other values and rolls them up into a score. To help allow SMI to gain traction in the industry, CA has donated the core technology to the Software Engineering Institute at Carnegie Mellon as part of what is called the SMI Consortium. This same group is responsible for the Capability Maturity Model Integration (CMMI) process optimization technology and other efforts. The second CA initiative is the funding of an industry online community called the Cloud Commons (http://www.cloudcommons.com/), the home page of which is shown in Figure 11.7.

FIGURE 11.7

The Cloud Commons (http://www.cloudcommons.com/web/guest) is a new online community founded by CA to promote information exchange on cloud services and the SMI standard.

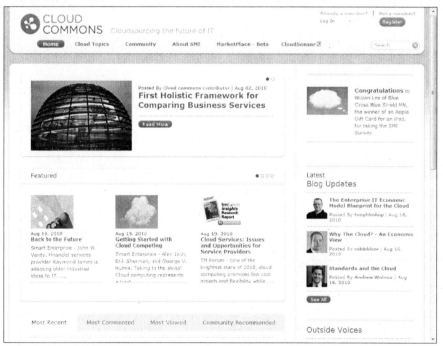

Because the Cloud Commons is brand new, it is hard to tell whether this group will have impact in the cloud community, but it is an interesting effort. The hope is that not only will this site establish CA's performance metrics, but that community users will eventually provide detailed information and ratings on particular services.

To demonstrate the potential of cloud-based metrics, the Cloud Commons has built a dashboard called the CloudSensor that monitors the performance of the major cloud-based services in real time.

This tool measures the performance of the following:

- RackSpace file creation and deletion
- E-mail availability (system uptime) based on Google Gmail, Windows Live Hotmail, and Yahoo! Mail
- Amazon Web Services server creation/destruction times at four AWS sites
- Dashboard Response Times for the consoles of AWS.Amazon, Google App Status, RackSpace Cloud, and Saleforce
- Windows Azure storage benchmarks
- Windows Azure SQL benchmarks

It is meant to demonstrate the value of cloud performance measurements. These metrics are based on real-time data derived from real transactions. Each chart shows the last two hours of activity. Figure 11.8 shows the CloudSensor performance dashboard.

The Service Measurement Index (SMI) is based on a set of measurement technologies forming the SMI Framework that CA donated to the SMI Consortium. It measures cloud-based services in six areas:

- Agility
- Capability
- Cost
- Quality
- Risk
- Security

These form a set of Key Performance Indicators (KPI) that can be used to compare one service to another. Figure 11.9 shows the different characteristics that make up each of the KPIs of the Service Measurement Index.

FIGURE 11.8

The CloudSensor (`http://dashboard.atgcloud.info:5001/cloudsensor/cloud-sensor.html`) dashboard displays real-time cloud service performance metrics.

FIGURE 11.9

SMI defined characteristics (Source: "The Details behind the Service Measurement Index" by Keith Allen, 2010)

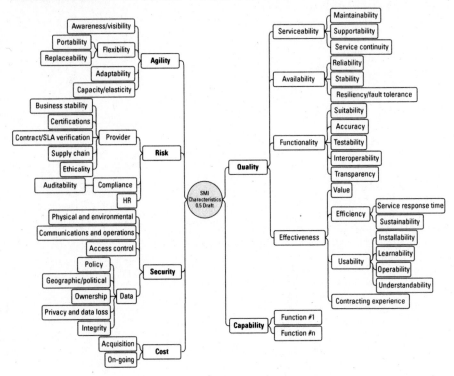

It's too early to determine whether SMI will gain traction, but the positioning of the technology as an open industry working group makes the project very interesting and worthy of note.

Summary

Cloud management is an important and growing area of technology. In this chapter, you learned about some of the products being offered or developed to address common management problems. Among the management tasks are deployment, monitoring, configuration, optimization, and often security. Nearly all network management software vendors are repositioning their products to work with cloud systems. Some network management is available from within the cloud service providers' platforms. Many of the software systems utilize the service provider's API to manage, monitor, and control resources. The use of virtualization has spawned many new products in this area.

In Chapter 12, you learn about security used in cloud computing. This is an extension of our discussion on network management, because security is another means of controlling access through network policies.

Understanding Cloud Security

Cloud computing has lots of unique properties that make it very valuable. Unfortunately, many of those properties make security a singular concern. Many of the tools and techniques that you would use to protect your data, comply with regulations, and maintain the integrity of your systems are complicated by the fact that you are sharing your systems with others and many times outsourcing their operations as well. Cloud computing service providers are well aware of these concerns and have developed new technologies to address them.

Different types of cloud computing service models provide different levels of security services. You get the least amount of built in security with an Infrastructure as a Service provider, and the most with a Software as a Service provider. This chapter presents the concept of a security boundary separating the client's and vendor's responsibilities.

Adapting your on-premises systems to a cloud model requires that you determine what security mechanisms are required and mapping those to controls that exist in your chosen cloud service provider. When you identify missing security elements in the cloud, you can use that mapping to work to close the gap.

Storing data in the cloud is of particular concern. Data should be transferred and stored in an encrypted format. You can use proxy and brokerage services to separate clients from direct access to shared cloud storage.

Logging, auditing, and regulatory compliance are all features that require planning in cloud computing systems. They are among the services that need to be negotiated in Service Level Agreements.

Also in this chapter, you learn about identity and related protocols from a security standpoint. The concept of presence as it relates to identity is also introduced.

Securing the Cloud

The Internet was designed primarily to be resilient; it was not designed to be secure. Any distributed application has a much greater attack surface than an application that is closely held on a Local Area Network. Cloud computing has all the vulnerabilities associated with Internet applications, and additional vulnerabilities arise from pooled, virtualized, and outsourced resources.

In the report "Assessing the Security Risks of Cloud Computing," Jay Heiser and Mark Nicolett of the Gartner Group (`http://www.gartner.com/DisplayDocument?id=685308`) highlighted the following areas of cloud computing that they felt were uniquely troublesome:

- Auditing
- Data integrity
- e-Discovery for legal compliance
- Privacy
- Recovery
- Regulatory compliance

Your risks in any cloud deployment are dependent upon the particular cloud service model chosen and the type of cloud on which you deploy your applications. In order to evaluate your risks, you need to perform the following analysis:

1. Determine which resources (data, services, or applications) you are planning to move to the cloud.

2. Determine the sensitivity of the resource to risk.

   Risks that need to be evaluated are loss of privacy, unauthorized access by others, loss of data, and interruptions in availability.

3. Determine the risk associated with the particular cloud type for a resource.

   Cloud types include public, private (both external and internal), hybrid, and shared community types. With each type, you need to consider where data and functionality will be maintained.

4. Take into account the particular cloud service model that you will be using.

   Different models such as IaaS, SaaS, and PaaS require their customers to be responsible for security at different levels of the service stack.

5. If you have selected a particular cloud service provider, you need to evaluate its system to understand how data is transferred, where it is stored, and how to move data both in and out of the cloud.

   You may want to consider building a flowchart that shows the overall mechanism of the system you are intending to use or are currently using.

One technique for maintaining security is to have "golden" system image references that you can return to when needed. The ability to take a system image off-line and analyze the image for vulnerabilities or compromise is invaluable. The compromised image is a primary forensics tool. Many cloud providers offer a snapshot feature that can create a copy of the client's entire environment; this includes not only machine images, but applications and data, network interfaces, firewalls, and switch access. If you feel that a system has been compromised, you can replace that image with a known good version and contain the problem.

Many vendors maintain a security page where they list their various resources, certifications, and credentials. One of the more developed offerings is the AWS Security Center, shown in Figure 12.1, where you can download some backgrounders, white papers, and case studies related to the Amazon Web Service's security controls and mechanisms.

FIGURE 12.1

The AWS Security Center (`http://aws.amazon.com/security/`) is a good place to start learning about how Amazon Web Services protects users of its IaaS service.

The security boundary

In order to concisely discuss security in cloud computing, you need to define the particular model of cloud computing that applies. This nomenclature provides a framework for understanding what security is already built into the system, who has responsibility for a particular security mechanism, and where the boundary between the responsibility of the service provider is separate from the responsibility of the customer.

All of Chapter 1 was concerned with defining what cloud computing is and defining the lexicon of cloud computing. There are many definitions and acronyms in the area of cloud computing that will probably not survive long. The most commonly used model based on U.S. National Institute of Standards and Technology (NIST; `http://www.csrc.nist.gov/groups/SNS/cloud-computing/index.html`) separates deployment models from service models and assigns those models a set of service attributes. Deployment models are cloud types: community, hybrid, private, and public clouds. Service models follow the SPI Model for three forms of service delivery: Software, Platform, and Infrastructure as a Service. In the NIST model, as you may recall, it was not required that a cloud use virtualization to pool resources, nor did that model require that a cloud support multi-tenancy. It is just these factors that make security such a complicated proposition in cloud computing.

Chapter 1 also presented the Cloud Security Alliance (CSA; `http://www.cloudsecurity alliance.org/`) cloud computing stack model, which shows how different functional units in a network stack relate to one another. As you may recall from Chapter 1, this model can be used to separate the different service models from one another. CSA is an industry working group that studies security issues in cloud computing and offers recommendations to its members. The work of the group is open and available, and you can download its guidance from its home page, shown in Figure 12.2.

FIGURE 12.2

The Cloud Security Alliance (CSA) home page at `http://www.cloudsecurityalliance.org/` offers a number of resources to anyone concerned with securing his cloud deployment.

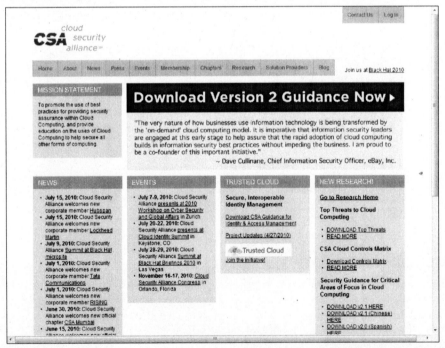

The CSA partitions its guidance into a set of operational domains:

- Governance and enterprise risk management
- Legal and electronic discovery
- Compliance and audit
- Information lifecycle management
- Portability and interoperability
- Traditional security, business continuity, and disaster recovery
- Datacenter operations
- Incidence response, notification, and remediation
- Application security
- Encryption and key management
- Identity and access management
- Virtualization

You can download the group's current work in these areas from the different sections of its Web site.

One key difference between the NIST model and the CSA is that the CSA considers multi-tenancy to be an essential element in cloud computing. Multi-tenancy adds a number of additional security concerns to cloud computing that need to be accounted for. In multi-tenancy, different customers must be isolated, their data segmented, and their service accounted for. To provide these features, the cloud service provider must provide a policy-based environment that is capable of supporting different levels and quality of service, usually using different pricing models. Multi-tenancy expresses itself in different ways in the different cloud deployment models and imposes security concerns in different places.

Security service boundary

The CSA functional cloud computing hardware/software stack is the Cloud Reference Model. This model, which was discussed in Chapter 1, is reproduced in Figure 12.3. IaaS is the lowest level service, with PaaS and SaaS the next two services above. As you move upward in the stack, each service model inherits the capabilities of the model beneath it, as well as all the inherent security concerns and risk factors. IaaS supplies the infrastructure; PaaS adds application development frameworks, transactions, and control structures; and SaaS is an operating environment with applications, management, and the user interface. As you ascend the stack, IaaS has the least levels of integrated functionality and the lowest levels of integrated security, and SaaS has the most.

The most important lesson from this discussion of architecture is that each different type of cloud service delivery model creates a security boundary at which the cloud service provider's responsibilities end and the customer's responsibilities begin. Any security mechanism below the security boundary must be built into the system, and any security mechanism above must be maintained by the customer. As you move up the stack, it becomes more important to make sure that the type and level of security is part of your Service Level Agreement.

FIGURE 12.3

The CSA Cloud Reference Model with security boundaries shown

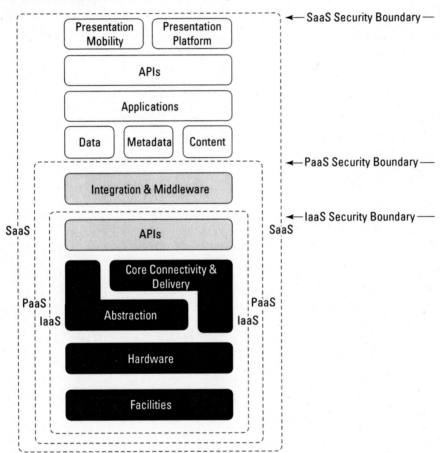

In the SaaS model, the vendor provides security as part of the Service Level Agreement, with the compliance, governance, and liability levels stipulated under the contract for the entire stack. For the PaaS model, the security boundary may be defined for the vendor to include the software framework and middleware layer. In the PaaS model, the customer would be responsible for the security of the application and UI at the top of the stack. The model with the least built-in security is IaaS, where everything that involves software of any kind is the customer's problem. Numerous definitions of services tend to muddy this picture by adding or removing elements of the various functions from any particular offering, thus blurring which party has responsibility for which features, but the overall analysis is still useful.

In thinking about the Cloud Security Reference Model in relationship to security needs, a fundamental distinction may be made between the nature of how services are provided versus where those services are located. A private cloud may be internal or external to an organization, and although a public cloud is most often external, there is no requirement that this mapping be made so. Cloud computing has a tendency to blur the location of the defined security perimeter in such a way that the previous notions of network firewalls and edge defenses often no longer apply.

This makes the location of trust boundaries in cloud computing rather ill defined, dynamic, and subject to change depending upon a number of factors. Establishing trust boundaries and creating a new perimeter defense that is consistent with your cloud computing network is an important consideration. The key to understanding where to place security mechanisms is to understand where physically in the cloud resources are deployed and consumed, what those resources are, who manages the resources, and what mechanisms are used to control them. Those factors help you gauge where systems are located and what areas of compliance you need to build into your system.

Table 12.1 lists some of the different service models and lists the parties responsible for security in the different instances.

TABLE 12.1

Security Responsibilities by Service Model

Model Type	Infrastructure Security Management	Infrastructure Owner	Infrastructure Location	Trust Condition
Hybrid	Both vendor and customer	Both vendor and customer	Both on- and off-premises	Both trusted and untrusted
Private/Community	Customer	Customer	On- or off-premises	Trusted
Private/Community	Customer	Vendor	Off- or on-premises	Trusted
Private/Community	Vendor	Customer	On- or off-premises	Trusted
Private/Community	Vendor	Vendor	Off- or on-premises	Trusted
Public	Vendor	Vendor	Off-premises	Untrusted

Security mapping

The cloud service model you choose determines where in the proposed deployment the variety of security features, compliance auditing, and other requirements must be placed. To determine the particular security mechanisms you need, you must perform a mapping of the particular cloud service model to the particular application you are deploying. These mechanisms must be supported by the various controls that are provided by your service provider, your organization, or a third party. It's unlikely that you will be able to duplicate security routines that are possible on-premises, but this analysis allows you to determine what coverage you need.

A security control model includes the security that you normally use for your applications, data, management, network, and physical hardware. You may also need to account for any compliance standards that are required for your industry. A compliance standard can be any government regulatory framework such as Payment Card Industry Data Security Standards (PCI-DSS), Health Insurance Portability and Accountability Act (HIPPA), Gramm–Leach–Bliley Act (GLBA), or the Sarbanes–Oxley Act (SOX) that requires you operate in a certain way and keep records.

Essentially, you are looking to identify the missing features that would be required for an on-premises deployment and seek to find their replacements in the cloud computing model. As you assign accountability for different aspects of security and contract away the operational responsibility to others, you want to make sure they remain accountable for the security you need.

Securing Data

Securing data sent to, received from, and stored in the cloud is the single largest security concern that most organizations should have with cloud computing. As with any WAN traffic, you must assume that any data can be intercepted and modified. That's why, as a matter of course, traffic to a cloud service provider and stored off-premises is encrypted. This is as true for general data as it is for any passwords or account IDs.

These are the key mechanisms for protecting data mechanisms:

- Access control
- Auditing
- Authentication
- Authorization

Whatever service model you choose should have mechanisms operating in all four areas that meet your security requirements, whether they are operating through the cloud service provider or your own local infrastructure.

Brokered cloud storage access

The problem with the data you store in the cloud is that it can be located anywhere in the cloud service provider's system: in another datacenter, another state or province, and in many cases even in another country. With other types of system architectures, such as client/server, you could count on a firewall to serve as your network's security perimeter; cloud computing has no physical system that serves this purpose. Therefore, to protect your cloud storage assets, you want to find a way to isolate data from direct client access.

One approach to isolating storage in the cloud from direct client access is to create layered access to the data. In one scheme, two services are created: a broker with full access to storage but no access to the client, and a proxy with no access to storage but access to both the client and broker. The location of the proxy and the broker is not important (they can be local or in the cloud); what is important is that these two services are in the direct data path between the client and data stored in the cloud.

Under this system, when a client makes a request for data, here's what happens:

1. The request goes to the external service interface (or endpoint) of the proxy, which has only a partial trust.

2. The proxy, using its internal interface, forwards the request to the broker.

3. The broker requests the data from the cloud storage system.

4. The storage system returns the results to the broker.

5. The broker returns the results to the proxy.

6. The proxy completes the response by sending the data requested to the client.

Figure 12.4 shows this storage "proxy" system graphically.

Note

This discussion is based on a white paper called "Security Best Practices For Developing Windows Azure Applications," by Andrew Marshall, Michael Howard, Grant Bugher, and Brian Harden that you can find at http://download.microsoft.com/download/7/3/E/73E4EE93-559F-4D0F-A6FC-7FEC5F1542D1/SecurityBestPracticesWindowsAzureApps.docx. In their presentation, the proxy service is called the Gatekeeper and assigned a Windows Server Web Role, and the broker is called the KeyMaster and assigned a Worker Role. ■

This design relies on the proxy service to impose some rules that allow it to safely request data that is appropriate to that particular client based on the client's identity and relay that request to the broker. The broker does not need full access to the cloud storage, but it may be configured to grant READ and QUERY operations, while not allowing APPEND or DELETE. The proxy has a limited trust role, while the broker can run with higher privileges or even as native code.

The use of multiple encryption keys can further separate the proxy service from the storage account. If you use two separate keys to create two different data zones—one for the untrusted communication between the proxy and broker services, and another a trusted zone between the broker and the cloud storage—you create a situation where there is further separation between the different service roles.

FIGURE 12.4

In this design, direct access to cloud storage is eliminated in favor of a proxy/broker service.

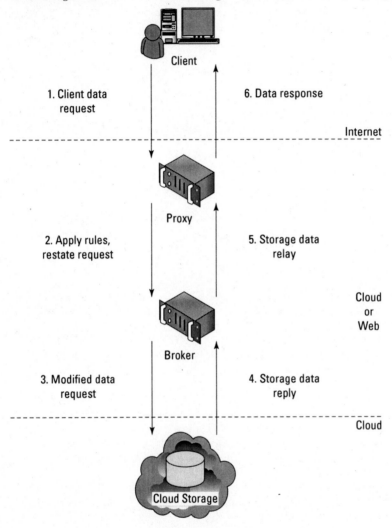

Even if the proxy service is compromised, that service does not have access to the trusted key necessary to access the cloud storage account. In the multi-key solution, shown in Figure 12.5, you have not only eliminated all internal service endpoints, but you also have eliminated the need to have the proxy service run at a reduced trust level.

FIGURE 12.5

The creation of storage zones with associated encryption keys can further protect cloud storage from unauthorized access.

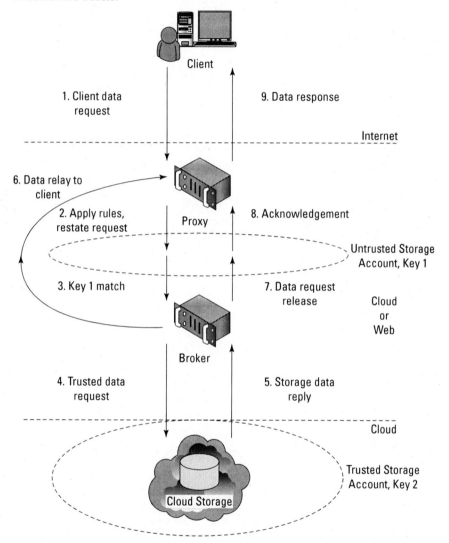

Storage location and tenancy

Some cloud service providers negotiate as part of their Service Level Agreements to contractually store and process data in locations that are predetermined by their contract. Not all do. If you can get the commitment for specific data site storage, then you also should make sure the cloud vendor is under contract to conform to local privacy laws.

Because data stored in the cloud is usually stored from multiple tenants, each vendor has its own unique method for segregating one customer's data from another. It's important to have some understanding of how your specific service provider maintains data segregation.

Another question to ask a cloud storage provider is who is provided privileged access to storage. The more you know about how the vendor hires its IT staff and the security mechanism put into place to protect storage, the better.

Most cloud service providers store data in an encrypted form. While encryption is important and effective, it does present its own set of problems. When there is a problem with encrypted data, the result is that the data may not be recoverable. It is worth considering what type of encryption the cloud provider uses and to check that the system has been planned and tested by security experts.

Regardless of where your data is located, you should know what impact a disaster or interruption will have on your service and your data. Any cloud provider that doesn't offer the ability to replicate data and application infrastructure across multiple sites cannot recover your information in a timely manner. You should know how disaster recovery affects your data and how long it takes to do a complete restoration.

Encryption

Strong encryption technology is a core technology for protecting data in transit to and from the cloud as well as data stored in the cloud. It is or will be required by law. The goal of encrypted cloud storage is to create a virtual private storage system that maintains confidentiality and data integrity while maintaining the benefits of cloud storage: ubiquitous, reliable, shared data storage. Encryption should separate stored data (data at rest) from data in transit.

Depending upon the particular cloud provider, you can create multiple accounts with different keys as you saw in the example with Windows Azure Platform in the previous section. Microsoft allows up to five security accounts per client, and you can use these different accounts to create different zones. On Amazon Web Service, you can create multiple keys and rotate those keys during different sessions.

Although encryption protects your data from unauthorized access, it does nothing to prevent data loss. Indeed, a common means for losing encrypted data is to lose the keys that provide access to the data. Therefore, you need to approach key management seriously. Keys should have a defined lifecycle. Among the schemes used to protect keys are the creation of secure key stores that have restricted role-based access, automated key stores backup, and recovery techniques. It's a good idea to separate key management from the cloud provider that hosts your data.

One standard for interoperable cloud-based key management is the OASIS Key Management Interoperability Protocol (KMIP; http://www.oasis-open.org/committees/kmip/). IEEE 1619.3 (https://siswg.net/index.php?option=com_docman) also covers both storage encryption and key management for shared storage.

Auditing and compliance

Logging is the recording of events into a repository; auditing is the ability to monitor the events to understand performance. Logging and auditing is an important function because it is not only necessary for evaluation performance, but it is also used to investigate security and when illegal activity has been perpetrated. Logs should record system, application, and security events, at the very minimum.

Logging and auditing are unfortunately one of the weaker aspects of early cloud computing service offerings.

Cloud service providers often have proprietary log formats that you need to be aware of. Whatever monitoring and analysis tools you use need to be aware of these logs and able to work with them. Often, providers offer monitoring tools of their own, many in the form of a dashboard with the potential to customize the information you see through either the interface or programmatically using the vendor's API. You want to make full use of those built-in services.

Because cloud services are both multitenant and multisite operations, the logging activity and data for different clients may not only be co-located, they may also be moving across a landscape of different hosts and sites. You can't simply expect that an investigation will be provided with the necessary information at the time of discovery unless it is part of your Service Level Agreement. Even an SLA with the appropriate obligations contained in it may not be enough to guarantee you will get the information you need when the time comes. It is wise to determine whether the cloud service provider has been able to successfully support investigations in the past.

As it stands now, nearly all regulations were written without keeping cloud computing in mind. A regulator or auditor isn't likely to be familiar with the nature of running applications and storing data in the cloud. Even so, laws are written to ensure compliance, and the client is held responsible for compliance under the laws of the governing bodies that apply to the location where the processing or storage takes place.

Therefore, you must understand the following:

- Which regulations apply to your use of a particular cloud computing service
- Which regulations apply to the cloud service provider and where the demarcation line falls for responsibilities
- How your cloud service provider will support your need for information associated with regulation
- How to work with the regulator to provide the information necessary regardless of who had the responsibility to collect the data

Traditional service providers are much more likely to be the subject of security certifications and external audits of their facilities and procedures than cloud service providers. That makes the willingness for a cloud service provider to subject its service to regulatory compliance scrutiny an important factor in your selection of that provider over another. In the case of a cloud service provider who shows reluctance to or limits the scrutiny of its operations, it is probably wise to use the service in ways that limit your exposure to risk. For example, although encrypting stored data is always a good policy, you also might want to consider not storing any sensitive information on that provider's system.

As it stands now, clients must guarantee their own regulatory compliance, even when their data is in the care of the service provider. You must ensure that your data is secure and that its integrity has not been compromised. When multiple regulatory entities are involved, as there surely are between site locations and different countries, then that burden to satisfy the laws of those governments is also your responsibility.

For any company with clients in multiple countries, the burden of regulatory compliance is onerous. While organizations such as the EEC (European Economic Community) or Common Market provide some relief for European regulation, countries such as the United States, Japan, China, and others each have their own sets of requirements. This makes regulatory compliance one of the most actively developing and important areas of cloud computing technology.

This situation is likely to change. On March 1, 2010, Massachusetts passed a law that requires companies that provide sensitive personal information on Massachusetts residents to encrypt data transmitted and stored on their systems. Businesses are required to limit the amount of personal data collected, monitor data usage, keep a data inventory, and be able to present a security plan on how they will keep the data safe. The steps require that companies verify that any third-party services they use conform to these requirements and that there be language in all SLAs that enforce these protections. The law takes full effect in March 2012.

Going forward, you want to ensure the following:

- You have contracts reviewed by your legal staff.
- You have a right-to-audit clause in your SLA.
- You review any third parties who are service providers and assess their impact on security and regulatory compliance.
- You understand the scope of the regulations that apply to your cloud computing applications and services.
- You consider what steps you must take to comply with the demands of regulations that apply.
- You consider adjusting your procedures to comply with regulations.
- You collect and maintain the evidence of your compliance with regulations.
- You determine whether your cloud service provider can provide an audit statement that is SAS 70 Type II-compliant.

The ISO/IEC 27001/27002 standard for information security management systems has a roadmap for mission-critical services that you may want to discuss with your cloud service provider. Amazon Web Services supports SAS70 Type II Audits.

Becoming a cloud service provider requires a large investment, but as we all know, even large companies can fail. When a cloud service provider fails, it may close or more likely be acquired by another company. You likely wouldn't use a service provider that you suspected of being in difficulty, but problems develop over years and cloud computing has a certain degree of vendor lock-in to it. That is, when you have created a cloud-based service, it can be difficult or often impossible to move it to another service provider. You should be aware of what happens to your data if the cloud service provider fails. At the very least, you would want to make sure your data could be obtained in a format that could be accessed by on-premise applications.

The various attributes of cloud computing make it difficult to respond to incidents, but that doesn't mean you should consider drawing up security incidence response policies. Although cloud computing creates shared responsibilities, it is often up to the client to initiate the inquiry that gets the ball rolling. You should be prepared to provide clear information to your cloud service provider about what you consider to be an incident or a breach in security and what are simply suspicious events.

Establishing Identity and Presence

Chapter 4 introduced the concept of identities, some of the protocols that support them, and some of the services that can work with them. Identities also are tied to the concept of accounts and can be used for contacts or "ID cards." Identities also are important from a security standpoint because they can be used to authenticate client requests for services in a distributed network system such as the Internet or, in this case, for cloud computing services.

Identity management is a primary mechanism for controlling access to data in the cloud, preventing unauthorized uses, maintaining user roles, and complying with regulations. The sections that follow describe some of the different security aspects of identity and the related concept of "presence." For this conversation, you can consider presence to be the mapping of an authenticated identity to a known location. Presence is important in cloud computing because it adds context that can modify services and service delivery.

Cloud computing requires the following:

- That you establish an identity
- That the identity be authenticated
- That the authentication be portable
- That authentication provide access to cloud resources

When applied to a number of users in a cloud computing system, these requirements describe systems that must provision identities, provide mechanisms that manage credentials and authentication, allow identities to be federated, and support a variety of user profiles and access policies. Automating these processes can be a major management task, just as they are for on-premises operations.

Identity protocol standards

The protocols that provide identity services have been and are under active development, and several form the basis for efforts to create interoperability among services.

OpenID 2.0 (`http://openid.net/`) is the standard associated with creating an identity and having a third-party service authenticate the use of that digital identity. It is the key to creating Single Sign-On (SSO) systems. Some cloud service providers have adopted OpenID as a service, and its use is growing.

In Chapter 4, you learned how OpenID is associated with contact cards such as vCards and InfoCards. In that chapter, I briefly discussed how OpenID provides access to important Web sites and how some Web sites allow you to use your logins based on OpenID from another site to gain access to their site.

OpenID doesn't specify the means for authentication of an identity, and it is up to the particular system how the authentication process is executed. Authentication can be by a Challenge and Response Protocol (CHAP), through a physical smart card, or using a flying finger or evil eye through a biometric measurement. In OpenIDL, the authentication procedure has the following steps:

1. The end-user uses a program like a browser that is called a user agent to enter an OpenID identifier, which is in the form of a URL or XRI.

    An OpenID might take the form of *name*`.openid.provider.org`.

2. The OpenID is presented to a service that provides access to the resource that is desired.

3. An entity called a relaying party queries the OpenID identity provider to authenticate the veracity of the OpenID credentials.

4. The authentication is sent back to the relaying party from the identity provider and access is either provided or denied.

According to a report by one of OpenID's directors called "OpenID 2009 Year in Review" by Brian Kissel (`http://openid.net/2009/12/16/openid-2009-year-in-review/`), there were over 1 billion OpenID accounts accepted by 9 million sites on the Internet.

The second protocol used to present identity-based claims in cloud computing is a set of authorization markup languages that create files in the form of being XACML and SAML. These protocols were described in Chapter 4 in detail, so I only mention them in passing here. SAML (Security Assertion Markup Language; `http://www.oasis-open.org/committees/tc_home.php?wg_abbrev=security`) is gaining growing acceptance among cloud service providers. It is a standard of OASIS and an XML standard for passing authentication and authorization between an identity provider and the service provider. SAML is a complimentary mechanism to OpenID and is used to create SSO systems.

Taken as a unit, OpenID and SAML are being positioned to be the standard authentication mechanism for clients accessing cloud services. It is particularly important for services such as mashups that draw information from two or more data services.

An open standard called OAuth (`http://oauth.net/`) provides a token service that can be used to present validated access to resources. OAuth is similar to OpenID, but provides a different mechanism for shared access. The use of OAuth tokens allows clients to present credentials that contain no account information (userID or password) to a cloud service. The token comes with a defined period after which it can no longer be used. Several important cloud service providers have begun to make OAuth APIs available based on the OAuth 2.0 standard, most notably Facebook's Graph API and the Google Data API.

The DataPortability Project (`http://dataportability.org/`) is an industry working group that promotes data interoperability between applications, and the group's work touches on a number of the emerging standards mentioned in this section. The group's Web site is shown in Figure 12.6.

FIGURE 12.6

The home page of the DataPortability Project, an industry working group that promotes open identity standards

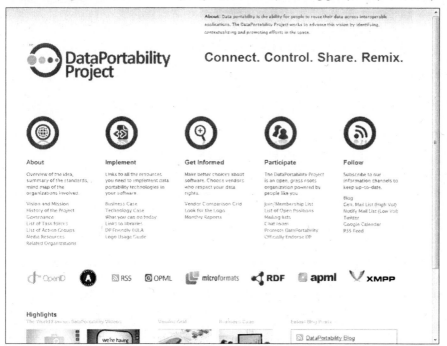

A number of vendors have created server products, such as Identity and Access Managers (IAMs), to support these various standards.

Windows Azure identity standards

The Windows Azure Platform uses a claims-based identity based on open authentication and access protocols and is a good example of a service implementing the standards described in the previous section. These standards may be used without modification on a system that is running in the cloud or on-premises, in keeping with Microsoft's S+S (software plus services) approach to cloud computing.

Windows Azure security draws on the following three services:

- Active Directory Federation Services 2.0
- Windows Azure AppFabric Access Control Service
- Windows Identity Foundation (WIF)

The Windows Identity Foundation offers .NET developers Visual Studio integration of WS-Federation and WS-Trust open standards. ASP.NET Web applications created with WIF integrate the Windows Communication Foundation SOAP service (WCF-SOAP) into a unified object model. This allows WIF to have full access to the features of WS-Security and to work with tokens in the SAML format.

WIF relies on third-party authentication and accepts authentication requests from these services in the form of a set of claims. Claims are independent of where a user account or application is located, thus allowing claims to be used in single sign-on systems (SSO). Claims support both simple resource access and the Role Based Access Control (RBAC) policies that can be enforced by Windows group policies.

Active Directory Federation Services 2.0 (AD FS) is a Security Token Service (STS) that allows users to authenticate their access to applications both locally and in the cloud with a claims-based identity. Anyone who has an account in the local Windows directory can access an application; AD FS creates and retains trust relationships with federated systems. AD FS uses WS-Federation, WS-Trust, and SAML, which allows users to access a system based on IBM, Novell, SAP, and many other vendors.

The final piece of the Windows Azure Platform claims-based identity system is built directly into the AppFabric Access Control (AC) service. You may recall from Chapter 10 that AppFabric is a service bus for Azure components that supports REST Web services. Included in AppFabric are authentication and claims-based authorization access. These can be simple logons or more complex schemes supported by AD FS. AC allows authorization to be located anywhere and allows developers to separate identity from their application.

The claims-based identity in AC is based on the OAuth Web Resource Authorization Protocol (OAuth WRAP), which works with various REST APIs. The Oauth 2.0 protocol seems to be gaining acceptance in the cloud computing industry, because SAML tokens can be accepted by many vendors.

Presence

Presence is a fundamental concept in computer science. It is used on networks to indicate the status of available parties and their location. Commands like the WHO command in Linux that list users logged into the network go all the way back to the first network operating systems.

Presence provides not only identity, but status and, as part of status, location. The status is referred to as the presence state, the identity is the presentity, and the service that manages presence is called the presence service. Many presence services rely on agents called watchers, which are small programs that relay a client's ability to connect. Among the cloud computing services that rely on presence information are telephony systems such as VoIP, instant messaging services (IM), and geo-location-based systems such as GPS. Presence is playing an important role in cell phones, particularly smart phones.

When you access an application such as AroundMe on the Apple iPhone, which lists businesses, services, and restaurants in your vicinity, you are using an example of a presence service. Figure 12.7 shows the AroundMe app with some sample results. The presence service is provided by the GPS locator inside the phone, which provides a location through AT&T (the service provider) to the application. Presence is an essential and growing component of cloud-based services, and it adds a tremendous amount of value to the ubiquity that a cloud network offers.

FIGURE 12.7

The AroundMe iPhone app is an example of an application that makes use of a presence service.

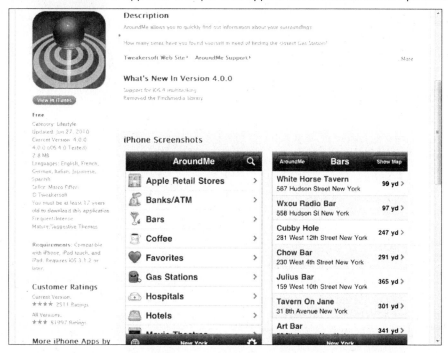

As cloud computing becomes more pervasive and vendors attempt to create federated systems, emerging presence services will become more important. Microsoft's Windows Identity Foundation (described in the previous section) created under the Geneva Framework project is one example of an attempt to create a claims-based presence system. WIF allows different systems to interoperate using a variety of authentication methods, including LDAP and Active Directory, OpenID, LiveID, Microsoft CardSpace, and Novell Digital Me.

The Internet Engineering Task Force (IETF) has developed a standard called the Extensible Messaging and Presence Protocol (XMPP) that can be used with a federation system called the Jabber Extensible Communications Platform (Jabber XCP) to provide presence information. Among the services that use Jabber XCP are the Defense Information Systems Agency (DISA), Google Talk, Earthlink, Facebook, the National Weather Service, Twitter, the U.S. Marine Corps, and the U.S. Joint Forces Command (USJFCOM).

Jabber XCP is popular because it is an extensible development platform that is platform-independent and supports several communications protocols, such as the Session Initiation Protocol for Instant Messaging and Presence Leveraging Extensions (SIMPLE) and Instant Messaging and Presence Service (IMPS).

The notion of applying presence services over the standard Service Oriented Architecture (SOA) protocols such as SOAP/REST/HTTP is that in SOA all these protocols support unidirectional data exchange. You request a service/data, and a response is supplied. SOA architectures don't scale well and can't supply high-speed data transfers required by the collaboration services that are based on presence service technologies. SOA also has the problem of services that have trouble penetrating firewalls. It was these barriers that Jabber and XMPP were created to solve, and you will find that protocol incorporated into a number of cloud computing SaaS services. AOL, Apple, Google, IBM, and others are using this technology in some of their applications today.

Summary

In this chapter, you learned about many of the issues concerning security and cloud computing. This is a rapidly changing area of great importance to anyone considering deploying systems or storing data in the cloud. Security may, in fact, be the single most important area of cloud computing that you need to plan for. Depending upon the type of service you use, you may find many security services already built into your system.

An issue you need to consider is how to protect data in transit to and stored in the cloud. Data encryption, access restrictions, and data protection services were described. Multi-tenancy, system virtualization, and other factors make monitoring, regulatory compliance, and incidence response more challenging than on-premises systems are. A key concept for controlling access to cloud resources is identity management.

In Chapter 13, the standards used to create cloud systems are described. These standards create what is called the Service Oriented Architecture. You also learn how cloud systems can be built from many different interoperable modular parts.

Part IV

Understanding Services and Applications

Understanding Service Oriented Architecture

S ervice Oriented Architecture (SOA) describes a standard method for requesting services from distributed components and managing the results. Because the clients requesting services, the components providing the services, the protocols used to deliver messages, and the responses can vary widely, SOA provides the translation and management layer in an architecture that removes the barrier for a client obtaining desired services. With SOA, clients and components can be written in different languages and can use multiple messaging protocols and networking protocols to communicate with one another. SOA provides the standards that transport the messages and makes the infrastructure to support it possible. SOA provides access to reusable Web services over a TCP/IP network, which makes this an important topic to cloud computing going forward.

You don't need SOA if you are creating a monolithic cloud application that performs a specific function such as backup, e-mail, Web page access, or instant messaging. Many of the large and familiar cloud computing applications are monolithic and were built with proprietary technologies—albeit often on top of open source software and hardware. However, as cloud computing applications expand their capability to provide additional and diverse services, SOA offers access to ready-made, modular, highly optimized, and widely shareable components that can minimize developer and infrastructure costs.

For over a decade now Service Oriented Architecture has been part of a collaborative effort on the part of both large and small vendors to come up with a common solution to architecting complex business software processes efficiently. As cloud computing matures and the applications offered become more capable, the key to being competitive and offering users the capability to customize their environments lays in the standardization that Service Oriented Architecture offers. The influence of SOA in cloud computing is therefore likely to grow.

This chapter provides the basis for understanding what SOA is, how SOA operates, what limitations and capabilities are part of the architecture, and the vocabulary that you need to know in this subject. SOA is an architecture, first and foremost, so in essence it is a blueprint for creating a system conforming to this standard. The environment it creates is a virtual message-passing system with a loose coupling between clients and services. The products that support SOA are a diverse lot. SOA components are meant to be modular and easily added to a business process, and this modularity makes them good candidates for Computer Aided Software Engineering (CASE) modeling tools. This chapter describes the software used to support SOA and some of the important ways in which the architecture is interpreted.

Cloud computing is not the next evolutionary step beyond SOA, as some think because of SOA's longer history. The two technologies are complementary. Whereas SOA can be used to construct large and complex applications that scale both horizontally and vertically, cloud computing applications tend to be scaled vertically. Horizontal scaling refers to applications with a large number of different business processes operating. Vertical scaling refers to large applications with a limited number of business processes operating. SOA techniques may be applied in both instances.

Introducing Service Oriented Architecture

Service Oriented Architecture (SOA) is a specification and a methodology for providing platform- and language-independent services for use in distributed applications. A service is a repeatable task within a business process, and a business task is a composition of services. SOA describes a message-passing taxonomy for a component-based architecture that provides services to clients upon demand. Clients access a component that complies with SOA by passing a message containing metadata to be acted upon in a standard format. The component acts on that message and returns a response that the client then uses for its own purpose. A common example of a message is an XML file transported over a network protocol such as SOAP.

Usually service providers and service consumers do not pass messages directly to each other. Implementations of SOA employ middleware software to play the role of transaction manager (or broker) and translator. That middleware can discover and list available services, as well as potential service consumers, often in the form of a registry, because SOA describes a distributed architecture security and trust services are built directly into many of these products to protect communication. Middleware products also can be where the logic of business processes reside; they can be general-purpose applications, industry-specific, private, or public services.

Middleware services manage lookup requests. The Universal Description Discovery and Integration (UDDI) protocol is the one most commonly used to broadcast and discover available Web services, often passing data in the form of an Electronic Business using eXtensible Markup Language (ebXML) documents. Service consumers find a Web service in a broker registry and bind their service requests to that specific service; if the broker supports several Web services, it can bind to any of the ones that are useful.

This architecture does not contain executable links that require access to a specific API. The message presents data to the service, and the service responds. It is up to the client to determine if the service returned an appropriate result. An SOA is then seen as a method for creating an integrated process as a set of linked services. The component exposes itself as an "endpoint" (a term of art in SOA) to the client.

The most commonly used message-passing format is an Extensible Markup Language (XML) document using Simple Object Access Protocol (SOAP), but many more are possible, including Web Services Description Language (WSDL), Web Services Security (WSS), and Business Process Execution Language for Web Services (WS-BPEL). WSDL is commonly used to describe the service interface, how to bind information, and the nature of the component's service or endpoint. The Service Component Definition Language (SCDL) is used to define the service component that performs the service, providing the component service information that is not part of the Web service and that therefore wouldn't be part of WSDL.

Note

Whatever protocol is used to negotiate a transaction, the formal definition of the transaction is referred to as the "contract." Indeed, the notion of a contract implies a certain level of service that is available to clients and that may be part of any paid service in SOA. ■

Figure 13.1 shows a protocol stack for an SOA architecture and how those different protocols execute the functions required in the Service Oriented Architecture. In the figure, the box labeled Other Services could include Common Object Request Broker Architecture (CORBA), Representational State Transfer (REST), Remote Procedure Calls (RPC), Distributed Common Object Model (DCOM), Jini, Data Distribution Service (DDS), Windows Communication Foundation (WCF), and other technologies and protocols. It is this flexibility and neutrality that makes SOA so singularly useful in designing complex applications. These services and the manner in which they interact in regards to SOA have been codified by a number of standards organizations, and some of the more prominent efforts are described later in this chapter.

Tip

To read the IBMs SOA Foundation White Paper, see `http://download.boulder.ibm.com/ibmdl/ pub/software/dw/webservices/ws-soa-whitepaper.pdf.` ■

SOA provides the framework needed to allow clients of any type to engage in a request-response mechanism with a service. The specification of the manner in which messages are passed in SOA, or in which events are handled, are referred to as their *contract*. The term is meant to imply that the client engages the service in a task that must be managed in a specified manner. In real systems, contracts may specifically be stated with a Quality of Service parameter in a real paper contract. Typically, SOA requires the use of an orchestrator or broker service to ensure that messages are correctly transacted. SOA makes no other demands on either the client (consumer) or the components (provider) of the service; it is concerned only with the interface or action boundary between the two. This is the earliest definition of SOA architecture.

FIGURE 13.1

A protocol stack for SOA showing the relationship of each protocol to its function

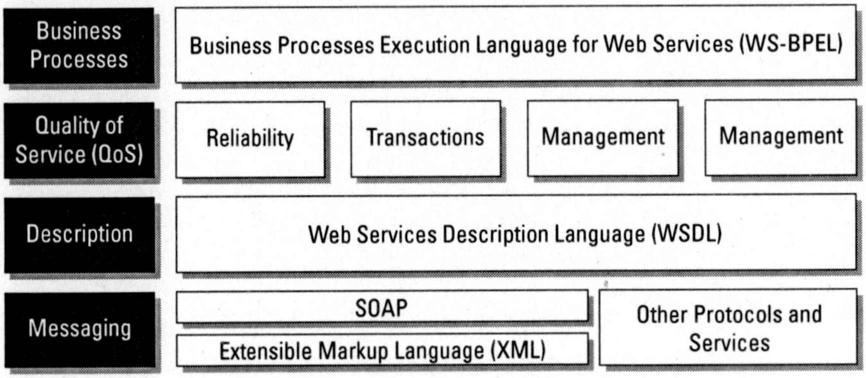

Business Processes	Business Processes Execution Language for Web Services (WS-BPEL)			
Quality of Service (QoS)	Reliability	Transactions	Management	Management
Description	Web Services Description Language (WSDL)			
Messaging	SOAP / Extensible Markup Language (XML)		Other Protocols and Services	

Components are often written to comply with the Service Component Architecture (SCA), a language- and technology-agnostic design specification that has wide, but not universal, industry support. SCA can use the services of components that are written in the Business Process Execution Language (BPEL), Java, C#/.NET, XML, or Cobol, and can apply to C++ and Fortran, as well as to the dynamic languages Python, Ruby, PHP, and others. This allows components to be written in the easiest form that supports the business process that the component is meant to service. By wrapping data from legacy clients written in languages such as COBOL, SOA has greatly extended the life of many legacy applications.

Tip

To read David Chappel's white paper on SCA, go to `http://www.davidchappell.com/articles/Introducing_SCA.pdf.` ∎

Components are coded with their service logic and their dependencies, QoS is established, and the service is instantiated. In the SCA model, data and messages are exchanged in a Service Data Object (SDO). This system of messaging using objects and services is sometimes referred to as a Data Access Service (DAS). Figure 13.2 shows how components of different types can communicate using different protocols as part of SOA.

When you combine Web services to create business processes, the integration must be managed. Two main methods are used to combine Web services: orchestration and choreography. In orchestration, a middleware service centrally coordinates all the different Web service operations, and all services send messages and receive messages from the orchestrator. The logic of the compound business process is found at the orchestrator alone. Figure 13.3 shows how orchestration is managed.

FIGURE 13.2

SOA allows for different component and client construction, as well as access to each using different protocols.

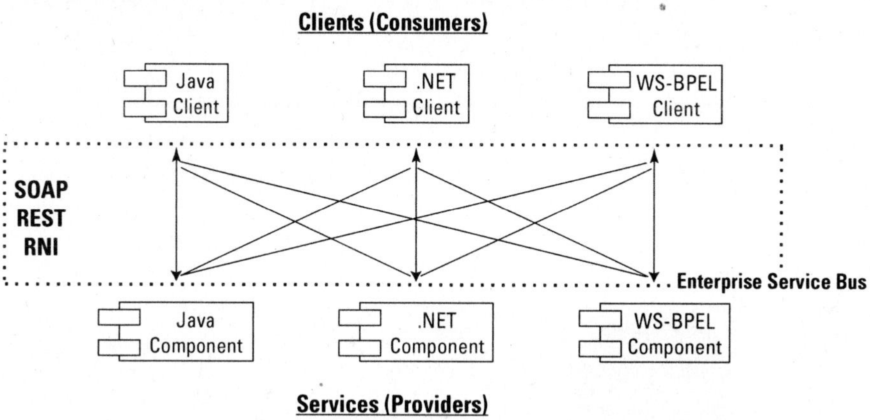

By contrast, a compound business process that uses choreography has no central coordination function. In choreography, each Web service that is part of a business process is aware of when to process a message and with what client or component it needs to interact with. Choreography is a collaborative effort where the logic of the business process is pushed out to the members who are responsible for determining which operations to execute and when to execute them, the structure of the messages to be passed and their timing, and other factors. Figure 13.4 illustrates the nature of choreography.

What isn't clear from Figure 13.2, but is shown in Figure 13.3 (orchestration) and Figure 13.4 (choreography) is that business processes are conducted using a sequence, in parallel, or simply by being invoked (called to). An execution language like WS-BPEL provides commands for defining logic using conditional statements, loops, variables, fault handlers, and other constructs. Because a business process is a collection of activity graphs, complex processes are often shown as part of Unified Modeling Language (UML) diagrams. UML is the modeling language of the Object Management Group that provides a method for creating visual models for software in the form of 14 types of diagrams. Some of the diagram types are structure, behavior, class, component, object, interaction, state, and sequence.

Tip

You can find a primer on BPEL by Matjaz Juric on Oracle's Web site at http://www.oracle.com/technology/pub/articles/matjaz_bpel1.html. For information on SOA modeling, refer to *Service-Oriented Modeling: Analysis, Design, and Architecture,* by Michael Bell, Wiley, 2008, and Bell's later book *SOA Modeling Patterns for Service-Oriented Discovery and Analysis,* Wiley, 2010. ■

FIGURE 13.3

An orchestrated business process uses a central controlling service or element, referred to as the orchestrator, conductor, or less frequently, the coordinator.

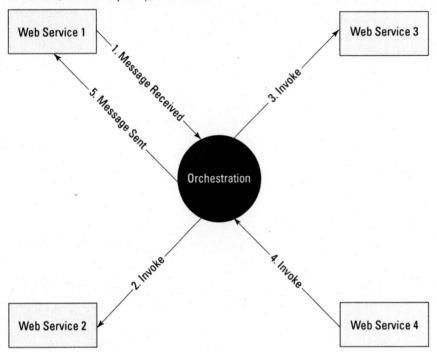

Most mature SOA implementations favor orchestration over choreography for a number of reasons. With orchestration a single central service manages the various processes, and changes to the business logic can be made in that one location. The integration of Web services into the architecture is easier than with choreography because these services don't need to know anything about the business process. Centralizing the business logic also makes it easier to put error handling mechanisms in place and to account for, manage, and analyze events that occur outside the business process that relate to a part of the process. Event handling is part of event-driven SOA or SOA 2.0, which extends Service Oriented Architecture to include both random and scheduled events that are triggered by a business process outside of a business process.

One way of performing orchestration is through the use of an Enterprise Service Bus or ESB. An ESB provides a middleware software layer for event management with a messaging infrastructure. ESBs are described later in the section called "The Enterprise Service Bus." An ESB isn't required by SOA, but it is often used to create a compliant and efficient service architecture.

FIGURE 13.4

With choreography, business process execution is a cooperative affair.

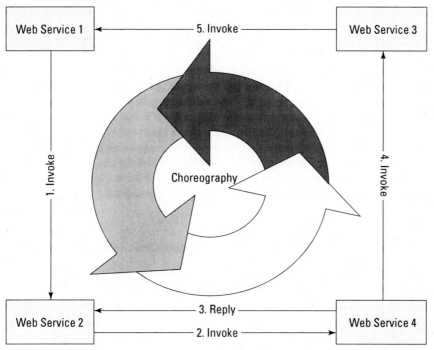

Event-driven SOA or SOA 2.0

Event-driven SOA or SOA 2.0 is an extension of the Service Oriented Architecture to respond to events that occur as a result of business processes or perhaps cause and influence a business process. For example, in a business process, sales at a certain Web site are processed. If the business process recognizes the rate at which sales are occurring, it could perform an analysis to determine what events might influence the buying decision. This is the sort of analysis that event-driven SOA is meant to address. SOA 2.0 can allow low-level events to trigger a business process, correlate events with information contained in the SOA design, inhibit a business process if the appropriate events don't appear, or invoke a reaction or response based on a trigger.

To perform these tasks in SOA 2.0, a Causal Vector Engine (CVE) with some built-in artificial intelligence must be added to the SOA design. Events are analyzed in terms of event sequences, event relationships, and event timing to establish whether a certain condition has occurred. The CVE then determines how to react to the condition using a set of rules that are built into the system. Many CVE systems display events in a console in different contexts so that an observer can analyze the display and take appropriate actions. A CVE application may include the ability to query event data in the same way that a stock ticker or trading application can query trading data. The CVE application provides the same kind of heartbeat and correlation functionality that a stock trading application does.

From the standpoint of the service requestor or consumer (client), the client simply needs to know the form required to initiate the action of the provider (service) and how to interpret the results returned from the service provider. The nature of the component's processing is unknown, the location where the processing is done is unknown, and the various operating systems and applications involved are unknown. The client is responsible for validating that the service returned the results that were expected. The SOA component is essentially a black box to the client. That is, SOA makes no demands of the component other than to conform to the rules of a standard endpoint. This level of abstraction offers operational advantages to Web service providers in that components can be continually upgraded, replaced, or moved to improve efficiencies without disrupting the clients that depend on those services, and the Quality of Service for that service can be accurately measured and delivered. In SOA, the service has been virtualized.

Cross-Ref
Communication protocols are discussed in detail in Chapter 3, "Understanding Cloud Architecture." ■

Any network service that spans different application types is a candidate for componentization. Consider a logon or authentication system. It would be wasteful to implement the same authentication functionality in several different applications when a single unified module could serve the same purpose. A single sign-on system for an accounting package, payroll module, or production database replaces three separate modules with attendant efficiencies in the amount of code that needs to be written and managed and the level of system overhead that is involved. SOA provides the rules so each application can access the authentication module in its own way, as required. What you gain with SOA is the ability to add significant capabilities with a fraction of the cost or effort and to federate applications if you desire. What you lose with SOA is the ability to perform fundamental customization of the service itself when that service is provided by a third party.

The Enterprise Service Bus

In Figure 13.5, those aforementioned hypothetical three different applications are shown interfaced with an authentication module through what has come to be called an Enterprise Service Bus (ESB). An ESB is not a physical bus in the sense of a network; rather, it is an architectural pattern comprised of a set of network services that manage transactions in a Service Oriented Architecture.

You may prefer to think of an ESB as a set of services that separate clients from components on a transactional basis and that the use of the word *bus* in the name indicates a high degree of connectivity or fabric quality to the system; that is, the system is *loosely coupled*. Messages flow from client to component through the ESB, which manages these transactions, even though the location of the services comprising the ESB may vary widely.

An ESB is necessary but not essential to a Service Oriented Architecture because typical business processes can span a vast number of messages and events, and distributed processing is an inherently unreliable method of transport. An ESB therefore plays the role of a transaction broker in SOA, ensuring that messages get to where they where supposed to go and are acted upon properly. The service bus performs the function of mediation: message translation, registration, routing, logging, auditing, and managing transactional integrity. Transactional integrity is similar to ACID in a database system—atomicity, consistency, isolation, and durability, the essence of which is that transactions succeed or they fail and are rolled back.

FIGURE 13.5

An SOA application of a shared logon or Authentication module

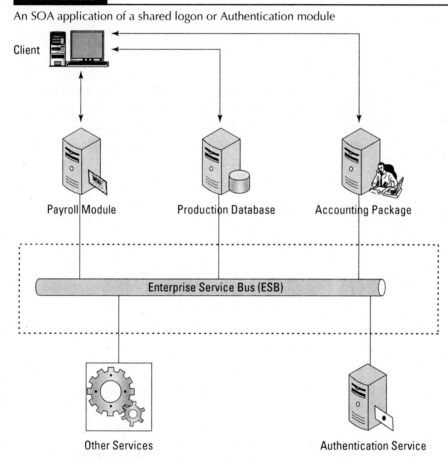

An ESB may be part of a network operating system or may be implemented using a set of middle-ware products. An ESB creates a virtual environment layered on top of an enterprise messaging system where services are advertised and accessed. Think of an ESB as a message transaction system. IBM's WebSphere ESB 7.0 is an ESB based on open standards such as Java EE, EJB, WS-Addressing, WS-Policy, and Kerberos security, and it runs on the WebSphere Application Server. It is interoperable with Open SCA. WebSphere ESB contains both a Service Federation Management tool and an integrated Registry and Repository function.

These typical features are found in ESBs, among others:

- **Monitoring services** aid in managing events.
- **Process management services** manage message transactions.
- **Data repositories or registries** store business logic and aid in governance of business processes.
- **Data services** pass messages between clients and services.
- **Data abstraction services** translate messages from one format to another, as required.
- **Governance** is a service that monitors compliance of your operations with governmental regulation, which can vary from state to state and from country to country.
- **Security services** validate clients and services and allow messages to pass from one to the other.

Figure 13.6 shows how these different services in an SOA relate to one another.

The difference between a repository and a registry in the context of a Service Oriented Architecture is subtle. Repositories and registries are both data stores, but a repository stores references to the components of the SOA, their source code, and linking information that are used to provide SOA services. An SOA registry contains references to rules, descriptions, and definitions of the services—that is, the metadata of the components.

A repository serves the role that a name server does in a network operating system infrastructure, while the registry plays the role of a directory service (domain). The service broker uses the rules contained in the SOA registry to perform its function as translator and delivery agent. For developers, the registry serves as the central location to store component descriptions that allow composite applications to be created and the place in which services may be published for general use.

These services in an SOA also include the provider interfaces and standard sets of network protocols that were mentioned previously. Developers may also choose to create a Business Process Orchestration module to coordinate the access and transactional integrity of multiple business applications that integrate into a larger platform, described in the next section in more detail.

FIGURE 13.6

This figure shows a network services model infrastructure for an SOA, which is based on the SOA meta-model of the Linthicum Group, 2007. A slightly different version of this diagram appears in *Networking Bible* by Barrie Sosinsky, Wiley, 2009.

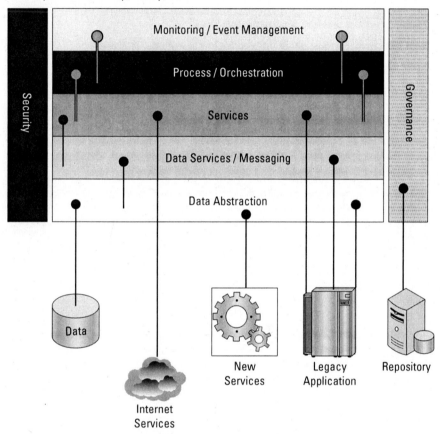

Service catalogs

Finding any particular service and locating the service's requirement in a large SOA implementation can involve a large amount of network system overhead. To aid in locating services, SOA infrastructure often includes a catalog service. This service stores information on the following, among other things:

- What services are available, both internal and external
- How to use a service
- Which applications are related to a particular service (dependencies)
- How services relate to one another
- Who owns the service and how a service is modified
- The event history of a service, including service levels, outages, and so on
- The nature of service contracts

Service catalogs are dynamic and under constant modification. Catalog servers have these features:

- They can be **standalone catalog servers** serving a single site.
- They serve the role of a **global catalog service** where two or more catalog servers are merged to include several sites. A global service usually requires some sort of synchronization or update to maintain a unified data store across the servers involved.
- They can be part of a **federated catalog service** where two or more global catalog servers have access to one another's information through a trusted query relationship.

Catalog services have an enormous impact on large system performance and eventually become essential as a SOA internetwork system grows. An internetwork is a network that is constructed through the consolidation of separate networks, in the same manner that the Internet has been built.

Note

The Information Technology Infrastructure Library (ITIL) developed by the United Kingdom's Office of Government Commerce (OGC) has developed a Service Catalog Management design specification as part of the ITIL v2 Service Design Package (SDP). Service Designs present best practice guidance for planned services. The ITIL Web site may be found at `http://www.itil-officialsite.com/home/home.asp.` ■

Defining SOA Communications

Message passing in SOA requires the use of two different protocol types: the data interchange format and the network protocol that carries the message. A client (or customer) connected to an ESB communicates over a network protocol such as HTTP, Representational State Transfer (REST), or Java Message Service (JMS) to a component (or service). Messages are most often in the form of the eXtensible Markup Language (XML) or in a variant such as the Simple Object Access Protocol (SOAP). SOAP is a messaging format used in Web services that use XML as the message format while relying on Application layer protocols such as HTTP and Remote Procedure Calls (RPC) for message negotiation and transmission.

The software used to write clients and components can be written in Java, .NET, Web Service Business Process Execution Language (WS-BPEL), or another form of executable code; the services that they message can be written in the same or another language. What is required is the ability to transport and translate a message into a form that both parties can understand.

An ESB may require a variety of combinations in order to support communications between a service consumer and a service provider. For example, in WebSphere ESB, you might see the following combinations:

- XML/JMS (Java Message Service)
- SOAP/JMS
- SOAP/HTTP
- Text/JMS
- Bytes/JMS

The Web Service Description Language (WSDL) is one of the most commonly used XML protocols for messaging in Web services, and it finds use in Service Oriented Architectures. Version 1.1 of WSDL is a W3C standard, but the current version WSDL 2.0 (formerly version 1.2) has yet to be ratified by the W3C. The significant difference between 1.1 and 2.0 is that version 2.0 has more support for RESTful (e.g. Web 2.0) application, but much less support in the current set of software development tools. The most common transport for WSDL is SOAP, and the WSDL file usually contains both XML data and an XML schema.

REST offers some very different capabilities than SOAP. With REST, each URL is an object that you can query and manipulate. You use HTML commands such as GET, POST, PUT, and DELETE to work with REST objects. SOAP uses a different approach to working with Web data, exposing Web objects through an API and transferring data using XML. The REST approach offers lightweight access using standard HTTP command, is easier to implement than SOAP, and comes with less overhead. SOAP is often more precise and provides a more error-free consumption model. SOAP often comes with more sophisticated development tools. All major Web services use REST, but many Web services, especially newer ones, combine REST with SOAP to derive the benefits that both offer.

Contained within WSDL are essential objects to support message transfer, including these:

- The **service** object, a container where the service resides.
- The **port or endpoint,** which is the unique address of the service.
- The **binding,** which is the description of the interface (e.g. RPC) and the transport (e.g. SOAP).
- The **portType,** or interface that defines the capabilities of the Web service, and what operations are to be performed, as well as the messages that must be sent to support the operation.
- The **operation** that is to be performed on the message.

- The **message** content, which is the data and metadata that the service operation is performed on. Each message may consist of one or more parts, and each part must include typing information.

- The **types** used to describe the data, usually as part of the XML schema that accompanies the WSDL.

Tip

A set of primers on WSDL may be found on the W3C Web site. The latest version, "Web Services Description Language (WSDL) Version 2.0 Part 0: Primer" may be found at `http://www.w3.org/2002/ws/desc/` `wsdl20-primer.` ∎

The code that follows is the WSDL 2.0 document that is created and analyzed in the W3C WSDL primer referenced in the accompanying tip.

```
<?xml version="1.0" encoding="utf-8" ?>
<description
    xmlns="http://www.w3.org/ns/wsdl"
    targetNamespace= "http://greath.example.com/2004/wsdl/resSvc"
    xmlns:tns= "http://greath.example.com/2004/wsdl/resSvc"
    xmlns:ghns = "http://greath.example.com/2004/schemas/resSvc"
    xmlns:wsoap= "http://www.w3.org/ns/wsdl/soap"
    xmlns:soap="http://www.w3.org/2003/05/soap-envelope"
    xmlns:wsdlx= "http://www.w3.org/ns/wsdl-extensions">

  <documentation>
    This document describes the GreatH Web service. Additional
    application-level requirements for use of this service --
    beyond what WSDL 2.0 is able to describe -- are available
    at http://greath.example.com/2004/reservation-documentation.html
  </documentation>

  <types>
    <xs:schema
        xmlns:xs="http://www.w3.org/2001/XMLSchema"
        targetNamespace="http://greath.example.com/2004/schemas/
resSvc"
        xmlns="http://greath.example.com/2004/schemas/resSvc">

      <xs:element name="checkAvailability"
type="tCheckAvailability"/>
      <xs:complexType name="tCheckAvailability">
        <xs:sequence>
          <xs:element name="checkInDate" type="xs:date"/>
          <xs:element name="checkOutDate" type="xs:date"/>
          <xs:element name="roomType" type="xs:string"/>
        </xs:sequence>
      </xs:complexType>
```

```
        <xs:element name="checkAvailabilityResponse" type="xs:double"/>

        <xs:element name="invalidDataError" type="xs:string"/>

   </xs:schema>
  </types>

  <interface name = "reservationInterface" >

    <fault name = "invalidDataFault"
           element = "ghns:invalidDataError"/>

    <operation name="opCheckAvailability"
           pattern="http://www.w3.org/ns/wsdl/in-out"
           style="http://www.w3.org/ns/wsdl/style/iri"
           wsdlx:safe = "true">
       <input messageLabel="In"
             element="ghns:checkAvailability" />
       <output messageLabel="Out"
             element="ghns:checkAvailabilityResponse" />
       <outfault ref="tns:invalidDataFault" messageLabel="Out"/>
    </operation>

  </interface>

  <binding name="reservationSOAPBinding"
    interface="tns:reservationInterface"
    type="http://www.w3.org/ns/wsdl/soap"
    wsoap:protocol="http://www.w3.org/2003/05/soap/bindings/HTTP/">

    <fault ref="tns:invalidDataFault"
      wsoap:code="soap:Sender"/>

    <operation ref="tns:opCheckAvailability"
      wsoap:mep="http://www.w3.org/2003/05/soap/mep/soap-response"/>

  </binding>

  <service name="reservationService"
       interface="tns:reservationInterface">

     <endpoint name="reservationEndpoint"
              binding="tns:reservationSOAPBinding"
              address ="http://greath.example.com/2004/
                   reservation"/>

  </service>

</description>
```

Notice the major elements of the document. The XML document sets up the namespace, defines the interface, specifies the binding, names the service, provides the documentations for the service, and then supplies a schema that may be used to validate the document. In the message descriptions, the message types are declared. XML schema can be separate files, but what we see here is normal for WSDL, an inline schema that is part of the WSDL document. For a much more complete step-by-step description, refer to the W3C tutorial.

A WSDL file contains essential message data for a transaction, but it doesn't capture the full scope of a Service Oriented Architecture design. Additional requirements need to be specified. The functional requirements for message passing between client and service in SOA are embodied in the concept of a *service contract*. A service contract codifies the relationship between the data to be processed, the metadata that accompanies that data, the intended service, and the manner in which the service will act upon that message.

Messages therefore must have some of the following pieces of information contained inside them:

- **Header:** The header contains the name of the service, service version, owner of the service, and perhaps a responsibility assignment. This is often defined in terms of a RACI matrix where the various roles and responsibilities for processes are spelled out in terms of a set of tasks or deliverables. The acronym designates the **R**esponsible party or service, the **A**ccountable decision maker, the **C**onsulted party, and person(s) or service(s) that must be **I**nformed on the use of the service.

- **Service Type:** Examples of service types include data, business, integration, presentation, and process types.

- **Functional Specification:** This category includes the functional requirements, what service operations or actions and methods must be performed, and the manner in which a service is invoked or initiated. Invocation usually includes the URL and the nature of the service interface.

- **Transaction attributes:** A message may define a transaction that may need to be managed or tracked or be part of or include another transaction operated at a specific Quality of Service and under a specific Service Level Agreement (SLA). Security parameters also are part of a transaction's attributes, as are the role the message plays in a process and the terms or semantics used to describe the interaction of the message with a service's interface.

Depending upon the degree of formalization a service contract may require messages to carry a variable amount of information in order to be successfully transacted. You can see, therefore, how SOA expands the definition of a Web service transaction from WSDL.

Business Process Execution Language

If a message represents an atomic transaction in a Service Oriented Architecture, the next level of abstraction up is the grouping and managing of sets of transactions to form useful work and to execute a business process. An example of an execution language is the Business Process Execution Language (BPEL) or alternatively as the Web Service Business Process Execution Language

(WS-BPEL), a language standard for Web service interactions. The standard is maintained by the Organization for the Advancement of Structured Information Standards (OASIS) through their Web Services Business Process Execution Language Technical Committee (WSBPEL-TC; see `http://www.oasis-open.org/committees/tc_home.php?wg_abbrev=wsbpel`.)

BPEL is a meta-language comprised of two functions: executable commands for Web services and clients, and internal or abstract code for executing the internal business logic that processes require. A meta-language is any language whose statements refer to statements in another language referred to as the object language. BPEL is often used to compose, orchestrate, and coordinate business processes with Web services in the SOA model, and it has commands to manage asynchronous communications.

BPEL uses XML with specific support for messaging protocols such as SOAP, WSDL, UDDI, WS-Reliable Messaging, WS-Addressing, WS-Coordination, and WS-Transactions. BPEL also builds on IBM's Web Services Flow Language (WSFL) and Microsoft's XLANG for data transport; the former is a system of directed graphs, while the latter is a block-structured language adding to additional verbs and nouns specific for business processes to BPEL, which were combined to form BPEL4WS and are being merged with BPEL. A version of BPEL to support human interaction is called BPEL4People, and it falls under the WS-HumanTask specifications of OASIS.

BPEL was designed to interact with WSDL and define business processes using an XML language. BPEL does not have a graphical component. A business process has an internal or executable view and an external or abstract view in BPEL. One process may interact with other processes, but the goal is to minimize the number of specific extensions added to BPEL to support any particular business process. Data functions in BPEL support process data and control flow, manage process instances, provide for logic and branching structures, and allow for process orchestration. Because transactions are long-lived and asynchronous, BPEL includes techniques for error handling and scopes transactions. As much as possible, BPEL uses Web services for standards and to assemble and decompose processes.

Business process modeling

SOA was created by the industry to solve a problem: how to make disparate, diverse, and distributed services talk to disparate and diverse clients. The final result of an SOA project isn't the access of services, per se; it is the creation of a business process. In a complex business project, the developers juggle many clients and many services, which can make visualization of the overall system difficult. To address this problem, various modeling tools have been developed to support SOA development and optimization, system and process management, change and life-cycle management.

Several methodologies have been developed to model SOAs. Working in a software package to model your business processes is similar in approach to designing and optimizing a relational database in entity-relationship, object-role modeling package, or another Computer Aided System Engineering (CASE) tool for data storage—and equally as valuable.

Commonly encountered system models include the following:

- **Unified Modeling Language (UML):** The UML standard is the work of the Object Management Group (`http://www.omg.org/`). UML creates graphical representations of software systems in the form of a set of diagram types. Elements in a UML architectural blueprint include actors, business processes, logic modules (components), program routines, database schemas, software components, and activities. UML diagrams are separated into seven structural types and four behavior types; structure types model the components of the system, while behavior types model states, actions, and events. UML is widely used in the industry for software system modeling. A developed system model can be reduced automatically to code.

- **XML Metadata Interchange (XMI):** XMI is another standard of the Object Management Group (OMG) and is used to exchange metadata using the Extensible Markup Language (XML). Metadata is structured into a metamodel that fits into the OMG's Meta-Object Facility. UML models often use XMI as their interchange format, although they can be used by other languages. XMI files are not generally interchangeable between the different modeling languages that can use them. XMI has been codified as an international standard by ISO, as ISO/IEC 19503:2005.

- **Systems Modeling Language (SysML)** is an open-source extension of the part of the UML system dealing with profiles. It is smaller, more focused, and easier to learn and work with than UML itself. SysML reuses 7 of UML 2.0's 13 diagrams. The effort to develop SysML was rolled into OMG in 2008, but remains open source. SysML can use XMI and is developing toward support of ISO 10303, which is the Standard for the Exchange of Product Model Data (STEP) AP-233. STEP aims to create the mechanisms for sharing information between the different software engineering tools described in this section (and others).

- **Business Process Modeling Notation (BPMN)** is a methodology for representing business processes as a set of connected visual objects that illustrate workflow in a Business Process Diagram (BPD). It is similar to UML. Originally developed in the Business Process Management Initiative (BPMI), it was incorporated into the Open Management Group in 2005. A BPD can be reduced to the OASIS standard WS-Business Process Execution Language, which is an executable language for information transfer between different Web services. However, this mapping is tool specific and standardized at this point.

- **Service-Oriented Modeling Framework (SOMF):** This framework was proposed by Michael Bell and combines a modeling language with a graphical display of the various SOA components so the system can be viewed as a map of objects and associated relationships. SOMF software allows developers to create an action plan to implement their business processes and can be valuable in system and architecture optimization, tracing message pathways, positioning software assets correctly, and providing a language for describing through abstraction and generalization how the processes operate. SOMF software not only allows you to determine what needs to be done, but also allows you to run "what-if" scenarios to see how changes will impact your SOA system.

Tip

The Enterprise Architect (EA) offered by Sparx Systems (`http://www.sparxsystems.com/`) is an example of a unified modeling language tool that supports software systems modeled in these various languages. ∎

A well-known SOMF modeling technology is IBM's Service-Oriented Modeling and Architecture (SOMA), introduced in 2004. SOMA reduces services to a set of service objects and breaks down relationships into three components: the services themselves, the service components that make use of those services, and the information flows required to interact between them. Flows consist both of processes as well as their internal composition. In SOMA, domains and functional groups are identified, variables that affect processes are analyzed, and component development and object oriented analysis are used to model specific cases. SOMA is meant to provide information on service and service boundaries, service granularity, and asset analysis.

In SOMF, the modeling is based on the elements of the service life cycle:

- **Conceptualization:** Defining the processes that will be supported
- **Discovery:** Determining how components are exposed
- **Analysis:** Identifying the relationships services have to clients
- **Integration:** Implementing the messaging infrastructure that connects clients to components
- **Logical design:** Building the system and process logic and determining how orchestration or choreography will be performed
- **Architecture design:** Creating the system component architecture and reducing design to software components with specified interfaces
- **System implementation:** Building and testing the system components

Figure 13.7 shows the various practices brought together in the SOMF modeling discipline.

Four modeling topologies for message passing are used in SOMF:

- **Circular topology:** A circular topology is one where message passing is carried out in a circular fashion. There is no orchestrator in this system, and each component providing a service is responsible for knowing which message to act on and where to send a message next. That is, the choreography of the system is maintained at the component.
- **Hierarchical topology:** In a hierarchical topology, services are arranged in a tree pattern with parent/child relationships. Messages from one service to another must traverse up the branch of the tree and down another branch from the root until the matching service is found. Hierarchical topologies offer the advantage of a well-defined set of relationships, a central location (the root) where logic may reside, and a clearly stated address space. The disadvantage of a hierarchical topology is that the overhead of passing a message from one service to another isn't optimized.
- **Network topology:** A network topology has a many-to-many relationship between services and their clients. The advantage of a network topology is that the overhead associated with message passing has been minimized (often there is a direct path), but there is considerable overhead built into the system in order to maintain the many links needed.
- **Star topology:** In a star topology, services are designed to connect through a central service. The star model is favored in orchestration processes and is useful for services that use broadcasting or multicasting services, publish and subscribe, and other related systems.

FIGURE 13.7

SOMF 2.0 practices, principles, and design methodologies

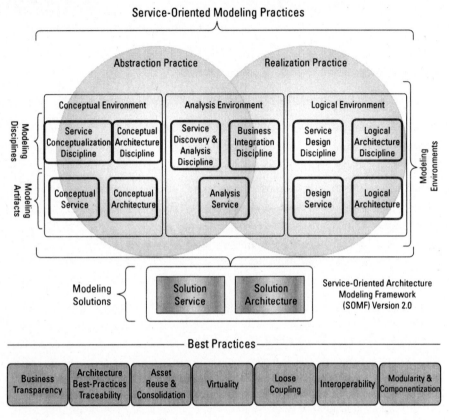

Figure 13.8 shows an interaction diagram of these four different topologies.

A service in SOMF that is granular and very narrow in scope is referred to as an atomic service. An atomic service cannot be decomposed into smaller services that provide a useful function. An example of an atomic service is a customer lookup that contains a customer ID and the customer's name and address. An address that doesn't contain the customer's name or lists a customer name without an ID wouldn't have much value, so this service stands alone. In Figure 13.8 an atomic service would be represented by one of the circles in the diagrams.

FIGURE 13.8

The four different message-passing topologies used in SOMF are shown above. The lines and arrows indicate message-passing pathways and relationships.

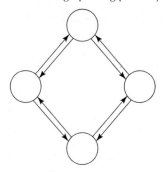

Circular topology

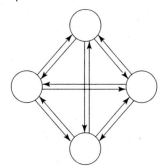

Network topology

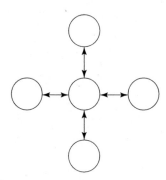

Star topology

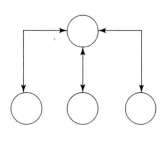

Hierarchical topology

Rarely do atomic services stand alone. A service that provides ID, name, and address might be part of a set of services that describe a bank account, customer purchase record, or any number of services. A collection of services that work together is referred to as a composite service. The Enterprise Service Bus described previously in this chapter is another example of a composite service; it contains functions for message routing, message interchange and translation, and process orchestration. A composite service is usually organized as a hierarchical topology and is multifunctional or a coarse-grained entity.

SOA describes a distributed collection of services performing business process functions. A collection of composite services that would form a process module is referred to as a *service cluster*. Service clusters may be composed of both atomic services and composite services. Large functions such as payroll modules would normally be composite SOA services.

Tip

To view a structured presentation on how to build an SOMF diagram, go to `http://www.modeling`
`concepts.com/pdf/SOMF_ANALYSIS_MODELING.pdf`. **The white paper "Enacting the Service Oriented**
Modeling Framework (SOMF) Using Enterprise Architect" by Frank Truyen (`http://www.sparxsystems.`
`com/downloads/whitepapers/EA-SOMF_Introduction.pdf`) **shows different SOMF diagram types.** ■

In an SOMF model, each of these three service types (atomic, composite, and clusters) appears as a
specific shape, and connections are made between them that generalize, specify, expand, or contract the services they provide. Services are typed, granular services are identified, and then services may be aggregated, decomposed, unified, intersected, or subtracted from other services to
suit the needs of the business process being modeled. The SOMF modeling notation has a symbol
for each analysis that relates one service to another. As you build a business process, you add services to the model and connect them in ways that make sense for your workflow. When the model
is complete and optimized, it is reduced to a conceptualized service that relates the business process to the specific implementation chosen. Some modeling technologies allow for the reduction of
the model to executable code.

Managing and Monitoring SOA

Software for monitoring and managing an SOA infrastructure plays an important role in large SOA
deployments. While SOA offers a logical design and reusable components, it does not make the
task of network management any easier. If anything, SOA management requires proactive over-
sight because you can't wait for a particular application to fail before taking corrective action.
Therefore, tools for managing SOAs tend to be multifaceted and run constantly.

SOA management tools

There are a number of network management frameworks products and suites, notably these:

- HP Software and Solutions OpenView SOA Manager (`https://h10078.www1.`
  `hp.com/cda/hpms/display/main/hpms_content.jsp?zn=bto`
  `&cp=1-10^36657_4000_100`)

- IBM Tivoli Framework Composite Application Manager for SOA (ITCAM; see `http://`
  `www-01.ibm.com/software/tivoli/solutions/`),

- Oracle BPEL Process Manager (`http://www.oracle.com/technology/bpel/`
  `index.html`)

These products have SOA tools for network management. IBM's product specializes in change
management and SOA lifecycle development, and it integrates with a WebSphere and other Tivoli
systems. HP SOA Manager provides dynamic mapping, monitoring, and optimization of SOA services such as Web services, software assets, and virtual services. These framework products create
a central console with a variety of management views. Oracle's BPEL Process Manager and
WebSphere are process managers for creating an Enterprise Service Bus.

The SOA management software technology is dynamic, with many small vendors' products some of which have been purchased and rolled into (or are being rolled into) larger systems. Oracle's recent acquisition of AmberPoint's SOA Management System is an example of this trend. BMC Software's AppSight (`http://www.bmc.com/products/product-listing/BMC-AppSight.html`) is an automated SOA problem-resolution package, as is Tidal Software's Intersperse package, which has root cause analysis services. The CA Wily SOA Solution (`http://www.ca.com/us/eitm/solution.aspx?id=8254`) is a monitoring and discovery service that can map SOA transactions and dependencies and discover components such as ESBs, Web portals, and various Web services. iTKO's LISA (`http://www.itko.com/products/index.jsp`). Enterprise SOA Testing platform specializes in testing Web service components that are used in SOA. Another example of an SOA transaction manager is OpTier's CoreFirst (`http://www.optier.com/corefirst_overview.aspx`).

Configuration and change management present a particular challenge in the area of SOA (and cloud computing in general). In addition to the fact that elements of an SOA infrastructure can be highly distributed and therefore require good discovery mechanisms, these environments also are highly virtualized. As workloads vary, solutions often provision virtual servers as needed and move these virtual servers' processing across physical servers. Virtualization will continue to challenge SOA management software well into the future.

SOA security

Any system that sends hundreds or thousands of messages across an internetwork as SOA does is subject to attack in all the traditional ways that network traffic is hijacked, spoofed, redirected, or blocked. Because SOA eliminates the use of application boundaries, the traditional methods where security is at the application level aren't likely to be effective.

Cisco has a family of products that enforce rules and policies for the transmission of XML messaging that they have named Application Oriented Networking (AON; `http://www.cisco.com/en/US/products/ps6480/`). A similar policy based XML security service may be found in Citrix's NetScaler 9.0 (`http://www.citrix.com/English/ps2/products/product.asp?contentID=21679`) Web application delivery appliance.

To address SOA security, a set of OASIS standards (`http://www.oasis-open.org/committees/tc_home.php?wg_abbrev=security`) was created, which includes the following:

- **Security Assertion Markup Language (SAML)** is an XML standard that provides for data authentication and authorization between client and service. The SAML technology is used as part of Single Sign-on Systems (SSO) and allows a user logging into a system from a Web browser to have access to distributed SOA resources.

- **WS-Security (WSS)** is an extension of SOA that enforces security by applying tokens such as Kerberos, SAML, or X.509 to messages. Through the use of XML Signature and XML Encryption, WSS aims to offer client/service security.

- **WS-SecureConversion** is a Web services protocol for creating and sharing security context. WS-SecureConversion is meant to operate in systems where WS-Security, WS-Trust, and WS-Policy are in use, and it attaches a security context token to communications such as SOAP used to transport messages in an SOA enterprise.

- **WS-SecurityPolicy** provides a set of network policies that extend WS-Security, WS-Trust, and WS-SecureConversion so messages complying to a policy must be signed and encrypted. The SecurityPolicy is part of a general WS-Policy framework.

- **WS-Trust** extends WS-Security to provide a mechanism to issue, renew, and validate security tokens. A Web service using WS-Trust can implement this system through the use of a Security Token Service (STS), a mechanism for attaching security tokens to messages and a set of mechanisms for key exchanges that are used to validate tokens and messages.

Another approach to enforcing security in SOA is to use an XML gateway that intercepts XML messages transported by SOAP or REST, identifies the source of the message, and verifies that the message was securely received. Providing XML Gateway SOA security requires a Public Key Infrastructure (PKI) so that encryption is enforced by digital signatures. Progress Software's Actional 8.0 (http://web.progress.com/en/actional/index.html) now includes Mindreef's SOAPscope Server and has an XML middleware service that performs diagnostic testing and Web services governance, adding that component to Actional's ability to monitor and map XML appliances and application servers.

The Open Cloud Consortium

The Open Cloud Consortium (OCC; see http://opencloudconsortium.org/) is an organization comprised of several universities and interested companies that supports the development of standards for cloud computing and for interoperating with the various frameworks.

OCC working groups perform these functions:

- They develop benchmarks for measuring cloud computing performance. Their benchmark and data generator for measuring large data clouds is called MalStone (http://code.google.com/p/malgen/).

- They provide testbeds that vendors can use to test their applications, including the Open Cloud Testbed and the Intercloud Testbed that are part of the work of the Open Cloud Testbed and Intercloud working groups.

- They support the development of open-source reference implementations for cloud computing. The Working Group on Standards and Interoperability For Large Data Clouds extends the architecture for data storage with a distributed file system, table services, and computing using MapReduce following the model that is part of Google's offering.

MapReduce is Google's patented software framework that supports distributed large data sets organized by the Google File System (GFS) accessed by clusters of computers. The Apache Hadoop (`http://hadoop.apache.org/`) open-source system is based on MapReduce and GFS.

- They support the management of cloud computing infrastructure for scientific research as part of the Open Science Data Cloud (OSDCP) Working Group's initiative.

Relating SOA and Cloud Computing

Cloud computing is still in its infancy, and although Web services can implement a Service Oriented Architecture, it is not a requirement. Most of the large implementations of cloud computing described in this book are single-purpose applications that have been optimized on a grand scale: Carbonite's backup, Google's Gmail e-mail, and Twitter's Instant Messaging (IM) are several examples. Applications of those types have less of a need for the flexibility and loose coupling that SOA provides. As cloud applications become more diverse in scope, SOA offers an architectural blueprint for accessing diverse optimized services through a loosely coupled standardized method that provides an ability to evolve that is difficult to implement in any other way.

SOA is loosely coupled because the service is separated from the messaging. If a component doesn't provide the capabilities required, it is an easy task to switch to a different component, and switching requires almost no programming. Developers lose some of the ability to customize modules, but gain a significant advantage in simplifying their applications. Taken as a whole, applications that rely on SOA components can be very complex and appear to be tightly coupled, when in reality they are not.

SOA components are often best-of-breed service providers that can provide a measured service level and can play a role in Business Process Management (BPM) systems. The separation of services from their design allows for much easier system upgrades and maintenance.

Many Web 2.0 applications use SOA components, and SOA will become increasingly useful in larger applications that require many Web services. Web 2.0 is an acronym coined by Tim O'Reilly to describe Web services that allow for user input and modification. These applications often rely on REST and feature AJAX components in a user interface that supports Web syndication (think of the Google customizable user page), blogs, and wikis. Some people regard mashups as Web 2.0 applications as well. A *mashup* is the combination of data from two or more sources that creates a unique service. The layers added to Google maps are examples of mashups.

AJAX stands for Asynchronous JavaScipt and XM. AJAX is a set of development tools that allow for client input into Web applications; it is not a standard. Rather AJAX describes a group of technologies that leverage HTML and CSS for styling, Web objects in the Document Object Model (DOM) for data, XML and XSLT for data interchange, the XMLHttpRequest for asynchronous communication, and JavaScript commands to request data from data sources.

The challenge SOA faces in designing systems to support Web 2.0 is the lack of standardization in how components in Web 2.0 are used. However, many people believe that SOA will play a role in creating what has been dubbed an "Internet of Services" where complex services will be available for use as a set of building blocks based on the convergence of SOA and Web 2.0. The Gartner Group refers to this trend as the development of "Advanced SOA," but features of SOA that are event-driven have been part of many vendors' middleware offerings for several years now.

Summary

This chapter described Service Oriented Architecture (SOA). SOA offers a design methodology for creating distributed applications using diverse clients and components. SOA defines a message-passing infrastructure from clients or consumers to and from service providers. Making SOA work correctly requires a certain set of middleware products in your infrastructure. These servers may aid in transaction management or brokering, message translation, or other services. Taken as a whole, these services are referred to as an Enterprise Service Bus (ESB).

Most message-passing protocols are based on a version structured XML, although that is not required in SOA. A variety of transport protocols are used, but SOAP and RPC are the most common ones. The nature of SOA messaging was explored. In a complex system of message passing and services, system management and security is an important consideration. Tools for setting up and running an SOA infrastructure were described.

Finally, this chapter described the relationship between SOA and cloud computing. You don't need to use SOA to build a massively scaled cloud computing application, but as cloud computing applications become more capable and user configurable, the logic and structure that SOA design imposes on infrastructure will prove to be invaluable to cloud applications. The two areas of technology benefit from their mutual convergence.

In Chapter 14, I consider the topic of transactional Web applications in cloud computing systems. That subject builds on what you have learned about SOA in this chapter, extending the discussion into the command Web APIs that are in use today.

14

Moving Applications to the Cloud

I n this chapter, you learn about some of the important considerations involved in moving an application from a local or on-premises installation to one that is either fully or partly in the cloud. Some applications benefit from cloud deployment, and the cloud enhances some features.

The process for determining whether, what, and when to move your applications to the cloud involves an analysis of what critical features of the application need to be supported. After those critical features are understood, you can determine the features supported by your particular cloud service provider to see whether the cloud can support the application's critical features. Factors such as access to data, latencies, data security, and so on often limit what applications are good candidates for porting.

Two examples of application porting to the cloud are discussed in this chapter. In one application, physical hardware is eliminated by moving the entire application to the cloud. In the second example, a system is essentially cloned to the cloud to provide an overflow capability, an example of a hybrid application technique called cloud bursting.

When you move an application to the cloud, you must use the APIs of your particular cloud service provider. There are APIs for each of the types of cloud services: infrastructure, software services, and applications in the case of platform providers. These APIs are generally not interoperable. So although the situation may change in the future, an application developer must make an informed choice to select the vendor that both best suits his needs and allows him to have the greatest flexibility.

IN THIS CHAPTER

Learning about cloud transactions

Determining the best features to move to the cloud

Seeing a cloud burst solution

Knowing the factors of cloud application development

Applications in the Clouds

When you deploy an application to the cloud, you start with the advantages and disadvantages of a distributed system that is the Internet and add to that mix the fundamental characteristics that clouds offer. In the cloud, your applications must account for system abstraction and redirection, scalability, a whole new set of application and system APIs, LAN/WAN latencies, and other factors that are specific to one cloud platform or another. In theory, any application can run either completely or partially in the cloud.

The question a developer needs to ask is whether his application's function is best served by cloud or local deployment. That answer depends upon the attributes of the application that the developer is trying to preserve or enhance, and how locating those services in the cloud impacts those attributes. This chapter takes a broad look at cloud computing from an application-specific viewpoint and attempts to highlight the factors that make cloud-based applications successful.

The location of an application or service plays a fundamental role in how the application must be written. An application or process that runs on a desktop or server is executed coherently, as a unit, under the control of an integrated program. An action triggers a program call, code executes, and a result is returned and may be acted upon.

Taken as a unit, "Request => Process => Response" is an atomic transaction. Because the transaction is executing locally within the purview of a monolithic application, the process is stateful and transaction is consistent. That is, the condition of the transaction is always known and the result is always accounted for. A coherent transaction either succeeds and is enacted, or fails and is rolled back. When rollback is not possible due to optimistic transaction commitment in a multiuser application, atomicity requires correcting the condition or performs some other compensating action at some later time.

The properties necessary to guarantee a reliable transaction in databases and other applications and the technologies necessary to achieve them have been called the ACID principle. The acronym stands for:

- **Atomicity:** The atomic property defines a transaction as something that cannot be subdivided and must be completed or abandoned as a unit.

- **Consistency:** The consistency property states that the system must go from one known state to another and that the system integrity must be maintained.

- **Isolation:** The isolation property states that the system cannot have other transactions operate on data that is currently being processed by a transaction.

- **Durability:** The durability property states that the system must have a mechanism to recover from committed transactions should that be necessary.

The ACID rules were developed by Jim Gray to apply to database technology in the late 1970s. The ACID principle is used today by any application that is reading and writing to a stored data set, which includes just about any application type you can think of.

An application that runs as a service on the Internet has a client portion that makes a request and a server portion that responds to that request. The request has been decoupled from the response because the transaction is executing in two or more places. In a distributed system, the transaction is stateless. In order to create a stateful system in a distributed architecture, a transaction manager or broker must be added so that the intermediary service can account for transactions and react accordingly when they succeed or fail.

When applications get moved to the cloud, they retain the features of a three-layered architecture, but now physical systems become virtualized systems. Virtual machines are not only stateless, but the place where program execution occurs is likely to be different every time the process runs. These fundamental properties must be accounted for in any cloud-based application.

Functionality mapping

Some applications can be successfully ported to the cloud, while others suffer from the translation. Understanding whether your particular application can benefit from cloud deployment requires that you deconstruct your application's functionality into its basic components and identify which functions are critical and can be supported by the cloud.

For example, any application that requires access to a data store quickly runs up against some of the limits that cloud computing imposes. Order transaction systems require that data in a database maintain the transactional integrity implied by the ACID model. For many non-relational cloud storage systems, such as the Amazon Simple Storage Service (S3), the newly announced Google Storage for Developers, and the Windows Azure Storage Service, the ability of the system to maintain transactional integrity through record locking isn't part of those systems. These types of storage systems are secure and store large amounts of data, but they have very slow access to that data and do not support query and retrieval well. These limitations are why all these vendors offer alternative relational cloud database systems such as SQL Azure.

In Figure 14.1, an attribute tree is constructed for an order transaction system where the functionality is decomposed into different functional areas. At the top are high-level attributes; some of these functions are essential to the operation of the application while others are not. Drilling down on the data management attribute, the second level explores data access and then access methods. A critical attribute for the application is the need to be able to access data when the client is both online and offline.

Note
This exercise isn't required for all attributes, just the critical ones, which should result in a manageable list. ∎

FIGURE 14.1

An attribute map is created to expose critical functionality.

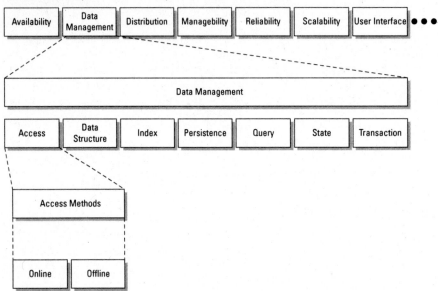

The choice to allow both online and offline data access determines the nature of your application's interaction with both cloud and local data stores. If the application needed to access data only when the client was online, then access to cloud-based storage would be the only data store your application would required. Perhaps the application could be entirely in the cloud and browser-based. The decision to allow both online and local data access means that you must create a hybrid application with a cloud component and a local component. Even if the access to data on the local system is a simple caching system, client-side support is needed. To support the application's data access, you may also be faced with building a synchronization or replication feature, which adds more overhead to the application.

This type of mapping exercise leads to some conclusions about the value of cloud computing to this particular application. You could safely conclude that an application that gets the most value from a cloud deployment is one that uses online storage without the need for offline storage. An application that needed offline storage alone might not benefit from a cloud deployment at all. In the case of a hybrid application, other factors such as scalability, costs, or ubiquitous access might offset the cost of offline access and make the cloud more attractive.

Application attributes

Table 14.1 lists some of the first- and second-level application attributes that you might want to consider in your analysis of an application's suitability to be ported to the cloud.

TABLE 14.1

Application Attributes

First Level	Second Level	First Level	Second Level
Application	Abstraction		Implementation
	Architecture		Language/locale
	Configuration		Monitoring
	Interoperability		Operations
	Modularity		Staffing
	Object model		Startup/recovery
	Reusability		Tools
Availability	Caching	Scalability	Caching
	Fault management		Expertise
	Geographic location		Licensing
	Pooling		Lifecycle management
	Resource access		Load balancing
	Reliability		Replication
	Uptime		Scale up or out
Costs	Development		
	Resources		Staging
Data Management	Application needs		
	Data exchange	Security	Access
	Database needs		Auditing
	Index		Authentication
	Online/offline access		Authorization
	Portability		Cryptography
	Query		Encryption
	State		Identity
	Store type		Regulations
	Structure		Remote access
	Transactions		Security rules
			Trust relationships
Maintenance	APIs	User Interface	Ease of use
	Configuration		Interface features
	Deployment		User interaction

Deconstructing an application's critical functionality is only half the process. Each cloud platform also has its own set of attributes that need to be mapped. In considering the needs of any feature, the key drivers for applications that benefit from deployment to the cloud are those that meet these criteria:

- Are not mission critical
- Are not core business functions
- Do not have sensitive data to protect
- Tolerate high network latencies or low network bandwidth
- Are legacy applications with no particular competitive advantage
- Are based on industry standard technologies
- Do not need to be customized
- Are mature enough and understood well enough to be successfully ported to the cloud

Cloud service attributes

You then want to match up application attributes to these key cloud service attributes:

- Applications
- Core services
- Infrastructure
- Platform features
- Storage

At the current stage in its development, it is impracticable to match the needs of an application to a set of cloud service providers. Each provider has a unique solution, uses its own APIs, and provides unique services. Therefore, each cloud provider needs separate developer skills, and integration between clouds would be a major chore. Perhaps someday this situation may change as more standards are developed, but at the moment application developers need to match their application to the single best vendor.

Table 14.2 lists some of the first- and second-level cloud features that you might want to consider in your analysis. You should map your critical application features to the features of a particular cloud platform to get the best match.

TABLE 14.2

Cloud Service Attributes

First Level	Second Level	First Level	Second Level
Application	Accounting		Operating system support (platform)
	Database		Resource pooling
	Event management		Scale up or out
	Messaging		Site location
	Location service		Redundancy and replication
	Relation management		Virtual machine types
	Web server		API
Core Services	Accounting	Platform Features	Application support
	Application support		Deployment technology
	Auditing		Development environment
	Data access		Language and locale
	Identity		Programming language support
	Index		Testing
	Query		API and commands
	Transaction management	Storage	Query
	Workflow		Non-relational
Infrastructure	Application support		Relational
	Availability		Reliability
	I/O (network) characteristics		Replication
	Load balancing		SQL support

System abstraction

The cloud turns physical systems into virtual systems. Organizations choose to deploy systems to the cloud entirely when they can recreate the essential part of their process and eliminate infrastructure. As an example, consider a service that does medical imaging. In the past, this service created patient scans and then rendered the image on a local computer. After the image was rendered, it was posted to the hospital LAN and made available to the people who read the scans. When the people reading the scans were outside the hospital, across the country, or around the world, those people would have to log into the hospital server via VPN to download the file.

The scanning service decided to eliminate infrastructure and streamline the process. The service began its redeployment by first moving the stored images off the hospital's LAN and onto shared storage in the cloud. This feature eliminated the need to maintain a great deal of managed storage locally. As the service began to outsource the reading of scans to other countries, it enabled a content delivery network feature that the cloud service provider had. CDN (Content Delivery Network) placed copies of recently used and created scans in locations that were closer to the readers and made the system faster.

The second stage in the redeployment was to eliminate the local processing associated with the scanning machines themselves. Most of the time the scanning machine was operating, it was collecting data, and an economic analysis revealed that it was significantly cheaper to process the files in the cloud.

In the new system, shown in Figure 14.2, the files are created locally and transmitted to the cloud. Virtual machines are provisioned to process the scans. The system leverages a message queuing server to create a steady stream of execution for the application server to process. At times of peak load, the system creates new machine instances to handle the load. As the application server completes the scan processing, it notifies the message queue, records the result in a database, and displays it on a Web page on a Web server, all of which are in the cloud.

This new system results in greater system efficiencies because the system is always processing at its optimum load. The rendered scans are available from anywhere viewed inside a browser. Also, because the system is scalable, the scanning service can expand to other sites and bring on new capacity to handle additional load. As the service loses sites, it can also release resources as well. When it is decided that the scans need to be converted into a different format, this can be done in a central location and doesn't need to be rolled out to the computers attached to individual scan systems.

Infrastructure, storage, and the queuing system all come together to eliminate a great deal of cost and operational complexity. This is a pure cloud play.

Cloud bursting

Many cloud deployments are hybrid applications: Part of the application is on a local system, and part is in the cloud. Often, this is the first stop on the path for many organizations migrating their applications to the cloud. There are many reasons why this is desirable, but one of the most common reasons is that the cloud can serve as excess capacity at times of high volume. This type of hybrid has been called *cloud bursting*. Examples of systems where there is high volume over short periods of time are transaction processing systems such as reservations systems.

In a reservation system, there is a certain low level of background transactions occurring at any time. At certain times, events trigger high demand. If the system builds infrastructure to accommodate peak demand, then that infrastructure is wasted.

FIGURE 14.2

An application deployed entirely to the cloud

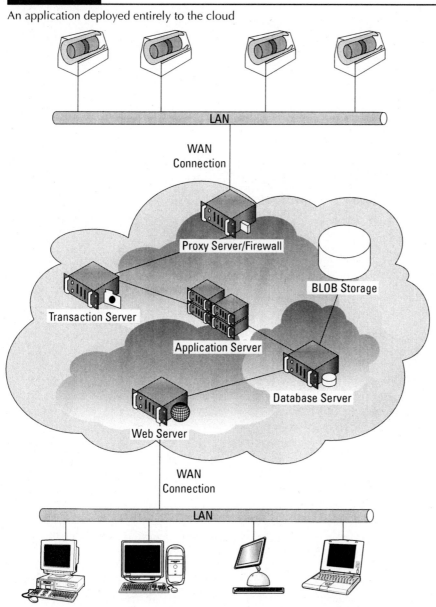

Most systems built to perform cloud bursting have a simple underlying design: clone the local system in the cloud. Often, there may be little activity in the cloud portion of the system, but when the activity grows, the copy of the system in the cloud picks up the extra activity and, when necessary, provisions extra resources. Figure 14.3 shows a simple reservations system set up for cloud bursting.

FIGURE 14.3

An application that provides for transaction overflow in a reservation system is an example of cloud bursting.

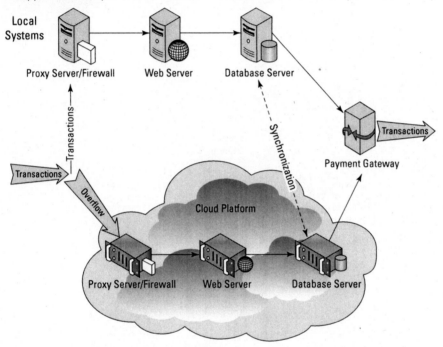

Reservation systems often require that transactions not only are atomic, but that when there is a pool of items being reserved, the system is consistent. When a transaction enters the local branch in Figure 14.3 and another transaction enters the cloud platform branch, they can't both reserve the same item. So there must be a transaction manager in this system to manage the pool. This is shown as a dotted line between the two database servers, labeled "Synchronization." The underlying mechanism is to perform record locking on a set of database records and when the transaction or a batch of transactions completes, the system performs a commit operation.

In most reservation systems, the actual transaction commitment is a small part of the traffic and processing. Most of the traffic is generated on the Web site as users browse the content. So it makes sense in this scenario to recreate the company Web site and create additional load-balanced Web server instances as needed. You also can optimize that Web site for faster transactions with less customization. If your Web site relies on dynamic data driven content, you can speed up its operation by switching more of the content over to static content. You'll need to synchronize changes between your on-premises and cloud-based Web servers in order to keep the information current.

The other step in a reservation system that is often a bottleneck is the payments gateway to credit card companies and financial institutions. It may make sense to move the payment portion completely to the cloud so that the processing of payments doesn't affect the other parts of the system. Because the commitment of the payment either is effective or not, this portion of the process does not need to be tracked. The fact that a virtual server is executing the payments and that the process is stateless has no impact in this point.

Eventually, developers will want to create composite applications that are built from the best-of-breed cloud services on multiple platforms. This offers the benefit of redundant suppliers, access to additional services and features, more data sources, and a whole host of other advantages. Cloud architectures offer enough advantages that over time large organizations will want to adopt them as a core architectural design. For example, in Figure 14.4, an internal cloud provides high-speed transactional services on the LAN, an external cloud services other needs of users, and the company cloud is replicated to multiple sites. Where services get located then depends upon factors such as cost, latency, and convenience.

FIGURE 14.4

For the users in large organizations, it is literally clouds everywhere in their future.

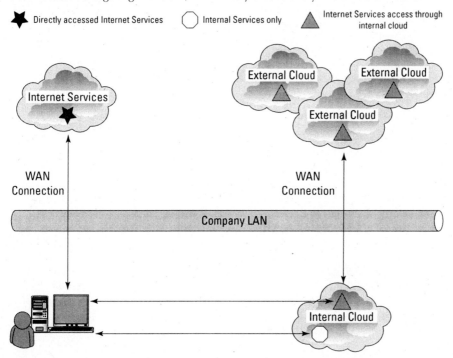

Applications and Cloud APIs

The nature of a cloud provider's Cloud API will impact your ability to move an application to the cloud and affect the way many of your application features operate. Cloud APIs are the Application Programming Interface to functions that exchange information in and with the cloud, request supported operations, and provide management and monitoring functions for applications running in the cloud.

At this stage in cloud computing's development, Amazon Web Service's Cloud API dominates the conversation, but that is probably subject to change. Each cloud vendor has its own specific API; most are exposed as REST, a few are exposed as SOAP, or some are both. Each API provides specific calls required by that vendor's infrastructure and service.

Most importantly, the cloud API contains the authentication and authorization mechanisms needed to access cloud services. When a vendor like Google allows other cloud application providers to access its ID mechanism (as is the case now), there is the same flexibility in using those services on other platforms.

Although efforts are underway to create more standardized cloud APIs, the situation limits the portability of any application developed for the cloud. The two cross-platform API initiatives are the Simple Cloud API (http://www.simplecloud.org/) and the work arising out of the Cloud Computing Interoperability Forum (http://www.cloudforum.org/). Several cross-platform cloud API projects are underway, including the Design Cloud, Deltacloud, jclouds, and libcloud APIs. These cross-platform APIs are based on generalizing the major cloud vendors APIs.

Each layer of a cloud application has its own specific API as well. So at the infrastructure level in addition to AWS EC2, you have the following:

- Windows Azure (http://www.microsoft.com/windowsazure/windows azure/)
- VMWare vCloud (https://www.vmware.com/products/vcloud/)
- Racksapce Cloud Servers (http://www.rackspacecloud.com/cloud_hosting_ products/servers/api)
- RimHosting (http://rimuhosting.com/)

All these present the developer with their own APIs. Individual services such as Windows Azure SQL, Flickr, and Google Maps present a service cloud API. If your application is developed in a platform such as Facebook, LinkedIn, or the Salesforce Force APIs, each platform has its own specific application API.

The point is that the decision to move an application to the cloud rapidly funnels you into a specific solution that provides a measure of vendor lock-in that, depending upon the nature of your application, can be anywhere from very easy to nearly impossible to port to any other cloud technology. This may not always be so, but it currently is true and it should give a developer some moments to pause.

Summary

In this chapter, you learned about some of the factors involved in deciding to move an application to the cloud. Cloud computing supports some application features better than others. To determine whether your application will port successfully, you should perform a functionality mapping exercise. This process involves determining the critical application features and then matching them to the cloud provider's offering to see if those features can be supported.

Examples of applications that were ported were presented. One application virtualized the entire application in the cloud and presented users with a browser-based service. The second scenario, called cloud bursting, is an overflow solution that clones the application to the cloud and directs traffic to the cloud during times of high traffic.

The role of a cloud vendor's specific API and the impact that it has on porting an application was also considered. This aspect of a migration isn't given enough thought beforehand and can cause problems later on should you wish to move to other solutions.

In Chapter 15, "Working with Cloud-Based Storage," various storage, backup, and disaster recovery solutions offered by cloud vendors are discussed.

Working with Cloud-Based Storage

T he world is creating massive amounts of data. A large percentage of that data either is already stored in the cloud, will be stored in the cloud, or will pass through the cloud during the data's lifecycle. Cloud storage systems are among the most successful cloud computing applications in use today. This chapter surveys the area of cloud storage systems, categorizes the different cloud storage system types, discusses file-sharing and backup software and systems, and describes the methods being used to get cloud storage systems to interoperate.

Cloud storage can be either unmanaged or managed. *Unmanaged storage* is presented to a user as if it is a ready-to-use disk drive. The user has little control over the nature of how the disk is used. Most user-oriented software such as file-sharing and backup consume unmanaged cloud storage. Applications using unmanaged cloud storage are Software as a Service (SaaS) Web services.

Managed storage involves the provisioning of raw virtualized disk and the use of that disk to support applications that use cloud-based storage. Storage options involved in formatting, partitioning, replicating data, and other options are available for managed storage. Applications using managed cloud storage are Infrastructure as a Service (IaaS) Web services.

Developing cloud storage interoperability standards are described in this chapter, notably those from the Storage Networking Industry Association (SNIA) and the Open Grid Foundation (OGF). The Cloud Data Management

Interface (CDMI) interoperability storage object protocol is described. This interface can store data objects, discover stored data objects, and supply these data objects to subscribing applications. The Open Cloud Computing Interface (OCCI) is another storage data interchange interface for stored data objects. The two protocols interoperate with one another.

Measuring the Digital Universe

The world has an insatiable hunger for storage. This hunger is driven by the capture of rich media, digital communications, the Web, and myriad other factors. When you send an e-mail with a 1GB attachment to three people, this generates an estimated 50GB of stored managed data. Only 25 percent of the data stored is unique; 75 percent of stored data is duplicated. You may be surprised to learn that 70 percent of the data stored in the world is user initiated; the remainder is enterprise-generated content.

Video cameras and surveillance photos, financial transaction event logs, performance data, and so on create what IDC (International Data Corporation; http://www.idc.com/), the research analysis arm of International Data Group has called the "digital shadow"—data that is automatically generated. Shadow data represents more than 50 percent of the data created every day. However, lots of shadow data does get retained, having never been touched by a human being.

Much of the data produced is temporal, stored briefly, and then deleted. That's a good thing, because there is a growing divide between the amount of data that is being produced and the amount of storage available.

The storage giant EMC has an interest in knowing just how much data is being stored worldwide. EMC has funded some studies over the past decade to assess the size of what it calls "The Digital Universe." The latest study done by IDC in 2007-2008 predicted that by 2011 the world will store 1800 exabytes (EB) or 1.8 zettabytes (ZB) of data. By the year 2020, stored data will reach an astonishing 35ZB. The number of managed objects stored in containers—files, images, packets, records, signals, and so on—is estimated to be roughly 25 quintillion (1018) containers. A *container* is a term of art in cloud storage.

These numbers are astronomical, and wrapping your mind around them can be hard. Even more astonishing is the fact that the amount of stored data is doubling roughly every five years. In 2007, the last year before the recession of 2008, the amount of stored data grew even faster, by 60 percent annually. You can visit EMC's Digital Universe home page, shown in Figure 15.1, to link to the IDC study, view the Digital Data Consumption Ticker, and get EMC's take on the problems associated with managing vast data sets.

Note

Here are some definitions of scale: a gigabyte is 10^9 bytes, a petabyte is 10^{15} bytes; an exabyte is equal to one billion gigabytes or 10^{18} bytes; a zettabyte is equal to one trillion gigabytes or 10^{21} bytes; and a yottabyte (YB) is 10^{24} bytes. ■

FIGURE 15.1

EMC's Digital Universe Web page located at `http://www.emc.com/leadership/digital-universe/expanding-digital-universe.htm`

To provide some measure of scale, the size of William Shakespeare's complete works downloaded as text from Gutenburg.org (`http://www.gutenberg.org/etext/100`) is 5.1MB. The amount of stored information in the United States Library of Congress is about 10 terabytes of data (10,000 gigabytes), and in 2009 Google was processing around 24 petabytes of data per day. Figure 15.2 shows a logarithmic scale with different data storage sizes.

FIGURE 15.2

Data storage plotted on a logarithmic scale

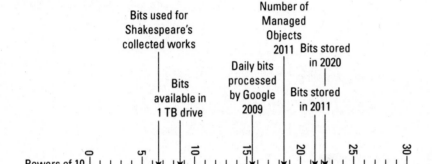

Cloud storage in the Digital Universe

A very significant fraction of this data is now or will be residing in cloud storage. Even more will pass through cloud storage in its use. IDC's 2010 study attempted to estimate the percentage of data that will be stored in the cloud or passed through the cloud in the year 2020. There will be a steady growth of cloud storage at the expense of online storage over the next decade. Figure 15.3 shows a graphical illustration of the impact of cloud storage systems on the overall Digital Universe in 2020.

FIGURE 15.3

Cloud storage data usage in the year 2020 is estimated to be 14 percent resident and 34 percent passing through the cloud by IDC. Source: IDC Digital Universe, May 2010.

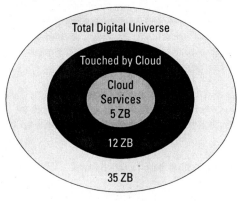

Cloud storage definition

Think of cloud storage as storage accessed by a Web service API. The characteristics that separate cloud storage include network access most often through a browser, on-demand provisioning, user control, and most often adherence to open standards so that cloud storage may be operating-system-neutral and file-system-neutral. These characteristics, taken as a whole define an offering that is best described as an Infrastructure as a Service model. However, most users do not provision storage under IaaS systems such as Amazon S3 (described in Chapter 9). Instead, most users interact with cloud storage using backup, synchronization, archiving, staging, caching, or some other sort of software. The addition of a software package on top of a cloud storage volume makes most cloud storage offerings conform to a Software as a Service model.

Storage devices may be broadly categorized as either block storage devices or file storage devices. A block storage device exposes its storage to clients as Raw storage that can be partitioned to create volumes. It is up to the operating system to create and manage the file system; from the standpoint of the storage device, data is transferred in blocks. The alternative type of storage is a file server, most often in the form of a Network Attached Storage (NAS) device. NAS exposes its storage to clients in the form of files, maintaining its own file system. Block storage devices offer faster data transfers, but impose additional overhead on clients. File-oriented storage devices are generally slower (with the exception of large file-streaming applications), but require less overhead from attached clients. Cloud storage devices can be either block or file storage devices.

Provisioning Cloud Storage

Cloud storage may be broadly categorized into two major classes of storage: unmanaged and managed storage. In unmanaged storage, the storage service provider makes storage capacity available to users, but defines the nature of the storage, how it may be used, and by what applications. The options a user has to manage this category of storage are severely limited. However, unmanaged storage is reliable, relatively cheap to use, and particularly easy to work with. Most of the user-based applications that work with cloud storage are of this type.

Managed cloud storage is mainly meant for developers and to support applications built using Web services. Managed cloud storage is provisioned and provided as a raw disk. It is up to the user to partition and format the disk, attach or mount the disk, and make the storage assets available to applications and other users.

The sections that follow describe these two storage types and their uses in more detail.

Unmanaged cloud storage

With the development of high-capacity disk storage starting in the mid- to late-1990s, a new class of service provider appeared called a Storage Service Provider (SSP). Fueled by venture capital and the dot.com boom, dozens of companies created datacenters around the world with the intent of doing for online storage what Internet service providers (ISP) did for communications.

With so much excess capacity in place, companies with names like iDrive (now at `http://www.driveway.com/`), FreeDrive (`http://www.freedrive.com/`) MyVirtualDrive (defunct), OmniDrive (gonzo), XDrive (kaput), and others were formed to offer file-hosting services in the form of unmanaged cloud storage. It is unmanaged storage in the sense that the storage is precon-figured for you, you can't format as you like, nor can you install your own file system, or change drive properties such as compression or encryption.

Storage was offered to users by these file-hosting services as fixed online volumes. These volumes were first accessible using FTP, then from a utility, and then from within a browser. Often the service offered a certain capacity for free, with the opportunity to purchase more online storage as needed. FreeDrive is an example of an unmanaged storage utility set up to do automated backups, a class of Web services that is discussed in the section "Exploring Cloud Backup Solutions" later in this chapter.

Three factors led to the demise of many of the early SSPs and to many hosted file services:

- The Dot.com bust in 2000
- The inability of file-hosting companies to successfully monetize online storage
- The continued commoditization of large disk drives, which led to free online storage from large vendors such as Google

These SSPs and file-hosting services were ahead of their time, but in many cases—through acquisitions and offspring ventures—their legacy remains.

The simplest of these unmanaged cloud storage services falls into the category of a file transfer utility. You can upload files to the service where that file is stored (for a while) and made available to you for downloading from another location. Some of these services allow the transfer of only a single file. File transfer services may be shared by other users you allow, and the files that are uploaded may be discoverable for some services. That is, you can query the system for a file or information that meets the criteria you set. The service FreeDrive is storage that allows Facebook users to view the content of others.

Dropbox, shown in Figure 15.4, is an example of a file transfer utility. You install the Dropbox utility on your system and create an account, and the Dropbox folder appears. Dropbox also installs a System Tray icon in Windows for you. You can then drag and drop files and folders to your Dropbox. When a remote user logs into a Dropbox account, he installs the Dropbox folder for that account on his system, creating what is in effect a shared folder over the Web.

FIGURE 15.4

Dropbox is a file transfer utility that creates a shared folder metaphor using a Web service.

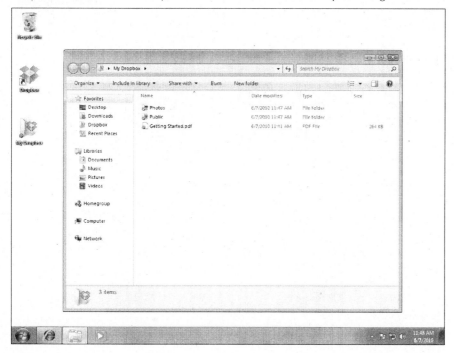

In an unmanaged cloud storage service, disk space is made available to users as a sized partition. That is, the remote storage appears as a mapped drive inside a folder like My Computer. File-hosting services allow the user to READ and WRITE to the drive and, in some cases, share the drive with other users, and often little more. As unmanaged storage offerings progressed in sophistication, they began to offer value-added software services such as folder synchronization and backup. Table 15.1 lists some of the current file-sharing services offered on unmanaged cloud storage.

TABLE 15.1

Unmanaged Cloud Storage

Service	Site	Storage Size	Maximum File Size	Direct Access	Remote Upload	Developer API
4Shared	http://www.4shared.com/	10GB free t0 100GB paid	200MB	Yes	Yes	WebDAV
Adrive	http://www.adrive.com/	50GB free to 1 TB paid	2GB	No, through a Web page	Yes	WebDAV
Badongo	http://www.badongo.com/	Unlimited	1GB	No, through Captcha	Only for paid users	
Box.net	http://www.box.net/	1GB free, 5 – 15GB paid	25MB free, 1GB paid	Yes		
Dropbox	https://www.dropbox.com/	2GB free, up to 8GB	Unlimited	Yes	Yes	No
Drop.io	http://drop.io/	100MB free	100MB	Yes	Yes	
eSnips	http://www.esnips.com/	5GB		Yes	Yes	
Freedrive	http://www.freedrive.com/	1GB		Yes	Yes	
FileFront	http://www.filefront.com/	Unlimited	600MB	Yes		
FilesAnywhere	http://filesanywhere.com/	1GB, more can be purchased		Yes	Yes	FA API
Hotfile	http://hotfile.com/	Unlimited	400MB free	No, through Captcha	FTP	

Service	Site	Storage Size	Maximum File Size	Direct Access	Remote Upload	Developer API
Humyo	http://www. humyo.com/	10GB free	None	Yes		
iDisk	http://www. apple.com/ mobileme/	20/40/60GB	1GB	Yes	Yes	WebDAV
Google Docs Storage	http://docs. google.com/#	1GB free, more can be purchased	250MB			
MagicVortex	http://magic vortex.com/	2GB	2GB	Yes	Yes	
MediaFire	http://www. mediafire. com/	Unlimited	200MB	Yes	Only for paid	
Megaupload	http://www. megaupload. com/	200GB free, Unlimited paid	2GB	No, through Captcha	Only for paid	
RapidShare	http://www. rapidshare. com/	20GB	200MB free, 2GB paid	No, imposed wait time	Yes	Yes
sendspace	http://www. sendspace.com/		300MB free, 1.5GB paid	Yes	Yes, through a wizard	
SkyDrive	http://sky drive.live. com/	25GB	50MB	Yes	Yes	WebDAV
Steek	http://www. steek.com/	1GB		Yes	Yes, through DriveDrive	
Wu.ala	http://wua.la/	1GB free, additional paid	None	Yes	Yes	
ZumoDrive	http://www. zumodrive.com/	2GB free, 10 – 500GB paid	None	Yes	Yes	

Source: Based on http://en.wikipedia.org/wiki/Comparison_of_file_hosting_services, June 7, 2010, and other sources.

If you are considering one of these services and require an automated backup solution, you also should consult Table 15.2 for those related products.

Managed cloud storage

The most basic service that online storage can serve is to provide disk space on demand. In the previous section, you saw examples of services where the service provider prepares and conditions the disk space for use by the user, provides the applications that the user can use with that disk space, and assigns disk space to the user with a persistent connection between the two. The user may be able to purchase additional space, but often that requires action by the service provider to provision the storage prior to use. That type of storage is considered unmanaged cloud storage because the user can't proactively manage his storage.

The second class of cloud storage is what I call managed cloud storage. You saw an example of a managed cloud storage system in Chapter 9 where Amazon's Simple Storage System (S3) was described. In a managed cloud storage system, the user provisions storage on demand and pays for the storage using a pay-as-you-go model. The system presents what appears to the user to be a raw disk that the user must partition and format. This type of system is meant to support virtual cloud computing as the virtualized storage component of that system.

Note

SNIA (Storage Networking Industry Association; `http://www.snia.org/`) has coined the term Data Storage as a Service (DaaS) to describe the delivery of storage on demand to clients over a distributed system. Others have called these types of system services Storage as a Service (STaaS). ∎

Managed cloud storage providers include the following:

- **Amazon.com Simple Storage Service** (S3; `http://aws.amazon.com/s3/`): This hosting service is described in Chapter 9.

- **EMC Atmos** (`http://www.emc.com/products/family/atmos.htm`): With Atmos, you can create your own cloud storage system or leverage a public cloud service with Atmos online.

- **Google Storage for Developers** (`http://code.google.com/apis/storage/docs/overview.html`): Code named "Platypus," this service currently in beta allows developers to store their data in Google's cloud storage infrastructure. It will share Google's authentication and data sharing platforms.

- **IBM Smart Business Storage Cloud** (`http://www-935.ibm.com/services/us/index.wss/offering/its/a1031610`): IBM has both infrastructure and software offerings that allow businesses to create and manage a private storage cloud.

  IBM is a major player in cloud computing (`http://www.ibm.com/ibm/cloud/`), particularly for businesses. The company offers a hardware platform called CloudBurst, as well as a portfolio of software that leverages cloud infrastructure such as IBM Smart Analytics Cloud, IBM Information Archive, IBM LotusLive, and LotusLive iNotes.

- **Iron Mountain** (`http://www.ironmountain.com/storage/storage-as-a-service.html`): Iron Mountain's service is mainly focused on backup and digital archiving, not on storage hosting.

- **Nirvanix** (formerly Streamload; `http://www.nirvanix.com/`): The company's MossoFS offers a managed cloud service.

- **Rackspace Cloud** (`http://www.rackspace.com/index.php`): Rackspace is a direct competitor to Amazon's S3 service.

Creating cloud storage systems

The Internet was designed to be a fault-tolerant network that could survive a nuclear attack. Paths between endpoints are redundant, message transfer is packetized, and dropped or lost packets can be retransmitted and travel different paths. Networks are redundant, name servers are redundant, and overall the system is highly fault tolerant. These features help make cloud-based storage systems highly reliable, particularly when multiple copies of data are stored on multiple servers and in multiple locations. Failover can involve a system simply changing the pointers to the stored object's location.

In Chapter 9, you saw how Amazon Web Services (AWS) adds redundancy to its IaaS systems by allowing EC2 virtual machine instances and S3 storage containers (bucket) to be created in any one of its four datacenters or regions. AWS S3 essentially lets you create your own cloud storage, provided you distribute your provisioned storage appropriately on Amazon's system.

AWS created "Availability Zones" within regions, which are sets of systems that are isolated from one another. In theory, instances in different availability zones shouldn't fail at the same time. In practice, entire regions can be affected, and storage and system redundancy needs to be established on a multi-regional basis. AWS can perform load balancing on multiple instances and can perform failover from one geographical location to another, but this is an additional service that you must purchase. The important point about redundancy is that for it to be effective, it has to be implemented at the highest architectural level.

Companies wishing to aggregate storage assets into cloud storage systems can use an enterprise software product like StorageGRID. This storage virtualization software from Bycast (now a part of NetApp; `http://bycast.com/`) creates a virtualization layer that pools storage from different storage devices into a single management system. You can potentially pool petabytes of data storage, use different storage system types, and transport protocols even over geographically dispersed locations. Figure 15.5 shows how SystemGRID virtualizes storage into storage clouds.

StorageGRID can manage data from CIFS and NFS file systems over HTTP networks. Data can be replicated, migrated to different locations, and failed over upon demand. The degree of data replication can be set by policy, and when storage in the pool fails, StorageGRID can failover to other copies of the data on redundant systems. StorageGRID can enforce policies and create a tiered storage system.

FIGURE 15.5

ByCast's StorageGRID allows you to create fault-tolerant cloud storage systems by creating a virtualization layer between storage assets and application servers.

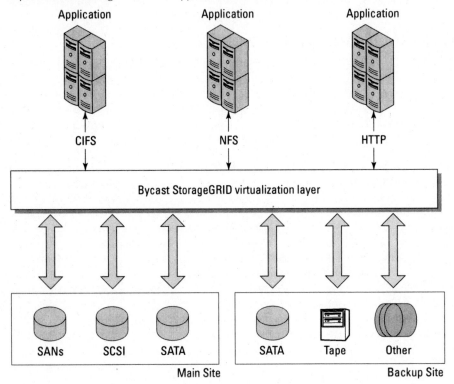

Virtual storage containers

In traditional pooled storage deployments, storage partitions can be assigned and provide a device label called a Logical Unit Number (LUN). A LUN is a logical unit that serves as the target for storage operations, such as the SCSI protocol's READs and WRITEs (PUTs and GETs). The two main protocols used to build large disk pools, particularly in the form of Storage Area Networks (SANs), Fibre Channel and iSCSI both use LUNs to define a storage volume that appears to a connected computer as a device. Unused LUNs are the equivalent of a raw disk from which one or more volumes may be created.

Traditionally, pooled online storage assigns a LUN and then uses an authorization process called LUN masking to limit which connected computers (or hosts) can see which LUNs. LUN masking isn't as strong a security feature as the direct identification of a physical Host Bus Adapters (HBAs), which are the storage networking equivalent of NICs (Network Interface Cards). LUN addresses can have their unique addresses spoofed more easily than a hardware address can. However, LUNs do protect against a server being able to write to a disk to which it shouldn't have access. Storage partitioning in large storage deployments also may be achieved using SAN zoning, as well as a partitioning disk based on physical location.

When online storage is converted for use in a cloud storage system, none of these partitioning methods allows for easy, on-the-fly storage assignment and the high disk utilization rates that are required in a multi-tenancy storage system. Delivering effective cloud storage solutions requires the use of a virtual storage container, which allows a tenant to perform storage operations on the virtual storage container consistent with the capabilities of the underlying storage system. Different storage vendors call their virtual storage containers by different names, but all use this entity as a construct to create high-performance cloud storage systems. LUNs, files, and other objects are then created within the virtual storage container. Figure 15.6 shows a model for a virtual storage container, which defines a cloud storage domain. This model, based on the SNIA model but modified somewhat, includes the interface operations that are needed to use that domain.

When a tenant is granted access to a virtual storage container, he performs standard disk operations such as partitioning, formatting, file system modifications, and CRUD (`Create`, `Read`, `Update`, and `Delete`) operations as desired. Data stored in a virtual storage container may be stored in chunks or buckets as the Amazon Simple Storage Service (Amazon S3) does, or it may be stored in containers that are in a hierarchical relationship typical of most file systems. The main requirement is that however cloud storage data is organized that data and its associated metadata may be discoverable.

Making cloud storage data discoverable on a TCP/IP network using HTTP or some other protocol requires that objects be assigned a unique identifier such as a URI (Uniform Resource Identifier) and that the relationship between objects and their metadata be specified. In the section "Developing Cloud System Interoperability," I describe the OCCI protocol for discovering and retrieving objects from a cloud.

Because virtual storage containers must be secured, these objects must carry a set of security attributes that protect a tenant's data from snooping, denial of service attacks, spoofing, inappropriate deletion, or unauthorized discovery. The main mechanism for securing one tenant's virtual storage container from another is to assign an IP address to the virtual storage container and then bind that container to a separate VLAN connecting storage to the tenant (host). Traffic flowing over the VLAN is encrypted, and the tenant is carefully authenticated by the system. Usually, data sent over the VLAN is compressed to improve data throughput over a WAN connection.

Different cloud storage vendors may implement their own proprietary management interfaces to connect distributed hosts or tenants to their provisioned storage in the cloud and to provide for security services. One open interface standard is the Storage Networking Industry Association's Cloud Data Management Interface (CDMI) described later in this chapter.

FIGURE 15.6

A cloud storage domain model and the interface commands needed to access those elements

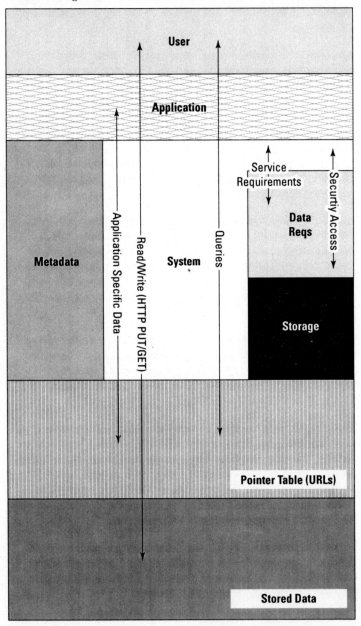

In evaluating cloud storage solutions, these factors are deemed to be important considerations:

- Client self-service
- Strong management capabilities
- Performance characteristics such as throughput
- Appropriate block-based storage protocol support such as iSCSI or FC SAN, or file-based storage protocol support such as NFS or CIFS to support your systems
- Seamless maintenance and upgrades

In addition to assigning security-provisioned cloud storage to a client or service requester, a cloud storage service provider must be able to deliver a measured level of service as captured by its stated Service Level Agreement (SLA). An SLA might specify that a particular Quality of Service (QoS) for a virtual storage container may be measured in terms of the I/O per second or IOPS that may be provided, as well as the reliability and availability of the service. QoS levels may be applied to different services against a single virtual storage container or a single service applied to the client's multiple assigned storage containers. In situations where multiple virtual storage containers are assigned to a client, a mechanism would need to be provided to federate the different containers into a consolidated management console.

One unique characteristic of cloud-based storage solutions is that they permit rapid scaling, both in terms of performance and storage capacity. To provide for scaling, a virtual storage container must be easily migrated from one storage system to another. To increase the capacity of a storage provision, it is necessary to provide the capability to scale up or scale out across storage systems. To scale up, the service must allow for more disks and more spindles to be provisioned. To scale out, the service must allow for stored data to span additional storage systems. Cloud storage systems that successfully scale their provisioned storage for clients often allow for the multiple storage systems to be geographically dispersed and often provide load-balancing services across different storage instances.

Exploring Cloud Backup Solutions

Cloud storage is uniquely positioned to serve as a last line of defense in a strong backup routine, and backing up to the cloud is one of the most successful applications of cloud computing. This area is a cornucopia of solutions, many inexpensive and feature rich.

Backup types

Backups may be categorized as belonging to one of the following types:

- **Full system or image backups:** An image backup creates a complete copy of a volume, including all system files, the boot record, and any other data contained on the disk. To create an image backup of an active system, you may need to stop all applications (quiesce the system). An image backup allows a system to do what is referred to as a bare metal restore. Ghost is an example of software that supplies this type of backup.

- **Point-in-time (PIT) backups or snapshots:** The data is backed up, and then every so often changes are amended to the backup creating what is referred to as an incremental backup. This type of backup lets you restore your data to a point in time and saves multiple copies of any file that has been changed. At least 10 to 30 copies of previous versions of files should be saved.

  The first backup is quite slow over an Internet connection, but the incremental backup can be relatively fast. For example, software such as Carbonite may take several days to backup a system, but minutes to create the snapshot.

Note

The amount of time needed to backup a system is referred to as its backup window. ■

- **Differential and incremental backups:** A differential backup is related to an incremental backup, but with some subtle differences in the way the archive bit is handled. During an incremental backup, any changed files are copied to the backup media and their archive attribute is cleared by the incremental backup. In a differential backup, all of the changed files since the last full backup are copied by the backup software, which requires that the software leave the archive bit set to ON for any differential backup, as only a full backup can clear all files' archive bit.

  An archive bit is used by backup software to specify whether a file should be backed up or not. The bit is set on for backup and cleared when backup has copied the file. In a sense, an archive bit is a directive to the software. The archive bit comes into play in backup software in the sense that an incremental backup solution must examine the full backup data and then analyze all subsequent increments to find the latest file(s). In a differential backup, the backup software can obtain the up-to-date backup from the last full backup and the last incremental backup alone. Files in intervening incremental backups may be taken as temporary or scratch versions. While incremental backups are faster and more efficient from a storage perspective, they are also less fault tolerant.

- **Reverse Delta backup:** A reverse delta backup creates a full backup first and then periodically synchronizes the full copy with the live version. The older versions of files that have been changed are archived so that a historical record of the backup exists. Among the software that uses this system is Apple's Time Machine and the RDIFF-BACKUP utility.

- **Continuous Data Protection (CDP) or mirroring:** The goal of this type of backup system is to create a cloned copy of your current data or drive. A cloud storage system contains a certain built-in latency, so unless the original data set is quiescent, the mirror lags behind the original in concurrency.

- **Open file backup:** Some applications such as database systems and messaging systems are mission critical and cannot be shut down before being backed up. An open file backup analyzes the transactions that are in progress, compares them to the file(s) at the start of the backup and the file(s) at the end of the backup, and creates a backup that represents a complete file as it would exist at the time the backup started after all the transactions have been processed. This is a difficult proposition, and open file backup systems are expensive and highly customized to a particular application such as SQL Server or Exchange.

3-2-1 Backup Rule

Peter Krogh's 3-2-1 Rule for data protection is a good one to follow. Krogh is a professional photographer, a member of the American Society of Media Photographers, and a consultant in the area of data storage and archiving. One of his clients is the Library of Congress, where data archival is a mission-critical task. As Krogh states on the site dpBestflow.org (`http://www.dpbestflow.org/backup/backup-overview#321`), a simple but effective backup scenario includes the following elements:

3. Retain **three** copies of any file—an original and two backups.

2. Files must be on **two** different media types (such as hard drives and optical media) to protect against different types of hazards.

1. **One** copy must be stored offsite (or at least online).

If you have a local version of a file, then a version of that file stored in the cloud conforms to all three of the 3-2-1 backup rules.

● **Data archival:** The term *archiving* is used to specify the migration of data that is no longer in use to secondary or tertiary long-term data storage for retention. An archive is useful for legal compliance or to provide a long-term historical record.

Note

Data archives are often confused with backups, but the two operations are quite different. A backup creates a copy of the data, whereas an archive removes older information that is no longer operational and saves it for long-term storage. You can't restore your current data set from an archive. ■

Cloud backup features

Features of cloud storage backup solutions that are valuable listed roughly in order of importance include the following:

● Logon authentication.

● High encryption (at least 128-bit) of data transfers, preferably end-to-end, but at least for the data that is transferred over the Internet.

● Lossless data compression to improve throughput. A related feature called differential compression transfers only binary data that has changed since the last backup.

● Automated, scheduled backups.

● Fast backup (snapshots) after full online backup, with 10 to 30 historical versions of a file retained.

● Data versioning with the ability to retrieve historical versions of files from different backups.

- Multiplatform support. The most important clients to back up are Windows, Macintosh, and Linux/Unix.

- Bare file/folder restore.

- Adequate bandwidth and perhaps scalable bandwidth options to which to upgrade.

- Web-based management console with ease-of-use features such as drag and drop, e-mail updates, and file sharing.

- 24x7 technical support.

- Backed up data set validation; checking to determine if the backed up data matches the original data.

- Logging and reporting of operations.

- Open file backups of mission-critical transactional systems such as enterprise databases or e-mail/messaging applications.

- Multisite storage or replication, enabling data failover.

Table 15.2 lists some of the current backup services offered on unmanaged cloud storage.

Caution

It is important that data backed up to the cloud cannot be viewed without adequate safeguards or restrictions due to legal regulations concerning stored data in the area of health care and other sensitive endeavors. ■

TABLE 15.2

Cloud Storage Backup Solutions

Service	Site	Windows/ Linux/ Mac	Encryption	Network Drive	Synchronization	File Hosting
ADrive	http://www.adrive.com/	Yes/Yes/Yes	Optional	Yes		
Backblaze	http://www.backblaze.com/	Yes/No/Yes	Yes; per user			
Barracuda Backup Service	http://www.barracuda networks.com	Yes/Yes/Yes	Yes	Yes	Yes	No
Carbonite	http://www.carbonite.com/	Yes/No/Yes	Optional	Yes (Pro)		Yes

Service	Site	Windows/ Linux/ Mac	Encryption	Network Drive	Synchronization	File Hosting
Crashplan	http://b5. crashplan. com/	Yes/Yes/Yes	Yes; per user			
Datapreserve	http://www. data preserve. com/	Yes/Yes/Yes	Yes	No	Yes	No
Dell Datasafe	https://www. delldata safe.com/	Yes/No/No	Yes	No	Yes	No
DriveHG	http://www. drivehq.com/			Yes	No (free); Yes (Premium)	
Dropbox	https://www. dropbox. com/.	Yes/Yes/Yes	Yes; per user		Yes	Yes
ElephantDrive	http://www. elephant drive.com/	Yes/Partial/ Yes	Yes			
Engyte	http://www. egnyte.com/	Yes/Yes/Yes	Yes		Yes	Yes
Evault (Seagate i365)	http://www. i365.com/	Yes/Yes/No	Yes	No	No	No
Humyo	http://www. humyo.com/	Yes/Partial/ Yes	Yes	Yes	Yes	Yes
IBackup	http://www. ibackup.com/	Yes/Yes/Yes	Yes	No	No	No
iDrive	http://www. idrive.com/	Yes/No/No	Yes	Yes	Yes	Yes
Jungle Disk	https://www. jungledisk. com/	Yes/Yes/Yes	Yes; per user			
KeepVault	http://www. keepvault. com/	Yes/No/No	Yes; per user			
Memopal	http://www. memopal.com/ en/	Yes/Yes/Yes	Yes		Yes	Yes

continued

TABLE 15.2 *(continued)*

Service	Site	Windows/ Linux/ Mac	Encryption	Network Drive	Synchronization	File Hosting
Mindtime Backup	http://www. mindtime backup.com/	Yes/Yes/Yes	No	Yes		No
MobileMe (Apple)	http://www. me.com	Yes/No/Yes	No	No	Yes	Yes
Mozy	http://mozy. com/	Yes/No/Yes	Optional; per user			
OrbitFiles	http://www. orbitfiles. com/	Yes/Yes/Yes	Yes			Yes
SOS Online Backup	http://www. sosonline backup.com/	Yes/No/No	Yes; per user			Yes
SpiderOak	https:// spideroak. com/	Yes/Yes/Yes	Yes; per user			
Steek	http://www. steek.com/	Yes/?/?				
SugarSync (formerly Sharpcast)	http://www. sugarsync. com/	Yes/No/Yes	Yes	Yes	Yes	Yes
Symantec Online Backup	http://www. spn.com	Yes/No/Yes	Yes	No	No	No
Ubuntu One	https://one. ubuntu.com/	No/Yes/No	Yes	N/A	Yes	No
Unitrends Vault2Cloud	http://www. unitrends. com/	Yes/Yes/Yes	No	Yes	Yes	No
UpdateStar Online Backup	http:// client.update star.com/	Yes/No/No	Yes; per user			
Windows Live Mesh	www.mesh.com	Yes/No/Yes	Partial; transmission only		Yes	
Windows Live SkyDrive	http://sky drive.live. com/	Yes/No/No			Yes	

Service	Site	Windows/ Linux/ Mac	Encryption	Network Drive	Synchronization	File Hosting
Windows Live Sync	`http://sync. live.com/`	Yes/No/Yes	Yes			
Wu.ala	`http://wua. la/`	Yes/Yes/Yes	Yes			
Yuntaa	`http://www. yuntaa.com/`	Yes/No/No	Yes	Yes	Yes	Yes
ZumoDrive	`http://www. zumodrive. com/`	Yes/Yes/Yes	Yes	Yes	Yes	Yes

Source: Based on `http://en.wikipedia.org/wiki/Comparison_of_online_backup_services`, June 7, 2010, `http://tomuse.com/ultimate-review-list-of-best-free-online-storage-and-backup-application-services/`, and other sources.

Cloud attached backup

The backup solutions described have been client- or software-based solutions that are useful for an individual desktop or server. However, some interesting hardware-based solutions are available for backing up your systems to cloud-based storage.

CTERA (`http://www.ctera.com/home/cloud-attached-storage.html`) sells a server referred to as Cloud Attached Storage, which is meant for the Small and Medium Business (SMB) market, branch offices, and the Small Office Home Office (SOHO) market.

The CTERA Cloud Attached Storage backup server has the attributes of a NAS (Network Attached Storage), with the added feature that after you set up which systems you want to back up, create user accounts, and set the backup options through a browser interface, the system runs automated backup copying and synchronizing of your data with cloud storage. Backed up data may be shared between users. Figure 15.7 shows how the CTERA Cloud Attached Storage Device is deployed in practice.

CTERA cloud backup provides a solution that optimizes the backup based on bandwidth availability. It performs incremental backups from the server, compressing and encrypting the data that is transmitted to CTERA's cloud storage servers where de-duplication is performed. The CTERA server performs the backups of clients without requiring any client-based software. Clients have browser-based access to the backups or can locally access files using CTERA's "Virtual Cloud Drive" network drive. Snapshots are captured on the CTERA Next3 file system, which is based on the open source Ext3 file system.

FIGURE 15.7

CTERA's cloud-attached storage network backup scenario

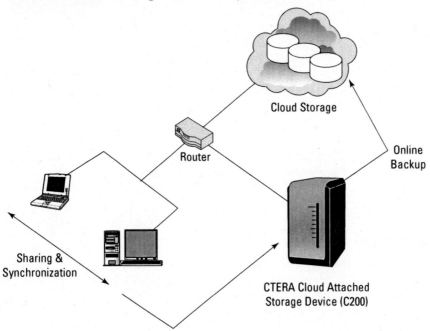

The development of systems on a chip has enabled CTERA to create a scaled-down version of the CTERA server called the CTERA CloudPlug for the SOHO market. This palm-sized low-power device converts a USB/eSATA drive and your Ethernet network and turns the hard drive into a NAS server. CloudPlug performs backup and synchronization services and then performs automated or on-demand backups and snapshots of your systems.

CloudPlug uses UPnP (Universal Plug and Play) and Bonjour to discover systems on the network and then installs a small agent on those systems. The software works with Microsoft Active Directory and allows for role-based user access. Among the protocols it supports are the Common Internet File Sharing (CIFS) used by Windows and Apple File Sharing (AFP) systems. It can back up NTFS, FAT32, EXT3, and the NEXT3 file systems. Laptops may be backed up from any location because they are assigned a roaming profile with dynamic IP support. The system also backs up locked files.

Cloud Storage Interoperability

Large network storage deployments tend to get populated by vendors who provide unique functionality for their systems by creating proprietary APIs for the storage hardware that they sell. This problem exists for online network storage, Storage Area Networks (SANs), and to an even greater extent for cloud storage systems. Storage vendors have encouraged adoption of their proprietary APIs by making them "open," but cloud system vendors have not responded by making any single API an industry standard. The development of Open Source APIs from the Open Source community has only added more storage APIs to the mix.

Cloud Data Management Interface (CDMI)

An example of an open cloud storage management standard is the Storage Networking Industry Association's (SNIA; http://www.snia.org) Cloud Data Management Interface (CDMI). CDMI works with the storage domain model shown in Figure 15.8 to allow for interoperation between different cloud systems, whether on public, private, or hybrid cloud systems. CDMI includes commands that allow applications to access cloud storage and create, retrieve, update, and delete data objects; provides for data object discovery; enables storage data systems to communicate with one another; and provides for security using standard storage protocols, monitoring and billing, and authentication methods. CDMI uses the same authorization and authentication mechanism as NFS (Network File System) does.

In the Cloud Data Management Interface (CDMI), the storage space is partitioned into units called containers. A container stores a set of data in it and serves as the named object upon which data service operations are performed. The CDMI data object can manage CDMI containers, as well as containers that are accessible in cloud storage through other supported protocols.

Figure 15.8 shows the SNIA cloud storage management model. In the figure, XAM stands for the eXtensible Access Method, a storage API developed by SNIA for accessing content on storage devices. VIM stands for Vendor Interface Modules, which is an interface that converts XAM requests into native commands that are supported by the storage hardware operating systems.

CDMI can access objects stored in the cloud by using standard HTTP command and the REST (Representational State Transfer) protocol to manipulate those objects. CDMI also can discover objects and can export and manage those exported objects as part of a storage space called a container. CDMI provides an interface through which applications can gain access to the storage objects in a container over the Web. Other features of CDMI are access controls, usage accounting, and the ability to advertise containers so that applications see these containers as if they are volumes (LUNs with a certain size).

CDMI uses metadata for HTTP, system, user, and storage media attributes accessing them through a standard interface using a schema that is known as the Resource Oriented Architecture (ROA). In this architecture, every resource is identified by a standardized URI (Uniform Resource Identifier) that may be translated into both hypertext (HTTP) and other forms. CDMI uses the SNIA eXtensible Access Method (XAM) to discover and access metadata associated with each data object.

Metadata is stored not only for data objects, but for data containers so that any data placed into a container assumes the metadata associated with that container. Should there be conflicting metadata at different levels of the hierarchy (container, object, and so on), the most granular level object's metadata attribute takes precedence.

FIGURE 15.8

CDMI allows data in cloud storage to be managed from a variety of resources.

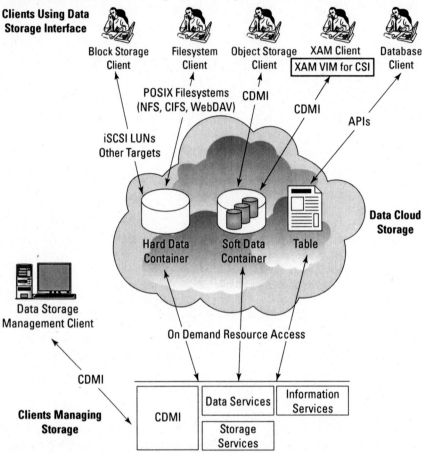

Source: *"Cloud Storage for Cloud Computing" SNIA/OGF, September 2009,* `http://ogf.org/Resources/documents/CloudStorageForCloudComputing.pdf.`

In CDMI, resources are identified as nouns, which have attributes in the form of key-value pairs, upon which actions in the form of verbs may be performed. Standard actions include the standard CRUD operations: Create, Retrieve, Update, and Delete; which translates into the standard HTTP action verbs POST, GET, PUT, and DELETE. Additionally, the HEAD and OPTIONS verbs provide a wrapper for metadata and operational instructions.

A typical action might be a PUT or GET operation, as follows:

```
PUT http://www.cloudy.com/store/<myfile>
GET http://www.cloudy.com/compute/<myfile>
```

The domain `cloudy.com` would be the service provider, *myfile* is the instance, and `compute` is the folder containing the file. In a `PUT` operation, the container (*store*) is created if it didn't exist previously. The metadata KEY/VALUE pair MIME is required in a `PUT`; other metadata KEY/VALUE pairs are optional in a `PUT`. A variety of KEY/VALUE pairs describing object attributes in CDMI is defined by the standard.

Open Cloud Computing Interface (OCCI)

SNIA and the Open Grid Forum (OGF; `http://www.ogf.org/`) have created a joint working group to create the Open Cloud Computing Interface (OCCI), an open standard API for cloud computing infrastructure systems. OCCI is meant to span the different vendors' standards and allow for system interoperability.

Note

To view the Cloud Standards Wiki with information about all the different standards groups working in this area of technology, go to: `http://cloud-standards.org/wiki/index.php?title=Main_Page`. **This page contains links to the work of groups in cloud storage, virtual machines, protocols, and more.** ■

The OCCI interface standard is based on the Resource Oriented Architecture (ROA) and uses the URI definition for OCCI that was previously defined by SNIA's Cloud Data Management Interface (CDMI) that OCCI interoperates with CDMI. Associations between resources appear in the HTTP header in the Atom Publishing Protocol (AtomPub or APP) that transfers the Atom Syndication Format (XML) used for XML Web news feeds. The OCCI API maps to other formats such as Atom/Pub, JSON, and Plain Text.

OCCI specifies, but does not mandate, what is called a *service life cycle*. In a service life cycle, a client (service requestor) instantiates or invokes a new application and through OCCI commands provisions its storage resources, manages the application's use, and then manages the application's destruction and the release of its cloud storage.

Cloud storage devices can be either a block or file system storage device, and in that regard they are no different than online network storage devices or even local storage. It is the ability to provide storage on a demand basis and pay as you go that is the key differentiator for cloud storage. The ability to provide storage on demand from a storage pool is referred to as *thin provisioning,* a term that also applies to compute resources such as virtual machines. Management of cloud storage is performed by *out-of-band* management systems through a data storage interface. Out-of-band refers to a management console that isn't on the storage network, but is most often on an Ethernet network inside a browser. From the management console, additional data services such as cloning, compression, de-duplication, and snapshots may be invoked.

As previously mentioned, CDMI and OCCI are meant to interoperate, and CDMI containers can be accessed through a data path and over other protocols. A CDMI container can be exported and then used as a virtual disk by Virtual Machines in the cloud. The cloud infrastructure management console can be used to attach exported CDMI containers to the Virtual Machine that is desired. CDMI exports containers so the information that is obtained from the OCCI interface is part of the exported container.

OCCI also can create containers that are interoperable with CDMI containers. These export operations can be initiated from either the OCCI or CDMI interfaces, with similar results. However, there are syntactical differences between using either interface as the export starting point. In Figure 15.9, CDMI and OCCI are shown interoperating with cloud resources of different types.

FIGURE 15.9

CDMI and OCCI interoperating in an integrated cloud system

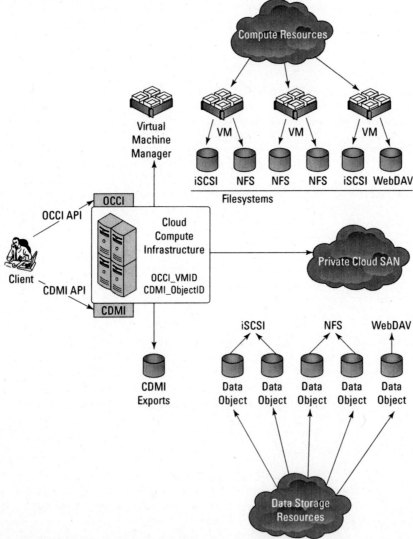

Source: "Cloud Storage for Cloud Computing" SNIA/OGF, September 2009, `http://ogf.org/Resources/documents/` `CloudStorageForCloudComputing.pdf.`

Summary

In this chapter, you learned about the nature of stored digital data and the role that cloud storage will play in the future in storing and processing data.

Cloud storage is classified as either unmanaged or managed storage. Most user applications work with unmanaged storage. The two major classes of cloud-based storage applications described in this chapter were file sharing and backup utilities. Managed storage is cloud storage that you provision for Web services or applications using cloud storage that you are developing. Managed storage requires you to prepare the disk and manage its use.

All cloud storage vendors partition storage on the basis of a virtual storage container. A model describing the virtual storage container is described. Efforts to make cloud storage systems interoperate, particularly the CDMI and OCCI protocols, were described.

In Chapter 16, "Working with Productivity Software," I consider desktop applications that replace office suite applications. These applications have the potential to displace a major portion of their commercial shrink-wrapped software counterparts over time, and while not as feature-filled as commercial software, they are surprisingly good. The chapter discusses the state of the art in this area and makes some predictions of what to expect over time.

Working with Productivity Software

O ffice productivity software is one of the most important categories of applications in use today. A vast majority of desktop computers have the applications that comprise office suites installed on their systems. Word processors, spreadsheets, presentation programs, and other programs that are typically bundled together by vendors such as Apple, Microsoft, Corel, IBM Lotus, Oracle/Sun, and others in their office suites are the most heavily used applications, with the exception perhaps of your system's browser.

It is no accident, therefore, that cloud software developers have targeted productivity software as the one area where cloud computing can have impact. The cloud offers a variety of benefits that make productivity software accessed over this medium attractive. Those benefits include lower software costs, ubiquitous and nearly universal access, ease of sharing and collaboration, and a standards-based approach that enables cross-platform capabilities.

These benefits must be weighed against the risks of requiring an Internet connection, storing sensitive data in the cloud, and the generally smaller feature sets that online productivity applications have than their desktop counterparts.

In this chapter, you learn about some of the major online office suites from vendors such as Adobe, Glide, Google, Microsoft, ThinkFree, and Zoho. Some of these sites offer a large array of tools and have been established since the mid-1990s. Others such as Acrobat.com and Microsoft Live Office and their Office Web Apps are relatively new and are being developed rapidly.

IN THIS CHAPTER

Defining productivity software

Assessing the benefits and drawbacks of online applications

Learning about office suites

Knowing the features of the most important cloud-based office suites

Using Productivity Applications

Everyone thinks he knows what the term "productivity software" means: It means Microsoft Office. In theory, anything you do on the computer that is faster and more productive than you could do any other way can be termed productivity software. So, I'm sorry; Instant Messaging, e-mail, and killing aliens in a video game probably don't qualify. A definition for productivity software is elusive, but try searching the term online and you'll see what I mean. ■

Productivity software is an archaic term based on office suites and includes the following:

- Word processors
- Spreadsheets
- Database management systems
- Presentation software
- Personal Information Managers
- Schedulers

Note

In the lists in this section, I have listed the importance of the application type from the most important application type at the top to the least important application type on the bottom. ■

You also would have to include in a secondary category applications that are used frequently, but that show up in some office suites and not others, or in none of the office suites. The following software categories are also in the mix:

- Graphics modules, most often bitmapped or paint programs, but less frequently vector-based or drawing packages
- Desktop publishing packages
- HTML editors and (less frequently) Web site managers and publishers
- Accounting packages
- Project planning programs
- The many utilities and tools that are used to support programs of these types

Cross-Ref

Because e-mail, collaboration, and media software are usually sold as separate products or part of the operating system, these three areas of software are described in Chapters 17, 18, and 19, respectively. ■

For the sake of this chapter, therefore, let me define productivity software:

> User-facing software that creates work product in the form of documents or files

If you want to define cloud-based productivity software, add the phrase "using resources accessed over a WAN" (Wide Area Network) to the end of that phrase.

User-facing software's inexorable migration from a user's personal computer to the cloud has been well underway for the past five or six years. The good reasons for this trend and some reasons that inhibit this migration are the subject of this chapter.

Software is fungible—subject to change and substitution. The inclusion of many of the modules in the original office suites beyond their word processors and spreadsheets was as much a matter of serendipity as it was due to planning. In only a few instances, a suite was completely written by its developers. By contrast, most of the productivity suites and applications that are cloud-based are the work of their original developers and represent the desire to displace desktop applications.

Characteristics of productivity software

The range of productivity applications is great. So if it isn't possible to define productivity software based on application type, at least we know the characteristics of productivity software. Those characteristics apply to online and to locally based applications.

Tip

This chapter does not describe many applications that are available online as standalone applications. Numerous programs, such as to-do lists, calendars, photo editors, and so forth, are often best-of-breed online software, but would require more space to describe than is available here. To learn more about these other programs, I refer you to survey books that cover these types of programs from a functional category basis. ■

To be included in the category of productivity software, an application must have the following characteristics:

- **User-centric and user-facing:** Productivity software is used daily.

- **Static features:** Productivity software offers limited customization. When a user sits down to use a productivity software package, the interface and command set should be roughly the same regardless of where and when the applications are used.

- **Ease of use:** Productivity software must follow a set of defined interface guidelines that make it easy for even inexperienced users to follow.

- **Standards for data interchange:** Productivity software should save data in file formats that are standardized, even if they are based on a vendor's format.

  Some of the options for saving data or for importing data should be through standardized data interchange formats. Examples of proprietary formats are Microsoft's DOC or Adobe's PDF format; two interchange formats might be the word processing RTF (Rich Text Format) or the database/spreadsheet CSV (Comma Separated Values) formats.

- **Modular interactivity:** Productivity application suites should enable a functionality that allows one application to interact with another. Interactivity can occur through operating system functionality such as the Clipboard or drag-and-drop or by using a mechanism that is proprietary to the application suite itself.

- **Inter Applications Communications (IAC):** IAC is the ability of one application to use the services of another to do productivity work. The level of IAC in a productivity suite may be seen to be a measure of the suite's sophistication. An example of IAC in action is when you create an object like a drawing in a word processor and the drawing tool becomes available to work on that object while it is in use.

Inter-Applications Communication and Cloud Computing

The development of systems to enable and encourage IAC reads like the history of networked application development itself. To enable IAC functionality over the years, we have seen these developed: Microsoft's Common Object Model (COM) and Distributed Common Object Model (DCOM) and the .NET Framework; the Object Management Group's Common Object Request Broker Architecture (CORBA); the inter-process communication (IPC) protocol Network Computing System (originally from Apollo Computer), Remote Procedure Calls (RPC); the Open Database Connectivity (ODBC) database drivers; and many others.

The cloud-computing-based applications that are described in this chapter rely on Service Oriented Architectures (SOA) to implement IAC using SOAP over HTTP, Web Services Flow Language (WSFL), the XML Remote Procedure Call XML-RPC, or a number of other Web service protocols that were discussed in Chapter 3. Thus, you can see that cloud computing enablement is simply a natural progression of trends that have a long history in the computer industry.

Online Office Systems

Online office systems are growing increasingly popular and are displacing shrink-wrapped office software for many users. Although the online systems have used traditional office products as their model, the nature of the Web and the services it provides makes some features hard to copy and other features that don't exist locally possible on the Web. In this section, I look at why online office suites are becoming popular and what features hinder their adoption.

These are benefits of using a cloud computing office suite:

- Generally lower costs for users
- Platform independence because the software runs inside a browser and is universally available
- Reduced maintenance costs because of fewer hardware requirements
- Centralized software patches and updates, whereby users have access to the latest version of the software
- Easier document sharing due to standard formats, and often easier document sharing for group collaboration

Using cloud-based productivity applications also has some disadvantages:

- An Internet connection is required to access your documents.

    Some cloud-based applications now offer what is called an "off-line" mode so you can work on documents on your local system when an Internet connection is not available.

- Performance can be slow, particularly when you have a slow Internet connection.

- Online productivity applications generally have fewer features than their shrink-wrapped competitors.

- Documents stored in the cloud may not be secure and are certainly not under a user's full control.

- Data in the cloud can be lost and must be managed and backed up.

- Documents created with desktop applications may not be fully compatible with cloud-based applications.

In the sections that follow, you learn about some of the major players that have office suites available for use on the Internet. Most of these vendors offer a free basic service, with premium or paid services available that extend their features. A subscription model based on monthly usage is common.

Acrobat.com

Acrobat.com is Adobe's application suite of cloud-based applications; it has been available worldwide since 2007. Unlike other office suites described in this section, Adobe's offerings on Acrobat.com are centered around preparing documents, manipulating graphics, and publishing the results. You can create a free account with limited functionality, or you can subscribe to a premium account, which removes or expands upon these limitations. Users of Adobe's software such as Acrobat will find that the online version of the product suite duplicates the core functionality. Acrobat.com is noted for very broad foreign language support.

These are among the tools you will find at Acrobat.com (`http://www.acrobat.com`):

- **Buzzword:** A really attractive word processor built with Flash graphics and full text-formatting features. Buzzword documents can be created and modified collaboratively with a managed revision history. Buzzword supports the roles of coauthor, reviewer, and reader for a document. Figure 16.1 shows a document being edited in Buzzword.

  Buzzword is cross compatible with other Office suites, including: text (`TXT`), Rich Text Format (`RTF`), Microsoft Word (`DOC` and `DOCX`), and Open Office (`ODT`) files. It also exports to Adobe `PDF`, `HTML`, and `EPUB`.

- **Tables:** A spreadsheet that can be shared or worked on collaboratively by multiple users.

- **Presentations:** A presentation package that can be shared and worked on collaboratively and that plays within a Web browser using the Adobe Flash Player.

- **ConnectNow:** An online conferencing and collaboration service. ConnectNow has a live text, audio, and video messaging system; a whiteboard; notes; and remote control and screen sharing features. The premium service allows for larger meetings.

- **File Sharing:** An online file-sharing service with live document preview and a file organizer for search by metatags.

- **Create PDF:** A PDF file converter. The basic service has a limit for file conversions and maximum size; a premium service allows for unlimited conversions but retains the 100MB file size limit.

FIGURE 16.1

Acrobat.com's Buzzword word processor offers a pretty and capable set of office applications, is particularly strong in graphic capabilities, and makes good use of Adobe Flash animation in its interface.

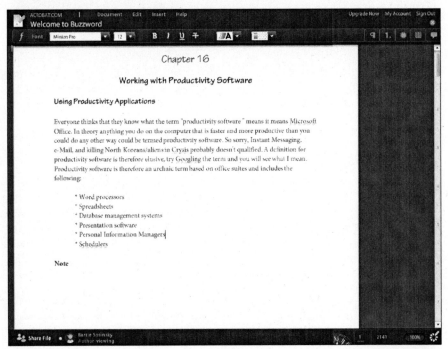

Create PDF supports the following file conversions to PDF: text (TXT, PS, RTF), Microsoft Office (DOC, DOCX, XLS, XLSX, PPT, PPTX, PRJ, PUB), Open Office (ODT, ODP, ODS, ODG, ODF), Star Office (SWX, SXI, SXC, SXD, STW), WordPerfect (WPD), and image files (BMP, GIF, JPEG, TIFF, PNG).

- **Workspaces:** A shared workspace or container that allows multiple users to create folders, upload and download documents, and manage the contents. Workspaces do not support audio or video file types.

The free plan allows for one workspace, the premium plan allows 20 workspaces, and the premium plus plan provides for unlimited workspaces. The workspace feature is similar to a Sharepoint folder. There is no limit to the number of invited users who may view a Workspace.

Acrobat.com has mobile phone support for Android, Blackberry, and iPhone phones. Among the features that it supports are picture upload from the phone to the online service, viewing files on the phone that are stored in the File Sharing service, sending faxes, and document sharing through published links to the online content. Mobile applications allow you to view the following file types: Adobe PDF, text (TXT, PS, RTF), Office (DOC, XLS, PPT, PRJ), Open Office (ODT, ODP, ODS, ODG, ODF), Star Office (SWX, SXI, SXC, SXD, STW), WordPerfect (WPD), and images (BMP, GIF, JPEG, TIFF, PNG).

Glide Digital

Glide Digital (http://www.glidedigital.com/) is a collection of integrated applications that are packaged within a complete desktop environment. TransMedia, the developer, calls the environment the Glide OS, which is now at version 4.0. Glide is compatible with Internet Explorer, Firefox, Chrome, and Safari.

Glide includes the following standard business applications:

- **Write:** A strong word processor
- **Crunch:** A spreadsheet
- **Presenter:** A presentation program
- **Calendar:** An individual and group collaborative calendar program
- **Contact:** An integrated address book
- **Email:** An e-mail client, with parental filters for children's accounts
- **Draw:** A drawing and coloring program
- **Media Player:** For playing audio and video files
- **Photo Editor:** A photo retouching and management tool that integrates with other online sites like Flickr
- **Portal:** A browser and a portal site with your bookmarks
- **Collaboration:** A meeting and blog tool
- **Glide HD:** An online storage drive that stores files within a container

Shown in Figure 16.2 is Glide Presenter, the presentation program on top of the Glide desktop.

Glide Digital OS4 (`http://www.glidedigital.com/`) is a complete suite with office software, e-mail, and other tools that replicate an online desktop. Shown is Glide Presenter, its presentation program in a window on top of the Glide desktop.

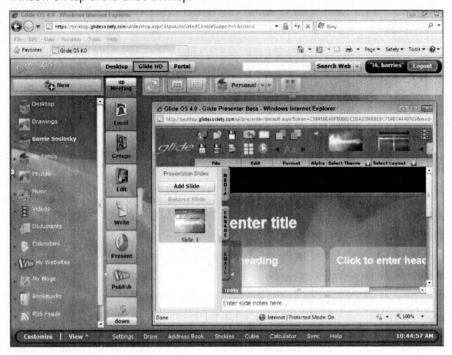

The Glide desktop and its applications represent one of the strongest offerings of an integrated cloud computing suite available today. While Google Docs and Zoho Office both offer a large number of applications and utilities, what makes the Glide OS environment so appealing is that its large collection of tools are well integrated.

Glide comes with tools for importing contacts from Microsoft Outlook, addresses from the Windows Address book, and bookmarks from Internet Explorer, Firefox, and Safari. For Macintosh users, addresses are imported from the Mac Address Book, events from iCal calendars, and bookmarks from Safari, Camino, and Firefox. Linux and Solaris users can have their contacts imported from Thunderbird LDIF files, and information is imported from iCalendar. Data can be exported in standard file formats based on the application type. For example, Write exports documents in DOC, DOCX, RTF, and PDF.

When you create an account, Glide creates an e-mail account for you in the `glidedigital.com` domain. Files that you create in Glide can be viewed on PCs, Macs, Linux, and OpenSolaris desktops; on cable company sites; and on several mobile platforms, with appropriate synchronization and conversions done by Glide itself.

Among the mobile platforms that Glide Mobile's (`http://www.glidemobile.com/`) Engage software supports are the Blackberry Storm, Tour, Curve, and Bold 9700; the Android MyTouch; Verizon Druid; and T-Mobile G1 Phones. A synchronization feature called Glide One keeps files created and managed on your desktop in sync with files on your other desktops and mobile devices.

Google Docs

Google Docs (`http://docs.google.com`) is a collection of office applications that users can create, modify, share, and work on documents collaboratively with others. Google Docs has a very large user base, mainly due to the dominant position of the search engine company in the marketplace and its free use.

Google Docs is supported on Linux, Macintosh OS X, and Microsoft Windows, as well as on Android and iPhone mobile phones. Only word processor and spreadsheets are supported by mobile phone applications at the moment; viewing presentations, database files, and PDFs are not. Figure 16.3 shows the document File Manager in Google Docs.

Google Docs creates native HTML files that are stored online. When you import files from Microsoft Word (DOC or DOCX), RTF, OpenOffice (ODF), data files in CSV, or PowerPoint (PPT), they are converted to HTML. You can export a Google Docs document to standard formats such as Microsoft Word DOC or Adobe PDF. Open documents are automatically saved, and Google Docs retains document revisions. You can tag and archive documents and use the tags to search your documents.

When you click the Share button, you can specify who can either view or collaborate on that document. The people you indicate are sent an e-mail with a link to that document in it. Collaboration on a document can be done simultaneously by two or more collaborators.

Cross-Ref
Google Applications, Google Gears, and other developer tools and online services are described in Chapter 8, "Using Google Web Services." ∎

Over the past year or two, Google has inked a number of high-profile contracts with government agencies, universities, and some corporations to serve as the office suite for their deployed desktops, displacing Microsoft Office. For commercial use, Google Docs requires a license agreement.

FIGURE 16.3

Google Docs (`http://docs.google.com`) File Manager is where you manage your online content.

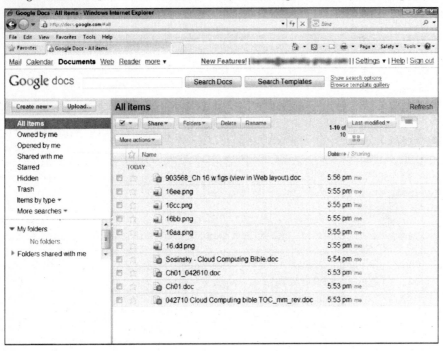

These are important features of Google Docs:

- **Google Docs:** This is a full featured word processor with an interface similar to Microsoft Office 2003. It has support for templates, a basic drawing function (Google Draw), and a LaTeX equation editor available in the word processor. The following file types can be imported into Google Docs: text (TXT), Word, RTF, HTML, Open Office (ODF), and StarOffice Writer (SXW).

  Figure 16.4 shows a document being edited in Google Docs.

- **Spreadsheets:** This allows you to create, import, modify, and share spreadsheets. You can collaborate on your spreadsheet and chat in real time, embed the worksheet in a document, or post your worksheets to a block or a Web site.

- **Presentation:** This is a presentation creation program. You can import and modify presentation files from PowerPoint (PPT or PPS) files or create new presentations that you can share. Presentations support images, audio, and video content. You can provide a real-time presentation from a remote site or publish your presentation to a Web page.

Tip

Using a feature called Google Gadgets, you can add functionality to various Google Docs modules. For example, gadgets can add an interactive motion chart or a temperature chart type to the spreadsheet. A list of gadgets for spreadsheets may be found at `http://docs.google.com/support/bin/answer.py?answer=99488`. ∎

FIGURE 16.4

Google Docs is Google's online word processor.

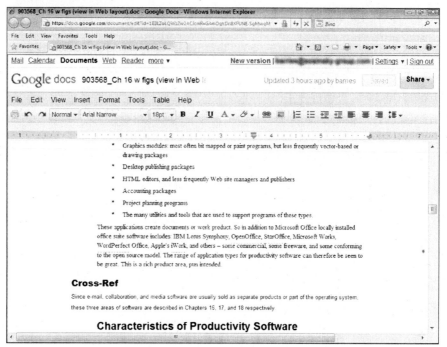

- **Reader** (`http://reader.google.com`): This RSS feed aggregator can be read online or offline.

  If you choose, you can populate Reader with your RSS feeds used on your iGoogle pages. The front page shows summaries of new items, and you can view a list or an expanded view of an item. Items may be imported or exported from Reader in an OPML file. Google also can search across all your feeds and updates in your subscriptions.

- **File Manager:** The central application in the Google Docs suite lets you upload documents, open documents, and share documents. When you open a document, the application that supports the file type launches.

The free account gives a user 1GB of disk storage. The current restrictions on content for a free account are 5,000 documents, 5,000 images, 1,000 spreadsheets, and up to 100 Adobe PDF files. Spreadsheets can have 256 columns maximum and up to 200,000 cells divided into no more than 99 worksheets. Images embedded in documents must be no more than 2MB in size.

- **Calendar** (`http://calendar.google.com`): Google's event and time management application uses an Ajax interface to support drag and drop of events between dates and times. Google Calendar is thought to be the most widely used online calendar today. It has a number of different viewing modes, including Day, 4 Day, Week, Month, and Agenda views; it also supports a To-Do list. Shown in Figure 16.5 is the Month view of the calendar.

FIGURE 16.5

The Month view shown in Google Calendar

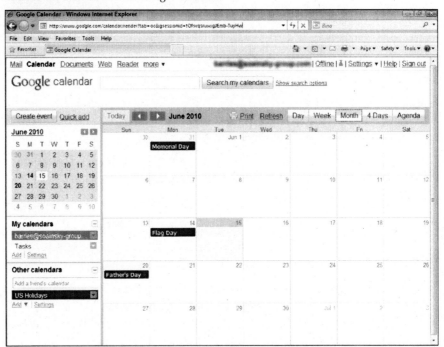

Tip

If you are interested in an online calendar program, you also may want to consider 30 Boxes (`http://www.30boxes.com/`**). A stronger online To-Do list, event manager, and time manager is the Remember the Milk (**`http://www.rememberthemilk.com/`**) application. Both are worthy competitors to Google Calendar.** ∎

Events in the calendar can be set up to generate SMS messages (called GVENTs) or e-mail through Google Gmail. You can use a gadget to populate your iGoogle home page with your events, and another gadget can allow you to search your calendars from within the Google Desktop application.

Calendar can import Microsoft Outlook calendar (CSV) and iCalendar (ICS) files. An account can support multiple calendars, which can be shared with other users and groups. Among the platforms supported by Google Calendar are Android, Blackberry, iPhone, and Pocket PC mobile devices, Apple Macintosh through iCal, and Microsoft Windows through Outlook.

Microsoft Office Web Apps

Microsoft's Office Web Apps are online slimmed-down versions of the Microsoft Office suite. They are written in Ajax and eventually are to be supplemented with Silverlight features. Files that you store on Windows Live SkyDrive can be accessed from a browser. You also can share files and collaborate with others using your online files.

Office Web Apps can be accessed through Windows Live SkyDrive using a SharePoint Server that is part of the Microsoft Software Assurance program or through a hosted Office Web Apps server using Microsoft's Online Services. SkyDrive can be a repository for your desktop office files or can serve as an online file share.

When you open Office Web Apps and view SkyDrive, the applications launch page appears as shown in Figure 16.6. Documents you create in SkyDrive and entire folders can be synchronized with other locations. Files you save in SkyDrive store a version history and are searchable within the service.

FIGURE 16.6

SkyDrive's Office Web page

Microsoft Office Web Apps includes versions of the following applications:

- Word
- Excel
- PowerPoint
- OneNote

Figure 16.7 shows the online version of PowerPoint with a single slide in design mode.

FIGURE 16.7

PowerPoint Office Live Web Apps is a Web-based version of the PowerPoint presentation program.

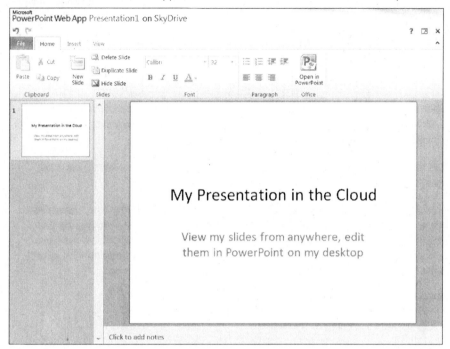

The approach Microsoft is using with Office Web Apps is to create a facility that supplements its desktop Microsoft Office products with applications in the cloud. Given Microsoft's position in the world of shrink-wrapped office software, the approach is a good one. The applications have the look and feel of their desktop counterparts, and they retain the fidelity of the originals, but they are minimalistic in their feature set.

While Office Web Apps is brand new, having just appeared as this chapter was being written, Microsoft's Office Live site (`http://office.live.com/`) is a work in progress. Microsoft Office Live is aimed at individual, SOHO (Small Office/Home Office), and small business users. The fundamental feature of the service is the ability to store and share documents online. The storage component is called Office Live Workspace and the online Web site creation facility is called Office Live Small Business.

If you are looking for a completely cloud-based application, you should probably look at other options. However, if you want the ability to work with your Office documents on the road, from another operating system, or from a cell phone, then Office Web Apps is a valuable complement to the desktop version. Microsoft's cloud-based offerings seem to be a work in progress.

ThinkFree Office

ThinkFree Office (`http://www.thinkfree.com`) is one of the earliest of the online office suites to be released, first appearing in 2001. Written in Java, with portions later added in Ajax, the current version supports Linux, Macintosh OSX, and Windows users in nine different languages and locales. Mobile support for core applications exists on the Android, Blackberry, iPhone, Nokia (S60), and Windows Mobile phone platforms.

After a trial period, you must subscribe to ThinkFree as a service. You can create a ThinkFree account or use your Google account to log into ThinkFree.

ThinkFree Online is very similar in look and feel to earlier versions of the Microsoft Office suite. Documents you create in Microsoft Office can be used within ThinkFree, and the site lets you create and export documents that Microsoft Office can use. Of the core applications, the word processor and spreadsheet are easy to use and feature rich. There is little interoperability among the three major modules; neither the clipboard nor drag and drop are supported.

Figure 16.8 shows the ThinkFree home page.

ThinkFree Office has the following components:

- **Write:** The word processor (shown in Figure 16.9)
- **Calc:** The spreadsheet
- **Show:** The presentation program
- **Note:** An HTML page and blog editor

Through the use of the Power Edit applet for Write, Calc, and Show, a history of document versions is retained. A Quick Edit mode for Write and Show allows for document modification. Documents created in ThinkFree Online can be saved to your desktop, an online share, or a mobile workspace. A synchronization manager maintains the latest copy of documents in all three locations.

ThinkFree has a collaboration feature called ThinkFree Docs where users can publish their documents. Other users can then view the documents, spreadsheets, or presentations that are made available to them.

FIGURE 16.8

ThinkFree.org's office suite login page

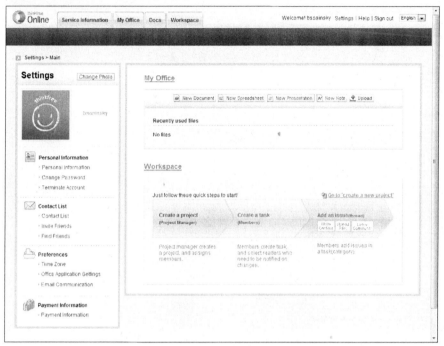

Zoho Office Suite

The Zoho Office Suite is one of the more highly regarded online office suites. With the exception of Google's apps, Zoho probably offers more modules than any of the other cloud-based office suite vendors. Zoho was created by an Indian company called AdventNet, Inc., which later rebranded itself as ZOHO Corporation. The first module, Zoho Writer, appeared in 2005.

Figure 16.10 shows the Zoho home page (http://www.zoho.com), with 15 named modules offered by Zoho directly linked to on that page. The Zoho applications are mostly free for basic functions, but they carry a charge as you use the application more heavily or access the more professional features.

FIGURE 16.9

ThinkFree's Write is one of the more capable online word processors available today.

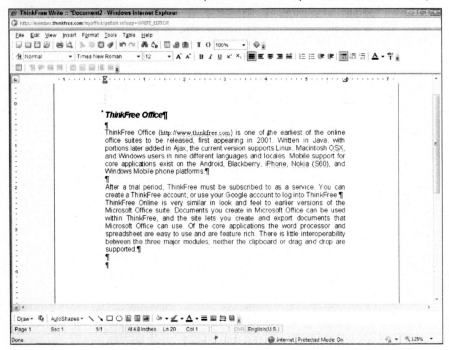

Note

Zoho supports a feature called pass-through authentication. You can either create a Zoho account or use your iGoogle, Google Apps, Yahoo!, or Facebook account to log into Zoho. ■

The Zoho Office Suite contains the following major applications:

- **Writer:** This full-featured word processor supports multiple author document creation and review. The program offers a LaTeX Equation Editor and works with MathMagic and MathType to incorporate formatted equations and expressions. Documents it creates can support embedded video files from sites such as Flickr. Figure 16.11 shows the Zoho Writer word processor.

  Writer supports the following standard file formats: text (TXT), Microsoft Word (DOC), RTF, Office Open XML (DOCX), OpenDocument text (ODT), OpenOffice.org text (SXW), HTML, and image files (JPEG, GIF, PNG).

- **Sheet:** This spreadsheet application is interoperable with Microsoft Excel and has a number of online features that make it valuable to users. For example, Sheet can be used to create and publish charts in Web pages and in blogs. It is available as an Excel plugin and a desktop widget. Facebook and box.net both offer Zoho sheet services.

FIGURE 16.10

Zoho's home page shows the wide range of cloud-based productivity software that it offers.

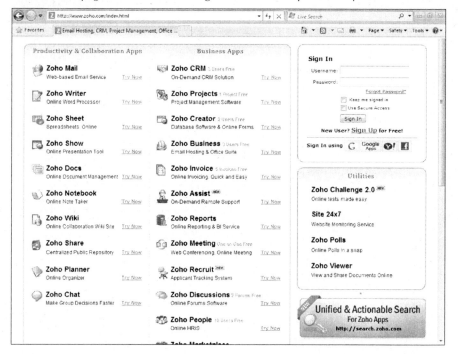

- **Show:** This presentation program interoperates with Microsoft PowerPoint (PPS and PPT), OpenDocument Presentations (ODP), and OpenOffice (SXI) presentations; it also can export to those formats.

- **Notebook:** The content creation and management system is similar to both Microsoft OneNote and Google Notebook. Pages in Notebook can include not only text, but images, audio, video content, RSS feeds, and allows you to launch and access other applications.

- **Creator:** This database system interoperates with Microsoft Access and other standard file formats. Database rules can be added to Creator using a drag-and-drop scripting engine, and it does not require a database language to implement.

  The module supports import of XLS, CSV, and TSV files and exports to XLS, CSV, TSV, HTML, PDF, JSON, and RSS files.

- **Projects:** The project management module creates and manages tasks, tracks milestones and deadlines, and provides reports and Gantt charts. Projects may be viewed by a group. In the free version of Zoho, you have access to only one project and a limited number of features. The premium version of Zoho removes these limitations.

- **Planner:** The calendar and event system compiles to-do lists, creates event reports, and has an alert e-mail system. Planner interoperates with Microsoft Outlook and Google Calendar.

FIGURE 16.11

Zoho Writer is a highly regarded online word processor.

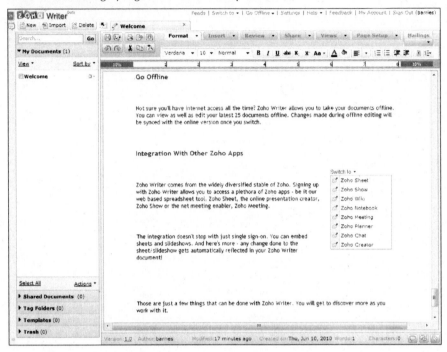

- **Mail:** The e-mail system integrates into Zoho Writer, Sheet, and Show modules. It provides such collaborative services as a calendar, contacts, document tools, and task management tools.

- **Chat:** This instant messaging application can be embedded into Web pages or blogs. Chat supports feeds to and from other chat system providers.

- **Discussions:** This is an online forum for groups that you either create or join.

- **Meeting:** This is a conferencing application with screen sharing technology. A presenter can designate that a participant be allowed to control the presenter's desktop. A Zoho Meeting Viewer can be embedded into a Web page or placed in a Zoho Show slide for viewing from that module.

  The creator must be on Microsoft Windows, but other meeting participants can be using a different operating system's browser. To view the meeting, the viewer must have Java, Flash, or ActiveX installed.

- **CRM:** This customer relationship management package provides a procurement and inventory function, along with invoicing and some other limited accounting support, as well as reporting.

- **People:** This is a Human Resource Information System and an Application Tracking System for a company.

- **Wiki:** This HTML editor creates Wiki pages from a graphical interface. When you create a Wiki on Zoho, you are given a URL that you can publish that allows others to add content to your page. Figure 16.12 shows the creation of a Wiki page from within a Zoho Personal page.

FIGURE 16.12

A Zoho Wiki can be created from your Zoho Personal page. This page gives you access to other applications and to your files and folders.

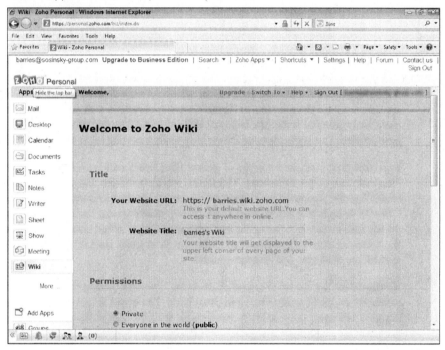

Zoho also offers an online test creation tool called Challenge and a survey tool called Polls; both can be added to a Web page. Other utilities include Site 24X7 Web site monitoring tool and a set of preview applications called Zoho Viewer. These tools are free for you to use.

Zoho has plugins for some of its applications that initiate support for a module within an office application or browser. Some of the Zoho modules also offer an open API for developers to use; at the moment the list of developer-customizable modules includes Writer, Sheet, Show, Creator, Meeting, and Planner. With Zoho for Google Apps, a number of the modules described above and some additional ones, including CRM, Projects, Invoice, Creator, and Creator Helpdesk can be used with a Google Apps account.

Icons for these functions can be placed on the Google navigation bar. With Zoho CRM for Google Apps, for example, you can provide for icon-initiated Sync Google Mail with Zoho CRM, Import Contacts from Google Apps, Attach Files from Google Docs, Export Events to Google Calendar, and Embed Gadgets into Google Sites. Similar icon support for Zoho Project, Creator, and Creator Helpdesk also exists.

Zoho was one of the first online office suites to offer the feature of offline content editing and synchronization. This feature allows users to work on documents even when they don't have an Internet connection. The system then makes their changes when the users become connected.

Zoho applications can be bundled by developers and sold as a service to users through a custom dashboard by its partners.

Summary

This chapter gave you a taste of the range of cloud-based applications available to users and of the relative sophistication of these applications relative to their desktop counterparts. Online productivity applications have the potential to displace local applications over time in many instances, but the more likely scenario is that the industry will arrive at a blended model that places some of the functionality of an application on the desktop while accessing other functionality through the cloud.

In this chapter, you saw examples of online office suites such as Acrobat.com, Glide, Google Docs, Microsoft Live Office Web Apps, ThinkFree, and Zoho Office. Google and Zoho offer a wide range of applications; Acrobat.com focuses on document creation and publishing; Microsoft's site offers Office Web Apps as a supplement to its desktop counterparts. Each vendor has a unique slant on the capabilities that it is providing and what its vision of office software in the cloud will be. All these sites leverage assigned storage containers as its users' data repository. For the most part, these systems are platform- and browser-neutral.

It's easy to see the appeal of online office suites. They offer reduced costs, universal access, better collaboration, and rapidly developing standards. The world is rapidly getting connected to the Internet, and many users are very comfortable with the idea of doing their work in the cloud.

In Chapter 17, "Using Webail Services," you learn about perhaps the most popular category of cloud-based applications in use today—messaging and e-mail outside of simple Web browsing. Chapter 17 covers traditional e-mail systems such as Google Mail or Gmail, Microsoft's Hotmail, Yahoo! Mail, and others. It also covers chat and Instant Messaging Services such as AOL Instant Messaging (AIM), Google Talk, and Skype, and Small Message Services such as Twitter.

Using Webmail Services

This chapter describes two of the most popular Web services that are deployed in the cloud: Webmail and syndicated content. Webmail sites are among the most popular Web sites in use today with the major services having hundreds of millions of user accounts.

Many Webmail services are free, and the rest are generally modestly priced. Webmail may be differentiated from hosted e-mail by its access through a Web browser. This makes them platform-independent. These services also sometimes use POP3 and IMAP, which allows them to be used to feed e-mail into traditional e-mail clients like Outlook and Thunderbird.

The current generation of Webmail services implements user interfaces based on Ajax and tends to follow a model that makes them look similar to the Microsoft Outlook e-mail client. These browser-based services provide filters, advanced search capabilities, sorting, tagging, and many other features. Most of these services use spam and virus detection to eliminate unwanted mail.

Syndication services are a method for publishing content from Web sites, blogs, wikis, and other services. It is a form of group e-mail, broadcast e-mail if you will.

There are both content providers and content consumers. Examples of content providers include not only the services just mentioned but also aggregation services and site. Many aggregation Web sites are well known for collecting content on the subject area in which they specialize.

RSS content can be read in most modern browsers. When you subscribe to an RSS feed, you create a bookmark or favorite that is updated automatically as new content appears. Another type of application called a newsreader allows you to collect subscriptions and view them all in one site. The iGoogle customization site is based on RSS and Atom news feeds.

Exploring the Cloud Mail Services

By any measure, browser-based hosted e-mail or "Webmail" is one of the great success stories of the Internet. It is the prototypical Software as a Service (SaaS) application. Webmail was also one of the first cloud computing applications to emerge and is today among the most heavily used services. Webmail is differentiated from hosted e-mail primarily by the use of browser-based client access. The underlying e-mail servers and the mail protocols are the same ones used for client/ server e-mail services, but the servers and services have been deployed on a massive scale.

Many of these services such as Gmail and Hotmail are free up to a certain level of service; it is certainly the price that has attracted such a large worldwide audience. When you layer on top of low price all the advantages that cloud computing offers—scale, ubiquitous access, platform independence, and others—it is not hard to understand Webmail's allure.

The first of the free hosted Webmail services to emerge was Hotmail. It was begun in 1996 by Sabeer Bhatia and Jack Smith with the name HoTMaiL. The capitalization indicated its origin as a Web- or HTML-based application. Microsoft acquired HotMail a year later and rebranded it as MSN Hotmail. The current version of the product is called Windows Live Hotmail, and it is part of the Windows Live suite of Web-based software products discussed in Chapter 10, "Using Microsoft Web Services."

It's anyone's guess who has the largest Webmail service. Based on the number of registered accounts, that honor would seem to be accorded to Microsoft, which has 360 million Hotmail accounts. Yahoo Mail! also claims to be the largest Webmail service with 260 million accounts. Google's Gmail by comparison has 176 million accounts as of the end of 2009, and AOL Mail (also called AIM Mail) is believed to be the fourth largest Webmail service.

Note

It is common practice among Webmail services to flag dormant accounts after a certain period of time and then to delete the accounts at some later time, should there be no activity. For Gmail and Hotmail, those actions occur after six and nine months, respectively. Yahoo! Mail deactivates accounts after only four months of inactivity. ∎

Accounts are one thing; active use of accounts is another. A much more accurate picture of how popular these services are may be obtained by examining the number of visits (hits) that the different Web sites get. A *hit* can be measured relatively accurately by looking at the DNS server logs at key points in the Internet backbone.

The Internet data analytics company Experian's Hitwise.com service maintains a dashboard (http://www.hitwise.com/us/datacenter/main/dashboard-10133.html) shown in Figure 17.1 with the current percentage of hits made on individual sites. As of the week of 7/17/2010, these were the three top Web sites:

- 1. Facebook (9.16%)
- 2. Google (7.45%)
- 3. Yahoo! (3.76%)

Webmail services occupy these slots:

- 4. Yahoo! Mail (3.59%)
- 8. Windows Live Mail (1.60%)
- 11. Gmail (0.87%)
- 14. AOL Mail (0.59%)

These figures give a much more accurate picture of how important the different services are in real-world usage.

FIGURE 17.1

Experian's Hitwise.com site publishes a dashboard with the leading Web sites by different categories.

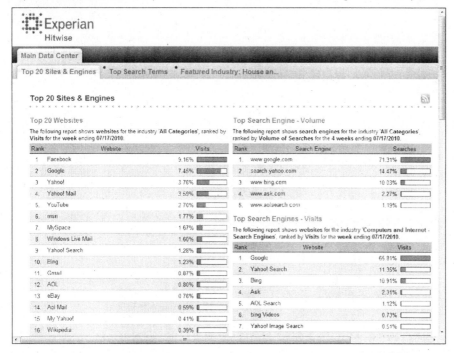

Table 17.1 summarizes the features of leading Webmail providers. The following sections describe the three largest Webmail services: Gmail, Hotmail, and Yahoo! Mail in detail.

TABLE 17.1

Webmail Features

Service/Owner	URL	Cost (U.S. $)	Storage/Max Attachment	IMAP or POP3 Support
AOL Mail AOL USA	https://mail.aol.com/	Free	Unlimited/25MB	Both
BlueTie BlueTie, Inc.	http://www.bluetie.com/	$4.99/mo	10GB/25MB	Both
ContactOffice Contract Office Group sa	http://www.contact office.com/	Free and paid	100MB to 10GB/25MB	Both
Excite IAC Search & Media	http://www.excite.com/	Free	1GB/25MB	No
FastMail.FM Opera Software Australia	http://www.fastmail.fm/	Free, $4.95/yr ad free, $34.95 enhanced	25MB to 15GB/10 to 50MB	IAMP for all, POP3 and SMTP paid
Gawab EgyptHome IT, Egypt	http://www.gawab.com/	Free	10GB/50MB	Both
Gmail Google USA	https://www.google.com/	Free	7.48GB/25MB	IMAP, POP3, POP+TLS, Microsoft Exchange
GMX Mail United Internet, Germany	http://www.gmx.net/	Free, paid for ProMail and TopMail	1 free or 5GB paid/20 to 50MB	Both (IMAP paid)
Hushmail Hush Communications Ltd.	http://www.hushmail.com/	Free, $34.99 premium	2MB free to 5GB premium/2MB free to 1GB premium	IMAP paid
Lavabit Lavabit LLC, USA	http://lavabit.com/	Two free options, and two paid options	128MB/32 to 128MB	Both (SSL optional)

Service/Owner	URL	Cost (U.S. $)	Storage/Max Attachment	IMAP or POP3 Support
LuxSci Lux Scientiae, Inc. USA	http://luxsci.com/	$9.99/mo	2GB+/100MB	IMAP, IMAP+SSL, IMAP+TLS, POP, POP+SSL, POP+TLS, Alternate Ports
Lycos Duam, Korea	http://www.lycos.com/	$19.95/yr	5GB/Unlimited	NA
Mail.com MMC, USA	http://www.mail.com/	Free, $3.99/mo or $19.99/ yr ad free	Unlimited/16MB	Free: None, Paid Both
Mail.ru Mail.ru, Russia	http://mail.ru/	Free, $5/ mo ad free	Unlimited/30MB	Both
Mail2World Mail2World, Inc. USA	http://www.mail2world.com/	Free, $19.95 premium	Unlimited/40MB	Both
MobileMe Apple, Inc. USA	http://www.mobileme.com	$99/yr	20GB/Unlimited	IMAP (POP3 optional
MyWay IAC Search & Media USA	http://www.myway.com/	Free	1GB/25MB	No
O2 Webmail Telefonica O2 UK	http://www.o2.co.uk/	Free	20MB/NA	POP3 only
Ovi Mail Nokia Finland	http://www.ovi.com/	Free	1GB/20MB	NA
Rackspace Email Rackspace USA	http://www.rackspace.com/	$1/mail-box month	10GB/50MB	Both
Runbox Runbox AS, Norway	http://www.runbox.com/	$49.95/yr	10GB/100MB	IMAP4 and POP3 with SSL
Seznam.cz Seznam.cz	http://www.seznam.cz/	Free	Unlimited/13MB	POP3
ThinkPost.net Thinkpost	http://www.thinkpost.net/	$5/mo	10GB/50MB	Both
Windows Live Hotmail Microsoft, USA	http://www.mail.live.com/	Free, $19.95 ad free	5GB/10 to 20MB	POP3

continued

TABLE 17.1 (continued)				
Service/Owner	URL	Cost (U.S. $)	Storage/Max Attachment	IMAP or POP3 Support
WWW.COM Email WWW.COM	https://mail.www.com/web-email	$28.99	7GB/25MB	Both (w/SSL option)
Yahoo! Mail Yahoo!	http://mail.yahoo.com/	Free, $19.99/yr for Plus	Unlimited/25MB	POP3 in most countries, with Plus), or with YPOPs!

Source: http://en.wikipedia.org/wiki/Comparison_of_webmail_providers.

Google Gmail

Google Gmail (http://www.gmail.com or alternatively http://www.mail.google.com) is the third most popular of the large Webmail services and became available first in beta in 2004 from Google Labs and then for the use of the public in 2007 as "beta." In July 2009 Google announced that Gmail and the Google apps were released products. Gmail is available worldwide in 52 languages, works in nearly all modern browsers, and comes in both a desktop and mobile browser version. Google markets Gmail for domains to organizations and has a Google Apps Partner Edition that Google allows to be branded by ISPs, large organizations, port Web sites, and other organizations as paid services.

Gmail is written to look like an Internet chat utility, as shown in Figure 17.2, and it sorts e-mails by conversations or threads. Conversations containing multiple e-mails can be edited to delete individual messages, but Gmail tends to perform most of its operations such as archiving on the conversation as a whole. A conversation cannot be split into multiple conversations, nor can a conversation be added to another conversation. When conversations get large, as they do with group e-mails, Gmail can be cumbersome to work in. When a conversation gets to be 100 messages long, Gmail splits the conversation into a second section.

At the time of its offering, Gmail created something of a sensation by offering 1GB of free storage when competitors would allow their free customers to have only a few megabytes of storage for their accounts. Today Gmail's free accounts come with up to 7.48GB of free storage. Figure 17.2 shows a Gmail screen for a new user account.

Gmail was notable for its early use of Ajax (Asynchronous JavaScript and XML), something that has become the standard development platform for Webmail applications across the industry. When you compose a message in Gmail's Rich Text Format interface, Gmail performs an Autosave of its content at 1-minute intervals.

The product is extensible both through a number of add-ons from Gmail Labs and through its multi-tabbed settings page (`https://mail.google.com/mail/?shva=1#settings`), shown in Figure 17.3. As these add-ons (or experiments if you will) are tested and mature, some of them make their way into Gmail's default setup. Among the features to have graduated into Gmail are the integrated chat with SMS messaging that you see in the lower left of Figure 17.3 (Google Talk, which is discussed in the next chapter), offline access using Google Gears, and the Tasks feature.

FIGURE 17.2

The Gmail service presents an interface that is reminiscent of an Internet chat utility.

FIGURE 17.3

Gmail's General settings page

Although many e-mail services use spam filters based on Bayesian algorithms, the developers of Gmail opted for a system where the entire user base's assignment of spam is used to grade and mark e-mail as potential spam. You can set your own flag for whether any particular e-mail or sender is spam overriding Gmail's setting. Gmail also scans both incoming and outgoing e-mail attachments for viruses and blocks the receipt of any file that it recognizes as an executable file.

In Gmail, you can construct searches with multiple operators using the Advanced Search feature, which accepts keywords, sender, location, and date. A number of additional search criteria, such as "language:<*languagename*>," can be used to narrow a search. When you set flags on messages, those flags can be used in filters to narrow what you see in the window. Some flags are set by performing operations such as reading the message, archiving, and so forth.

Google uses an advertiser-driven model to supply its free service to users. In its search function, Google uses the keywords from your search and your search history to match sponsors to you. In

Gmail, Google scans the content of the e-mail and extracts keywords from your messages. This has raised the concern that mail sent through Gmail isn't as private as some advocates might like. Although you have agreed to Google's privacy policy, the people sending you e-mail have not.

In one of the General settings shown earlier in Figure 17.3, you can set an option to force Gmail to use the HTTPS transfer protocol instead of the non-secure HTTP protocol. This is the default setting in the current version of the program. For POP3 and IMAP access to your Gmail account through a mail client, the transport protocol is TLS (Transport Layer Security). Not all e-mail clients receive mail from Gmail's servers using TLS; some, such as Thunderbird, get the message transmitted to them over the wire as clear text. Using the Mail Fetcher feature, up to five POP3 accounts can be automatically retrieved and displayed within a Gmail account.

These are the Gmail POP3 settings:

- **POP server address:** pop.gmail.com.
- **POP user name:** Your full Gmail address (including @gmail.com); Google Apps users may have to enter <Username>@your_domain.com>.
- **POP password:** Your Gmail password.
- **POP port:** 995.
- **POP TLS/SSL required:** Yes.

The fact that Google scans and stores e-mail for up to 60 days makes it a target for hackers. The recent kerfuffle concerning hackers gaining access to human rights activists' Gmail accounts in China led to Google moving its servers from Beijing to Hong Kong and tends to validate these concerns. However, Google isn't unique in the way it handles Webmail, and these concerns apply to nearly every service described in this chapter.

Mail2Web

Mail2Web is the prototypical POP3 Webmail mail retrieval service, established in 1997. You log into your e-mail account from a browser using your account name and password, and then Mail2Web queries your mail server and downloads the messages that are unread for display. From the Mail2Web interface, you can read messages, reply, and create new messages, as shown in Figure 17.4. The basic service is free, but the company based in Toronto, Canada, has additional paid services for hosted Microsoft Exchange accounts.

Mail2Web also has a mobile e-mail service based on Exchange called Mail2Web.com Mobile E-mail. The mobile service works with RIM Blackberry cell phones. The company's instant messaging service for mobile devices allows users to connect to their AOL, ICQ, MSN, and Yahoo! IM accounts.

FIGURE 17.4

Mail2Web.com provides online access to any POP3 account.

Windows Live Hotmail

Windows Live Hotmail is Microsoft's Webmail offering and with localized versions in 36 languages. The original version of the product was found at http:www.hotmail.com and was rebranded as MSN Hotmail. Today, that URL redirects you to the login page for Windows Live Hotmail at http://mail.live.com. After you establish an account with the domain address of either *<Username>*@hotmail.com or *<Username>*@live.com, you are directed to your Windows Live Hotmail inbox, and the welcome message is displayed, as shown in Figure 17.5.

Windows Live Hotmail is one of the central applications in Microsoft Windows Live product portfolio, and it's integrated with other Windows Live applications. As you can see in Figure 17.5, Hotmail provides one-click access to Windows Live Calendar, Contacts, Messenger, and Spaces. The last version of Hotmail was released in June 2010 and added further integration to Windows Live Office and to your Windows Live SkyDrive online storage.

Although the interface looks similar to an Outlook client in that it has a folder-based navigation tree (the left panel), Windows Live Hotmail was created with Ajax technology. The current version of Hotmail is compatible with Internet Explorer, Firefox, and Chrome, but not Safari.

A welcome message shown in Windows Live Hotmail, a central offering of Windows Live Services

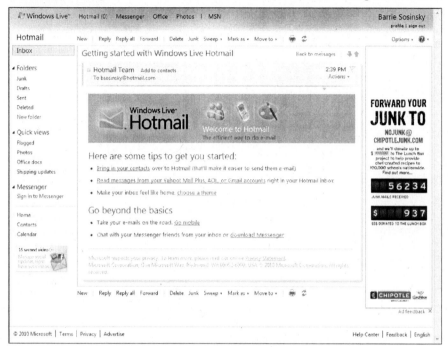

Hotmail has a strong feature set. This includes the ability to navigate the interface with a keyboard, automatic completion of input fields, and strong contact management and group e-mail support. Built into the product is a spam filter and virus scanning. You can support multiple e-mail accounts in Hotmail, allowing the product to serve as a central repository of your e-mail from different services.

The newest version of Hotmail added the ability to set a spam filter directly with your mouse, called 1-Click Filters; to set a junk mail collection, called Inbox Sweeping; and to send attachments up to 10GB in size. Also new is a set of special content folders called Quick views, which can show messages you flag, display photos and Office documents, and show shipping update notices from shipping carriers.

One of the stronger features of Hotmail is its Advanced Search function, shown in Figure 17.6. You can search on addresses, domains, keywords, and dates, and you can perform a search scoped to different folders. The search terms you enter create a compound structured query.

You can get your Hotmail account using POP3 inside a traditional e-mail client or using a POP3 Web service such as Mail2Web.com.

Hotmail's Advanced Search creates a structured query across multiple fields.

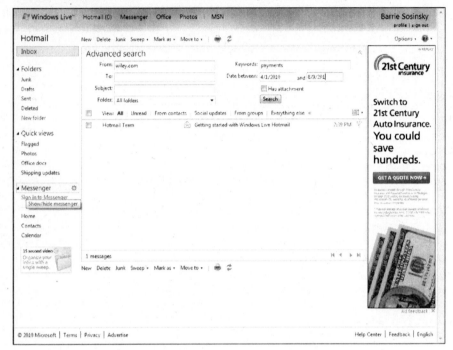

The POP3 settings for Hotmail are as follows:

- **POP server:** pop3.live.com (Port 995).

- **POP SSL required:** Yes.

- **User name:** Enter your Hotmail account, *<Username>*@hotmail.com or *<Username>*@live.com.

- **Password:** Enter the password you use to log into Hotmail, or if you are using a Windows Live account, use that password.

- **SMTP server:** smtp.live.com (Port 25 or 587).

- **Authentication required:** Yes; this matches your POP username and password.

- **TLS/SSL required:** Yes.

Hotmail also can be viewed in Microsoft Office Outlook using the Outlook Connector or using Windows Live for Windows Mobile phones on that phone's operating system. The Microsoft Office Outlook Connector (for Outlook 2003, 2007, and 2010) lets you access messages, contacts, and your calendar from Outlook in your Hotmail account. If you have a premium subscription to

Hotmail, you also can access your notes and tasks using the connector. Windows Live Mail and Microsoft Outlook can synchronize messages with Hotmail using Microsoft's DeltaSync protocol, but only on the Windows platform. Another synchronization feature called Exchange ActiveSync adds the ability to synchronize messages, contacts, and calendars on any mobile phone that has ActiveSync.

Yahoo! Mail

Yahoo! Mail, or as it is now rebranded "Y! Mail," is the largest Webmail service on the Internet. It is also one of the oldest, having appeared at the same time as Hotmail did in 1997. The original Y! Mail interface is still available for clients on older operating systems and other retro fan boys; it is shown in Figure 17.7.

In 2006, Yahoo! added a version of the user interface based on Ajax that looks like a form of Microsoft Outlook that has become something of an industry standard. This Ajax interface is based on the work of Oddpost, which the company acquired in 2004. Gmail also was heavily influenced by Oddpost's work. Figure 17.8 shows Y! Mail in the Ajax form.

FIGURE 17.7

Yahoo! Mail shown in the "Classic" interface format

FIGURE 17.8

The Ajax form of Y! Mail, referred to as the "All New Mail" option

Mail is meant to mimic a desktop client and has drag-and-drop capabilities, keyboard equivalents, tabbed widows, an advanced search, address auto-completion, and supports RSS feeds. You can send SMS messages to others in some countries using Y! Mail. Yahoo! Mail provides an unlimited amount of mail storage and a limit of 10MB per message and 25MB per attachment in the United States.

Y! Mail supports POP3 client access and mail forwarding. The service also runs a set of IMAP servers that you can access for free. The login to the service requires that a special command be sent, so you may need to either obtain a mail client that supports Y! Mail IMAP or make appropriate modifications to your own client. Versions of Mozilla Thunderbird and Mutt support the IMAP feature. In some countries, you can use Yahoo! SMTP server (smtp.mail.yahoo.com) to send messages.

These are the POP3 and SMTP settings for Yahoo! Mail:

- **Incoming Mail (POP3) Server:** pop3.mail.yahoo.com (use SSL, port: 995)

- **Outgoing Mail (SMTP) Server:** smtp.mail.yahoo.com (use SSL, port: 465, use authentication)

- **Account Name/Login Name:** Your Yahoo! Mail ID (your email address without the "@ yahoo.com")
- **Email Address:** Your Yahoo! Mail address (*<Username>*@yahoo.com)
- **Password:** Your Yahoo! Mail password

Yahoo! Mail has a filter feature that lets you create up to 100 filters per account. The paid versions of the service expand this limit to 200 filters. Those filters operate in addition to the built-in spam filter called SpamGuard that Yahoo! applies to its e-mail. SpamGuard works on messages before filters are applied. The system also flags some mail that it suspects of being spam to deferred delivery, a feature referred to as greylisting. While the details of greylisting aren't fully revealed, they probably work by seeing if additional mail of this type arrives in a certain period, and if not, the block is lifted.

Mail is authenticated by Y! Mail using DomainKeys, which is a service that verifies the DNS domain of the person sending the e-mail and establishes the messages integrity. DomainKeys is based on the IETF protocol call Identified Internet Mail, which was enhanced to create a new protocol called DomainKeys Identified Mail (DMIK; http://www.dkim.org/), so that DMIK now replaces the original version of DomainKeys. You can also filter messages and archive messages to your local drive. Y! Mail also allows a sender to send messages with other domains listed as the origin.

Y! Mail has been integrated with a number of Yahoo! Web services. Y! Mail is integrated with Yahoo! Messenger, so you can check your mail and connect with others using instant messaging. This integration has become a standard feature in Webmail offerings; both Gmail and Hotmail offer this feature. Yahoo! Messenger can exchange messages with Windows Live Messenger. You also can access Yahoo! Calendar from within the program. Some other applications that are accessible from Y! Mail are Flickr, Piknic, and Wordpress.

Yahoo! offers a premium subscription version of Y! Mail called Yahoo! Mail Plus. Another service called Yahoo! Business E-mail provides Webmail, POP3, IMAP, and SMTP services along with 10 accounts of the Plus version for a $25 setup charge with a $9.99 monthly subscription. You also can register accounts with two other Yahoo! e-mail service domains: ymail.com and rocketmail. com.

Working with Syndication Services

A syndication service is another way for people to send messages to a group of people; it's a form of published e-mail. To receive syndicated content, you must opt into the system and subscribe to the "feed" from one of the many content management system services. You can read RSS and Atom formatted content inside special applications called newsreaders, or as they are called more often "readers," as well as in many Webmail applications. After you subscribe to a feed, the reader uses the link provided to download content from a site that you haven't downloaded already.

The technology behind syndication is simple, but the value of the content can be impactful. It's a shame that more people don't make better use of this free Web service, although Web service providers have proved themselves to be creative consumers of syndication. Your personalized Google home page can be altered to include information from any of thousands of feeds, serving the role of a reader or aggregator application, and with Ajax you can rearrange pages of feeds into various channels. Web feeds also are used to follow blogger and wikis entries.

Note
RSS and Atom are prototypes of a class of XML specifications called syndication markup languages. ■

The RSS and Atom Protocols

Two technologies are behind most of the syndicated content being used on the Internet: RSS and Atom. The first of these technologies, RSS, stands for Really Simple Syndication. A typical RSS document or feed contains text and metadata that can be used to indicate publication dates, authors, keywords, and more. RSS uses an XML file format and the concept of an RSS world or module. Several modules exist that are XML namespaces, including Ecommerce RSS 2.0, Media RSS 2.0, and OpenSearch RSS 2.0 modules. The major browser providers use the feed icon shown in Figure 17.9 to indicate that you can subscribe to content on that Web page; the icon applies equally to RSS and Atom content.

FIGURE 17.9

The RSS syndication feed icon used in today's browsers.

The format has a long history of development starting as far back as 1995 as an effort to summarize content of Web pages. Dave Winer and UserLand Software were instrumental in developing the format specification, which exists in two main forms: RDF (RSS 0.91, 1.0, and 1.1), and RSS 2.* (RSS 0.91, 0.92-0.94, and 2.0.1). Winer added the ability for subscription to include audio files in RSS feeds at the end of 2000. Most consumers of RSS can work with either branch of the standard. Currently, the RSS Advisory Board (http://www.rssboard.org/rss-specification) manages this format.

RSS feeds are the basis of podcasts that are carried on the Apple iTunes store and in many other locations and helped spark a revolution in media distribution (and for which this author is eternally grateful).

Because of the number of people involved in the development of RSS and the absence of a standards body endorsing it, an alternative version of XML syndication called the Atom Publishing Protocol was developed by the IETF. That standard was released as part of the Proposed Standard RFC 4287 (`http://tools.ietf.org/html/rfc4287`), with the Atom Publishing Protocol published as RFC 5023 (`http://bitworking.org/projects/atom/rfc5023.html`). Atom has some structural differences with RSS, but is similar in approach and technology.

Most of the major browsers support RSS and Atom, but some ask you to choose between them. Blog and wiki content tends to use Atom as the format. When you view a syndication content management application, the aggregators tend to list feeds by content. This is possible because a feed contains keywords in its metadata.

Newsreaders

Most major Web sites support Web feeds, either as a consumer or a provider. An example of a consumer is your favorite browser or the reader applications described below. An example of a provider is a Web site or aggregator service.

A browser that is a consumer of RSS feeds shows you an RSS icon in the browser's address bar (or somewhere else). Often, the site's RSS feed appears as a link in the menu bar. In Mozilla Thunderbird, clicking the icon in the address bar opens a dialog box asking if you want to subscribe to the feed. Essentially, you are creating a bookmark. In Internet Explorer, the RSS icon is in the Command toolbar and takes you to the RSS feed page. In Figure 17.10, the RSS feed page for NYTimes.com is shown. If you click the Subscribe link, you see a dialog box to create the bookmark that is added to your Favorites and is updated regularly.

To view your subscriptions in your browser, you would open the Feeds section of your bookmarks or in your Favorites folder or toolbar. The page you see in your browser is identical to the one shown in Figure 17.10.

There is a class of applications whose entire purpose is displaying RSS content. These are the three best-known newsreaders:

- Google Reader (`http://reader.google.com`)
- Bloglines (`http://bloglines.com`)
- Newsgator Online (`http://newsgator.com`)

Google Reader is shown in Figure 17.11.

FIGURE 17.10

The New York Times RSS feed page and the Subscription dialog box in Internet Explorer

News Aggregators

A news aggregation Web site is one that relies on collecting the syndicated content from other Web sites in a form that can be viewed together. Most are themed. Many of the most popular Web sites that take the form of an online magazine such as the Huffington Post, Drudge Report, and NewsNow are displaying syndicated content with short descriptions and stories mixed in. In these cases, there is human intervention to structure the content in a way that works better with the original material on the site.

FIGURE 17.11

Google Reader is an application for collecting messages sent in RSS and Atom format from information providers. These applications are sometimes referred to as newsreaders or aggregators.

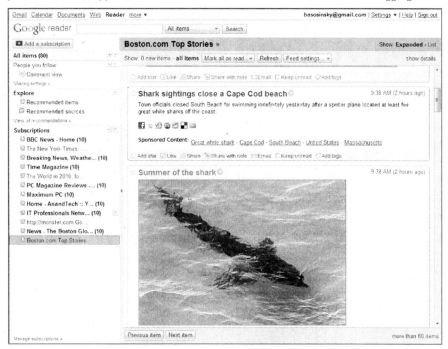

Web syndication is popular because it allows a Web site to receive content from other sites, which makes the site score higher with search engines. If you have a site that aggregates content the way RealClearPolitics.com does for political content or the way ArtsandLettersDaily.com does for the literary arts content, these sites score highly in search engine optimization algorithms because they have more of the same type of keyword in their contents or appropriate links, which moves the site toward the top of a search in its dedicated area because of its aggregation. Figure 17.12 shows the site ArtsandLettersDaily.com as an example of an aggregation site.

FIGURE 17.12

Arts & Letters Daily (`http://www.artsandlettersdaily.com`) is an example of a Web site news aggregator.

Aggregation also can be done within software creating a custom Web page. An example of this is the type of personal magazine you can create in an iGoogle or My Yahoo! account. When you create these accounts, you are provided a page you can subscribe to for content. The Add Stuff link in iGoogle takes you to the content management system shown in Figure 17.13 where you can select the content you want to subscribe to. When you return to iGoogle, the feed appears within an Ajax frame that can be moved around on the page or moved to additional tabs that you can create, as shown in Figure 17.14.

FIGURE 17.13

iGoogle's syndication aggregation site, an example of a content management system

FIGURE 17.14

Syndicated content appears in iGoogle inside Ajax frames that can be arranged in pages.

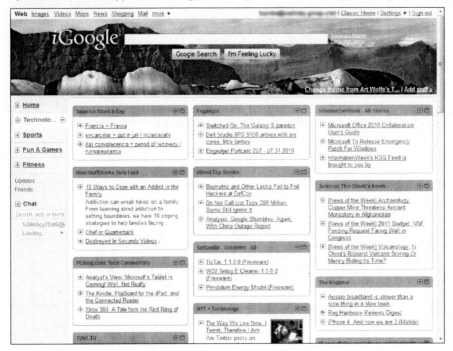

Summary

In this chapter, you learned about Webmail and the various services that offer it. The Webmail sites such as Yahoo! Mail, Windows Live Hotmail, Gmail, and AOL Mail are among the most heavily visited sites on the Internet. Webmail services are often free, browser-based, and platform-independent. Features such as filtering and search make these services very capable and very popular. Webmail has broken out and is becoming widely adopted in companies and governments.

Also described in this chapter are syndication services. RSS and Atom are protocols for publishing messages in the form of XML that can be displayed in application. Web sites, bloggers, wikis, and many more places serve as content providers. Browsers and readers can be used to view syndicated content. Syndication shows up in personalized Web pages and in news and magazine Web sites.

Chapter 18 describes another set of collaboration applications that are popular cloud computing applications. These applications include instant messaging, collaboration applications, and community or social sites.

Communicating with the Cloud

In this chapter, you learn about some of the cloud-based messaging and social interaction services that have greatly affected the use of the Internet for many people. The sites described in this chapter are among the most heavily visited in the world. The names of the services—Twitter, LinkedIn, MySpace, Facebook, and others—are so well known that the services they perform will enter the vocabulary of users as common verbs.

Instant messaging has been a product category for a long time. The cloud has made these services more numerous, easier to access, and much more popular. AOL Instant Messenger was a pioneer in this category, but now IM is integrated into all the major Webmail platforms. This chapter describes some IM services, along with how to get some of them to interoperate with one another.

Small Message Service (SMS) systems allow short text messages to be exchanged. Twitter was described as the prototypical example of this type of service.

Social networks arise from the desire to share personal information with others. These services provide the means to create a mini-personal Web site and your profile. There are tools to share resources, join groups, follow people, e-mail and IM, and more from these sites. Literally hundreds of these sites are devoted to all manner of activities, and many are listed here.

Because working in multiple sites and following many people can be a major chore, a number of services that perform site aggregation are described. These sites let you add feeds from other sites and view them together.

Exploring Instant Messaging

Instant messaging (IM) is a software category that has benefited greatly from the growth of large user communities. Instant messaging builds on the older concept of Internet chat to add a more immediate response to text messages between individuals and groups. Whereas online chat is aimed at exchanging information between people in a forum or multiuser environment, instant messaging is most often a peer-to-peer communication.

Instant messaging fills the gap between e-mail, which is asynchronous, and telephony, which is synchronous communication. A good description of IM is that it is "near-real-time" communications.

In the preceding chapter, you saw that each Webmail service offers its own IM client in its Webmail interface. While IM is meant to be instant communication between people, the merger of Webmail and IM means that many systems support sending messages to other people who are not currently logged into the system. This form of offline messaging blurs the differences between IM and regular e-mail.

Instant messaging clients

It is difficult to avoid exposure to instant messaging applications: Operating systems, Webmail services, video games, enterprise messaging systems, and many other applications install IM clients. Any application that wants to foster a sense of community can benefit from instant messaging.

Instant messaging applications have the following forms:

- Discrete instant messaging desktop clients
- Enterprise messaging services with IM capabilities
- Browser-based IM clients (often in conjunction with Webmail)
- Mobile device clients, either embedded and client specific or mobile browser-based

You can get some sense of the diversity of instant messaging clients by looking at the home page for AOL Instant Messenger (`http://www.aim.com`), shown in Figure 18.1. AIM comes in desktop, browser, and native client formats on multiple platforms. The tendency recently has been to connect instant messaging systems to social media sites.

For a long time, AIM was the undisputed leader of IM with a dominant market share on the desktop. AIM is still is a heavily used service, but Yahoo! Instant Messenger (`http://messenger.yahoo.com/`) and to a lesser extent Windows Live Instant Messenger (`http://messenger.live.com/`) have eclipsed AIM. The popularity of Gmail has helped to make Gmail's embedded IM client widely used as well.

FIGURE 18.1

The AIM (AOL Instant Messenger) home page emphasizes the range of client types and interconnections to which products in this category aspire.

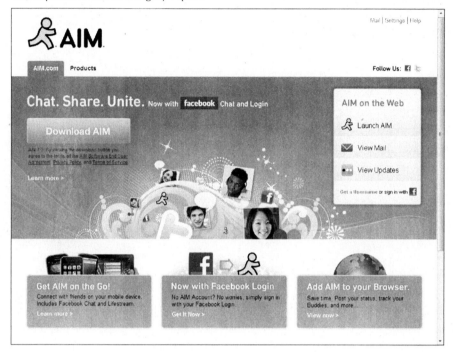

IM is a very rich product category that adds the following to the older concept of Internet chat:

- Directed messages
- Rich contact management
- Message logging and archiving
- File transfers
- E-mail integration
- Voice and video feeds
- Connections to social media

Shown in Figure 18.2 is Windows Live Messenger's main window, which lists contacts by categories and groups. These dialog boxes are often referred to as *buddy lists,* a phrase that was popularized by AIM. You can set options and use the icons to link to other social networking services. To send a message to someone, you click the name. The system opens a window with a text box for you to enter your message. When messages arrive, the system shows an alert over the System Tray icon, sounds a bell, or performs other actions to let you know.

FIGURE 18.2

The Windows Live Messenger native client contact or "buddy" list

Instant messaging is as popular in business as it is in personal communications. Many organizations use it as a second kind of e-mail. That's the main reason you find IM clients embedded in the major Webmail services, as well as in the clients of messenger servers such as these:

- Cisco Jabber XCP (`http://www.cisco.com/web/about/ac49/ac0/ac1/ac258/JabberInc.html`), part of Cisco Unified Presences Server and Personal Communicator

- IBM Lotus Sametime (`http://www.ibm.com/software/lotus/sametime/`)

- Microsoft Office Communications Server (`http://www.microsoft.com/communicationsserver/en/us/default.aspx`)

- Oracle Beehive (`http://www.oracle.com/products/middleware/beehive/index.html`)

This category of software is sometimes referred to as Enterprise Instant Messaging (EIM) and is part of a unified collaboration software suite. Servers of this type support IM, e-mail, document stores, and other features.

Instant messaging interoperability

Some IM clients use peer-to-peer messaging, but not all. IM software aimed at businesses such as XMPP, Lotus Sametime, and Microsoft Office Communicator use a client/server architecture based on their message server products such as Domino and Exchange. Early developers in this field have tended to create their own proprietary messaging standards, which has made communications between different IM clients difficult or impossible.

Interoperability between different instant messaging clients has been a major area of contention. In an effort to create an interoperability standard between different IM clients, several instant messaging protocols have been created. The most important are the three IETF (Internet Engineering Task Force) standards: Session Initiation Protocol (SIP), SIP for Instant Messaging and Presence Leveraging (SIMPLE), and Extensible Messaging and Presence Protocol (XMPP). The Open Mobile Alliance also has an IM communications standard called IMPS (Internet Messaging and Presence Service) for cell phones.

For a long time, each of the top IM services was locked into its own proprietary protocol. However, there has been some movement in this area over the last several years. The top three IM service providers (AOL, Microsoft, and Yahoo!) have adopted SIP/SIMPLE as their interoperability protocol, and they allow their users to connect with the other services' public users for a fee.

Several third-party IM clients aim to allow their users to connect to the different major IM services, including these:

- Adium (http://www.adium.im/)
- Digsby (http://www.digsby.com/)
- Meebo (http://www.meebo.com/)
- Miranda IM (http://www.miranda-im.org/)
- Pidgin (http://pidgin.im/)
- Trillian (http://www.trillian.im/)

Most notable among these is Trillian, which runs on Windows, Macintosh, IOS (iPhone OS), Android, Blackberry, and inside browsers. Trillian connects to the IM services AIM, ICQ, Windows Live Messenger, Yahoo! Messenger, IRC, Novell GroupWise Messenger, Bonjour, XMPP, and Skype. Additionally, Trillian can be used to send and receive messages from Facebook, MySpace, and Twitter.

BigBlueBall.com, a site that follows instant messaging and social networking, has published a chart with the current state of IM interoperability as of March 8, 2009. That chart is shown in Figure 18.3.

As a general rule, Enterprise IM software has been much more accommodating to the notion of interoperability than the large consumer IM networks have been. Microsoft and Lotus Enterprise IM products not only talk to one another, but also to public services such as AOL, Windows Live Messenger, and Yahoo! Instant Messenger.

BigBlueBall.com's published list of instant messaging clients interoperability is found at `http://www.bigblueball.com/im/interoperability/`.

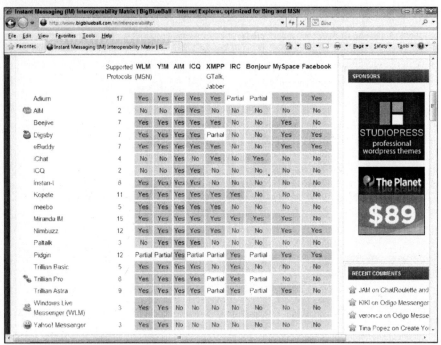

A number of IM services available are aimed at specific industries. Bloomberg Messaging (`http://www.bloomberg.com/professional/communities/`) and Thomson Reuters Messaging (`http://thomsonreuters.com/products_services/financial/financial_products/products_az/messenger`) are two examples that provide IM services for the financial industry. Often these services are private, but they are set up to interoperate with the other public services in some way. Figure 18.4 shows a screen from the Thomson Reuters service.

Micro-blogs or Short Message Services

The form of text messaging most widely used today is SMS, which stands for Short Message Service. When a service collects your messages in a conversation, it is called a micro-blog. Nearly all cell phones come with an SMS client, putting the capabilities of SMS in the hands of billions of users. SMS limits the size of messages sent to around 150 characters. SMS was originally developed as part of GSM networks, but it's now in use on CDMA, 3G, and a variety of other proprietary networks. SMS clients also appear on desktops and, in the case of Twitter, a combination of all platforms.

FIGURE 18.4

A sample session in Thomson Reuters Messaging shows how financial companies can integrate IM into their daily information flow.

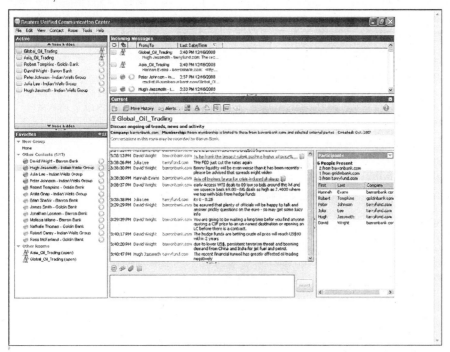

Cross-Ref

Because the bulk of SMS usage is on cell phones, a fuller discussion of the topic may be found in Chapter 21, "Working with Mobile Web Services." ■

Twitter is a good example of an SMS service organized into a social network and blog. It is sometimes referred to as the SMS of the Internet or as a form of Internet Relay Chat (IRC). Users send messages of up to 140 characters called *tweets,* which are displayed on the user's page. The system is opted out so messages you send are shown by default unless you mark the option to show them only to your friends. Although the service is free to use, when you send a tweet over a cell phone, your service provider may attach its normal SMS message fees for sending it.

Your friends are subscribers to your tweets; they are called followers. When you create tweets, they are sent to your followers and posted in reverse chronological order on your user profile page. If you are a follower of multiple people, their tweets appear in reverse chronological order in your Twitter client. There are also lists belonging to people such as Oprah Winfrey that you can join; these lists have tens to hundreds of thousands of followers.

Twitter has published an API that allows developers to add the ability to send and receive SMS messages on the Twitter system. According to Twitter, there are now over 70,000 applications that incorporate the Twitter SMS system. The Twitter Web client was built using Ruby on Rails and deployed on the Ruby Enterprise Edition, with the message queue server written in Scala. Wikipedia maintains a jump page of Twitter clients that you can download and install at `http://en.wikipedia.org/wiki/List_of_Twitter_services_and_applications`. A set of reviews of Twitter clients may be found also at `http://alltwitterapps.com/`. The Twitter app for the iPhone is shown in Figure 18.5.

Twitter has had an enormous impact, even though it was only launched in 2006. Often the first indications of news stories such as the earthquake in Haiti were tweets. Several people in that disaster were rescued from collapsed buildings because they could tweet their location.

People and businesses use Twitter to publicize their work, and the ability to search content by keywords offers insight into real-time trends that have considerable value. People tweet about almost anything, and you often get a faster answer to a question like "what's the best Chinese restaurant near me" from your followers at Twitter than you can from books or an Internet search.

FIGURE 18.5

The Twitter app on the iPhone (from Twitter, Inc.) has real-time search and can display trends, topics, maps, and location-aware messaging.

The rapid growth of the service has led to some embarrassing outages in its early years. Twitter's popularity in foreign countries led to the system being attacked at times of conflict. Of more concern is the fact that Twitter collects your personal information and sells the information to interested third parties. Twitter's service has no advertising, but the practice of sharing data allows companies to advertise directly to users based on their tweets. There have been several break-ins on Twitter accounts, which has led to the Federal Trade Commission charging Twitter with lax security in a recent lawsuit. The settlement in June 2010 requires Twitter to add more layers of security and undergo audits biannually.

Twitter has proved itself to be immensely popular, with over 190 million accounts. Twitter doesn't release its traffic figures, but in 2009 it was estimated that the site got over 2 million page views per day, putting it in the top 50 of all Web sites worldwide. According to Alexa.com, Twitter is the 11th ranked Web site worldwide. To give you some idea of Twitter's popularity, the Library of Congress recently announced that every public message ever sent over Twitter will be archived in the library's collection.

Exploring Collaboration Technologies

The emergence of cloud networks, the lowered cost of computing, and the high cost of travel also have helped spur the popularity of collaborative software for conferencing and workgroup support. You could define collaborative software as software that enables real-time or near-real-time communication, and that definition could include many of the applications described in this chapter. In this section, the focus is on groupware and collaborative work systems.

Collaborative software is an old concept with roots in many different types of systems. The first true collaboration platform that I recognized was Lotus Notes, which appeared as an enhanced form of client/server e-mail. Lotus Notes added document management, content management, and groups, and it supported mobile users. Lotus Notes actually predates the Internet, but its impact on the market has been significant. Microsoft's Exchange platform added features to compete with Notes. As the Internet matured, companies added the ability to perform Voice over IP telephony and video streaming either point-to-point or multicast. These tools have been migrated to the Web and are being migrated to the cloud.

Citrix GoToMeeting (http://www.gotomeeting.com/) is one of the best-known collaboration software products because the company heavily advertises the service. It also has a strong feature set and is very reliable. The service installs an address book that you use to initiate meetings and control attendance. When the service is connected, users see the portion of your desktop that you allow them to see. It is usually the entire desktop, but it can be a particular window such as a browser.

The product allows users to share their desktop, do presentations, and even let a user remotely take over another user's computer in real time. Meetings can be scheduled and recorded for later playback. You can use the service to work on documents cooperatively and annotate them with drawing tools.

The Zimbra Collaboration Suite (ZCS; `http://www.zimbra.com/`) is another groupware product that provides e-mail, calendar, and content management support. ZCS can synchronize e-mail, contacts, and calendars with a number of mail services, including mobile phones. Yahoo!, the owner of ZCS, makes the source code available under their Yahoo! Public License (YPL), which is a form of open-source arrangement.

For conferencing that requires a richer multimedia collaboration, Dimdim (`http://www.dimdim.com/`) offers a service that is a strong Web conferencing platform. You can give presentations, talk, chat, and show video feeds from Webcams to users. DimDim is a direct competitor to GoToMeeting.

Although this section presents three examples of this type of software, it is anticipated that there will be many more services like these three that will be supported by the cloud in the years to come.

Using Social Networks

The rise of low-cost commodity computing has fostered a number of large social networking services that are having great impact in the world. The recent use of Twitter and Facebook by opposition parties in Iran is a good example of the power of these social networks.

The SMS service Twitter can be considered a social network, but it's as much a telephony service as it is a Web service. Some of the largest Web sites now operating are dedicated to social networking and use the full power of Web 2.0 to allow people to communicate in a number of ways. According to Alexa.com, Facebook is the second most heavily visited Web site on the Internet, with Google being first. On August 3, 2010, Alexa.com had Blogger as 8th, Twitter as 11th, Wordpress as 19th, LinkedIn as 28th, MySpace as 29th, Flickr as 34th, Vkontakte.ru as 38th, and Google's Orkut as 69th. By any measure, this kind of media penetration for any one category of Web site is astonishing.

Friendster, MySpace, and Facebook represent one category of social networks. These sites let you create your own small personal Web site, which you give people access to view. Information on these pages is of the nature of personal profile. There are tools for leaving comments, chats, alerts when new information is listed, and many other features.

Friendster was the earliest of these three services, followed by MySpace, which was more successful, and then Facebook, which is truly a phenomenon. Facebook claims to have recently created its 500 millionth user account. Figure 18.6 shows the Facebook page for Mark Zuckerberg, the founder of Facebook.

Messaging between people is an important part of social networking. The success of services like Facebook has encouraged all Webmail providers to create personal profile sites of their own. Examples of this trend are Google Buzz and Windows Live Spaces.

FIGURE 18.6

Shown here is Facebook's founder Mark Zuckerberg's wall page where people can post comments.

Features

These are the central elements of social networking sites:

- **Personal profile:** In this section, you enter your biographical data, your likes and dislikes, personality traits, and whatever else you want to share with your friends and the world. With certain sites that specialize in a theme such as job networking, as Linked In does, your profile contains information relating to your career and skills.

- **Friends, buddies, or connections:** These are people who are allowed to view your site and post comments to your profile. They can also send you e-mail. Most social networking sites require that you be a member in order to use their site. Friends are designated within the service, with some control over the level of trust afforded.

- **Groups:** Nearly all social networks have a feature called groups where people interested in a similar topic can post messages to one another. Groups can be related to your high school classmates, a topic of interest, or just about anything you can think of.

- **Discussions:** Discussions are message boards where people who are usually in a group post messages on a topic. The conversation, referred to as "the thread," represents the evolved thinking of two or more people. You often see discussions with useful links and media.

  Discussions are often indexed by the major search engines, so it is often the case that when I'm trying to solve a technical problem, I find my answer in a discussion on one of these social network sites.

- **Blogs:** Blogs are personal Web logs, collections of journal entries you make, shown in reverse chronological order. Most social networking sites have the ability to create blogs and either show them on your pages or post them to one of the leading blog hosts, such as Blogger or Wordpress.

- **Widgets:** A widget is a small utility that you can add to your page. Many social networking sites have widget galleries that contain clocks, calendars, animations, weather information, electronic Post-It notes, and many more. The use of Ajax as a programming medium for these types of sites makes the use of widgets even more prevalent than in the past.

List of social networking sites

Table 18.1 lists some of the more well-known social networking sites.

TABLE 18.1

List of Social Networking Sites

Site	URL	Description
Advogato	http://www.advogato.org/	Software developers
Amie Street	http://amiestreet.com/	Music
aNobii	http://www.anobii.com/	Books
aSmallWorld	http://www.asmallworld.net/	Social networking
Athlinks	http://www.athlinks.com/	Athletics
BabyCenter	http://www.babycenter.com/	Parenting
Badoo	http://badoo.com/	Social networking
Bebo	http://www.bebo.com/	Social networking
Bigadda	http://www.bigadda.com/	Indian social networking
Big Tent	http://www.bigtent.com/	Portal for groups
Biip.no	http://www.biip.no/	Norwegian community
BlackPlanet	http://www.blackplanet.com/	African American social networking site
Blogster	http://www.blogster.com/	Blogging
Bolt	http://boltagain.ning.com/	Social networking
Buzznet	http://www.buzznet.com/	Music and pop culture

Site	URL	Description
CafeMom	http://www.cafemom.com/	Mothers
Care2	http://www.care2.com/	Ecology and activism
Cellufun	http://www.cellufun.com/	Mobile social games
Classmates.com	http://www.classmates.com/	School, military, and work
Cloob	http://www.cloob.com/	Iranian social networking
Crunchyroll	http://www.crunchyroll.com/	Anime
DailyBooth	http://dailybooth.com/	Photo-blogging
DailyStrength	http://www.dailystrength.org/	Anime
Delicious	http://www.delicious.com/	Photo-blogging
deviantART	http://www.deviantart.com/	Health topics
Disaboom	http://www.disaboom.com/	European and American social elite
Elftown	http://www.elftown.com/	Social bookmarking
Epernicus	http://www.epernicus.com/	Art
Eons.com	http://www.eons.com/	Disabilities
eSnips	http://www.esnips.com/	Fantasy and sci-fi
Experience Project	http://www.experienceproject.com/	Research science
Exploroo	http://www.exploroo.com/	Baby boomers
Facebook	http://www.facebook.com/	Large social networking site
Faceparty	http://www.faceparty.com/	Life experiences
FilmAffinity	http://www.faceparty.com/	Travel
Flixster	http://www.flixster.com/	Movies
Flickr	http://www.flickr.com/	Photo sharing
Fotoblog	http://www.fotoblog.com/	Spanish photo-blogging site
Foursquare	http://foursquare.com/	Location-based mobile social network
Friends Reunited	http://www.friendsreunited.com/	UK school, sports, and streets
Friendster	http://www.friendster.com/	Social networking; popular in Asia
Gaia Online	http://www.gaiaonline.com/	Anime and games
GamerDNA	http://www.gamerdna.com/	Computer and video games
Gather.com	http://www.gather.com/	Article, photo, and video sharing
Gays.com	http://gays.com/	LBGT social network
Grono.net,	http://grono.net/	Polish social network
Google Buzz	http://www.google.com/buzz	Social network
Hotlist	http://www.thehotlist.com/	Location-aware network
Hyves	http://www.hyves.nl/	Dutch social network

continued

TABLE 18.1 (continued)

Site	URL	Description
Ibibo	http://www.ibibo.com/	Talent-based social network
Indaba Music	http://www.indabamusic.com/	Musicians
IRC-Galleria	http://irc-galleria.net/	Finnish social network
Italki.com	http://www.italki.com/	Language learning
Itsmy	http://www.itsmy.com/	Mobile social network
JammerDirect.com	http://jammerdirect.com/	Creative resources
Kiwibox	http://www.kiwibox.com/	General social network
Jaiku	http://www.jaiku.com/	General social network
LaFango (formerly TalentTrove)	http://lafango.com/	Talent network
LastFM	http://www.last.fm/home	Music
LibraryThing	http://www.librarything.com/	Books
LinkedIn	http://www.linkedin.com/	Business and professional networking
LiveJournal	http://www.livejournal.com/	Blogging, popular in Russia
Livemocha	http://www.livemocha.com/	Language learning
Mixi	http://mixi.jp/	Japanese social network
MocoSpace	http://www.mocospace.com/	Mobile community worldwide
Mubi (formerly The Auteurs)	http://mubi.com/	Cinema
Multiply	http://multiply.com/	Asian relationships
MyBlogLog	http://www.mybloglog.com/	Blogging network
MyHeritage	http://www.myheritage.com/	Genealogy
MyLife (formerly Reunion.com)	http://www.mylife.com/	Locating friends and family
My Opera	http://my.opera.com/community/	Blogging, sharing, social networking
MySpace	http://www.myspace.com/	Social networking
myYearbook	http://www.myyearbook.com/	General social network, charity
Netlog (formerly Facebox and Redbox)	http://www.netlog.com/	Social networking; popular in Europe, the Middle East, and Quebec
Nexopia	http://www.nexopia.com/	Canada
Odnoklassniki	http://www.odnoklassniki.ru/	Russian school social network
Orkut	http://www.orkut.com/	Social networking site; popular in India and Brazil
Plaxo	http://www.plaxo.com/	Site aggregator

Site	URL	Description
Plurk	http://www.plurk.com/	Micro-blogging, RSS; popular in Taiwan
Qzone	http://qzone.qq.com/	Large Chinese social networking site
Raptr	http://raptr.com/	Video games
Renren	http://www.renren.com/	Chinese social networking
ResearchGATE	http://www.researchgate.net/	Science research
ReverbNation.com	http://www.reverbnation.com/	Music
Ryze	http://www.ryze.com/	Business
ScienceStage	http://sciencestage.com/	Science
Shelfari	http://www.shelfari.com/	Books
Skyrock	http://www.skyrock.com/	French social networking
Something Awful	http://www.somethingawful.com/	Humor
Sonico.com	http://www.sonico.com/	South American, Spanish, and Portuguese social networking
Stickam	http://www.stickam.com/	Video streaming and chat
StudiVZ	http://www.studivz.net/	German universities
StumbleUpon	http://www.stumbleupon.com/	Smart bookmarks
Tagged	http://www.tagged.com/	Social networking
Taringa!	http://www.taringa.net/	Social networking
TravBuddy.com	http://www.travbuddy.com/	Travel
Travellerspoint	http://www.travellerspoint.com/	Travel
Tribe.net	http://www.tribe.net/	Social networking
Trombi.com	http://www.trombi.com/	French school network (Classmates.com)
Tuenti	http://www.tuenti.com/	Spanish school network; popular in Spain
Tumblr	http://www.tumblr.com/	Micro-blogging, RSS
Twitter	http://twitter.com/	Micro-blogging, RSS
Vkontakte	http://vk.com/	Russian social networking
Vampirefreaks.com	http://vampirefreaks.com/	Gothic and industrial
Viadeo	http://www.viadeo.com/en/connexion/	Social and school networking, worldwide
Virb	http://virb.com/	Art, music, and photography
Vox	http://www.vox.com/	Blogging
Wakoopa	http://wakoopa.com/	Computers

continued

TABLE 18.1	(continued)	
Site	**URL**	**Description**
Wattpad	http://www.wattpad.com/	Books
WAYN	http://www.wayn.com/	Travel and lifestyle
WeeWorld	http://www.weeworld.com/	Teens
Wer-kennt-wen	http://www.wer-kennt-wen.de/	Germany's largest social networking site
Windows Live Spaces	http://spaces.live.com/	Blogging
Xanga	http://www.xanga.com/	Blogs and metro area focus
XING	http://www.xing.com/	European and Chinese business
Yammer	https://www.yammer.com/	Corporate social networking
Yelp, Inc.	http://www.yelp.com/	Local matters
Zoo.gr	http://www.zoo.gr/	Greek Web meeting point
Zooppa	http://zooppa.com/	Talent

Source: http://en.wikipedia.org/wiki/List_of_social_networking_websites.

Privacy and security

When you place so much personal information into the hands of a third party, you are always at risk should the information be compromised. Social networks have had the normal history of infrequent break-ins by hackers, often because a person's password isn't set to a strong one. Because many of these sites are free, their business model must use advertisement or the sale of user demographics or information to monetize themselves. That puts lots of pressure on social networks to disclose information in aggregate or by individual.

However, two other aspects of security are more troubling: privacy rights and the fungibility of the data over a long time period. Ideally, social networking sites should be opt-in systems. When you sign up, you are presented with a list of options that you select to belong to. Unfortunately, these networks often have lots of options, so some sites set their accounts to be opt-out by default. That is, the site itself determines the default options and assigns those options to any new account. If you want out of an option, you need to change the setting in your profile's settings. For a site like Facebook with many options, this has been a problem, and it has caused an uproar. Facebook has had to change its privacy policy several times over the last couple of years.

When you post data on a social network, you have to realize that the data may have a long lifecycle. A picture or story you post on your page as a teenager might influence your candidacy for a job a few years later. So it is very important to protect your data and retain your privacy rights. One of the issues encountered is the ownership of the data; do you or does the Web site have ownership rights? This is an evolving area of law.

Interaction and interoperability

Participating in multiple social networks is a major chore, and it is easy to be overwhelmed. Not only do you have to manage the data you are entering into the system, but if you are following or subscribing to different individuals on different services, you may find yourself logging into each of those services separately during your day or week.

As the sites get bigger and their technologies get better defined, there has been a trend in the industry to get different sites to interoperate with one another. One imitative to create a common API is the OpenSocial (`http://www.opensocial.org/`) API that Google and MySpace support. OpenSocial has yet to achieve critical mass in the industry, but is indicative of the direction of this technology to interoperate.

A new class of social network aggregators has appeared that collects information from other sites into a consolidated data store. Some of these sites also allow you to create a universal personal profile that can be shared with several social networks.

In order to perform aggregation, these applications have to tap into the social network's API, provided that the service is given consent by the user in the form of supplying his username and password for the social networking service. This is similar to OpenID, and in fact several of the major sites are adopting OpenID as their authentication.

These are the best known of the social network aggregators:

- ContextMine (`http://www.contextmine.com/`): This site monitors brand presence.
- FriendFeed (`http://friendfeed.com/`): This site is a real-time aggregator of social networking, blogging, and RSS/Atom feeds. It is one of the more heavily used aggregators.
- Gathera (`http://www.gathera.com/`): Gathera offers a desktop application or browser add-in for aggregating Webmail and social network accounts.
- Gnip (`http://www.gnip.com/`): Gnip offers an aggregation API for developers.
- Mybloglog (`http://www.mybloglog.com/`). This Yahoo! service provides a record of the people visiting your blog.
- myZuzu (`http://www.myzazu.com/`): This site allows you to create and manage the information you send or get from multiple sites.
- Network Insights (`http://www.networkedinsights.com/`): Network Insights offers an SaaS service that provides online analysis and measurement of social media tools.
- NutshellMail (`http://nutshellmail.com/`): This site aggregates social networks into your own personal e-mail systems from multiple sources.
- OrSiSo (`http://www.orsiso.com/`): This really pretty aggregator creates multiple channels for incoming content organized by the people you follow from different services. Figure 18.7 shows the OrSiSo Web site.
- Plaxo (`http://www.plaxo.com/`): This online address book and content management service can be shared with other services.
- Plocky (`http://plocky.com/`): This is an e-mail and social networking service aggregator.

FIGURE 18.7

OrSiSo is an aggregator that takes content from multiple sources and lets you organize it as channels in a very visual way.

Aggregator sites may offer some of the following features:

- Search across multiple sites
- Tools for managing messages
- RSS readers for social networking feeds
- Tools to manage bookmark from multiple sites
- Tools to track friends, buddies, or connections over time

For the more capable of these aggregators, the term *lifestream management* has been applied by the digerati who see their digital output as the complete total sum of their existence. The addition of real-time feeds and location-based information are two trends that are shaping the features that social networking services are developing. The notion of a lifestream may be fanciful, but perhaps that is where this technology is leading us.

Summary

In this chapter, you learned about a variety of communications and social services that you can access over the Web, most of which already follow the cloud computing. The first of these services are the Instant Messaging applications such as Windows Live Messenger, Yahoo! Instant Messenger, and AIM. IM is a valuable adjunct to e-mail, which is why you find many vendors offering the two services within the same interface.

A subset of IM is the Small Message Service (SMS) exemplified by Twitter. Growing out of telephony, Twitter creates a stream of messages that can be followed, and it's indexed and searchable. Twitter provides a unique way of accessing the knowledge of a community in real time. For that reason, many people find it invaluable.

A major portion of this chapter was dedicated to social networking sites. The best known of these sites—Facebook, MySpace, LinkedIn, and others—are household names. Social networking sites let you share personal information with others and create and manage a community of your own. There are so many sites of this type and they are so popular that it is hard to keep up with this area of technology. The emerging category of social network aggregators is a helpful way of managing information coming from multiple streams that you follow.

In Chapter 19, "Using Media and Streaming," you learn about Web-enabled telephony and video streaming services.

Using Media and Streaming

S treaming files is a way of delivering large content in pieces so playback can begin more quickly. Streaming is used for broadcasting current events, showing TV and movies on your computer or cell phone, listening to Internet radio, making phone calls, and using many other applications.

Cloud computing has a number of advantages that aid content providers and delivery systems. Cloud computing provides large storage for maintaining libraries, large networks where content can be deployed worldwide, compute power for streaming servers, and an engine for encoding/decoding/transcoding content. This chapter describes some of these advantages, introducing you to early products and services in this field.

Audio streaming was among the first media applications to find widespread use on the Internet. Cloud computing has expanded the use of streamed audio to make radio, Web casts, music sites, and other services widely available.

VoIP is a form of audio streaming with a set of specialized protocols. Cloud computing is bringing a whole new class of applications to Internet users. Two applications in this area, Skype and Google Voice, are highlighted in this chapter.

Broadband connections and low-cost infrastructure have made video streaming services widely available. The formats used for video streaming are described here.

Cloud computing has made many of these services available at low cost or for free. This chapter presents some of the best and most widely known video services on the Internet, many of which are household names and among the most heavily visited sites. One trend worth watching is the move of TV into the cloud. A number of video sites bring this type of content to you. The video sharing site YouTube is described in some detail.

Understanding the Streaming Process

Streaming media are files that are sent in pieces by a service and played back by a client as the delivery continues. Streamed material can be live or on-demand. Live streaming is called progressive streaming or progressive download, while on-demand streaming is from material that is already stored to disk. In order to stream content successfully, the system requires that the network bandwidth be adequate to support the transfer of enough material to support user playback. For cloud computing where the media files are large and the connection is a low latency WAN connection, this is a major consideration and potential bottleneck.

The amount of data transferred during streaming can be enormous. Assuming that you have a one-hour video file transferred at 300 kbps and encoded into a widow that is 800X600 pixels in size, on-demand streaming would require the following:

Size (MB) = Time (seconds) x bit rate (bps)/(mebibyte), where a mebibyte (MiB) is 8 x 1,024 x 1,024 bits

(3,600 x 300,000 bps)/ 8,388,608 = 128 MiB or about 135 MB/hour

Because 1 kbs is equal to 1,000 bps, in the line above 300 kbs is equal to 300,000 bps. Notice that this calculation uses mebibytes (MiB). A MiB is a measurement of the number of binary bytes in units of 2^{20}, which is what the prefix *mebi-* indicates. A MiB is equal to 2^{20} or 1,048,576 bytes.

When a live stream is sent multicast to 1,000 concurrent users at 500 kbps, the number of megabytes transferred is calculated like this:

MB transferred = Bandwidth x Time x Number of Users

MB transferred = 500 kbps x 3600 s x 1000/(8 x 1,024) = 220 GB

These figures are based on calculations found at http://en.wikipedia.org/wiki/Streaming_media.

When this stream is sent unicast to users, it uses a bandwidth of 300 kbps. Unicast is a stream sent from a service to an individual user. For many content services, such as the music services Last.fm and Rhapsody, a vast number of files are being served to individual users and they go out using unicast protocols as individual streams. The more users being served by the same content, the less efficient unicast is, and multicast protocols are employed. In a multicast scenario, the same content is being pushed out to multiple users. The system can send an individual copy or stream of the content to an intermediary server, which then uses the replicated copy to service users.

Because we know that live streaming requires 220GB be transferred per hour, a multicast system would require that we transfer 220GB to each of the relay servers in the multicast network. The amount of data sent per 1,000 customers would then be a function of the amount of fanout in the system. Here's where a content delivery network deployment in the cloud really pays for itself. Let's assume that you choose to serve the content out of 20 datacenters worldwide to 1,000 users and that your,system load balances the clients using an algorithm that determines the closest 1,000/20 or 50 users to each site. Then you have transferred 20 x 220GB or 4.4TB of data to your servers from the service, but your relays have then transferred 50 x 4.4TB or 220TB to end users. If those relay servers are on LANs with their clients, then the speed-up can be greatly enhanced. Even if delivery is always over a WAN connection, CDN (Content Delivery Network) still offers enormous efficiencies.

The second requirement is that the service sending content be able to deliver the material in sequence or nearly in sequence to the client. As material is streamed to a client, the material can be buffered to memory and the system can use the sequence number in the packets received to structure playback. Depending upon the player application in use, the downloaded information can be viewed and then discarded, or it can be viewed in sequence in parts until the file is completely downloaded. In the latter case, the technology is performing what is called progressive downloads, which is so similar to streaming that it also is called pseudo-streaming. Applications that protect streamed content by playing part of the file and discarding it are more aptly referred to as streaming.

Protocols in Use

A digital audio or video file is partitioned into many small pieces and played back at high speed. Depending upon the nature of the material, playing streamed material can suffer a certain amount of loss of transmitted packets, which is displayed as dropped frames or missing notes without the viewer noticing. This difference between streamed media and transferred media is fundamental in deciding which transfer protocol to use. For transferred media, the entire file must be transmitted with fidelity, thus TCP (Transmission Control Protocol) is the transmission protocol. In a streamed media scenario, fidelity isn't a prerequisite, thus UDP (User Datagram Protocol) is the transmission protocol.

Note
You can find a fuller discussion of TCP and UDP in the book *Networking Bible* by Barrie Sosinsky, Wiley, 2009. ■

A number of network control protocols have been developed to stream media. Prominent among them are Real-time Transport Control Protocol (RTCP), Real-time Streaming Protocol (RTSP), and Real-time Transfer Protocol (RTP). RTP and RTCP are used exclusively with UDP, while RTSP is used with several different protocols. These three protocols are Application layer protocols, whereas TCP and UDP are Transport layer protocols.

All the streaming protocols in use take raw files and compress them in some way. If the material is to be protected, then the files also are encrypted prior to transmission and decrypted when they arrive.

The cloud computing advantages

People in the streaming media community are very excited about cloud computing, and for good reason. Cloud computing has some unique features that make it a very suitable platform for large scale audio and video streaming to customers on demand. Cloud systems offer the following:

- Access to large scale storage, which enable the storage of large media files and on-demand media libraries.

  Amazon S3, Microsoft Windows Azure Blob Storage, Nirvanix, EMC Atmos Online, Mezo, Google Storage for Developers. Rackspace CloudFiles, and Eucalyptus are examples of some of the large cloud storage systems available to content providers. Some of these systems, such as Microsoft Azure and Google Storage, support the applications developers' position on those SaaS services.

- Access to scalable compute engines and network storage that can serve as the streaming server to large audiences.

- Access to a scalable compute engines that can be useful when you want to perform encoding/decoding or transcoding on media files.

    The company Encoding.com is an example of a transcoding service where you can use an Adobe AIR application to drag and drop files that are encoded right to your desktop.

- Access to content delivery networks or edge systems that can push content out to users based on geographical location.

    Examples are Akamai, Amazon's CloudFront, and Limelights' edge streaming systems that are part of its content delivery networks.

Encoding.com, whose home page is shown in Figure 19.1, offers a great example of how the cloud can be leveraged to provide a service on demand. Encoding.com advertises itself as the world's largest encoding/transcoding service. The company uses a cloud infrastructure to convert files that you send them to the formats you require. Multiple formats and devices are supported, and you can use an Adobe AIR application or a browser plug-in to drag and drop files that the service converts. The conversions are done in the cloud on your uploaded file, and the results are then downloaded to your desktop when complete.

Encoding.com supports static picture file conversions (JPEG, GIFF, TIFF, and so on), audio file conversions, and video file conversions. Most of its business is focused on streaming file formats used in audio and video work, and it supports the many different formats that services need to support diverse device types. These are the most popular conversions on the site currently:

- AVI to WMV

- MP4 to WMV

- video to 3GP

- WMV to MPEG

- FLV to MPG

- AVI to MPEG-4

- 3GP to WMV

- MP4 to 3GP

- FLV to MOV

- H.264 to AVI

- VP6 to AVI

- H.264 to MPEG

- VP6 to MPEG

- H.264 to WMV

FIGURE 19.1

Encoding.com is an example of a company that provides an encoding/decoding solution directly from your desktop using its cloud infrastructure.

Encoding.com supports conversions to third-party services such as Wordpress, Brightcove, JW Player, Flowplayer, Bits on the Run, and Drupal by providing a set of plug-ins. There are also encoding profile supports for Amazon S3 and Rackspace CloudFiles.

Audio Streaming

Audio streaming makes much lower demands on network bandwidth than video streaming does. An audio file is roughly 500 times smaller than a correspondingly long video file. Therefore, the first streaming services that appeared even before broadband became widely available were audio streaming services. An early entrant into this area was Real Networks' Real Player technology and its associated protocol suite. There was a time when many content providers required you to use RealAudio technology and the RealPlayer media player. Two other competing formats appeared that have gotten general acceptance: Windows Media Player and Apple QuickTime. These players play video formats as well as audio formats, and all are available as stand-alone players or as browser plug-ins.

Many sites still offer content in one of these three formats, but the trend over the past five years has been to shift away from proprietary formats to standard formats. Today MP3 is king, and all three

407

of the aforementioned players will play streamed MP3 files in addition to their native formats. The bulk of the large services that have migrated to the cloud have stored their material in MP3 format. Some services protect their audio content by making sure that only their player can play back material from their service, and that the sound can't be recorded digitally; Last.fm is an example of this type of service.

Another type of streamed service is SHOUTcast, a proprietary server solution for streaming media on the Internet. SHOUTcast is best known for its SHOUTcast Radio, which maintains a directory of SHOUTcast servers. These servers stream content in the form of channels or streams that form the basis for Internet radio stations. More than 60 million people listen to Internet radio every week. Several other competitive streaming services exist.

National Public Radio is a very good example of how audio streaming has evolved. The goal of NPR is to be available on all platforms in current use. NPR started out providing RealAudio files for streaming and then added Windows Media files as a second format. Today, NPR provides an audio stream from Internet Explorer on Windows inside Windows Media Player, as shown in Figure 19.2. Programs are recorded as MP3 files. If you subscribe (via RSS) to an NPR program using a program like iTunes, MP3 files are transferred to your system. RSS stands for Really Simple Syndication, a protocol for providing Web feeds from publication sources such as blogs, news sites, and others.

FIGURE 19.2

NPR has offered a variety of audio formats in the past, but has consolidated on MP3 files for its current audio downloads.

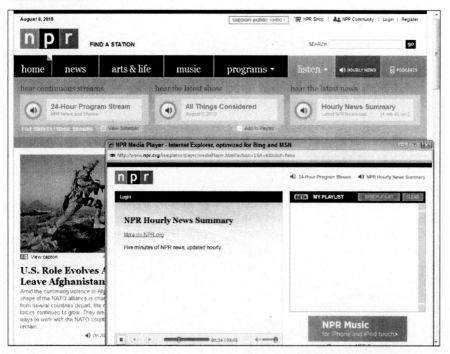

Working with VoIP Applications

Voice over IP or VoIP is a set of communication protocols for delivering voice over the Internet. Some of these services have been migrated to the cloud, particularly those services that require the involvement of large number of servers. VoIP uses additional protocols and standards other than audio streaming; these are the most commonly used VoIP standards:

- H.323
- IP Multimedia Subsystem (IMS)
- Media Gateway Control Protocol (MGCP)
- Session Initiation Protocol (SIP)
- Real-time Transport Protocol (RTP)
- Session Description Protocol (SDP)

The older protocol H.323, while still used on long transmission lines, is being replaced with more lightweight protocols such as MGCP and more particularly SIP. VoIP is a growing market, displacing older switching technologies used in the public telephone system, what has come to be called the "Plain Old Telephone Service" or POTS. As such, it is a technology that benefits from deployment in clouds. To illustrate the kind of impact that cloud computing can have on VoIP and telephony applications, the examples of Skype and Google Voice are presented here.

Note

POTS is also referred to as the Public Switched Telephone Network (PSTN), although the latter term includes many of the more modern switching technologies. The ITU-T is the standards body for PSTN. ∎

Skype

Skype is an example of a VoIP application. The Skype protocol is a proprietary (closed-source) protocol, parts of which use the Global Index P2P protocol. Unlike standard VoIP, which uses a client/server model, Skype uses the peer-to-peer model that was based on Kazaa. Kazaa was a P2P file-sharing network developed by the Estonian company BlueMoon Interactive, which went on to develop Skype. Because Skype is a P2P application, the nature of the deployment of the directory must be distributed in some way, but it is not clear how this is done.

Skype communication is encrypted using standard encryption methods: RSA key negotiation and Advanced Encryption Standard (AES) encryption algorithms. Accounts on Skype do not require that the name of the caller be identified during a call, only his username. It is not certain that communication on Skype is entirely secure; there is speculation that the company or government agencies may have access to communications. However, in the United States, the FCC has stated that Skype is subject to the Communications Assistance for Law Enforcement Act (CALEA), although Skype claims exemption. The company also refuses to state whether it can listen in on the system's phone calls.

Skype is perhaps the most widely used telephony application in the world. The Skype client exists for Windows, the Macintosh, Linux, Android, Blackberry, iPhone, Symbian, Nokia Internet Tablets, Windows Mobile Phone, and many other devices.

Depending upon the client, Skype supports the following:

- Instant messaging
- Voice telephony
- File transfers
- Group chats
- Message logging
- Video conferencing

Figure 19.3 shows a video conference in action within the Skype Window client.

Caution

Skype does not support calls to emergency numbers such as 911 in the United States; for these calls, you need access to a land line. ■

FIGURE 19.3

Skype is a universal communications platform that supports chat, SMS, VoIP, and video conferencing for free.

As long as the connection is between Skype clients, the communication is free. When you use Skype to call out to phones, charges accrue. In some countries, Skype offers a SkypeIn service that allows a user to receive calls on their computers from telephones. Skype can assign you a local number in these countries and charges for calls to that number based on the local rate.

Skype's popularity is enormous; it has some 500 million registered user accounts worldwide. The verb "to Skype" has entered into the vocabulary of many of its users. An estimated 50 million calls are placed on the service daily. You can see the number of currently connected users at the bottom of the Skype client. Because Skype isn't a web site, its popularity can't be measured by services such as Alexa.com.

Google Voice and Google Talk

Google has two streaming services that use VoIP protocols: Google Talk (`http://www.google.com/talk/`) and Google Voice. Google Talk, or G Talk, is Google's Voice over IP service combined with an Instant Messaging service. Google Voice is Google's telephony application, which is also a VoIP service. Both applications are free, and Google Voice has some powerful features that make it a very attractive service.

Google Talk is a service that uses the XMPP/Jabber protocol for the Google Chat IM client. Because IM was described in Chapter 18 and the focus here is on the Google Talk VoIP application, no more need be said.

Google Talk is a Windows only VoIP service on the desktop that uses the Jingle protocol; it supports communication with mobile XMPP clients such as the Nokia N900 Smartphone, Blackberry, iPhone, and Android phones. You also can find Google Talk on the Sony mylo and the Nokia 770 Internet Tablet. Some third-party applications such as Nimbuzz (`http://www.nimbuzz.com/en`) and Fring (`http://www.fring.com/`) support Google Talk VoIP on and Android, iPhone, Symbian, and Windows Mobile phones, along with some other platforms. A Google Talk gadget has also been released that lets any platform with an Adobe Flash Player work with Google Talk from within an iGoogle page. With Google Talk, you can get voicemail in your contact's mailbox.

The more interesting application is Google Voice, the settings screen of which is shown in Figure 19.4. Google Voice was acquired when Google purchased the Company GrandCentral in 2005, and it appeared for release in March 2009.

Google Voice lets you select a phone number in one of many area codes out of the 1 million telephone numbers that it has reserved. After you select a number, that number is yours and is assigned to your Google account. That phone number is yours to give out to others, and when they call you, the call is forwarded to the numbers you specify: your cell phone, home phone, or whatever. The system stores voicemail as MP3 files, handles SMS text, and can send alerts as well. Google's voicemail system does voicemail transcription, blocks callers, allows you to listen in, records calls, does conference calling, and more. It is hard to believe that this service is free in the United States and Canada, but it is free for users in those countries.

In an interesting development, Google submitted a Google Voice app for the iPhone in June 2009, which Apple rejected for its iTunes app store. The reason Apple gave was that the app replaced some of the iPhone core functions. This matter is now under review at the Federal Communications Commission (FCC). Google also apparently is working on a Google Voice desktop application.

FIGURE 19.4

Google Voice is an integrated telephony application that gives you a unique phone number, message forwarding, and more for free. Shown here is the voicemail and text settings page.

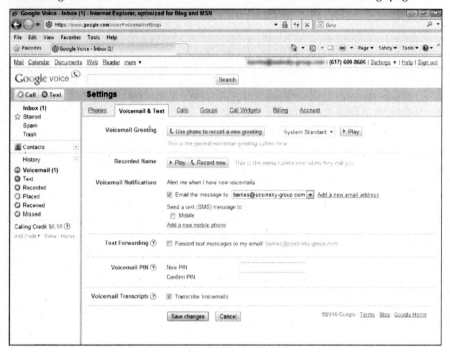

Video Streaming

Video streaming over the Internet has become one of the major broadcast transmission media in a rather short time. Many trends have come together to help make this transition a reality, including broadband networks, high-capacity commodity disk drives, low-cost computing power, and now cloud computing. Video streaming is one of these technologies that benefits greatly from deployment in the cloud.

Many of these services already have a cloud-based infrastructure. Some of them are content servers, others are systems for caching and storing content, and some services can be used to modify content so it is in an appropriate format, with many other services besides. Because this area is still in its infancy, many surprises are likely waiting for us in the years to come. The best way to get an idea of the impact of cloud computing is to consider some of the services that already exist.

Among the video streaming services in widespread use are the following:

- **blip.TV** (http://blip.tv/): Blip.tv airs independent full-length shows that you might see on television.

- **Break.com** (`http://www.break.com/`): This site, formerly called Big-boys.com, targets a male audience of 18-35 and has comedy, flash games, and pictures on its site.

- **Dailymotion** (`http://www.dailymotion.com/`): This video-sharing service is based in Paris, France.

- **Flickr** (`http://www.flickr.com/`): This is a picture- and video-sharing site.

- **Hulu** (`http://www.hulu.com`): This is a TV-show- and movie-streaming site.

- **Internet Archive** (`http://www.archive.org/`): The Internet's "Wayback Machine" stores past versions of the Internet and includes some interesting and significant out-of-copyright video content.

- **Kyte** (`http://www.kyte.com`): This is a video platform for live and on-demand content streamed to online, mobile, and social media platforms.

- **Metacafe** (`http://www.metacafe.com/`): This is an entertainment site with movie trailers, TV shows, video games, and more.

- **Nico Nico Douga** (`http://www.nicovideo.jp/`): This is a popular Japanese video-sharing site.

- **RuTube** (`http://rutube.ru/`): This is a popular Russian video-sharing site.

- **Todou** (`http://www.tudou.com/`): Based in Shanghai, China, this large video-sharing site allows users to upload and download large video files with entire episodes of TV and full-length movies.

- **UStream.tv** (`http://www.ustream.tv/`): This is a live video event streaming service.

- **Veoh** (`http://veoh.com/`): Veoh serves TV and movie content from major studios, along with uploaded user content.

- **Yahoo Video** (`http://video.yahoo.com/`): This is a video-sharing site.

- **YouTube** (`http://www.youtube.com`): The largest of the video-sharing sites, this is the second most heavily visited site on the Internet. It is described in detail later in this section.

- **YuMe** (`http://www.yume.com`): YuMe is a video advertising company.

The services listed above had more than one million unique visitors a month or an Alexa rank (most heavily visited Web sites) of 150 or lower. A lower Alexa ranking indicates a more popular site.

A more complete list along with some of the formats and specifications supported by these services may be found at `http://en.wikipedia.org/wiki/Comparison_of_video_services`.

Television in the cloud

Television is a very important industry. The average American watches five hours of TV a day, and $70 billion a year is spent on advertising. The number of TV watchers dwarfs the 1 billion PC users, and even the 2 billion cell phone users. Worldwide, there are 4 billion TV watchers.

As video streaming becomes ever cheaper in the cloud, many TV stations have begun to put their series episodes and movies on Internet sites such as ABC.com, CBS.com, NBC.com, Syfy.com,

Hulu.com, and others. The model that seems to have been adopted is that these stations post their episodes a day or a week after the show airs, allowing viewers to catch up on their shows or to view an entire season at one time. The popularity of these services has shifted many TV watchers, particularly younger viewers, away from cable TV and onto these sites connected through their broadband connection. This trend is likely to accelerate.

Hulu.com is a particularly interesting example of TVIP or TV over the Internet. Hulu, shown in Figure 19.5, was launched in 2007 as a joint venture by ABC, Fox, and NBC to offer content to viewers in the United States. There are plans to launch Hulu in other countries, and it is speculated that the UK and Japan are the next target markets, but plans have not been formally announced.

The site also offers a Web syndication service for sites such as AOL, Facebook, fancast.com (part of Comcast), MySpace, and Yahoo!. In the three years since its founding, the service has become immensely popular and now serves up to a billion videos a month, and it's profitable. On Hulu, you can find network shows from A&E, Bravo, E!, FX, G4, NFL Network, Onion News Network, Oxygen, PBS, Speed, Syfy, Style, Sundance, and others.

Shows that run on Hulu are interrupted every 15 minutes for a 30-second commercial. The revenue from the advertising stream is split according to the New York Times so that 50-70 percent goes to the content provider and the remainder goes to YouTube. Hulu is also starting a new service called Hulu Plus, which (for a subscription fee of $9.99/month) offers more premium content and content served for the iPhone and iPad, your TV, and in HD format.

The popular movie subscription service Netflix is another example of a service that has moved to the cloud. In May 2010, the company announced that it will expand significant portions of its Web site onto Amazon Web Services. The company had previously moved its member movie lists, the movie search engine, and its recommendation engine onto AWS. The second and much larger deployment moves its 17,000 titles and the ability to use the Watch Instantly online service to AWS. Netflix has found that 55 percent of its subscribers are streaming video instead of swapping DVDs by mail in Q1 2010. That figure is up from 36 percent in Q1 2009.

Netflix also is expected to use the cloud deployment to expand the support of other devices. The company hopes to have Netflix available on TVs from LG, Samsung, Sony, and Vizio; on the three major gaming consoles, XBox, Playstation, and Wii; on the Apple iPad; on TiVo DVRs; on Roku boxes; and on set-top boxes and a few Blu-ray players. This diverse group of devices requires that numerous encodings and file formats and different resolutions be available for streaming; Netflix will use the Amazon service to transcode and store the different versions of digital files that must be produced.

Over the years, software and hardware vendors in the computer industry have introduced products aimed at bringing the Internet to TV, and vice versa. Microsoft has made several attempts to enter the set-top box market, introduced its media center PC interface (an enhanced version of TV), and used the thin client device originally known as WebTV (now MSN TV).

FIGURE 19.5

Hulu.com is one of the most popular sites for viewing TV and movies on the Internet. The site is currently available only in the United States.

Apple has Apple TV (http://www.apple.com/appletv/), which can best be described as a digital media receiver. None of these products has really had much penetration in the market. Although Apple TV is highly regarded by many who own one, Steve Jobs has talked about Apple TV as being a "hobby" for Apple and hasn't promoted the product well. That may change. There are rumors that Apple is working on a new version of Apple TV, based on the iPhone IOS 4 operating system, and that it will be a small form factor device for under $100.

Several cloud vendors are gearing up to introduce new products that bring the Internet and TV together using the cloud as a content platform. The most notable announcement is probably Google TV (http://www.google.com/tv/), due out in Q3 2010. Google TV is a media center software platform that will appear in some HDTVs (Sony Internet TV) and Blu-ray players from Sony, in some set-top boxes, and in some other devices that you connect to the Internet and to your TV. The project uses the Android operating system and has an open-source standard API for developers to work with. Using Google's Chrome browser, you can search the Internet for video content that you can stream to your TV. You also can download and use apps from the Google app store with your TV as the viewing device.

Streaming video formats

The history of streaming video on the Internet has progressed from the raw video formats supported by Real Media to media that is embedded directly into Web pages in the form of Apple QuickTime or Windows Media. The predominant format at the moment is the platform based on Adobe Flash, although other formats, such as Microsoft's Silverlight, are constantly being introduced as competitors. As the industry is moving more and more to the cloud, there has been a push to develop open-source video standards such as the new HTML 5 video format.

To view streaming content in HTML5 video players, you need a compatible browser and a site like YouTube that supports H.264 and WebM (VP8 codec) formats. At the time this book was written, the following browsers were listed as being HTML5 compatible by YouTube (`http://www.youtube.com/html5`):

- Firefox 4 (WebM)
- Chrome (h.264 supported now, WebM enabled version available via Early Release Channel)
- Opera 10.6+ (WebM)
- Apple Safari (h.264, version 4+)
- Microsoft Internet Explorer 9 (h.264, Platform Preview 3)
- Microsoft Internet Explorer 6, 7, or 8 with Google Chrome Frame installed

You should expect HTML5 to be standard in the official release versions of these browsers before 2010 ends.

You also can view HTML 5 content in the following media players:

- Media Player Classic (`http://mpc-hc.sourceforge.net/`)
- Moovida Core (`http://www.moovida.com/`)
- VLC (`http://www.videolan.org/`)
- Winamp (http://www.winamp.com/media-player/)
- XBMC (`http://xbmc.org/`)

Video formats are only half of the story when it comes to video file formats. The second half of the story is the format for the streaming protocol that encodes the video file. Several of these container formats are in use.

The most widely used streaming video file container format is H.264/MPEG-4 Part 10. MPEG-4 Part 10 is also known as MPEG-4 AVC, which stands for Advanced Video Coding. This standard was designed for the recording and playback of home theater or HD video, and it supports lower-quality video played on mobile devices. The ITU-T Video Coding Experts Group (VCEG) and the ISO/IEC Moving Picture Experts Group (MPEG) created the Joint Video Team (JVT), and the result is that both standards are technically identical. You may therefore see streamed video content in the form of H.264, AVC, or MPEG-4 Part 10, all of which refer to the same file format. H.264 can carry Flash, HTML5, and other video file formats.

You will find H.264 used as the streaming format for most large video sites, such as YouTube and iTunes, in cable and satellite TV services, and for video conferencing software. Older and less capable formats such as H.263, MPEG-4 Part 2, and MPEP-2 are still in use, but they aren't deployed in the new cloud-based implementation meant for large audiences.

In order to support a range of devices, the Advanced Video Coding defines a set of profiles to support specific device types. These profiles define resolution and bitrates, among other features. One profile might be used on the Apple iPhone, another on a standard definition DVD, and yet a third on HDTV. The profiles in most widespread use are Main and High, with the Baseline and Extended profiles in use for mobile devices. Within each profile are a set of levels that determine which features are available to support a specific application. For example, High Level 2.1 has a resolution of 480X272 and can play at framerates of 23.97, 25, or 29.97 fps (frames per second); this level supports the Sony PSP. Level 4 has a resolution of 1920X1080 and can play at framerates of 24, 25, 29.97, or 30 fps (frames per second); this level supports the Blu-ray and HD DVD devices.

The codec that compresses/decompresses the video content uses a block-oriented motion-compensation scheme. It is important to understand that H.264 defines a standard for encoding content, but that the implementation of a codec can vary. Some codecs may choose to encode some features and not others. When content is encoded in H.264/MPEG AVC, any codec may decode the file, but some do a better job decoding the file than others. Some decoders may ignore features that others won't.

The newest of the video streaming file formats is WebM. WebM (`http://www.webmproject.org/about/`) is an open-source royalty-free media file format (.`WEBM`) that has been optimized for the Web and is used to carry HTML 5 video content. This container file format is encoded/decoded by the VP8 video codec, which was developed by On2 and now owned by Google. WebM uses the Vorbis audio codec and the Matroska container file structure. Introduced in September 2008, WebM builds on the earlier VP6 codec that is the industry standard built into Adobe Flash. VP8 improves on the compression algorithms in VP6 and is supposed to allow WebM to deliver more content with a lower client-processor overhead than content carried by H.264.

Jan Ozer at StreamingMedia.com has done an analysis (see http://www.streamingmedia.com/Articles/Editorial/Featured-Articles/First-Look-H.264-and-VP8-Compared-67266.aspx and `http://www.streamingmedia.com/Articles/ReadArticle.aspx?ArticleID=68594&PageNum=1`) of WebM versus H.264 and concludes that at this early point in WebM's development, the minor differences in quality will probably escape notice and that WebM's client-side overhead still requires more optimization and doesn't yet deliver a significant bandwidth advantage over H.264. Hardware acceleration support in upcoming devices may provide the boost that WebM's developers have promised. The royalty-free distribution of WebM is its primary appeal over H.264.

YouTube

YouTube is the iconic flash video-sharing service now owned by Google. When Google acquired YouTube in November 2006 for $1.65 billion, it bought a company with little revenue, large bandwidth expenses, and an uncertain monetization model. It was a brilliant purchase. YouTube has dominated the area of cloud-based video streaming.

To put this in perspective, Alexa's Top 500 Web Site rankings has YouTube rated #3 behind only Google (#1) and Facebook (#2) and ahead of sites like Yahoo! (#4), Windows Live (#5), and all the other well-known names in the industry. Why is YouTube so popular? The answer is obvious. YouTube is more fun than a barrel of monkeys. By the way, the search phrase "Barrel of Monkeys" yields 726 hits on YouTube.

YouTube is also highly significant. Along with the BBC, CBS, MGM, and others, many government agencies are using YouTube to host their video messages. Many of the pages you visit on WhiteHouse.gov have a YouTube message embedded in them. Figure 19.6 shows you one example. The list of governments that have blocked YouTube at various times include China, Pakistan, Iran, Libya, Turkey, and Morocco speaks to the impact that its content can have in those countries.

FIGURE 19.6

President Obama gives the news on the new Web site HealthCare.gov, courtesy of YouTube, from his virtual office on Whitehouse.gov.

YouTube technologies

To use YouTube inside a browser, you need to have Adobe Flash installed on your computer. Steve Jobs hates Flash (for a few good reasons), but YouTube was important enough for his audience that the iPhone ships with a native app for displaying YouTube content. To get YouTube onto iPhones, iPod Touch, iPad, and other Apple platforms requires that the video be transcoded into the H.264 format. YouTube Mobile uses RTSP streaming to make video available on other mobile phone platforms. You also may encounter YouTube on TiVo, as well as a service called "YouTube for TV" that can be used in devices such as set-top boxes and game consoles like the PlayStation 3 and Wii. Recently, YouTube developed a simplified interface for TV display called YouTube XL, a sample screen of which is shown in Figure 19.7.

Although the majority of online video is in Flash format (about 75 percent according the BBC), YouTube launched a new site in January 2010 that presents H.264 or WebM format video that can be viewed inside an HTML5 browser (and doesn't require Flash).

Anyone can watch videos on YouTube for free. In order to upload a video to the service, YouTube requires that you register. For a user, there is no limit to how many videos can be uploaded, nor is there a fee. Clips are limited to 15 minutes in length and a file size of under 2GB for free accounts. For content providers who want to use YouTube as a distribution medium, the company has a YouTube partnership program with a fee structure in place. YouTube also pays some content providers for the use of their content.

FIGURE 19.7

The YouTube XL interface, coming to a TV near you soon (maybe)

YouTube allows video to be uploaded in the following formats:

- 3GP
- AVI
- DivX
- FLV
- MKV
- MOV
- MP4
- MPEG MPEG-4
- OGG and OGV
- WMV

YouTube has been evolving its support for audio and video over time. The original video support was for 320X240 pixels and used the Sorenson Sparc codec. Audio was in the form of mono MP3. There is now support for 240p, 360p, 480p, 720p, 1080p, with experimentation to add the 4k resolution standard. The original aspect ratio was 4:3 (like a TV), but the widescreen movie standard 16:9 was added at the end of 2009 as part of 1080p HD support. The current audio standard is AAC, and the video is H.264/MPEG-4 AVC. YouTube also has recently been experimenting with 3D video content.

YouTube and the law

The sheer volume of content uploaded to YouTube on a daily basis is staggering. YouTube posts a notice asking that copyrights be obeyed, and the company subjects content to automatic filters, but it's impossible to police all the content that gets onto a site. As a general rule, YouTube removes content that receives what it sees as valid complaints from individuals or organizations, but after the content is online, often the damage has already been done. YouTube relies on its users to police its content.

This has led to some well-known lawsuits, such as the one Viacom has pursued asking for $1 billion in damages for posted content. As of June 2010, the District Court in Southern New York ruled in favor of Google, but this case could be headed to the Supreme Court. In another case, the artist now/formerly known as Prince sued a mother who posted a clip of her infant son dancing to the song "Let's Go Crazy." That case was resolved in favor of the posting party on the "fair use" doctrine. Fair use as defined by the U.S. Copyright act of 1976 allows portions of a copyrighted work to be used when:

1. The use is for non-profit educational purposes and not for commercial gain.
2. The nature of the copyrighted work allows its use in part as a natural course.
3. The amount used is not a substantial amount of the overall work.
4. The effect of the use doesn't diminish the overall value of the copyrighted work.

Courts are supposed to balance these four factors when deciding whether a posting or use falls under fair use, and so should you. Without fair use, newspapers, magazines, educational institutions, and a myriad of other public goods would be significantly diminished.

YouTube doesn't win them all. In a recent case in the Italian courts on February 24, 2010, three Google executives were convicted of violating privacy laws when a video of a group of Italian boys harassing a boy with Down syndrome was shown on the site. Although YouTube removed the video after two hours and the judge gave community service to the minor boys who posted the video, the conviction of the executives could have a chilling effect on YouTube's content policy—at least in Italy and perhaps in the European Union. The disposition of this ruling will be interesting to watch.

Summary

In this chapter, you learned about streaming content over the Internet and how cloud computing helps enable content providers and distributors. Audio streaming has enabled low-cost distribution of news and entertainment, podcasting, Internet radio, and even new telephony applications. Skype and Google Voice were highlighted in this chapter.

Video streaming is a high data-rate transfer activity that benefits greatly from the cloud. Many video services are already cloud-based, and this chapter introduced you to many interesting sites. The notion of television moving to the Internet and being enabled by cloud computing was also presented. Among the many worthy video services, this chapter highlighted the second most popular Web site in use, Google's YouTube.

Networked media is a rich and constantly changing area of computer technology.

In the next chapter, the impact of cloud computing on mobile devices is described. Chapter 20 looks at some of the devices, their operating systems, communication methods, and other features. Chapter 21 advances the discussion for a closer look at mobile applications that are impacted by cloud computing.

Part V

Using the Mobile Cloud

Working with Mobile Devices

I n this chapter, you learn about mobile phones and their interaction
with the cloud. The impact that cellular phone technology has had on
civilization is dramatic. The most popular consumer device is the Nokia
1100, and the billionth cell phone that Nokia sold was an 1100 in Nigeria.
Cell phones have had nearly universal worldwide adoption.

Cell phones fall into two categories. As this chapter explains, there are feature
phones, which are phones with added capabilities, and smartphones that run
recognized operating systems, install applications, and have persistent
Internet connectivity. Feature phones are being replaced by smartphones,
and for many people in the world, smartphones are the only computer that
they will ever own.

Cloud services are having a major impact on cellular phone technology, and
vice versa. Many smartphones come with native applications that consume
Web services, many of which are currently deployed in the cloud. Some of
these applications do little more than point a micro-browser at a Web site
that has been specifically formatted for mobile phone consumption. Other
applications consume RSS feeds, and many more are simply frontends for
applications that run in the cloud. Mobile application developers are staging
their apps in the cloud, and a number of hosting services provide support for
this. Amazon Web Service and the iAWSManager app are provided as an
example.

The five major smartphone operating systems to consider are Google's
Android, Apple's iOS (iPhone OS), RIM BlackBerry, Symbian, and Windows
Mobile Phone. Each of these platforms supports installable applications, and
Android and the iPhone support hundreds of thousands of third-party
applications. Many of these applications running in part or fully in the cloud
contribute greatly to the value proposition of these leading edge mobile
platforms.

IN THIS CHAPTER

**Learning about the cell phone
market**

**Discovering the key
smartphone Web features**

**Understanding how cloud
services are changing phone
services**

**Discovering the different
smartphone operating
systems**

Defining the Mobile Market

Here's an astonishing figure to consider. As of 2009, the world's population was 6.8 billion people, and the number of mobile phones estimated to be in use was 4.6 billion units. That means that nearly 68 percent of the people in the world have a cell phone. In some countries people own multiple cell phones and the penetration of phones appears to be more than 100 percent of the population—which is physically impossible, of course.

The top 10 countries and the percentage of their populations with cell phones in 2009 were as follows:

1. China, 797 million, 60.8 percent of the population

2. India, 635 million, 53.8 percent of the population

3. United States, 286 million, 91.0 percent of the population

4. Russia, 214 million, 147.3 percent of the population

5. Brazil, 187 million, 97.6 percent of the population

6. Indonesia, 140 million, 60.5 percent of the population

7. Japan, 107 million, 84.1 percent of the population

8. Germany, 107 million, 130.1 percent of the population

9. Pakistan, 98 million, 59.6 percent of the population

10. Italy, 89 million, 147.4 percent of the population

Some experts have contended that the cell phone has done more to bring people out of poverty in the Third World than almost any other invention in history. The idea of grub-staking people with "40 acres and a mule" in the 21st century needs to be replaced by the phrase: "40 acres, a mule, and a cell phone." With a cell phone in hand, a farmer in India or Africa can find out what crops to plant and which buyer to sell to with a phone call.

You may compare these numbers with the estimated number of personal computers in use worldwide in 2010, which according to the Computer Industry Almanac (`http://www.c-i-a.com/compuseexec.htm`) was 1.4 to 1.5 billion units, to judge how much greater the potential impact of cell phones is worldwide. Indeed, for nearly 3.2 billion people, their cell phone is potentially their main computing device, and the trends appear to favor increased cell phone penetration in the future.

Note

You can read the full list of countries and their cell phone usage on Wikipedia at http://en.wikipedia.org/wiki/List_of_countries_by_number_of_mobile_phones_in_use. The International Telecommunications Union does yearly studies of cell phone penetration. You can read its latest study at `http://www.itu.int/ITU-D/ict/publications/idi/2010/Material/MIS_2010_Summary_E.pdf`. ■

Connecting to the cloud

One important trend fueling the rise of pervasive cell phone Internet access is the availability of mobile broadband to the world. When you examine the way in which people connect to the Internet as a function of the type of broadband subscription that is used, you find a dramatic increase in the number of mobile broadband subscriptions worldwide. Figure 20.1 taken from the ITU report illustrates these trends. This chart shows the percentage of inhabitants that have different types of broadband connections, and it is notable that mobile broadband subscriptions have doubled from 2005 to 2009.

FIGURE 20.1

Number of broadband mobile subscriptions per 100 users; source: ITU World Telecommunication/ICT indicators database

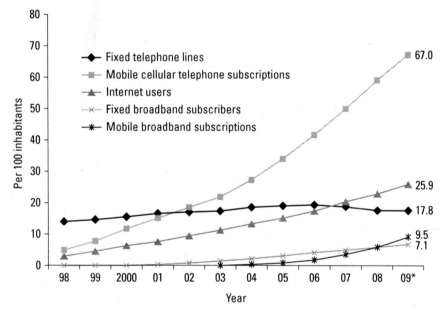

In 2009, the ITU estimated that there were 640 million mobile and 490 million fixed broadband connections. There are still many more cell phone users connected using low speed networks, but the trends all point to a dramatic shift to broadband over the next few years. There's plenty of room to grow broadband, because only 23 percent of people in developed countries have broadband access and 4 percent have access in developing countries. This study finds that the cost of fixed broadband Internet is a major impediment for its adoption, and presumably this factor favors mobile broadband connections.

Adopting mobile cloud applications

When you consider the term "mobile cloud computing," you are describing a model where processing is done in the cloud, data is stored in the cloud, and the mobile device serves as the presentation platform or the display. For this model to work a phone, tablet, or laptop requires a reliable Internet connection and the ability to run a browser (a micro-browser, really) or another viewing application. Currently, most of the computing applications that run on mobile devices run on the local device itself, with a few exceptions. Those exceptions include applications such as Google Earth, Google Maps, the major cloud mail services, and applications that provide navigation, among others. For the most part, though, applications that run on the current generations of smartphones such as Android, iPhones, RIM BlackBerry, and Windows Mobile, among others, are processed locally on the phone. These smartphones are essentially miniaturized computers.

In 2009, cell phone sales totaled 1.2 billion units, while smartphones sold 172 million units. Smartphones currently represent only 14 percent of the overall market. While smartphone sales grew from a level of 139 million units in 2008 versus 1.2 billion sales of cell phones, it is and will remain for a while only a small albeit highly profitable part of the cell phone market.

When you live in the United States, Europe, or another affluent society, you tend to view the world through the prism of your own experience. Many readers of this book who are technological cognoscenti have smartphones, but most of the world's roughly 4.6 billion cell phone users do not; they have what are described as "feature phones." What cloud computing offers the world's cell phone users is the potential to have a smartphone or rich Internet media experience on a cell phone and the potential for smartphones to become technologically "thinner" devices. By thinner, I mean that the devices will require less processing, consume less power, and have better battery life.

Currently, when you want to buy a cell phone or a smart phone, you trundle into a service provider's store and buy a phone that is supported by that network. To have an application run on the different cell phone types or smartphone operating systems, you need a Nokia developer, a Symbian developer, a RIM developer, an iPhone developer, and so on. When you develop an application for the cloud, you need just one type of developer and then all the connected phones can use that application. This is one of the main reasons why cloud computing represents a disruptive technology for mobile computing and cell phones.

Another reason is the avoidance of vendor lock-in. When you "commit" to a cell phone (particularly a smartphone), many people essentially lease these phones and are trapped in one- or two-year commitments. Worse than that, the data and applications they use are associated with their current phone and platform. Cloud computing frees those huddled cell phone masses yearning to be free from having to migrate their data and apps. If you think mobile service providers aren't concerned about their customers being free to vote with their feet, think again. The recent "announcement" (http://googlepublicpolicy.blogspot.com/) by Google and Verizon Wireless (with the support of AT&T) that they support a tiered pricing model for content transferred over wireless networks is nothing more than an attempt to control Web applications on their network and for Google to retain unrestricted access (for a cost) on willing carriers.

With such a large audience relying more and more on mobile technologies, and cell phones in particular, it is incumbent on software developers to think about extending their applications to the mobile space. What better way to do so than to build a cloud application? For mail servers, that means migrating your platform to a mail service. For a PaaS vendor such as Salesforce.com, that means modifying your Web service so the application can be experienced on the 960x640 pixel iPhone 4, the 480x800 HTC Touch HD, or the 360x480 BlackBerry 9500 (Storm). These are all relatively large displays that can render a window to a near-PC experience. Indeed, as Figure 20.2 attests, that's exactly what Saleforce.com has done with its Mobile Lite Service and Salesforce CRM Mobile Service applications for the iOS, Windows Mobile, and RIM operating systems, respectively. Mobile Lite is an extension of the Salesforce.com cloud service.

FIGURE 20.2

Salesforce.com's Mobile Lite (`http://www.salesforce.com/mobile/lite/`) illustrates an important trend in software to extend its products as cloud services for mobile access.

Feature phones and the cloud

Feature phones have nowhere near the resolution that the current smartphones do, nor is it likely that they will in the near future. A feature phone is more capable than a "dumb phone," but often it has a screen that is limited to text or very low-end graphics. Feature phones own 83 percent of the cell phone market in the U.S. as of 2009, and they are categorized by having lower prices, longer battery lives, and simpler APIs. Of the top 10 best selling phones listed on Wikipedia (`http://en.wikipedia.org/wiki/List_of_best-selling_mobile_phones`), only the Nokia 5230, which runs Symbian OS v9.4, is a smartphone:

1. Nokia 1100 (200 million)
2. Nokia 3210 (150 million)
3. Nokia 5230 (145 million)
4. Motorola RAZR V3 (130 million)
5. Nokia 3310 (126 million)

As feature phones go upscale and smartphones extend their market downscale, the industry is beginning to add to inexpensive feature phones the capability to run lightweight operating systems such as Oracle's (nee Sun's) Java Platform Micro Edition (Java ME; `http://www.oracle.com/technetwork/java/javame/index.html`) or Qualcomm's Binary Runtime Environment for Wireless (BREW; `http://brew.qualcomm.com/brew/en/`). This gives feature phones the capability to run applications such as browsers that make cloud computing on these phones more attractive. Qualcomm is slated to add both the Opera Mini 5 and Opera Mobile 10 browsers to the Brew mobile platform. There's little uniformity in the features and interoperability in the micro-browser arena, but that could change quickly. While carriers have been quick to offer us repackaged games like Atari on feature phones, the race is on to move to Web applications at service providers like AT&T where a new messaging service has just been added for a number of their feature phones that provides access to e-mail, Facebook, and other services.

Feature phones are worldwide leaders today, but could rapidly be overtaken as the price of smartphones decline. All the trends point in that direction. Smartphones are up nearly 48 percent according to a study by AdMob (`http://metrics.admob.com/wp-content/uploads/2010/06/May-2010-AdMob-Mobile-Metrics-Highlights.pdf`) from Q1 2009 to Q1 2010 worldwide, while feature phones are declining. In Europe, where Nokia's Symbian S60 phones once dominated, their share has fallen to 7 percent, while Android and iOS dominate with a 16 percent and 73 percent market share, respectively. Indeed, worldwide smartphones account for 46 percent of the network traffic, feature phones account for 42 percent, and mobile internet devices (MID) account for 12 percent. Smartphones move roughly 30 times the data that feature phones do because of smartphone's use of applications.

The conclusion you can reach from this data is that phones are getting cheaper, and as smartphones become cheap enough, they replace feature phones. As feature phones are retired, newer lightweight operating systems are being added to lower-end phones to give them smartphone capabilities. Access to the cloud where data and processing are outsourced and the phone is a display platform will tend to level the playing field, making feature phones appear to be smarter and all phones cheaper.

Using Smartphones with the Cloud

There are many different ways in which you can define a smartphone, but these are the essential characteristics:

- A smartphone has a recognizable operating system.
- A smartphone can run installable applications.

- A smartphone offers advanced calling features such as video calls or conferencing.

- A smartphone offers messaging features.

- A smartphone comes with a touchscreen; the bigger the touchscreen the smarter the phone.

- A smartphone offers keyboard entry, either physically or virtually.

- A smartphone has a persistent Internet connection.

So my definition of smartphones goes like this:

> Smartphones are small computers on which you can make phone calls, send messages, and access Internet data in real time.

So much for smartphones, but what about the cloud? As it stands today cloud computing is based around the idea that large industrial-sized information appliances can serve up data to any and all comers. The smartphone and eventually feature phones too, as well as tablets, laptops, and mobile internet devices, are all cloud clients. But smartphones and the cloud, well that is dynamite because the two technologies are synergistic: you couple a client that requires a ubiquitous service with a service that is ubiquitous, and then you provide the combination with a nearly universal worldwide market penetration. Each technology enhances and drives the other.

Consider what we haven't seen yet in smartphones that clouds can offer. If you move smartphone execution to a virtual machine running in the cloud, smartphones are no longer constrained by their processing power, memory, or storage capacity. The only two factors of importance are network bandwidth and display quality. You have to think that someone will build the equivalent of a thin client/terminal service using the cloud.

We also haven't seen phone networks using peering. If you design a phone so that each phone is a node in a large distributed network, then the overall computer has almost infinite capability and power. Some of the most powerful supercomputers in the world are built with large numbers of commodity computers in a cluster or grid, and some of the largest computing projects ever attempted run on the spare cycles of hundreds of thousands of computers. So why not a peer-to-peer cell phone network too? This isn't cloud computing, but it is something you have to wonder about.

One thing that smartphones have made perfectly clear is that people love apps. On the mobile platforms described in the following sections, each vendor (with the exception of Symbian) has an application marketplace. Each vendor also puts lots of effort into getting third-party applications written for its platform. Many of the applications using Web services are doing so through sites that are specially formatted for a particular platform. Nearly every major Web site or service has a version that is optimized for mobile computing and accessed using a mobile URL. When you point a micro-browser at one of these sites, you get a smartphone-optimized cloud-based experience.

Android

Android (`http://www.android.com/`) is the mobile device operating system originally developed by Android Inc., purchased and further developed by Google, and supported by the industry working group called the Open Handset Alliance (`http://www.openhandset`

alliance.com/). Android is based on Linux and GNU software. The software is licensed to OEMs under the Apache license. The current version of the OS is 2.2 and is called Froyo (for Frozen Yoghurt); the next two versions are codenamed Gingerbread, which is due out in Q4 2010, and Honeycomb, which will be released sometime in 2011.

Phones using the Android operating system were first sold by Google, branded as the Nexus One, and manufactured by HTC. A long list of these phones is maintained at `http://en.wikipedia.org/wiki/List_of_Android_devices`, but many people will recognize current market leaders such as the HTC Evo, Hero, and Incredible, the LG Optimus, the Motorola Droid and Droid X, Samsung Galaxy, and Sony Ericsson XPERIA, among others on this list.

As of Q2 2010, Android was the leading smartphone OS in the U.S., and it sells worldwide at a run rate of 5 million phones per month. It has been remarked that as Windows was to Macintosh, Android is to the iPhone. Google's policy of licensing phones to all service providers and doing many incremental releases instead of Apple's yearly release is helping Android phones to pull away from the iPhone in terms of features and quality.

Android was built to serve as a mobile platform for Internet computing and, by extension, as a consumer or client for cloud computing services. The Android software is based on Java and runs in a Dalvik virtual machine. Among the core modules are a surface manager, the OpenGL and SGL graphics engines, SQLite RDBMS, WebKit rendering engine, and the OpenCore media framework.

The Android Market currently has 75,000 applications listed in it, and it's a very active site. According to some sources, 100,000 more applications have been submitted to Google for potential distribution. Google's participation in the Android Market has extended to offering several of its Web services in the form of Android applications.

Notably, you will find the following Google applications:

- **Google Voice**, the telephone service
- **Google Finance**, a financial service
- **Google Translate**, a language searching program
- **Google Shopper**, a shopping search program
- **Google Listen**, a podcatcher and player
- **My Tracks**, a jogging program
- **Places Directory,** for local search
- **Google Goggles**, an image recognition program
- **Google Chrome to Phone Extension**, which sends links and information from a Chrome browser to an Android phone
- **Voice Actions for Android**, a voice command and speech recognition program

The last two applications are new and worth a moment to consider. Google Chrome to Phone Extension places a button in your Chrome browser that can push links, maps, selected text, or phone numbers out to your Android phone. The application is available on Market and works for Froyo (Android 2.2).

Voice Actions for Android allows you to use spoken commands to control your Android phone. This includes dialing a contact, getting a map, sending text or e-mail, playing a music file, browsing the Web, and performing other actions. Voice Actions is accessed with the microphone button inside the Google search box on the Android home screen.

Cross-Ref

Many of these Google programs are described in Chapter 8. ■

The Android Market is available on Android phones through the Market application. Not all phones come with Market preinstalled. Market is a utility for downloading Android Package Files (APK) to the /data/app directory, where they require Linux root access to view and modify. A convenient place to browse featured applications is a showcase site that Google maintains, as shown in Figure 20.3.

FIGURE 20.3

Google's showcase of Android Market applications may be found at http://www.android.com/market.

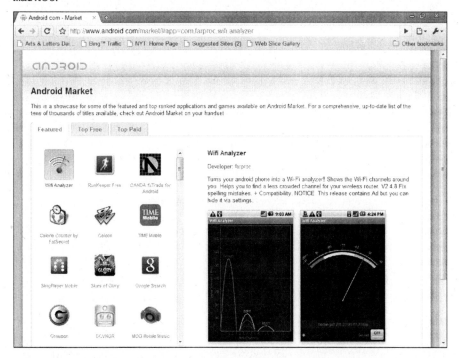

Apple iPhone

The Apple iPhone is considered by many people to be the leading Internet-enabled smartphone in the market today. The first generation of the iPhone running the iPhone OS appeared in January

2007, and in every subsequent year, Apple has released a next generation model. You can view a list of iOS devices at `http://en.wikipedia.org/wiki/List_of_BlackBerry_products`. The current generation is the iPhone 4, which runs the iOS operating system. The Apple iPhone and the iTouch (an iPhone without the phone portion) run a version of the Darwin operating system found in Mac OS X bundled with Core Animation software that supplies motion graphics routines based on OpenG ES 2.0.

The iPhone is really a handheld computer more than it is a phone, and the current model ships with two cameras for video telephony (FaceTime), GPS navigation, a three-axis accelerometer, a gyroscopic sensor, a proximity sensor, and a number of other built-in devices. Upon its introduction, the iPhone was noted for its multi-touch capacitive touchscreen, which accepts finger input and gestures, something that has become more common today.

The iPhone, like the iPod before it, is managed with the Apple iTunes program. It would be hard to overestimate the impact that iTunes has had on the music industry and that the App store has had on the smartphone industry. It is my impression that the overwhelming success of the App store caught Apple entirely by surprise. In the days when Personal Digital Assistants got apps from software vendors over the Internet, the experience was a miserable one. When you found an application, you needed to know if it was compatible for your device, how to install and use it, and how to manage and update it.

The App Store

What Apple did with the App Store is to create a unified distribution with a large installed based and an automated server push and client poll update service. This in turn gave developers a large installed base of devices to write to, a uniform set of tools to write with, and a mechanism for monetizing their applications. As a result, applications for the iPhone got much cheaper, and what an application lost in price, it made up in volume. Apple did for mobile applications what eBay did for auctions and Amazon did for books—with all the associated benefits and drawbacks. It is hard to imagine today a successful smartphone platform that doesn't also come with an application library service. There were in excess of 252,000 iPhone apps on the App Store as of September 2010.

The iPhone connects to the Internet either through Wi-Fi, wide area GSM (Global System for Mobile Communications), or an EDGE (Enhanced Data rates for GSM Evolution) network. Wi-Fi is an 802.11 standard, while GSM and EDGE are cellular phone networks. The iPhone 3g has a reported download speed of 7.2Mbps, and file transfers over cellular networks are limited in size to prevent congestion. There are no limits to file transfers over Wi-Fi. The large amounts of data transferred over the AT&T network have proven to be a problem for that service provider and have led to congestion in some major metropolitan areas.

Apple has not included support for Adobe Flash or Java on its platform or on the iPad, which means that many sites viewed within the Safari micro-browser are not completely rendered, something for which Apple has been criticized. Apple's contention is that Flash is very vulnerable software, and given the number of recent exploits who can argue with that point of view? Other people have suggested that Apple has excluded Adobe Flash to maintain control over the graphics part of the iOS 4 platform.

The iPhone has also been noted for being a good consumer of Web services, but according to some industry observers, due to the closed nature of the platform, it may be a bad potential consumer of many major cloud services that don't support Apple's native applications. Third-party applications that run on the iPhone can access cloud services with no problem, so the iPhone is a champion cloud client in that regard. (Indeed, my iPhone has 31 cloud applications on it out of my 72 total applications.) Many core Web services are locked out of the iPhone platform. For example, only recently did Apple add a streaming service to its iDisk feature of Mobile Me (see the next section). So it will be interesting to see whether Apple chooses to open up the iPhone to more cloud computing services as the platform evolves.

MobileMe

MobileMe is Apple's cloud service. This subscription-based Internet suite incorporates services that were once part of iTools and .MAC into a single collection adding tools for productivity, synchronization, and communication. The tools that are built into MobileMe use Ajax and DHTML to create the appearance of a desktop application inside a browser. The central application in the suite is Apple's hosted e-mail service. The home page for MobileMe is Me.com, shown in Figure 20.4.

FIGURE 20.4

Apple's Mobile Me (`http://www.me.com/`) contains a number of cloud services such as iDisk, hosted e-mail, and more.

MobileMe offers the following features:

- **e-Mail** is available at the @me.com domain for iOS, Mac OS X, and Windows OS; or through the Web interface at `http://www.me.com`. The older .MAC service used the domain Mac.com for e-mail accounts.

  MobileMe Mail adds a number of features to hosted e-mail including better screen control and formatting, picture handling, and a rich Web experience. MobileMe Calendar is an updated version of the online calendar application.

- **Online storage** provides 20 to 200GB/month data transfer. Certain features such as the address book, calendar, notes, and to-do lists are synchronized between systems.

  With MobileMe installed on Windows, you can synchronize data with your MobileMe account to Windows.

- **iDisk** is an online storage drive that can be browsed and from which items can be shared. The sharing feature can be done by granting individual access or through a public folder.

- **MobileMe Gallery** is a photo- and video-sharing service.

- **Find My iPhone** is a device tracking service that shows a message or displays a sound when activated. You can also use this service to change the password or erase the memory of an iPhone remotely.

- **iWeb Publish** is a hosted Web site that can be accessed either through your own personal domain or through a personal page at Me.com.

- **iChat** is Apple's instant messaging service that interoperates with AIM.

If the iPhone, iTouch, and iPad have one Achilles heel, it is their relatively limited storage capacity. A capacity of 16, 32, or even 64GB isn't really enough to make these devices portable libraries in the way that a big 'ole hard drive is. This means that to consume mass quantities of media, these devices must rely on data transfer to the cloud. That's probably why Apple invested in the music streaming service LaLa.com. It is not improbable to believe that Apple will set up its media business so you can stream content from its servers to your Apple devices, move the content from an Apple device to other devices, and allow iTunes to wirelessly synch content. If Apple goes this route, then what you have is a situation where applications live on local devices and data is stored in the cloud.

iPhone apps hosting services

iPhone applications are hosted on the iTunes App Store, but many applications are heavy users of Internet or Web services and require dedicated infrastructure to stage. When an iPhone application is released, there is often no way to accurately predict demand, and success can hinge on the performance of the application at the time it was released. For this reason, many mobile developers are using cloud-based infrastructure for the elastic scaling of their Web services. There are several IaaS vendors available for deploying applications; RackSpace and Amazon Web Services are probably the two largest choices. RackSpace even has an app on the iPhone to manage its service deployments.

Amazon Web Services has a specific iPhone Application Hosting page, shown in Figure 20.5, for iPhone developers. As AWS notes, when you create an iPhone application, you can structure the application so it is a rich client frontend to services in the cloud. The full range of AWS is available for a deployment may be monitored and controlled; these various services were discussed in detail in Chapter 9.

Of course, if you are developing for the iPhone, you probably want to be able to control your infrastructure with an app. In Figure 20.6 is the iAWSManager, a third-party application that uses the AWS APIs to control the various components and instances you have running.

An advantage of Android and Windows Mobile is that they have their own dedicated infrastructure on which developers can host their applications, if they want to. For Google, that hosting service is the Google AppEngine and Google's infrastructure; for Microsoft, that hosting service is the Windows Azure Platform and Microsoft's infrastructure. Chapter 8 describes the Google AppEngine, and Chapter 9 describes Windows Azure in detail.

FIGURE 20.5

Amazon Web Service offers an iPhone application hosting service. To read about it, go to `http://aws.amazon.com/iphone-application-hosting/`.

FIGURE 20.6

There's a cloud app for that; iAWSManager lets you control your AWS EC2, ELB, S3, CF, SQS, and SDB Web services from an iPhone.

Research In Motion BlackBerry

The Canadian company Research In Motion BlackBerry mobile e-mail devices and smartphones are hugely popular with many devotees. BlackBerry owns 21 percent of the world's smartphone market, making it number 2 overall. President Obama is a well-known crackberry addict, as are many in government and large corporate enterprises. A "crackberry" is someone who is on their BlackBerry so much that it affects their normal lives.

BlackBerry started out as an enhanced pager in the mid-1990s and developed a push e-mail service that is well suited to business applications. You can find a list of BlackBerry models at `http://en.wikipedia.org/wiki/List_of_BlackBerry_products`. The roots of the BlackBerry phones as a PDA can be seen in the way in which the BlackBerry OS structures its interface and in the range of applications it supports. The OS has support for both Java and WAP.

BlackBerry is known primarily for its messaging capabilities, which is probably the most advanced in the industry. In addition to push e-mail through Wi-Fi or cellular network connections, there are push notification services available from a range of cloud services such as Facebook, Myspace, Ebay, and others. BlackBerry has an IM service called BlackBerry Messenger, and it supports other IM services, such as Google Messenger, ICQ, Windows Live Messenger, and Yahoo Messenger, which makes the BlackBerry the most agnostic and interoperable IM platform you can have. The newer BlackBerry devices come with the BlackBerry Messenger (BBM) Instant Messaging application that can send media-rich instant messages to another BlackBerry whose PIN (eight-digit ID) are known. BBM supports location sensing, group communication, and (through third-party software) CRM (Customer Relationship Manager) and DBMS (Database Management System) systems.

The BlackBerry can also serve as a Microsoft Exchange Server, Lotus Domino, and Novell GroupWise messaging server client, synchronizing e-mail and calendar data. Large deployments of BlackBerry devices are supported by the BlackBerry Enterprise Server (BES), which is an e-mail relay software add-on for Exchange, Domino, and GroupWise.

The BES Mobile Data-Service Connection Service (MDS-CS) can connect to mobile BlackBerry devices through a TCP/IP connection, and through the use of the API and Java ME runtime, developers can create applications that can communicate with these devices. Google offers a Connector to BES for Google Apps. Later versions of the BlackBerry do not require MDS-CS to connect to the Internet, but the connector is still required if you want to create a secure connection.

The BlackBerry Internet Service (BIS) is the alternative connection for a BlackBerry that doesn't use the BlackBerry Enterprise Server as its connection. Communication between BlackBerry's servers and devices using the BIS are highly encrypted and compressed. The service is available in 91 countries and through nearly all the major cellular providers, and it's the way an individual would connect to a large service provider. BIS is provisioned by service providers, but the service runs on RIM servers. A BIS account gives a customer a POP3 and IMAP mail connection, up to 10 accounts, and access to other e-mail services such as AOL, Gmail, Hotmail, and Yahoo!.

BlackBerry supports an applications store called BlackBerry App World that isn't as extensive as its Android or iPhone competitors. The store opened in April 2009 and is available through the Blackberry via the App World application. Users can browse the store's catalog online using their desktops or other devices. Users can access this service using the BlackBerry App World 2.0 application, which was released in August 2010 and is part of BlackBerry OS 4.5.0 and later. Figure 20.7 shows the BlackBerry App World Web site.

FIGURE 20.7

BlackBerry App World is a new application store for BlackBerry devices. Browse applications at `http://na.blackberry.com/eng/services/appworld/`.

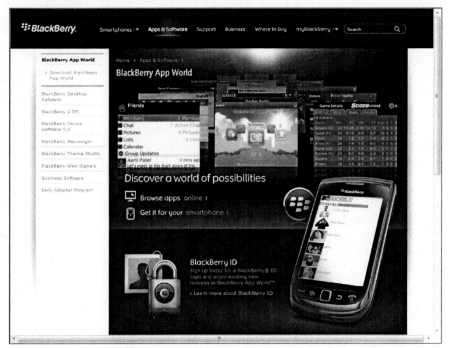

Symbian

Symbian refers to the Symbian open-source operating system and the Symbian platform that runs the operating system on feature phones and smartphones made by various OEMs. Symbian is the leading platform for cell phones, with 41 percent of the world market, due primarily to Nokia's dominance in the industry worldwide for so many years. Nokia had an app store a decade ago for its phones, but never extended the concept.

The Symbian Foundation (`http://symbian.org/`), which maintains the open-source OS, was formed in 2009 by Nokia, NTT, Sony Ericsson, and Symbian Ltd., and the software is made available under the Eclipse Public License (EPL). The Symbian Foundation is an official backer of the Open Cloud Manifesto (`http://opencloudmanifesto.org/`) and runs many of its systems and services on the cloud.

The Symbian kernel, which is currently at EKA2, is a microkernel architecture designed to work with a single processor. Unlike other OSs, Symbian includes device drivers in the kernel itself. The Symbian^4 OS (to be released in 2011) uses the Orbit interface built on Qt application framework and libraries, and it comes with a graphics toolkit called avkon. Avkon is the next generation of S60 routines that take commands either from the device touchpad or a keyboard.

Starting with Symbian^3 in 2005, devices include a WebKit browser. The Symbian OS is modular with different technology domains, each containing software packages, and with each domain having its own separate roadmap. All the Symbian phones on the market are Symbian^1 or Symbian^2 phones. The Nokia N8 is the first Symbian 3 phone. No Symbian^4 phones have yet been announced. Wikipedia maintains a list of Symbian phones at `http://en.wikipedia.org/wiki/List_of_Symbian_devices`. Symbian^3 and eventually Symbian^4 will lead to the release of next-generation smartphones that will be better cloud consumer devices. In this regard, it will be particularly insightful to see how the Nokia N8 is received; Nokia bills this device as a portable entertainment center and provides Web access to a variety of services native on the device, as well as various social networking features.

Windows Mobile

Windows Mobile is the last of the four major smartphone operating systems that this chapter considers. The platform has undergone continuous upgrade and revisions since it was first introduced in 2000 as the Pocket PC 2000. The current version of the operating system is Windows Mobile 6.5, with the new version called Windows 7 slated to release about the time this book appears in the stores.

Microsoft has worked hard to make Windows Mobile devices a natural extension for Windows developers upon which to position their products. The Windows CE 5.2 kernel is a suite of Microsoft applications optimized for a smaller display size and using the Windows API. Early editions of these devices had a Windows look and feel, and they required the use of a stylus, which made the screen look cluttered and data entry difficult. As the platform has developed, Microsoft has streamlined the interface and improved the product.

Given the compatibility of Windows Mobile phones with Exchange Server infrastructures and the ability to create Windows-based programs on a mobile platform, Windows Mobile phones have been popular with many businesses, but less so with the consumer, where phones based on this OS have been losing market share of late. The upcoming Windows Phone 7 continues the trend toward a more modern smartphone interface and is by all accounts a substantial departure from previous efforts.

Note

You can read more about the Windows Phone 7 in Paul Thurrott's Windows Phone 7 Secrets, Wiley, 2010. ■

Windows Mobile has always had strong connection to Microsoft Enterprise Server technology, but has never achieved great success in the consumer market. Windows Phone 7 is meant to rectify this situation. The emphasis in this new phone is on consumer experience, and there are smart links and features associated with social networking on the phone, as well as a completely new interface code named "Metro." Microsoft has used several of the features of its Zune HD platform in its design of Windows Phone 7. One feature of note is a Bing button that launches that search engine directly and can use voice input. Figure 20.8 shows the Windows Phone 7 Web site.

FIGURE 20.8

The Window Phone 7 Web site may be found at `http://www.windowsphone7.com/`.

Applications for the Windows Phone 7 are based on the .NET Compact Framework 4, XNA, and Silverlight Applications. The applications that ran on older versions of Windows Mobile Phone will not run on the Windows Phone 7. Indeed, applications that run on Windows Phone 7 will run in some entirely new ways for Microsoft. The phone is much less customizable for OEMs than previous phones were, and even user access to the file system has been severely limited. The earliest versions of the phone will come with Internet Explorer Mobile and will initially ship without Adobe Flash or HTML 5 support. Flash support is expected a few months after launch.

Based upon what I've seen from Microsoft, I conclude that the company is a passionate supporter of cloud computing. As was discussed in Chapter 10, a significant portion of the company is currently working on projects related to cloud computing. Windows Mobile fits into the company's strategy of Software + Services by offering another platform on which Microsoft developers can stage their products and by using the Windows Azure platform through which cloud-based services can be delivered. In many ways, Windows Phone 7 and Azure represent a reboot for Microsoft's mobile business. The company has lots of experience in this area and a good strategy, so it will be interesting to watch the company's progress on this platform.

Summary

In this chapter, you learned about the mobile phone market. In total, the cell phone market dwarfs the PC market, with a majority of the world's inhabitants owning one or more cell phones. Mobile phones are differentiated into feature phones and smartphones. Many more feature phones have been sold than smartphones, but the market for smartphones is increasing dramatically. It is anticipated that in the next few years smartphones will dominate the market.

Cloud computing offers the capability to run cell phone applications and Web services and to store data remotely. Many applications that run on smartphones, and in many cases features found in feature phones, are dependent upon the Web services found in the cloud. This trend is likely to accelerate. The eventual impact of the cloud on mobile devices will be to make them thinner (as a client), cheaper, and seemingly much more powerful.

Smartphone technology is advancing rapidly, and the market for them is very dynamic. In the past four years, Apple's iPhone has gone from 0 to more than 200,000 applications and has become immensely profitable. Google's Android phones seem to have an even faster trajectory. RIM BlackBerry has a leadership position in the messaging area—and a very large market share. The most dominant operating system is Symbian, which is losing market share but is developing new versions of its operating system. Even Microsoft's mobile platform is being relaunched with a brand new class of devices called the Windows Phone 7. It is likely that this market will support several successful operating systems and many different vendors and models for some time to come.

Working with Mobile Web Services

Mobile devices use more network traffic in consuming Web services than do fixed-line systems. Most people find that their use of Web services is increasing dramatically year after year. Indeed, as this chapter shows you, the Web is becoming a source of rich content for mobile devices.

Mobile devices present some challenges for Web services. Specifically, their device characteristics don't match the resolution and detail of desktop computers. For that reason, many service protocols are specifically aimed at providing the necessary translation required to make Web sites look good on mobile devices.

To use a Web service, a device needs to know about that service and know how to access it. This chapter describes some of the methods used for Web service discovery based on standard methods.

Mobile devices can transmit specific information about the condition of the device and its user. This information, when properly parsed and logically analyzed, can be used to create context-aware services. Location-based services are offered as the prime example of this feature.

Push services are an important mechanism in e-mail and in certain forms of publishing. In this chapter, you learn about different push services, including how BlackBerry does push and the Lemonade Profile. The Short Message System (SMS) is a form of message push service and is described in this chapter. The chapter is rounded out by a look at the Wireless Access Protocol (WAP), which is a push mechanism for publishing Web site data that is device-specific. You also learn about some of the data synchronization standards used in mobile technology.

Understanding Service Types

Mobile Web services are those in which information is transferred between applications (especially a browser) and services over an Internet connection. As you saw in Chapter 20, more information is transferred over mobile connections now than is transferred over fixed lines. Early cell phones and feature phones depended upon native applications for most of their enhancements. Web services have made the development of mobile Web applications much easier and more powerful, and thus these types of applications are steadily replacing native applications that are usually platform-specific and proprietary. The tendency to include sensors of all types in mobile devices is making the mobile Web a very rich service indeed.

Mobile interoperability

In the current market, the mobile Web is fractured into many different competing operating systems and proprietary hardware. This isn't going to change anytime soon, and the market will probably be supporting many different products for years to come. The fact is that the approach Apple has taken with the closed iOS products, the iPhone, iTouch, and iPad does tend to make these devices more reliable, and because they are more predictable, they are easier to use. For these benefits, you tender a certain amount of flexibility. The lack of expandable storage on these devices is a classic example of vendor lock-in.

There are open-system alternatives to systems like the iOS or BlackBerry OS. The two best examples are the Android OS and the Symbian OS. Open-system hardware and software tends to evolve more quickly than proprietary systems because there are more players and the work tends to get wider review. There's also a higher emphasis placed on interoperability in open systems.

One effort to make mobile devices more interoperable is the W3C Mobile Web Initiative (http://www.w3.org/Mobile). This initiative sought to make browsing the Web with mobile devices more reliable by setting standards that Web site designers can use to make their sites mobile-friendly. There are guidelines on the Mobile Web Initiative Web site that you can read on best practices, as well as a site-checking tool that does an assessment of a site for you.

The problem with mobile site optimization is that many different devices exist, and it is impossible to support more than a few of them. These factors need to be addressed, among others:

- Variable screen sizes and resolutions
- Slow transmission over the connection and limited rendering speeds on the device (something that is improving over time)
- Different methods of navigation through the interface
- Limited use of windows and lack of some standard graphical user interface controls
- Exclusion of certain file formats such as PDF, rendering engines such as Adobe Flash, and cookies
- Message size limitations
- Nonstandard and often onerous transmission costs

Vendors approach the problem of interoperability in several ways. A common way is to create individual sites within a Web site for different devices. Content is served up to a device based on the device's identity and content negotiation. With the rise of smartphone applications, many organizations are creating application frontends to their sites. To my mind, the best of these sites have been created by the major news organizations: BBC, CNN, AP, and the *New York Times*.

Compare the front page for the Web site of the *New York Times* on a standard 1024x768 resolution monitor in Figure 21.1 versus the same content displayed on an Apple iPhone 480x320 resolution screen. These two screenshots taken of the page (`http://www.nytimes.com/`) on September 1, 2010, illustrate the different approaches that designers have taken to show dense content on different resolutions screens. While the computer display is loaded with ads, the iPhone app displays on a single large advertisement. The content is displayed on the application with much less leading content, and in a strictly hierarchical navigational system. Each story is a link in the form of a large button to the full text of the story. Many large links on the display have been replaced by fewer, but easier to select, buttons. There is also less use of graphics and images on the application.

FIGURE 21.1

The *New York Times* home page on a standard computer monitor (left), and the *New York Times* home page on the same day within the iPhone 3g application (right)

One approach to improving interoperability that was considered by the Mobile Web Initiative's Device Description Working Group (`http://www.w3.org/2005/MWI/DDWG/`) was to create a database of device characteristics, called a Device Description Repository. This repository would then be used in concert with the DDR Simple API to modify content so screen size, markup language, and image format support is delivered to a device correctly. This work ended in December 2008 with a recommendation for adoption to the W3C, but it hasn't resulted in an industry standard, although it might be incorporated into some later work.

A specific top-level domain has been created for the producers and consumers of mobile services and products called .MOBI, which is maintained as a registry called the Mobile Top Level Domain (mTLD). The purpose of this domain is to create sites that render correctly on mobile devices. This domain is a sponsored domain and was created by a group of companies in the mobile space that include Ericsson, Google, GSM Association, Hutchison Whampoa, Microsoft, Orascom Telecom, Samsung, Telefónica Móviles, Telecom Italia Mobile, Syniverse Technologies, T-Mobile, Visa, and Vodafone. The domain received ICAN approval in July 2005.

Figure 21.2 shows the dotMobi (`http://mtld.mobi/`) registration service for this domain. Afilias (`http://www.afilias.info/`) acquired the registry service in February 2010 and serves as its DNS service provider.

dotMobi participated in the work of the Mobile Web Initiative and has a tool called Ready.mobi that analyzes Web sites and scores them. However, dotMobi doesn't mandate that a Web site use any specific technologies, only that it be mobile-device-friendly.

FIGURE 21.2

The .MOBI domain is specifically set aside for mobile Web products and services; shown here is the dotMobi registration service home page.

The establishment of the .MOBI domain has been subject to criticism from the W3C's director, Tim Berners-Lee, on the grounds that the Web sites on the Internet should be device-independent. It is suggested that a better mechanism for content compatibility on the mobile Web is to use content negotiation, cascading style sheets, or other devices. In HTTP, *content negotiation* is a mechanism by which user agents can be served a different document or file format based on going to the same URI. For example, if a device goes to the URI and is recognized as belonging to a supported type, then the program logic serves up the appropriate content.

Another effort aimed at promoting standards on mobile networks is the Open Terminal Platform (OMTP; `http://www.omtp.org/`). The group was an industry association formed in 2004 by several mobile vendors, including Huawei, LG Electronics, Motorola, Nokia, Samsung, and Sony Ericsson. On July 1, 2010, OMTP became part of the Wholesale Applications Community (WAC; `http://www.wholesaleappcommunity.com/`), a group that exists to promote the market for mobile applications. The members of the WAC are AT&T, Deutsche Telekom AG, KT, Orange, Smart Communications, Telecom Italia, Telefónica, Telenor, and Vodafone; the sponsors are Ericsson and Nokia. Figure 21.3 shows the WAC's home page.

The OMTP worked in many areas, including creating universal charging standards for micro-USB devices, mobile security, position measurements, device management, and standardized APIs. They have an initiative called the BONDI API (`http://bondi.omtp.org/`) based on a set of JavaScript APIs and a security framework based on XACML for creating mobile interfaces and subsystems. An open-source project has released an SDK (`http://bondisdk.org/`) for this API. BONDI, which is named for the Australian beach near Sydney, is one of several efforts to create standard mobile APIs. Two others are:

GSMA OneAPI (`http://www.gsmworld.com/oneapi/`)

Joint Innovation Lab (JIL; `http://www.jil.org/`)

The Wholesale Applications Community is an industry group aimed at standardizing and promoting mobile applications.

Performing Service Discovery

Web services are useful only if they can be discovered by mobile devices and accessed by those devices by mutually supported protocols. If protocols are standard and open, the chances of being able to exchange information is increased. Web services are a form of publishing: In some cases, they involve messaging; in others, they use a publish/subscribe metaphor; and in other cases, they are broadcast. The nature of the protocol supports the mechanism for data transfer that is required.

One standard for publishing a Web service that is used in cloud computing and contributes to the Service Oriented Architecture (SOA) is the Web Service Description Language (WSDL). This protocol was described in Chapter 14. In WSDL, the service is described in terms of an interface or endpoint that can be accessed to send information to and get information back from the service.

Note

The Web site for these various OASIS Web service discovery protocols may be accessed at http://www.oasis-open.org/committees/tc_home.php?wg_abbrev=ws-dd. ∎

Several mechanisms exist for aggregating WSDL documents into a searchable form. The Universal Description, Discovery, and Integration (UDDI; `http://www.oasis-open.org/committees/uddi-spec/`) service is an open registry of business services. UDDI is an OASIS standard that is searchable and is in the XML format. Documents stored in UDDI conform to the Web Service Inspection Language (WSIL) format, which makes the information searchable. IBM has a UDDI federated search technology in its Business Explorer for Web Services product (BE4WS; `http://www.alphaworks.ibm.com/tech/be4ws`).

UDDI publishes information in the following forms:

- White pages with identification information
- Yellow pages with industry categorization based on standard schema or taxonomies
- Green pages that specify the service endpoints

The WS-Discovery service provides a means for advertising services on small networks using a multicast protocol. Typically, the service is delivered using SOAP over UDP. WS-Discovery is an OASIS standard and is used as part of network discovery in Windows (WSDAPI), in the Device Profile for Web Services (DPWS), and in the Windows Rally technologies. Microsoft uses Windows Rally to provision network nodes such as computers, access points, printers, and other network-connected devices.

ebXML, which stands for Electronic Business using eXtensible Markup Language is a joint standard of OASIS and UN/CEFACT and aims to create a searchable global registry of business services. The standard is maintained by the freebXM (`http://www.freebxml.org/`) initiative.

Context-aware services

As mobile computing has grown, each mobile device contains and is capable of transmitting a large amount of information concerning the condition or state of the device and the user who carries the device. When parsed properly, this information can provide intelligent systems with not only the user's identification, but the context in which that user finds himself.

Location is the prime example of context. When we search for something near us, the search engine returns results that are location-based and thus have context. When a phone transmits its GPS coordinates to a service, that service may be able to compare that location to the customer's registered home or work address and then send information appropriate to each environment back to the user. Or more specifically, if a phone transmits its location as being in a specific building or room to a service, then the service can display a map showing where the nearest restroom is or where the light switches are located, or it can provide instructions for how to work the overhead display in the room. You can see how this very tailored and specific information could be incredibly valuable and useful.

Note

Keith Jones, an SOA Designer at IBM, published an article, "Building a context-aware service architecture" (`http://www.ibm.com/developerworks/architecture/library/ar-conawserv/index.html?ca=drs-`), that goes into more detail on this topic and addresses different approaches. ∎

When a mobile user is connected to her mobile service, she is exchanging two different sets of information:

- **Physical context:** Information derived from measurements made from the mobile device or its sensors
- **Logical context:** Information derived from the user or from the manner in which the user has interacted with services over time

As an example to demonstrate the difference between the two, the identification string associated with your cell phone's SIM card is a physical attribute, and your service login ID and its associated password are a logical attribute. Physical context provides location, ambient device conditions, device states, and more. Logical contexts are information about the purpose a location serves, a digital identity and its associated attributes, relationships, interests, past searches, Web sites visited, privileges, and preferences.

Chapter 14 covers Service Oriented Architectures. An SOA provides a set of methods for using modules to construct loosely coupled complex systems from standard parts. You may recall from that discussion that the essence of SOA is that the method of construction of the modules is abstracted out of the system and encapsulated, and what SOA requires is a standard method for exposing the services that a module provides as a standard interface exposed by an API. The API's methods remain invariant, even when the module is moved, re-architected, or subsumed into another module. SOA requires a standard messaging protocol and a form of federated database system.

In a Web service, the mobile client plays the role of a service consumer and the Web service is the service provider. In Figure 21.4, a system for processing contextual information is shown, based on the ideas of a Service Oriented Architecture.

A system of this type provides a much richer environment in which to respond to requests and allows both service providers and content providers to either narrowcast or tailor information for a specific user based on his current context. The Context Logic Processor plays the role of the orchestrator providing programmed logic that works with the data parsed by the Context Parser.

The Context Parser takes all the input data (digital signals in many cases) and applies a logical schema to create the needed structured objects for the Logic Processor's use. This infrastructure can be placed in the cloud. The concept of creating a structured representation of concepts and their relationship in a domain is referred to as ontology. Ontology is a formal way of specifying a shared abstraction. Ontologies are used in all fields of computer science and are at the heart of efforts to create the Semantic Web, in artificial intelligence, library classification scheme, and so on. The specific ontology that applies to a mobile SOA is the Web Ontology Language (OWL; http://www.w3.org/TR/owl2-overview/), and the formal semantics and Resource Data Framework (RDF/XML; http://www.w3.org/TR/rdf-primer/) serializations are under active development.

FIGURE 21.4

A Service Oriented Architectural approach to processing requests using contextual data from mobile users

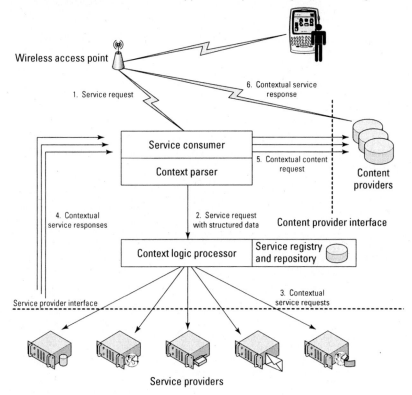

MEMS

MEMS stands for microelectromechanical systems and is a class of very small sensor or actuator devices where small mechanical systems are driven by electricity to indicate a position. MEMS as a class can be between 1 and 1000 micrometers in size, and they are packaged into components that often include a microprocessor, memory, and other components. Several MEMS are packaged in smartphones, and their numbers and complexity are growing over time.

The incorporation of low-cost geo-sensors in the form of Global Positioning System (GPS) chips into mobile devices opens the mobile user to a whole range of services based on the client's location. This type of service is sometimes referred to as context-aware services, but location is just one context that can be used in processing client requests and returning relevant information. There are many more.

The following are built into the latest cell phones:

- Accelerometers for measuring relative motion changes
- Gyroscopes

- Image sensors in the form of CCD chips
- Proximity sensors
- Light sensors
- Sound sensors
- Compasses
- Pressure sensors (barometer)
- Thermisters (resistance thermometer devices or RTDs)

The iPhone uses the proximity sensor to turn the screen off when a user puts the phone to his face. The Droid, Nexus One, and iPhone have dual microphones so they can perform Active Noise Cancellation (ANC). These sensors have the ability to measure the physical world around the user and translate an analog signal into a digital one that can be used to enhance a cloud-connected user's experiences. These types of devices are called Micro-Electro-Mechanical systems or MEMS for short, and the MEMS industry is experiencing explosive growth.

MEMS are everywhere you look. They are in smart watches like the Casio Pathfinders, cars, the Wii-mote, Rock Band instruments, on the suits actors wear to do green-screen work, in Qualcomm's mirasol Display (`http://www.qualcomm.com/qmt/`) used for e-readers, and (as previously mentioned) in smartphones. Without MEMS, smartphones would be stupid phones, and smartphones are driving both innovation and demand for these 21st-century devices. MEMS are turning smartphones into the ultimate digital Swiss Army knife.

Location awareness

The idea behind context-aware services is that your device is constantly being polled for or sending data from its sensors that indicate the condition of the device. For a desktop that never moves anywhere, knowing the location is a one-time thing. Suppose you type a search in Google on your desktop like this:

```
pizza 02052
```

Google returns a search that shows you the pizza joints in that ZIP code. You can see how this kind of search would be helpful for shopping, social networks, services, and other location-based information.

However, when you are motoring around with your smartphone, laying rubber to the road, and cutting the night with your beams, you don't need to tell Google what your zip code or location is because your phone has already given that information to Google's Web service. If you're lucky, your iPhone might ask you if you want to share your location with this service, but usually the information is simply passed on through with your query. There are many examples of location-aware services based on GPS data, where your location is found to within a few feet through the triangulation of three or more overhead satellite distances and positions.

Skyhook Wireless operates services, as shown in Figure 21.5, that are based on a Wi-Fi Positioning System (WPS). The advantage of WPS is that there are hundreds of millions of Wi-Fi access points worldwide and they are closer to the mobile device, so there isn't the significant lag time during triangulation that you experience with GPS. Skyhook holds a patent on a hybrid positioning system it calls XPS, which uses several location technologies in concert: WPS, GPS, and cellular tower triangulation to obtain accurate user location to within a few feet and taking just a few seconds.

FIGURE 21.5

Skyhook Wireless (`http://www.skyhookwireless.com`) provides a location service that identifies a Web site visitor's location.

The system uses a large reference database of Wi-Fi access points and cell tower IDs, raw position data from each location source (a signal), and the company's proprietary algorithm to locate the device. The XPS system is constantly polling locations to update them and recalibrating data points to improve accuracy over time. Failing that, the system performs a location analysis based on your IP address and your known service provider.

Loki (`http://www.loki.com`) has a Java API that works with the Skyhook network and its browser plug-in to locate users for subscribing Web sites.

Push services

Push services are a technology where the transaction is initiated on a server and sent automatically to the client. The opposite of a push is a pull technology, in which the client polls for and requests a transaction. In some instances, push can be a form of publishing and is described as conforming to the publish/subscribe model. The following services are examples of push technologies:

- Automated software updates
- Comet, an Ajax application data transfer (Comet uses either HTTP streaming or long polling, described below.)
- Instant Messaging
- e-mail
- HTTP streaming (also known as HTTP server push)
- Java pushlet
- RSS services
- Software installations
- Teleconferencing

Not all push technologies used in mobile applications are server-based. The IRC protocol and the XMPP IM and VoIP protocol are two examples of peer-to-peer push technologies. Bidirectional Streams Over Synchronous HTTP (BOSH) is a transport protocol that, when combined in XMPP Over BOSH (`http://xmpp.org/extensions/xep-0124.html`), can be used for push service. The XMPP PubSub extension is how Apple creates a push service for MobileMe.

Cross-Ref
WAP Push is covered in the section "Defining WAP and Other Protocols" later in this chapter. ■

Push e-mail is the penultimate example of a push service. In push e-mail, the service is always connected to the client, and it sends out to the client more or less immediately any new e-mail that arrives at the server. In the parlance of system design, the active transfer process is referred to as "push," the server is called the Mail Delivery Agent (MDA), and the client is called the Mail User Agent (MUA). The concept of push is that the mail is sent without the client asking for it, whereas the process of sending mail when the client asks for mail is referred to as "polling."

The well-known e-mail protocol POP3 is a polling protocol; IMAP can support both push and polling. Push-IMAP is a push technology, as is the SMTP protocol. Push-IMAP (`http://tools.ietf.org/html/rfc3501`) stands for the Push extensions for Internet Message Access Protocol (P-IMAP); it is an addition to the IMAPv4 protocol that was added for mobile clients. P-IMAP allows an IMAP server to automatically keep a connection alive and update using what essentially amounts to a heartbeat signal and response. These signals are short and compressed, can contain commands and macros, and can be sent in three ways: using the IMAP `IDLE` command (`http://tools.ietf.org/html/rfc2177`), as SMS, or using WAP Push. P-IMAP contains a feature that sends rich e-mail in a manner similar to SMTP.

Some polling mechanisms set the polling interval so short that the system appears to behave as if it is a push technology, so it can sometimes be hard to tell the difference. With a technique called long polling, the client requests information from the server, and if the server doesn't have information to send back to the client, it queues the request until a response with data is possible.

When the server sends a response, the client typically sends another request to add to the queue, thus maintaining the apparent connection. A mobile device that is polling is constantly activating its antenna and network services and draining its battery. This is one reason that the BlackBerry and its push service gives a noticeably longer battery life between charges than other smartphones, Blackberry turns on its antenna only when required.

Both push and polling have pluses and minuses associated with them. Polling offers the advantages that the client need not be permanently connected to the network and that the MDA (Mail Delivery Agent) can identify the location of the client from the details of the query. However, polling requires the client and the server to engage in handshaking, so it imparts lots of overhead to mail transfers. Whereas a delay of a minute or more doesn't matter for many applications, for some applications—like stock market information—time is critical.

The following are examples of services that use push e-mail:

- Apple MobileMe (`http://www.apple.com/mobileme/`).
- DataViz Roadsync (`http://www.dataviz.com/`) for Android and Symbian S60 using Microsoft Exchange ActiveSync.
- Fifth C BlacMail Server (`http://www.fifthcsolutions.com/`).
- Google Gmail (`https://mail.google.com/`).
- Mail2Web (http://www.mail2web.com/).
- Microsoft Exchange ActiveSync (`http://www.microsoft.com/windowsmobile/activesync/default.mspx`).
- Microsoft Windows Mobile (`http://www.microsoft.com/windowsmobile/`).
- RIM's BlackBerry Enterprise Server (BES; `http://na.blackberry.com/eng/services/server/5/`). BlackBerry devices use their own proprietary e-mail protocols.
- Seven (`http://www.seven.com/`). Seven provides push e-mail, messaging, and sync for multiple mail and IM services and devices.
- Yahoo! Mail (`http://mail.yahoo.com/`).

The immense popularity of the BlackBerry devices' push e-mail system has led to a widespread adoption of this technology by many e-mail service providers. Thus, you also find push e-mail with Push-IMAP on some Nokia Symbian S60 and its Intellisync Wireless Email, Sony Ericsson Smartphones, and Cybershot phones among others.

The BlackBerry Push Service

Developers use the BlackBerry Push Service to push application updates, images, text, audio, and other content to BlackBerry users using Java applications or BlackBerry Widgets that they develop using the service. The Push Service transfers up to 8KB messages directly. If the content is larger than that, the content provider sets up its system so the notification is a push service and the device downloads the data from the content provider.

BlackBerry Push Service uses the following steps:

1. Content provider sends a push request to the server.

2. BlackBerry servers send a response back to the content provider.

3. BlackBerry servers push the data out to BlackBerry clients.

4. BlackBerry clients send a response to the BlackBerry server that the message was received.

5. BlackBerry servers forward the acknowledgement to the content provider.

6. The content provider sends a read notification to the BlackBerry server.

Figure 21.6 illustrates the BlackBerry Push service.

Note

You can read more about the BlackBerry Push Service at `http://na.blackberry.com/eng/developers/javaappdev/pushapi.jsp.` ■

FIGURE 21.6

An illustration of the BlackBerry push technology

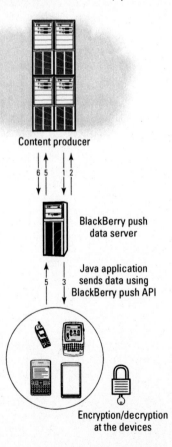

Content producer

6 5   1 2

BlackBerry push
data server

5   3   Java application
sends data using
BlackBerry push API

Encryption/decryption
at the devices

The Lemonade Profile

The Lemonade Profile (`http://www.lemonadeformobiles.com/`) uses a set of e-mail extensions to provide access to mobile devices. It builds on the IMAP protocol for delivery and on the Message Submission SMTP profile. The Lemonade Profile is an alternative mechanism for push e-mail. When a message is available, a timely notification is provided and the Mail Submission Agent (MSA) used in SMTP can be used to retrieve the e-mail from an IMAP data store. The advantage of the Lemonade Profile is that it uses both IMAP and SMTP and can be used by any IMAP client.

This mechanism is an alternative to a Push-IMAP specification, but uses instead a combination of short notification and the `IDLE` command in IMAP. The Lemonade Profile is a specification of the IETF as RFC 5550 (`http://tools.ietf.org/html/rfc5550`). A Push-IMAP specification has been developed but not standardized.

Using SMS

The Short Message Service (SMS) is a text-notification service that has evolved into a primary communications protocol for near-real-time message passing. SMS, or texting, forms a secondary method for mobile users to communicate with one another, and it's valuable because it occupies a middle ground between an Instant Message and a Chat. Internet Service Providers have noticed a drop in e-mail volume over the past years that they attribute to the widespread use of SMS. The majority of cell phone subscribers have SMS text-message accounts.

The word *short* refers to the limitation of the number of characters that can be sent in a single message. A message can be only 140 octets (or 140 * 8 bits = 1120 bits).

This maximum size in characters is as follows:

- For 7-bit characters (upper ASCII), which includes numbers, letters, and symbols, the limit is 160 characters.
- For 8-bit characters (full ASCII), the limit is 140 characters.
- For 16-bit character representations, like those used by pictographic languages, there's a lower limit of no more than 70 characters.

A form of SMS called Concatenated SMS or Long SMS allows longer messages to be sent using multiple packets containing a User Data Header that contains the segment number. The limit for this multipart or segmented SMS is 153 characters for 7-bit, 134 for 8-bit, and 67 for 16-bit encoding. The practice of sending this type of SMS is relatively rare.

SMS was designed to operate over the control channel during times of low traffic. A control channel is sending and receiving handshake information so the connection is maintained correctly; it also is used to send messages with commands that control phone features such as ringtones. Every so often, the control channel is synchronized and for a while no messages need to be exchanged. It is during those periods that SMS packets are transmitted. This arrangement makes SMS a very low-overhead messaging service.

SMS is a store-and-forward system for communications. In a unicast message sent using Short Message Service Point-to-Point (SMS-PP), when a phone or PC sends an SMS message, that message is sent over the control channel to a Message Controller, and then onto a Short Message Service Center (SMSC). The SMSC forwards the SMS message to a Message Controller connected to the party receiving the SMS, and then the SMS message is sent onto the recipient. If the recipient moves to another location, the SMSC can send the SMS message to the appropriate SMS controller. The SMSC keeps trying to send the message until it receives a response from the receiving party that the message was received.

An SMS message can be retained at the SMSC for many days until the message reaches its intended recipient. Also, SMS messages are retained on the sending and receiving systems in their SIM cards until they are deleted. SMS also supports broadcasting, sending the message from one person to many.

SMS is not a particularly secure method of communication. Over a GSM network system, transfers use a weak encryption. One-way authentication is also performed, which is another vulnerability. An SMS message also can pass through multiple networks, which exposes the message to various attacks, and there is no protection for a message that appears on a stolen phone. SMS over GSM is also the target of SMS spoofing, which is where a message comes from a party who misidentifies himself as someone else.

SMS is a subscription service; you can purchase a certain amount of message transfers, after which you are charged for additional messages, usually on a per-byte basis. The cost on a usage basis can be onerous. Certain plans allow for unlimited texting. While SMS is certainly convenient, you can't count on getting timely delivery with your message. It can take minutes or hours for a message to arrive. Also, basic SMS is strictly text and doesn't allow you to send media files or any other binary content.

Many of the smartphone providers offer upgrade versions of SMS, including the following:

- **Enhanced Messaging Service** (EMS): EMS allows you to attach sounds, pictures, icons, and even formatted text with your message.
- **Multimedia Messaging Service** (MMS): MMS supports the sending of audio, video, and even animation with the SMS text. (MMS uses a combination of WAP and SMS for its transport.)

SMS was initially developed for GSM networks. Over time, SMS has moved to 3G networks and even has satellite phone network.

Not all texting systems are SMS, even if they appear so. RIM BlackBerry and NTT DoCoMo i-mode use SMTP to send short messages. Other exceptions include NTT DoCoMo ShortMail and J-Phone SkyMail.

Some SMS services go through an *SMS gateway*. This service works by aggregating SMS traffic or using what is called the SS7 (Signal System No. 7) telephony signaling protocols. An SMS gateway service works by taking the messages received at the SMSC and sending those messages over aggregated or enhanced networks. An SMS gateway is more reliable and faster than SMS itself, so these services can be used in mission-critical notification systems, for businesses, and even in polling or voting. Examples of some SMS gateways include the following:

- Direct to SMSC gateway
- Direct to mobile gateway appliances
- Skype clients
- Some GSM e-mail like the M-Mail service
- Microsoft Outlook and Windows Live Messenger
- Yahoo! Messenger

To view a list of SMS gateways, see the following Web sites:

```
http://en.wikipedia.org/wiki/List_of_carriers_providing_SMS_transi
```

```
http://www.dmoz.org/Computers/Mobile_Computing/Wireless_Data/
Short_Messaging_Service/
```

For most SMS users, their SMS phone number is their mobile phone number. However, some SMS services offer *a short code* as an SMS phone number. The short code is usually 4 to 6 digits in length and often can be reserved so the numbers represent words and phrases. Many short code numbers provide automatic services. For example, when you are given a short code and told to put the word "Haiti" or "Pakistan" in the subject line, sending the SMS to that number may make a donation to the agency of your choice and charged on your phone bill. Some companies use short codes to narrowcast advertisements. They have been used as updating services, subscription list opt-ins or opt-outs, and for many other purposes.

Defining WAP and Other Protocols

The Wireless Application Protocol (WAP) is an application-layer network protocol that allows a WAP browser on a mobile device to communicate with a WAP-enabled Web site. Data is transferred between the two in the form of the Wireless Markup Language and is specially formatted to fit on that mobile device. Web sites can be composed in WML, or the data can be automatically converted to WML.

WAP was originally created by the WAP Forum in 1997, but is now part of the Open Mobile Alliance (OMA; `http://www.openmobilealliance.com`). Figure 21.7 shows the home page of the Open Mobile Alliance, which is the standards body for many of the protocols described in this chapter.

WAP has had a mixed history of success. It is widely used in Asia, but has had limited success in Europe and the U.S. With the advent of MMS services (described in the preceding section), there has been a broader adoption of WAP over the last couple of years. WAP's usage has been limited due to limitations in WML (Wireless Markup Language), developer tools, and problems with being able to successfully transmit mobile device characteristics. As mobile devices get more capable and with the new versions of the protocols, some of these difficulties are being addressed.

FIGURE 21.7

The Open Mobile Alliance is a standards body administering many mobile Web service protocols.

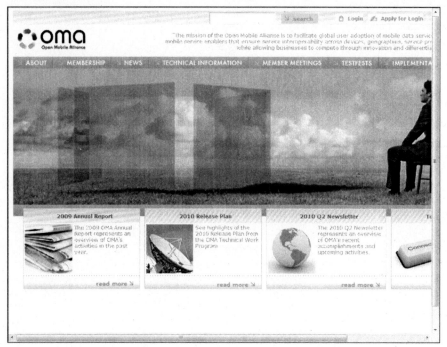

WAP 1.2 is a protocol suite that consists of a number of different technologies that are designed to work over different wireless networks such as GSM or CDMA. Essentially, this WAP 1.2 serves the role of a gateway.

The WAP 1.2 protocol stack from top to bottom includes the following:

- **Wireless Application Environment (WAE):** A set of application specific markup languages, of which WML is an example
- **Wireless Session Protocol (WSP):** Similar to a compressed version of HTTP
- **Wireless Transaction Protocol (WTP):** A transaction monitoring service based on a request/response mechanism
- **Wireless Transport Layer Security (WTLS):** A public-key encryption method that is used for the same purpose as TLS and SSL before it
- **Wireless Datagram Protocol (WDP):** Provides unreliable data transport data formatting
- **Wireless Data Network, GSM, CDMA,** or another network type

The last update for WAP was version 2.0 released in 2002. Version 2.0 uses the lightweight eXtensible Hypertext Markup Language Mobile Profile (XHTML MP) for its modified Web page rendering. Used with XHTML MP is the WAP CSS Cascading Style Sheet. In WAP 2.0, HTTP is used for complete transport and the gateway and protocol stack described above is eliminated. There is a new specification for XHTML that is part of the release of HTML 5.

WAP Push is a form of WAP added to version 1.2 that allows content to be pushed from content providers to mobile clients using a gateway service. WAP Push works sending messages that contain the link to the WAP address over a WDP carrier such as GPRS or SMS. GSM networks don't use GPRS and must use SMS. When a WAP Push Service Indication (SI) notification is received, the user has the option to download the content using this service. Figure 21.8 shows how the WAP Push system works.

FIGURE 21.8

WAP Push uses a set of gateways to push content onto wireless clients.

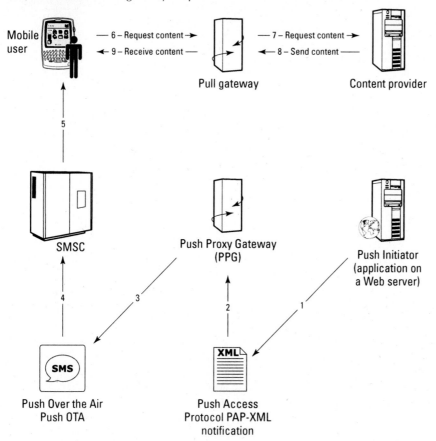

Performing Synchronization

Data synchronization is an important Web service for mobile devices. Contact, calendar, and information on devices often need to be synchronized between multiple systems. The most commonly used standard for performing synchronization is SyncML (Synchronization Markup Language).

All or some the following data types may be synchronized by SyncML:

- Bookmarks
- Calendar
- Contacts
- E-mail
- Files
- Memos
- Music
- Photos
- SMS
- Tasks
- Video

SyncML is implemented using a SyncML server or alternatively as a SyncML hosted service. The client portion of SyncML is either a browser plug-in or client connector software. Different servers and clients allow for the synchronization of different data types. Some backup software also uses SyncML. The standard is an open platform-independent protocol maintained by the Open Mobile Alliance as part of the Data Synchronization and Device Management group (http://www.openmobilealliance.org/Technical/DS.aspx).

The SyncML protocol finds support in a number of products from major mobile software and hardware vendors. It has the advantage over standard Internet protocols. SyncML also can be used to share iCalendar data. Tables of SyncML servers, services, clients, and plug-ins may be found at http://en.wikipedia.org/wiki/SyncML.

Several proprietary synchronization technologies are in wide use. Microsoft Exchange and Windows Mobile use a technology called ActiveSync (http://www.microsoft.com/windowsmobile/activesync/default.mspx) that has gone through several development cycles. Exchange server is so widely used that many other vendors have licensed ActiveSync from Microsoft for use in their mobile mail clients. You can find ActiveSync on the Apple iPhone, on certain models of Google Android, in the WebOS operating system developed by Palm and now part of HP, and in Lotus Domino and Novell GroupWise e-mail servers. Exchange ActiveSync is a push e-mail service. An open-source version of ActiveSync called SynCE (http://www.synce.org/moin/) exists.

The desktop-to-mobile sync application Windows Mobile Device Center (previously called ActiveSync) allows a mobile client to synchronize to a desktop or Microsoft Exchange Server. Desktop ActiveSync is also supported by some third-party mail servers. Windows Mobile Device Center (`http://www.microsoft.com/windowsmobile/`) can synchronize the following data between Windows Mobile phones and desktops:

- Personal Information Management (PIM) data with Microsoft Outlook
- Music and videos with Windows Media Player
- Photos with Windows Photo Gallery
- Files and folders from Windows Explorer
- Favorites with Internet Explorer

Figure 21.9 shows the current version of Windows Mobile Device Center.

FIGURE 21.9

The Windows Mobile Device Center

Summary

In this chapter, the use of Web services on mobile devices was considered. Mobile devices present a number of challenges for Web services and Web site designers. There are many different device types, different mobile operating systems, and in many cases competing standards. Some of the methods used to standardize Web services for mobile devices were presented.

This chapter considered how mobile devices are becoming increasingly smarter and how that intelligence can be used to create Web services that are highly customized for an individual user and the context in which they find themselves.

A number of different Web services use a push mechanism for sending data to mobile devices. You learned about how the BlackBerry performs this task, how SMS uses push for messaging, the Wireless Access Protocol, and other services of this type.

This chapter ends *Cloud Computing Bible*, but is not the end of the story. As you well know, we are really only at the beginning of what is possible in computer science and in human/machine interaction. Computers have the potential to unify the human race, to correct human deficiencies, and to enhance the human condition. As a species, we face great challenges in the years to come. It is my fervent hope that the technologies you have read about in this book contribute to an understanding and solution to these problems so that all of us, our children, and our planet have a better future.

Index

Index

Index

W

Index

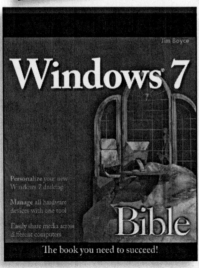

Everything You Need to Craft Killer Code for Apple Applications

Whether you are a seasoned developer or just getting into the Apple platform, Wiley's Developer Reference series is perfect for you. Focusing on topics that Apple developers love best, these well-designed books guide you through the most advanced and very latest Apple tools, technologies, and programming techniques. With in-depth coverage and expert guidance from skilled authors who are proven authorities in their fields, the Developer Reference series will quickly become your indispensable Apple development resource.

The Developer Reference series is available wherever books are sold.

CPSIA information can be obtained at www.ICGtesting.com
Printed in the USA
BVOW00n1944050913

329983BV00009B/14/P